W9-ANG-318

Oz Clarke's

NEW ENCYCLOPEDIA OF FRENCH WINES

OZ CLARKE'S NEW ENCYCLOPEDIA OF FRENCH WINES

SIMON AND SCHUSTER
New York London Toronto Sydney Tokyo Singapore

SIMON AND SCHUSTER
Simon & Schuster Building
Rockefeller Center
1230 Avenue of the Americas
New York, New York 10020

Originally published in Great Britain
by Websters International Publishers in 1989
as *French Red and Rosé Wines* and *French White Wines*

Created and designed by Webster's Wine Price Guide Ltd,
Axe & Bottle Court, 70 Newcomen Street, London SE1 1YT

Typesetting by Dorchester Typesetting Ltd, Dorchester, England
Color reproduction by Spectrum Reproduction, Colchester, England
Printed in Hong Kong

1 3 5 7 9 10 8 6 4 2

Library of Congress Cataloging in Publication Data

Clarke, Oz.
[French red and rosé wines]
Oz Clarke's new encyclopedia of French wines / Oz Clarke.
p. cm.
Combines the author's French red and rosé wines, and his French white wines.
"Originally published in Great Britain by Websters International Publishers in 1989" – T.p. verso.
ISBN 0-671-72456-8
1. Wine and wine making – France – Dictionaries. I. Clarke, Oz. French white wines. 1990. II. Title. III. Title: New encyclopedia of French wines.
TP553.C542 1990
641.2'2'0944 – dc20 90 – 32237

Opposite title page: Autumn in Languedoc-Roussillon
Opposite: Winter vines in Meursault

Contents

INTRODUCTION

I'd like to say I fell in love with French wine from the very first sip. But sadly it wouldn't be true. I was 13 at the time of the momentous first gulp, paralysed with shyness, staying with a French family who placed brimming bottles of 11 per cent wine – that's what they called it, *l'onze degrés* – on the table at every meal. I tossed back my first glass and thought it was horrible. Hardly an auspicious beginning to a great love affair, I'll admit, yet all the same, the episode must have meant something to me, because the deep and lasting involvement with the wines of France has never diminished.

Some years after this false start, older, wiser, the experience of the *gros rouge* obliterated by glasses a little higher up the quality scale, I worked my first vintage at Château d'Angludet in the Haut-Médoc, and took my first steps in learning how wine is made. Since those days I have blended Champagne, tasted still-fermenting new Burgundy, seen oak casks being made, and travelled to every corner of France in the search for more and more information on this most traditional and influential of wine-growing countries. I've talked to winemakers in Chile and Australia, seen the vine flower and bear fruit in Tuscany and the Napa Valley. But it's always France that I come back to with most affection, that proves to have the most irresistible lure.

The wine-making world is very different now from when I first took those juddering mouthfuls of *gros rouge*. We all know so much more about the secrets of harnessing fruit and aroma, of exerting more control over these wayward charges. These days, the wines of France are imitated on a worldwide scale – everyone, it seems, wants to know the secrets of making luscious white Burgundy, delicate and creamy Champagnes, sturdy Rhônes. The sons and daughters of the great Châteaux and Domaines travel to California and Australia to see how it's done there – and vice versa. You discover that the wines emerging from a co-op in the Midi have suddenly taken a turn for the better – and they tell you a New World winemaker has taken over! The good news for us is that the quality of wine throughout the world has never been better. And we owe a significant proportion of this international debt – to France.

Visit the producer of a top Pinot Noir red in California or Oregon, and as you congratulate him on his wine he will confide that he believes he has at last found a way to make French red Burgundy – in the United States. An Australian producer will want the world to know that his toasty, oaky Victorian Chardonnay has just been identified as white Burgundy Bâtard-Montrachet in a blind tasting. Savour the remarkable Sauvignon Blanc wines of New Zealand's Marlborough or the Cabernets of California's Napa Valley and the way to send the producer into paroxysms of pleasure is to say you really feel Marlborough/Napa Valley wines are the New World's closest equivalents to the great Sancerres of the Loire or the Classed Growths of the Médoc in France. And the latest fashion in the US? Planting Syrah vines – to emulate the great peppery, spicy wines of the Northern Rhône.

All the internationally recognised classic wine types originate in France. All the greatest wine grape varieties are French, with the honourable exception of Riesling. (And there's some of that in Alsace anyway.) All the methods of wine-making now accepted worldwide as the text-book procedures for production of great wines, red or white, are based on French tradition. Take the *barrique*, for instance. The 225-litre barrel used to age the great Classed Growths of Bordeaux can now be found in cellars all over the world, from Sonoma to Piedmont. Not only that, but the French methods of quality control, as laid out in the *Appellation d'Origine Contrôlée* (Controlled Appellation of Origin) have formed the basis for quality control regulations all over the world.

France's geographical position provides it with every kind of growing conditions. In fact, France has the luck to be able to grow virtually every type of grapevine within its boundaries. Would your vines prefer an Alp for comfort? No problem. Or is well-drained gravel their choice? France seems to be able to cope with the temperamental vine and with the high-yielding

▲ Château Canon-de-Brem in Canon-Fronsac; its red wines are two-thirds Merlot blended with one-third Cabernet Franc.

vin ordinaire varieties. At 50 degrees of latitude north the vines struggles to ripen at all, yet can produce light and intensely flavoured wines. At 40 degrees it is getting so torrid that delicacy is all but impossible, yet the superripeness makes it possible to create wines like the wonderfully rich, heady Muscats of southern France and the beefy red wines of the Rhône or Provence. Whatever your preferred wine style – from wispy, pale and dry whites to big, round and alcoholic reds, from the tart and tangy to the deeply luscious, from reserved to exotic, from sparkling to still – France has far more to offer than any other wine-producing nation.

And if there is one thing which to me exemplifies the French wine style, it is balance – the balance between overripeness and underripeness, too much fruit flavour and not enough, too much new oak flavour and not enough. And this is the result of almost 20 centuries of trial and error, experimentation and refinement which began with the Romans and still continues today. Generation after generation of winemakers have patiently matched grape varieties with the most suitable soils in the most suitable sites so that from far north to far south, the most appropriate ripening conditions have been found for all the great table wine grapes. With the result that the Cabernet Sauvignon and Merlot of red Bordeaux and the Pinot Noir of Burgundy, or the white Sauvignon of the Loire and the Chardonnay of Burgundy, have been planted throughout the world. And when you ask the growers where they bought their vines, they'll tell you, from the nurseries of Burgundy, or, oh, I bought cuttings from Château d'Yquem, my sparkling wine yeast came from Champagne.

The French, you see, have had 2000 years of practice at the wine-making game. And I reckon that however strong the challenges from the world's vineyards, it's going to be some time before France's supremacy is shaken.

The Wine Regions of France

France lies between latitudes 50 and 40 north, and within the boundaries set by these two extremes, every kind of wine style is possible, and is created by the genius of French winemakers.

Champagne, in the far north, is cold and uninviting for most of the year, but in the folds of the Marne valley and on the neighbouring slopes near Reims and Épernay, the chalky soil produces the thin acid white which is the perfect base for sparkling wine. Champagne! The name says it all: the world's greatest fizz, and it only comes from this single area of France.

The eastern frontiers of France are a series of mountain ranges and all of these produce highly individual wines. The Vosges mountains in Alsace slope into the Rhine valley opposite Germany's Baden, and the east-facing vineyards, warm and dry long into the golden days of autumn, produce fabulously spicy, perfumed white wines, unlike any other. In the Jura mountains further south they make strange, unforgettably flavoured wines and from Savoie – the old alpine kingdom on the Italian border – come whites which are sharp, tasty and mouthwateringly good.

Inland from these mountainous redoubts is the great swathe of land which used to make up the Duchy of Burgundy. It has been famous for wine and food since Roman times and it is still the birthplace for some of the most irresistible wine flavours in the world. Burgundy built its reputation on red wines, but several of its most famous wines are white – and most famous of all is Chablis, a dowdy little town between Paris and Dijon, yet the home of a stone-dry white as celebrated as any in France. Red wine production gets into full swing south of Dijon with the Côte d'Or – a narrow slope of south-east facing land which produces many of the most famous red and white wines in the world – but in extremely limited quantities.

South of the Côte d'Or is the Côte Chalonnaise – a less spectacular, but extremely good source of Burgundy, reds from the Pinot Noir and whites from the Chardonnay, while the Mâconnais exists primarily as a white wine producer of very varying quality. In nearby Beaujolais the red Gamay grape can perform brilliantly but frequently doesn't.

The Rhône valley is on the whole a paradise for red wine drinkers, though good rosés can be tracked down and the white Viognier grape makes startlingly good wine at Condrieu. On the steep, positively cliff-like vineyards of the northern Rhône valley, the Syrah grape offers power and fiery force with some of France's grandest reds from Côte Rôtie, Hermitage and Cornas. But the valley spreads out beneath the hill of Hermitage and the flavours soften too as the Grenache blends in with the Syrah, the Carignan and the Cinsaut to produce enormous amounts of easy-fruited Côtes du Rhône and much smaller amounts of concentrated, super-ripe Châteauneuf-du-Pape.

The whole of the south of France is dominated by red wine – although Provence is more famous for its rosé – and though there aren't many well-known names yet, we're going to see more and more of Corbières, Minervois, Fitou and Côtes du Roussillon as some of the world's most reliable, good-value reds.

In the Loire valley the white Sauvignon Blanc, Chenin and Muscadet grapes produce some of France's most distinct wine styles. In the Upper Loire, Sauvignon creates world classics in the tangy, dry white stakes with Sancerre and Pouilly-Blanc-Fumé. The ultra-dry, almost smoky green flavour has spawned imitators the world over, and made the Sauvignon Blanc a superstar. The Sauvignon also thrives in Touraine, the Loire's centre, but the Chenin now takes over, both at Vouvray, and further west in Anjou. Although difficult to ripen, Chenin can produce good sparkling wines as well as dry, medium and sweet whites, all depending on the weather and the whim of the winemaker. The Cabernet Franc in a warm year makes thrilling reds at Chinon and Bourgueil. And the Muscadet grape makes – Muscadet, the perfect easy-going light, soft, fresh dry white. If ever there was an all-purpose white, this has to be it.

Bordeaux could well lay claim to the title 'red wine capital of the world'. The Merlot dominates the clay-rich vineyards of St-Émilion and Pomerol, while the gravelly soils of the Graves and the Haut-Médoc, especially at Margaux, St-Julien,

Pauillac and St-Estèphe, provide the perfect conditions for Cabernet Sauvignon to produce a string of stunning wines. Bordeaux produces whites too, using Sémillon and Sauvignon Blanc grapes. Entre-Deux-Mers is increasingly providing easy-to-drink, fruity but dry whites, while for true greatness, just look at the tangy, intense, dry styles of Graves and Pessac-Léognan. And as for Sauternes and Barsac – their unctuously sweet, rich wines set the standard for sweet wines throughout the rest of the world.

And between these great classic areas, there are the little backwaters of wine; the byways which usually get forgotten as the big producers surge to the fore. Well, we don't forget them. As well as covering all the major areas, in great detail, the minor areas also get their due, sometimes even a little more than they deserve, but that simply means that they've given me particular pleasure on some picnic lost in a high mountain valley or in some little country café as I tucked into the *plat du jour* heading south to the sun.

Great and small, famous and unknown, red, white and rosé, they all add up to the magical world of France and its wines.

MAKING RED AND ROSÉ WINES

Wine is created by fermentation – yeasts turning grape sugar into alcohol. It's as simple as that, and if you bought a few bunches of ripe grapes, squashed them, put the resulting goo into a bucket and left it somewhere warm like the airing cupboard – well, a wine of sorts would almost certainly be produced. It might taste more like vinegar, but technically it would be wine.

Of course, if it was as easy as that, we'd all be doing it ourselves instead of spending our hard-earned money on the many different bottles which are now crowding wine-shop shelves. But this simple chemical reaction has been refined by hundreds of years of experience, and, more recently, by the application of high technology and microbiological know-how. Today the making of *good* wine is a complicated, high-tech affair, and more and more it is scientists who are in charge – rather than the guy who never went to wine school, but with something in his soul which spurs him on to make great wine time and again. We are now in the age of the white-coat winemaker. The result is more attractive, affordable wine than ever before, to balance the declining influence of many-flavoured brilliance from the old-style wine magicians.

The wine-making process begins when the grapes are brought in from the vineyard and are prepared for fermentation. With the exception of Beaujolais and a few other wines using the 'whole bunch' method of fermentation (also called carbonic maceration, see page 34), black grapes are put through a crusher to break their skins and release the juice. Usually a crushing machine also removes the stalks as these have a tough tannic taste, but in some areas – especially the Rhône – they are left on to produce a firmer wine. The resulting 'must' – pulpy mush of flesh and juice and skins (which give red and rosé wines their colour) – is pumped into a big vat, ready for fermentation.

Yeasts are naturally present on grapes, but increasingly, cultivated yeasts are used to ensure a rapid start to fermentation. At this stage, in the cooler areas of France, the addition of sugar is permitted if the grapes aren't fully ripe. Similarly, in the hottest regions, a little acid may be added if the grapes are overripe. A light red ferments for less than a week, whereas a full-bodied red takes around two weeks – sometimes even three or four – to extract all the flavour and colour from the skins. With rosés, the fermenting juice is drawn off the skins after a day or less.

Throughout the process, skins – and any other debris like stalks and pips – surge upwards, pushed by the stream of carbon dioxide released during fermentation. At the top, they form a thick 'cap' which must be mixed back in continually – partly so that the wine can extract maximum colour and flavour.

When red wine fermentation is finished – all the sugar having been converted to alcohol – the juice is drawn off the vat, and the residue of skins is pressed, to produce a dark, tannic wine called 'press wine'. This may be added to the free-run juice to create a deeper, tougher style, or it may be stored apart – it all depends on what the winemaker wants.

Technically, the wine is now made – but it is pretty raw stuff, in need of further care and attention. To begin with, it probably has a sharp, green-apple acidity. This is reduced through a second fermentation – the 'malolactic' – which converts that tart malic acid into mild lactic acid. Almost all reds undergo this second fermentation – becoming softer and rounder in the process.

If the wine is to be drunk young it is put in large tanks of stainless steel or concrete to rest a short while before bottling. Almost all rosé is treated this way. Red wine for ageing, however, is stored – often in oak barrels of various sizes – for anything from nine months to over two years. If the barrels are new or only once-used, they impart a strong flavour of spice, herbs, perfume and vanilla as well as adding to the wine's tannic structure.

During this pre-bottling period, wine throws a deposit. Since this contains murky-flavoured dead yeast cells, it must be separated from the wine. This is done by racking – carefully transferring the wine to clean barrels. For cheaper wines, the same effect is achieved through filtration, but here some of the wine's body and flavour is always lost as well.

▲ Fermentation is closely monitored. Too high a temperature and the wine will lose fruit and finesse. Here, at Château Langoa-Barton, Haut-Médoc, the winemaker uses a hydrometer to measure the sugar content of the must.

◀ Inside the co-operative at Juliénas, one of the Beaujolais *cru* villages. Fermentation is over; the light, fresh free-run wine has been drawn off and now the grapy residue from the vats is being piled into horizontal presses. The resulting wine – *vin de presse* – will be dark and tannic.

With top-quality wines, the last stage before bottling is 'fining' – removing any particles held in suspension by means of a clarifying agent. The agent – typically egg white or isinglass or gelatin – is added to the surface and, as it falls down through the wine, it collects all impurities with it. Most other wines are filtered; ones for immediate drinking often receive quite a fierce filtration to ensure no deposit forms in the bottle. Some of the best wines that have been fined are also filtered – but very lightly as preservation of their personality is all-important. In top red wines, a slight deposit is inevitable, if not essential.

For best results, bottling should be cold and sterile, with an inert gas like nitrogen filling the gap between wine and cork to prevent oxidation. But fine wines, destined to mature in bottle, need that tiny amount of air – not nitrogen – to continue the ageing process. Many everyday wines, however, are either 'hot-bottled' or pasteurized. Both treatments, which involve heating the wine, ensure its stability but they also undoubtedly detract from its personality.

So, that's the outline. Of course at every single stage, numerous fine-tunings occur and even the most technocratic winemaker indulges in little personal adjustments – otherwise all our wines would end up tasting the same, which would defeat the whole purpose of the exercise – and make this book redundant!

Making White Wines

The creation of any wine begins in the vineyard, but the wine-making process proper starts with the annual grape harvest. When it comes to white wines, this involves choices: pick early and make a snappily fresh wine for quick-drinking, or pursue ripeness until the grapes fill with sugar or, in certain parts of Bordeaux and the Loire, leave the grapes to overripen and hope for an attack of the sweetness-intensifying noble rot.

When the grapes arrive at the winery, choices continue. Traditionally the bunches are immediately pressed and the juice run off into tanks or barrels to settle – any bits of gunge fall naturally to the bottom. Alternatively, crush the grapes lightly and leave the juice and pulp to steep together for between 12 and 48 hours *before* fermentation. This dramatically increases the fruit flavour in a young white wine.

Once the juice has cleared itself of solids, or been filtered or centrifuged to quicken the process (although filtration will invariably remove some potential flavour as well), it is pumped into a tank – generally of stainless steel, if the objective is to make a young fresh white. A suitable yeast culture will normally be added at this stage, as with red or rosé wines, to ensure the fermentation is both efficient and controlled.

The advantage of fermenting in a stainless steel tank is that this is the easiest material to keep sterile-clean, and the easiest in which to control temperature. Either through inserting heat-exchange coils into the tank, or by wrapping the tank in insulation jackets full of coolant, maintained temperatures of about 64–68°F (18–20°C) give a fruitier, fresher style of white. For the fullest white styles, the juice is fermented in a wooden barrel which imparts a rich, mellow flavour even to a dry wine.

After the primary alcoholic fermentation, there is a second fermentation, called the malolactic in which green, appley, malic acid is turned into soft, creamy, lactic acid. Most classic whites undergo the malolactic, but as it reduces fresh-fruit character and tangy acidity, it is generally prevented – by filtration – i modern quick-drinking whites.

A wine for drinking young is generally store in a stainless steel tank for a short time, racke off its lees, if necessary, fined, filtered t produce a star-bright, stable liquid and the bottled – often at only six months old – t maximize its fresh, fruity character. Howeve the best wines of Burgundy and Bordeaux, a well as occasionally in Alsace, the Loire, th Rhône and the south, may have a period c maturation in 225-litre *barriques* (barrels). If th barrels are new or fairly new, they give a stron buttery or spicy character to the wine. Olde barrels merely soften and round out the win due to the slight contact with oxygen – rathe than impart any particular flavour. This matura tion can take up to 18 months but, in genera six are quite long enough for a white wine.

Finally, the bottling. The objective is to have totally clean product, but intensity of filterin varies. Ideally, the very best wines are hardl filtered at all, since the process also removes little of the flavour. Sterile conditions are cruci to avoid bacterial spoilage and sulphur dioxid is generally added as anti-oxidant.

SWEET French wines achieve a measure c sweetness in three different ways. Firstly, ther are lots of wines which are medium in style fruity, vaguely sweet; these demand the reter tion of *some* sugar. So fermentation needs t be stopped while there is still some sugar le unconverted to alcohol. Traditionally, this wa done by pumping in sulphur dioxide to kill th yeasts, but nowadays it is much more commo to remove the yeasts either by chilling the win right down or by centrifuging it, which elimi ates all the solids, including yeasts, and leaves stable wine, sweetness and all. It is als possible to add back a little sterilized grap juice after the wine has fermented to dryness.

Secondly, the wine can be fortified. The ric Muscats of the south use this method. Th sugar-rich juice is partially fermented and the high-strength neutral spirit is added whic raises the alcohol level to between 17 and 2 per cent. Yeasts cannot operate at more tha about 15–16 per cent alcohol, so fermentatio stops and the remaining sugar stays in the win as sweetness.

However, the great sweet wines of Sauterne

and the Loire valley do not rely on anything being added to the fermenting juice. The grapes are left on the vine well into the autumn when they are attacked by a horrid-looking fungus called 'noble rot' (*Botrytis cinerea*). This sucks out the water from already overripe grapes, concentrating the sugar. During the fermentation, the sugar is converted by yeasts into alcohol and the more sugar in the grape juice, the higher the alcoholic strength. But yeasts can only work in alcohol levels of up to about 15 per cent (and frequently the winemaker will add a little sulphur dioxide to stop fermentation at around 12–13 per cent). So when the yeasts stop, *all* the rest of that grape sugar remains in the wine as sweetness – full of potential lusciousness.

SPARKLING The secret to making sparkling wine is the fact that carbon dioxide is a very soluble gas. Carbon dioxide is given off during fermentation and if the fermenting wine is kept in a pressurized container – either a bottle or tank – the gas is absorbed by the wine – for as long as the pressure remains. That explains why as soon as you open a bottle of sparkling wine there is a whoosh of froth and bubbles as the pressure is released.

That sounds simple enough, but there is one major problem – the dead yeast cells form a deposit after they've finished fermenting out the sugar, leaving a nasty sludge in the container. So let's look at ways of getting the bubbles into the wine, then at how to get the sludge out.

The most basic method is simply to carbonate the wine by pumping gas into it. I've never had a decent example of 'carbonated' fizz yet, and a slug of lemonade would considerably improve most of them.

The tank method involves putting wine into a pressurized tank and then adding sugar and yeast to start a second fermentation. The carbon dioxide dissolves in the wine, which is then filtered and bottled under pressure. Most cheap fizz is made this way and the only reason so much of it tastes nasty is that the base wine was foul in the first place. The Italians make delicious Asti Spumante wine using the tank method, so it *can* be done.

All the greatest sparklers are made by inducing a second fermentation in the actual bottle from which the wine will be served. This is called the Champagne method. The wine is initially fermented in tanks or barrels in the usual way. It is then bottled with the addition of sugar and yeast, corked up, and stored in a cool cellar for anything from a few months to several years. The second fermentation slowly takes place, creating carbon dioxide which is trapped in the wine. It also leaves a yeasty sludge which has such an attractive creamy taste that the best sparkling wines will spend a couple of years on their yeast, becoming softer and richer in flavour.

▲ These noble-rot-affected grapes will be used to make Monbazillac, a sweet white wine from the Bergerac region in France's south-west.

So the wine is sparkling – but what about the sludge? Well, in the tank method it is quite simply filtered out before the wine is bottled under pressure. The Champagne method calls for more care. Firstly, the sludge must be dislodged from the side of the bottle. So the bottles go through a process called *remuage*: they are gradually transferred from the horizontal to the vertical – but upside down – as well as being regularly turned and tapped, causing the deposit to slide down inside the glass and collect on the cork.

The next stage – removing the sediment – is called *dégorgement*. The neck of the upturned bottle is frozen in brine. The bottle is then turned upright, the cork is whipped out, and a small pellet of frozen sludge is ejected. If done properly there is almost no loss of wine.

So now you top up the bottle with varying amounts of sugar and wine, depending on how sweet you want the final taste to be. You bang in a cork, secure it with wire, finish it off with foil – and there it is – a lovely inviting bottle of sparkling wine.

CLASSIFICATIONS

France has the most complex and yet the most workable system in the world for controlling the quality and authenticity of its wines. First and foremost it is based on the belief that the soil a vine grows in, and the type of grape variety employed, are crucial to the character and quality of the wine.

There are three levels of specific quality control for French wines above the basic *Vin de Table* – table wine – level. At the top is *Appellation d'Origine Contrôlée* (Controlled Appellation of Origin) usually abbreviated to AOC or AC. All the great classics and most other top wines belong in this group.

The second level is *Vin Délimité de Qualité Supérieure* (Delimited Wine of Superior Quality), usually abbreviated to VDQS. This is a kind of junior *appellation contrôlée*, and many wines – after a probationary period as VDQS – are promoted to AC. It is also used for the oddballs which don't quite match AC requirements but are nonetheless interesting.

Third is a relative newcomer – *Vin de Pays* (Country Wine, see page 220). This was created in 1968 (and finalized in 1973) to give a geographical identity and quality yardstick to wines which had previously been sold off for blending. Many good wines are appearing under the *vin de pays* label at very fair prices. It is a particularly useful category for adventurous winemakers because the regulations usually allow the use of good quality grape varieties which are not traditional to an area and thus debarred from its AC. Some of southern France's most exciting new wines come into this class.

There are seven major areas of control in the AC regulations, which are mirrored to a greater or lesser extent in both VDQS and *vin de pays*:

LAND The actual vineyard site is obviously at the top of the list. Its aspect to the sun, elevation, drainage – all these crucially influence the grape's ability to ripen. The composition of the soil also affects flavour and ripening.

GRAPE Different grape varieties ripen at different rates given more or less heat and on different sorts of soil. Some wines are traditionally made from one grape variety – like Beaujolais from the Gamay, or white Burgundy from Chardonnay: some are made from several – like Bordeaux's Cabernet Sauvignon and Merlot grapes. Over the centuries the best varieties for each area have evolved and only these are permitted so as to preserve the individuality of each AC.

ALCOHOLIC DEGREE A minimum alcoholic degree is always specified as this reflects ripeness. Ripe grapes give better flavour – and their higher sugar content creates higher eventual alcohol levels.

VINEYARD YIELD Overproduction dilutes flavour and character – this is as true for vines as it is for pears and plums. So a sensible maximum yield is fixed which is expressed in hectolitres of juice per hectare.

VINEYARD PRACTICE The number of vines per hectare and the way they are pruned can dramatically affect yield and therefore quality. So maximum density and pruning methods are decreed.

WINE-MAKING PRACTICE The things you can or can't do to the wine – like adding sugar to help fermentation, or removing acidity. Each area has its own particular rules.

TESTING AND TASTING The wines must pass a technical test for soundness – and a tasting

▲ Château Olivier, like the other Classed Growths of the Graves region, is now in the Pessac-Léognan AC, but it will continue to be described as *cru classé de Graves*.

panel for quality and 'typicality'. Every year a significant number of wines are refused the AC.

You may also see words like *grand cru, grand cru classé* or *premier cru* on the label. Sometimes, as in Alsace and Burgundy, this is part of the AC.

But in the Haut-Médoc in Bordeaux, it represents a historic judgement of excellence. In the 1855 Classification 60 red wines from the Haut-Médoc – and one from the Graves (now Pessac-Léognan) – were ranked in five tiers according to the prices they traditionally fetched on the Bordeaux market. Although there are some underachievers, there are at least as many overachievers, and, in general, the 1855 Classification is still a remarkably accurate guide to the best wines of the Haut-Médoc.

Sauternes was also classified in 1855, but Graves had to wait till 1953 for its reds and 1959 for its whites. Pomerol has no classification, though St-Émilion does – and it is revised every ten years.

However, these Bordeaux classifications, though obviously influenced by the best vineyard sites, are actually judgements on the performance of a wine over the years – something which is often as much in the hands of the winemaker as inherent in the soil.

Alsace and Burgundy have a classification, enshrined in the AC, which delineates the actual site of the vineyards. So the potential for excellence is rewarded with either *grand cru* (the top in both areas) or *premier cru* (the second rank, so far only in Burgundy). Ideally this is the better method – although a bad grower can still make bad wine anywhere.

BORDEAUX CLASSIFICATIONS

Single property names started appearing in Bordeaux in the eighteenth century. As people started to realize the importance of factors like the gravel ridges in the Médoc, more and more attention became focussed on naming sites and defining vineyard areas. But it wasn't until the Paris Exhibition of 1855 that any kind of ranking was devised. Wanting to exhibit a selection of Bordeaux wines, a group of brokers drew up a classification, divided into five levels, based on the prices of the wines. Red Haut-Médoc, plus one red Graves and white Sauternes were classified at this point, red Graves had to wait until 1953, and white Graves until 1959. The impact can be assessed by the fact that the only alteration ever made to the 1855 Classification was when Château Mouton-Rothschild, after years of campaigning, was admitted to the ranks of First Growths in 1973. The St-Émilion classification, drawn up in 1954, is re-assessed every ten years – which is perhaps the fairest system of all. No doubt those brokers who drew up the first lists in 1855 would be astonished to realize that their decisions would stay in force for so long!

Of course discussing and trying to re-arrange the Classification of 1855 is virtually a regional pastime. Any Médoc château that wasn't on the list was effectively condemned as second best, and yet perhaps inevitably there are many examples of wines at Fifth Growth that people say should be Second or Third, and some at Second or Third Growth that people say should be Fifth!

THE 1855 CLASSIFICATION OF RED BORDEAUX

FIRST GROWTHS (*PREMIERS CRUS*)
Latour, *Pauillac*
Lafite-Rothschild, *Pauillac*
Margaux, *Margaux*
Haut-Brion, *Graves*
Mouton-Rothschild, *Pauillac* (since 1973)

SECOND GROWTHS (*2ÈME CRUS*)
Rausan-Ségla, *Margaux*
Rauzan-Gassies, *Margaux*
Léoville-Las-Cases, *St-Julien*
Léoville-Poyferré, *St-Julien*
Léoville-Barton, *St-Julien*
Durfort-Vivens, *Margaux*
Lascombes, *Margaux*
Gruaud-Larose, *St-Julien*
Brane-Cantenac, *Cantenac-Margaux*
Pichon-Baron, *Pauillac*
Pichon-Lalande, *Pauillac*
Ducru-Beaucaillou, *St-Julien*
Cos d'Estournel, *St-Estèphe*
Montrose, *St-Estèphe*

THIRD GROWTHS (*3ÈME CRUS*)
Giscours, *Labarde-Margaux*
Kirwan, *Cantenac-Margaux*
d'Issan, *Cantenac-Margaux*
Lagrange, *St-Julien*
Langoa-Barton, *St-Julien*
Malescot-St-Exupéry, *Margaux*
Cantenac-Brown, *Cantenac-Margaux*
Palmer, *Cantenac-Margaux*
la Lagune, *Ludon-Haut-Médoc*
Desmirail, *Margaux*
Calon-Ségur, *St-Estèphe*
Ferrière, *Margaux*
Marquis d'Alesme-Becker, *Margaux*
Boyd-Cantenac, *Cantenac-Margaux*

FOURTH GROWTHS (*4ÈME CRUS*)
St-Pierre, *St-Julien*
Branaire-Ducru, *St-Julien*
Talbot, *St-Julien*
Duhart-Milon-Rothschild, *Pauillac*
Pouget, *Cantenac-Margaux*
la Tour-Carnet, *St-Laurent-Haut-Médoc*
Lafon-Rochet, *St-Estèphe*
Beychevelle, *St-Julien*
Prieuré-Lichine, *Cantenac-Margaux*
Marquis-de-Terme, *Margaux*

FIFTH GROWTHS (*5ÈME CRUS*)
Pontet-Canet, *Pauillac*
Batailley, *Pauillac*
Grand-Puy-Lacoste, *Pauillac*
Grand-Puy-Ducasse, *Pauillac*
Haut-Batailley, *Pauillac*
Lynch-Bages, *Pauillac*
Lynch-Moussas, *Pauillac*
Dauzac, *Labarde-Margaux*
Mouton-Baronne-Philippe, *Pauillac*
du Tertre, *Arsac-Margaux*
Haut-Bages-Libéral, *Pauillac*
Pédesclaux, *Pauillac*
Belgrave, *St-Laurent-Haut Médoc*
de Camensac, *St-Laurent-Haut-Médoc*
Cos Labory, *St-Estèphe*
Clerc-Milon-Rothschild, *Pauillac*
Croizet-Bages, *Pauillac*
Cantemerle, *Macau-Haut-Médoc*

◀ Château Pichon-Lalande, a Pauillac property classified a Second Growth in 1855, still producing consistently remarkable wines.

THE 1855 CLASSIFICATION OF SAUTERNES

GREAT FIRST GROWTH (*GRAND PREMIER CRU*)
d'Yquem, *Sauternes*

FIRST GROWTHS (*PREMIERS CRUS*)
Climens, *Barsac*
Coutet, *Barsac*
Guiraud, *Sauternes*
Haut-Peyraguey, *Bommes*
Lafaurie-Peyraguey, *Bommes*
Rabaud-Promis, *Bommes*
Rayne-Vigneau, *Bommes*
Rieussec, *Fargues*
Sigalas-Rabaud, *Bommes*
Suduiraut, *Preignac*
la Tour-Blanche, *Bommes*

SECOND GROWTHS (*2ÈME CRUS*)
d'Arche, *Sauternes*
Broustet, *Barsac*
Caillou, *Barsac*
Doisy-Daëne, *Barsac*
Doisy-Dubroca, *Barsac*
Doisy-Védrines, *Barsac*
Filhot, *Sauternes*
Lamothe, *Sauternes*
Lamothe-Guignard, *Sauternes*
de Myrat, *Barsac*
Nairac, *Barsac*
Romer-du-Hayot, *Fargues*
Suau, *Barsac*
de Malle, *Preignac*

THE 1959 CLASSIFICATION OF WHITE GRAVES

CLASSED GROWTHS (*CRUS CLASSÉS*)
Bouscaut, *Cadaujac*
Carbonnieux, *Léognan*
Domaine de Chevalier, *Léognan*
Couhins, *Villenave d'Ornan*
Haut-Brion, *Pessac*
la Tour-Martillac, *Martillac*
Laville-Haut-Brion, *Talence*
Malartic-Lagravière, *Léognan*
Olivier, *Léognan*

A–Z of Wines, Grapes and Wine Regions

The lists on the following pages cover all the *appellations contrôlées* for French red, white and rosé wines, plus a selection of the most important VDQS and *vins de pays*, so unless you are travelling in some *very* obscure corner of France you should find here a description of any wine you are likely to come across. There are also profiles of those Bordeaux châteaux and Champagne houses which I consider to be the best. Often these are the most famous names, but not always! There are also entries on France's main wine grape varieties and wine regions.

The wine entries all follow the same format, the left-hand column containing the name of the wine, the classification, the region and the main grape varieties (up to a maximum of four) in order of importance (see below).

The most important wine regions of France (including Alsace, Beaujolais, Bordeaux, Burgundy, Champagne, Loire, Rhône) are each given a whole spread to themselves with maps and a list of the main wines and grapes of the region. The items in these lists can be found in the A–Z. There is also a section on French *vins de pays*.

The name of the wine; in this case it's a claret (red Bordeaux) and these wines are generally known by the château name (ch. = château). Most wines are listed under their AC name.	**BEYCHEVELLE, CH.**	The classification; some wine regions (for example, Médoc, Côte d'Or, St-Émilion) have particular local systems of classification by which wines are allowed to style themselves *grand cru, premier cru* and so forth. The Médoc's famous classification dates from 1855. This wine is a Fourth Growth.
The *appellation contrôlée* (AC) name.	**St-Julien AC, *4ème cru classé***	
The region; Haut-Médoc is a major sub-area of Bordeaux.	HAUT-MÉDOC, BORDEAUX	
	🍷 Cabernet Sauvignon, Merlot, Cabernet Franc, Petit Verdot	The grape varieties listed in order of importance.

The wine name and *appellation* (this wine is a Vin Délimité de Qualité Supérieure – VDQS).	**SAUVIGNON DE ST-BRIS VDQS**	
	CHABLIS, BURGUNDY	The region.
The grapes in order of importance up to a maximum of four named varieties.	🍸 Sauvignon Blanc	The symbols stand for red 🍷, rosé 🍷 and white 🍸 wines.

◀ An aerial view of Château Suduiraut in the Sauternes area of Bordeaux.

AJACCIO AC
CORSICA

🍷🍷 Sciacarello

🍷 Vermentino, Ugni Blanc

Of all the Corsican ACs this is the only one which seems to break away from the Corsican mould of rather flaccid reds, head-banging rosés and stale fruitless whites. With the shining exception of Comte Peraldi whose excellent white shows real class in both oak-aged and non-oaked versions, the whites are still all potential and little realization, as are the distinctly orange-hued rosés. To be frank, the best white wines coming out of Corsica are not *appellation contrôlée* at all, but are the *vins de pays* being made by the more innovative co-operatives, and using such mainland classic grape varieties as Chardonnay. However, the reds *can* show a bit of form, even if the rather sour edge of acidity still intrudes more than I'd like into the fairly plummy fruit. Again, Comte Peraldi is in a different league from the others, but there are rather rustic but tasty efforts from Clos Capitoro and Domaine de Paviglia.

ALIGOTÉ

Aligoté plays the same role in the white Burgundy world as Gamay does in the red – everyone says how inferior it is, picks out its worst features at the expense of its good ones, and manages to forget, first, that it never claimed to be a world-beater, and second, that in one or two places it can make extremely nice wine. Its basic characteristic is a positively lemony tartness, even though the wine may be quite full, but it can also have a misleading ripe smell rather like buttermilk soap, with sometimes a whiff of pine, and of eucalyptus. It is a grape which gives immeasurably better wine from old vines, and many of the best Aligoté wines in Burgundy come from vines 50 years old. In ripe years it can resemble a Chardonnay, especially if a little new oak is used.

The best area for Aligoté is Bouzeron, the northernmost village in the Côte Chalonnaise where the wine has its own AC, but several Côte d'Or villages also produce fine Aligoté from old vines, though these are only allowed the Bourgogne Aligoté AC. Pernand-Vergelesses makes particularly good examples. Apart from in the Côte d'Or and the Côte Chalonnaise there is some Aligoté planted in the Hautes-Côtes, in the Mâconnais and around Chablis – not in the Chablis AC but in the nearby villages of St-Bris-le-Vineux and Chitry-le-Fort.

Virtually every single one of the 2500 acres (1000 hectares) of French Aligoté is in Burgundy, except for a few vines in the Rhône's Châtillon-en-Diois – where the wine is rather nutty and not half bad.

ALOXE-CORTON AC
CÔTE DE BEAUNE, BURGUNDY

🍷 Pinot Noir

🍷 Chardonnay

An important village at the northern end of the Côte de Beaune producing mostly red wines. Its reputation is based on the wines that come from the hill of Corton, which completely dominates the village. The hill is thick with vines from the east side, through the south-facing swathe to almost due west, right up to the tree-covered brow.

The large Corton vineyard is the Côte de Beaune's only red *grand cru*. It is also the cheapest – and most variable. The other vineyards of Aloxe-Corton used to offer some of Burgundy's tastiest wine at a fair price but the reds now rarely exhibit their delicious blend of ripe fruit and appetizing savoury dryness. Although there are a number of *premiers crus* vineyards, these are hardly ever named on the label, but 'premier cru', denoting a blend of several *premier cru* wines, is quite common. Best years: 1988, '87, '86, '85, '83, '82, '78. Best producers (reds): Bize, Chandon de Briailles, Drouhin, Dubreuil-Fontaine, Latour, Senard, Tollot-Beaut, Voarick. Almost all of the white wine of Aloxe-Corton is now sold as *grand cru* (both Corton and Corton-Charlemagne), and straight Aloxe-Corton Blanc is very rare, seldom exceeding 3000 bottles a year. Best producers (whites): Chanson Drouhin, Leflaive, Jadot, Latour, Tollot-Beaut.

▶ An estate in Aloxe-Corton, the smallest village in the Côte de Beaune but famous for its *grand cru* Corton wines.

ALSACE EDELZWICKER
Alsace AC
ALSACE

🍷 Chasselas, Sylvaner, Pinot Blanc and others

In the mid-nineteenth century Edelzwicker was very highly regarded ('edel' means 'noble'), being a blend of the best grape varieties – Riesling, Gewürztraminer and Pinot Gris. Since Alsace gained its AC in 1962 the move has been towards *all* the best grape varieties being vinified separately, so now Edelzwicker is generally a blend of Chasselas, Sylvaner and Pinot Blanc, beefed up with a splash or two of Gewürztraminer or Riesling. Never expensive, it can be good value. Best producers: Dopff & Irion, Éguisheim co-operative, Ehrhart, Schoech.

ALSACE GEWÜRZTRAMINER
Alsace AC
ALSACE

🍷 Gewürztraminer

One of Britain's more respected wine authorities described Gewürztraminer to me as smelling 'like a tart's boudoir'. I forbore from asking how he came to be cognizant of such forbidden delights, but found myself thinking that Gewürztraminer's problem is that it is absurdly easy to enjoy. Our rather Puritan ethic of wine appreciation can't stand its willingness to be enjoyed with no pain and no recrimination. Well, I hope you don't suffer from this torture, because Gewürztraminer must be wallowed in to get the best out of it! Given that Alsace wines are renowned for their flowery spice, the 'Gewürz' (as it is often called) is the most *alsacien* of flavours because the smell is an explosion of roses, grapes, lychees, mangoes and peaches. Sometimes there's just not enough acidity to cope, but the effect is so luscious, I often don't mind. It's worth emphasizing that these wines are *dry*! The flavours are most evident in late-picked wines from hot years, but even cheap Gewürztraminer from a co-operative will be flowery, exotic and unmistakable. Best years: 1988, '85, '83, '76, '71. Best producers: Becker, Beyer, Cattin, Faller, Ginglinger, Hugel, Kientzler, Kuentz-Bas, Rolly Gassmann, Schleret, Schlumberger, Schoech, Trimbach, Zind-Humbrecht.

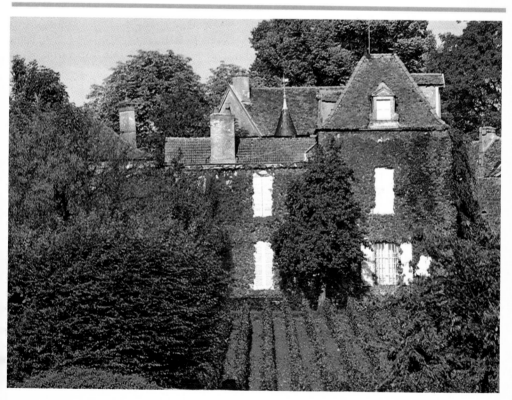

Alsace

Some of the most deliciously individual white wines in France come from Alsace yet, at first sight (rather than taste), you might well mistake them for German. Alsace bottles are tall, slender and green – just like the bottles from the Mosel region of Germany. The name of the producer is almost certain to be Germanic, and also, in many cases, the name of the wine – Riesling, Sylvaner, Gewürztraminer...

Despite the German influence – and years of German rule – Alsace is proudly, independently French. Many of the grapes used may be the same but Alsace winemakers create completely different flavours from them – drier, yet riper, fuller of alcohol, yet quite disturbingly scented.

The key to producing wine so far north lies in the Vosges mountains – rising high to the west, they draw off the moisture from the damp westerly winds and leave an east-facing slope to enjoy the second driest climate in all of France. Only the Pinot Noir, Alsace's lone red variety, has difficulty ripening here, needing the exceptional summers to make red rather than rosé.

Although it is now commonplace for us to see bottles labelled according to grape type from all over the world, Alsace was the first area of France to enshrine this practice in its own wine laws. A single AC was created – Alsace AC – and apart from the blends, called Edelzwicker, all table wines are called by the grape name. Usually this is the only description of wine type on the label but the best vineyards have now been designated *grand cru*. Occasionally the grapes are left to overripen in the hottest years and make intense, late-picked wines of positively monumental flavour. And for the grapes which don't ripen, there is a thriving sparkling wine industry making Crémant d'Alsace.

WINE ENTRIES
Alsace Edelzwicker
Alsace Gewürztraminer
Alsace Grand Cru
Alsace Muscat
Alsace Pinot Blanc
Alsace Pinot Gris (Tokay)
Alsace Pinot Noir
Alsace Riesling
Alsace Sylvaner
Alsace Vendange Tardive
Crémant d'Alsace

GRAPE ENTRIES
Chasselas
Gewürztraminer
Muscat
Pinot Blanc
Pinot Gris
Pinot Noir
Riesling
Sylvaner

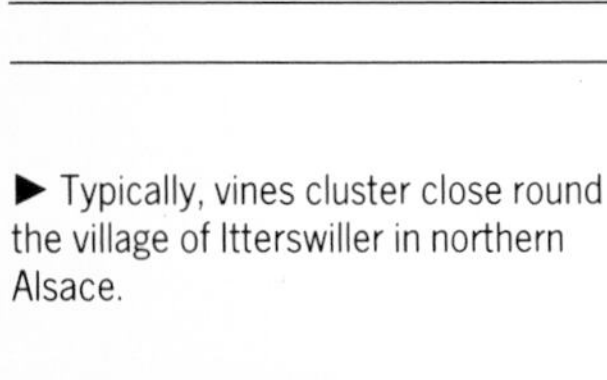

► Typically, vines cluster close round the village of Itterswiller in northern Alsace.

APPELLATION ALSACE CONTRÔLÉE
DEPUIS 1626
TRIMBACH
SYLVANER
70cl
F.E. TRIMBACH NÉGOCIANT A RIBEAUVILLÉ - HUNAWIHR HAUT-RHIN
PRODUCT OF FRANCE
BOTTLED IN ALSACE

FRANCE
VIN D'ALSACE
APPELLATION ALSACE CONTROLÉE
JOSMEYER
Depuis 1854
PINOT
AUXERROIS
e 0,7 l

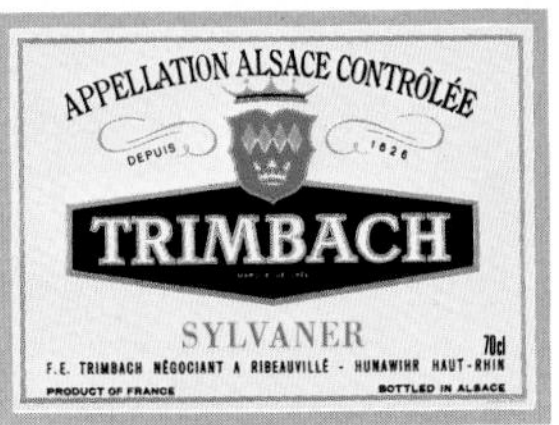

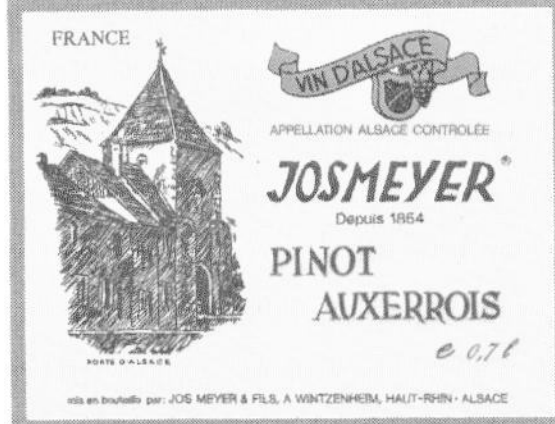

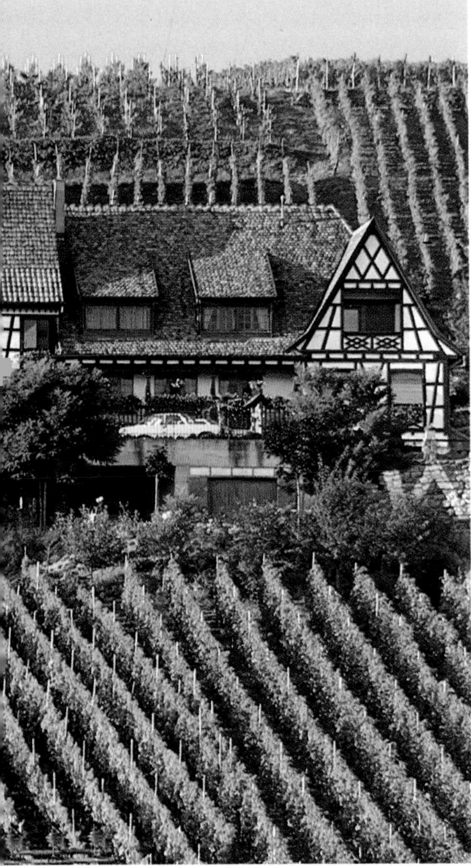

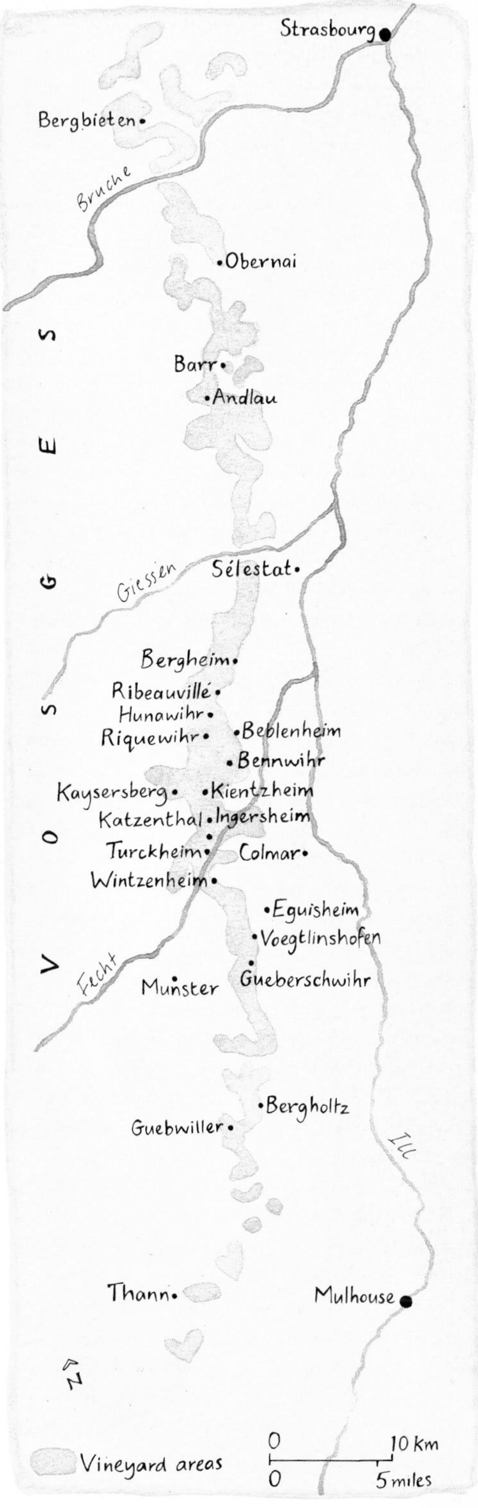

Strasbourg
Bergbieten
Bruche
Obernai
Barr
Andlau
VOSGES
Giessen
Sélestat
Bergheim
Ribeauvillé
Hunawihr
Riquewihr
Beblenheim
Bennwihr
Kaysersberg
Kientzheim
Katzenthal
Ingersheim
Turckheim
Colmar
Wintzenheim
Eguisheim
Voegtlinshofen
Fecht
Munster
Gueberschwihr
Bergholtz
Guebwiller
Ill
Thann
Mulhouse
N
Vineyard areas
0
10 km
0
5 miles

ALSACE GRAND CRU AC
ALSACE

🍷 Riesling, Gewürztraminer, Pinot Gris or Muscat

This *appellation* is an attempt, beginning with the 1985 vintage, t classify the best vineyards in Alsace. It is fiercely resisted by th merchant *négociants*, who argue that a blend from several vineyard always makes the best wines, but this just isn't so. It is the sam now-discredited argument used for generations by the merchants o Burgundy who, anxious to keep tight control over their profitable shar of the market, would deny a grower the right to say, 'This slope ha always been special and I can show you why'.

At the moment 48 vineyards are classified, mostly in the souther Haut-Rhin section, though there are other sites under consideration Only Gewürztraminer, Riesling, Pinot Gris and Muscat grapes qualify fo *grand cru* status and the grape varieties must be unblended. Sinc several great Alsace wines are blends and since, for instance, th non-designated Sylvaner is capable of very fine wine but cannot use th term *grand cru* even if it comes from a *grand cru* quality vineyard, th arguments are not over yet – and we may see a *premier cru* second tie of vineyards just as in Burgundy. Things do look hopeful, howeve especially since the minimum natural alcohol level for *grand cru* is muc higher (10 degrees for Muscat and Riesling, 11 degrees for Gewürztra miner and Pinot Gris) and the yield allowed is 70 hectolitres per hectar – as against 100 hectolitres for AC wine – which can dramaticall improve quality. Best sites: Brand, Eichberg, Frankstein, Geisberg Goldert, Hengst, Kitterlé, Mandelberg, Rangen, Rosacker, Schlossberg Schoenenbourg, Sporen, Zinnkoepflé, Zotzenberg.

ALSACE MUSCAT
Alsace AC
ALSACE

🍷 Muscat Ottonel, Muscat à Petits Grains

This can be sheer heaven. If it continually amazes me how few wine have any taste of grape at all, it also amazes me how Alsace Muscat ca seem like the purest essence of fresh grape – and yet be totally dry. It i a magical combination – the heady hothouse smell of a vine in lat summer, the feel in your mouth delicate and light, yet the gentle fruit a perfumed and refreshing as the juice crunched from a fistful of muscate grapes. A little green acidity and a slight muskiness, like fresh coffee add to the pleasure. The Muscat à Petits Grains variety used t predominate, but its susceptibility to rot meant that producers turne increasingly to Muscat Ottonel. The two varieties cover less than fou per cent of the vineyard area in Alsace, because they are prone t disease and often only ripen well one year in two. If you see one – sna it up, chill it for an hour, and serve it either as the perfect aperitif or afte dinner – the Muscat flavour in a light, dry wine is far more reviving than bumper of port or brandy! Best years: 1988, '87, '86, '85. Bes producers: Albrecht, Becker, Cattin, Dirler, Dopff & Irion, Ginglinge Klipfel, Kreydenweiss, Kuehn, Kuentz-Bas, Zind-Humbrecht.

ALSACE PINOT BLANC
Alsace AC
ALSACE

🍷 Pinot Blanc, Auxerrois Blanc

For such a simple wine Pinot Blanc can have an awfully complicate make-up. Usually it is a blend of Pinot Blanc and the similar, bu unrelated Auxerrois and is a soft dry white, slightly appley, slightl creamy – perfect wine-bar white with or without food. However, Pino Blanc wine can also be made from *three* other grape varieties: whit wine from the red Pinot Noir is called Pinot Blanc and can be deliciou full and creamy; Pinot Gris wine can be called Pinot Blanc too; and the is a little Chardonnay planted which is *also* called Pinot Blanc! The wine all share a fresh, soft, easy-drinking style, excellent young, but capabl of ageing surprisingly well. Klevner or Clevner, the Alsace name for Pino Blanc, seldom appears on a label – if it does, it generally applies to Pinot Blanc-Auxerrois blend. Best producers: Bechtold, Cattin, Gisse brecht, Hugel, Josmeyer, Kreydenweiss, Schleret, Sipp, Willm.

ALSACE PINOT GRIS
Alsace AC
ALSACE

🍷 Pinot Gris

Well, *I* love Pinot Gris. If that sounds a bit defensive, it's because so many people criticize this delicious wine as being flat and mawkish. I mean, what is mawkish supposed to imply? As far as I'm concerned, top-line Pinot Gris wines are frequently the greatest wines in Alsace and even the basic ones have a lovely lick of honey to soften and deepen their attractive peachy fruit. But first things first – that name, Tokay.

The legend is that an Alsatian soldier, de Schwendi, attacked the Hungarian fortress of Tokaj in 1565, captured 4000 vats of their Tokay wine, and liked it so much that he sent his servant to fetch some Tokay vine cuttings. Hungarian Tokay is made from Furmint grapes. The servant brought back Pinot Gris, already well-known in much more hospitable Burgundy. So perhaps he really went there and only pretended to go to Hungary. Anyway, the name Tokay stuck, and it is always made from Pinot Gris, although nowadays the label usually says Tokay Pinot Gris.

It is golden wine, often seeming too dark in colour for its own good. Acidity *is* low, but that doesn't stop the wine ageing brilliantly, blending a treacle, honey and raisin richness with flavours like the sweet essence from the skins of peaches and apricots, and a smokiness like lightly burnt toast. And, as I keep saying, in Alsace this is a *dry* wine! The Vendange Tardive styles are particularly exciting but even at the basic level you should glimpse these flavours. The wine can be drunk straight away or matured for some years. Best years: 1988, '85, '83, '81, '78, '76. Best producers: Adam, Albrecht, Boxler, Cattin, Gisselbrecht, Hugel, Josmeyer, Kreydenweiss, Kuentz-Bas, Muré, Ostertag, Schaller, Schleret, Schlumberger, Zind-Humbrecht; co-operatives at Éguisheim, Gueberschwihr and Pfaffenheim.

ALSACE PINOT NOIR
Alsace AC
ALSACE

🍷🍷 Pinot Noir

It's bad luck on Alsace that, although the region boasts one of the greatest cuisines in France, it can't produce the great red wines many of the dishes cry out for. I don't remember a single visit to Alsace when I haven't gazed down at my plate groaning with hare, or pheasant, or venison . . . and sighed wistfully for a really full-bodied glass of red. Well, you have to go south to Burgundy, Beaujolais and the Rhône for that, because up in Alsace the only red grape they manage to ripen is the Pinot Noir – and only in the warmer years. Frankly, it hardly ever achieves much colour or much weight, although in years like 1976 or '83 some quite impressive specimens triumphantly revealed themselves.

But I *do* like Alsace Pinot Noir, even if it is closer to pink than red: it often reveals a hauntingly spring-like perfume rare in a red wine, and a gentle soothing strawberry flavour that slips down pretty easily (chilling it for an hour isn't a bad idea). One or two producers are now putting the wine into new oak barrels to age, which is stretching things a bit since these wines don't have the guts to cope with oak-barrel ageing. In any case, I drink them for their bright, cherry-red fruit and that's the first thing to disappear if you leave the wine in an oak barrel for six months. Best producers: Cattin, Faller Frères, Hugel, Rolly Gassmann and co-operatives at Bennwihr, Éguisheim and Turckheim.

ALSACE RIESLING
Alsace AC
ALSACE

🍷 Riesling

Wherever Riesling is planted people call it the 'king of wines'. OK. If the king is the least approachable, the slowest to unwind and the most reserved in manner, then I suppose I'll buy that – just! Certainly Riesling does have a haughty, austere style in contrast with the perfumed headiness of Gewürztraminer and Pinot Gris, and the easy-come drinkability of Pinot Blanc and Muscat. Even among the Alsace winemakers themselves it is the most revered variety. I suspect the

reason it is so popular with the producers is that although it is the great grape of Germany they take positively provocative pleasure in asserting that their totally dry, yet full-bodied style is superior to Germany's lighter, sweeter product. And although Germany is now making dry 'Trocken' styles, none of them are a patch on Alsace Rieslings.

About 18 per cent of the region is planted with Riesling and this is increasing. When the wines are young they should have a steely streak of acidity, cold like shining metal splashed with lemon and rubbed with an unripe apple. As they age, sometimes after two years but sometimes not until ten years or more, a pure, strangely unindulgent honey builds up, a nutty weight balancing the acid which itself slowly turns to the zest of limes and the unmistakable wafting pungency of petrol fumes. Alsace Riesling is not so easy to appreciate as Muscat or Gewürztraminer, but it certainly is 'something else'! Vendange Tardive and special Sélection wines are most likely to show this style. Ordinary blends can be a bit bland. Don't age these, but do age the 'specials' – and don't neglect lesser years. 1984, '86 and '87 all produced good, lean, steely Rieslings. But the best years are: 1988, '85, '83, '81, '79, '76. Best producers: Adam, Albrecht, Bennwihr co-operative, Beyer, Blanck, Cattin, Deiss, Faller, Ginglinger, Josmeyer, Kientzler, Kreydenweiss, Lorentz, Rolly Gassmann, Schaetzel, Schoech, Sick-Dreyer, Sparr, Trimbach, Weinbach, Willm, Zind-Humbrecht.

ALSACE SYLVANER
Alsace AC
ALSACE

Sylvaner

Sylvaner used to be the most widely planted of Alsace's grapes and as recently as 1982 accounted for 20 per cent of the vineyard area. It is gradually being supplanted by Pinot Blanc and Riesling, both superior non-aromatic varieties (Gewürztraminer, Pinot Gris and Muscat are the 'aromatics'). It has quite good acidity and ripens well in the less-than-ideal vineyards of the northern Alsace *département* of the Bas-Rhin, and down on the plain. From a good producer, young Sylvaner can be pleasant and slightly tart in an appley way. Mature Sylvaner *can* get an earth and honey fullness to it, though it often brings along a whiff of tomato too – *not* really what you expect in a white wine! Best producers: Boeckel, Kientzler, Rolly Gassmann, Schlumberger, Seltz.

ALSACE VENDANGE TARDIVE AC
ALSACE

Riesling, Muscat, Pinot Gris, Gewürztraminer

Vendange Tardive means 'late-harvest'. The grapes are picked almost overripe, giving much higher sugar levels and therefore much more intense exciting flavours. The minimum natural strength is 12·6 degrees for Riesling and Muscat and 14 degrees for Gewürztraminer and Pinot Gris. Fourteen degrees is quite a mouthful, and given the aromatic personality of Alsace wines, there are some exceptional late-picked wines to be had from years such as 1983 and '85. The wines are totally dry, but usually rich and mouthfilling, and often they need five years or more to show their personality. They can be disappointingly 'shut-in' at two to three years old, but superb five years later.

There is a further subcategory of special wines – Sélection de Grains Nobles – from very late-picked grapes affected by noble rot (the fungus which creates the sweetness in Sauternes). The minimum natural alcohol here is 14·6 degrees for Riesling and Muscat and 16 degrees for Gewürztraminer and Pinot Gris. In years such as 1976 and '83 the actual sugar levels are often much higher. Since the yeasts cannot ferment the wines much beyond 15 degrees, they are often notably sweet and incredibly concentrated, able to age for decades. Very little is made, and it is always wildly expensive. Best years: 1983, 1976. Best producers: Beyer, Dopff & Irion, Faller, Heim, Hugel, Muré, Schlumberger, Trimbach, Wolfberger from the Éguisheim co-operative, Zind-Humbrecht.

'ANGÉLUS, CH.
t-Émilion AC, *grand cru lassé*
ORDEAUX

Cabernet Franc, Merlot, abernet Sauvignon

Judging by the price, you would expect Château l'Angélus to be a leading *premier grand cru classé* – and the rich, warm, mouth-filling flavour would confirm this. Yet l'Angélus is only *grand cru classé*. It is an example of how one must not take wine classifications as gospel, because the influence of an energetic owner, a talented winemaker or investment in the winery can upgrade the quality of a vineyard's wine – just as laziness, incompetence and penny-pinching can dilute it.

L'Angélus is well placed on the lower part of the *côtes* (slopes) to the west of St-Émilion, and the soil is rather heavy. Until 1979 this resulted in fruity, though slightly bland, wine. But in the 1980s new oak-barrel ageing was introduced, adding a good, sturdy backbone to the easy-going fruit. 1988, '86 and '85 showed glorious fruit and richness but also a gratifying firmness that will allow them to age beautifully.

)'ANGLUDET, CH.
Margaux AC, *cru bourgeois upérieur exceptionnel*
IAUT-MÉDOC, BORDEAUX

Cabernet Sauvignon, Merlot, abernet Franc, Petit Verdot

If you were in a cynical mood, you *could* take any remarks I make about Château d'Angludet with a substantial pinch of salt, because this was the first Bordeaux château I stayed at, did the vintage at, surreptitiously sampled the new wine of . . . So when I say that this English-owned property, set well back in the woods behind the village of Cantenac, makes one of my favourite wines, do bear with me. When I say the wine possesses a delicious, approachable burst of blackcurrant-and-blackberry fruit that makes you want to drink it as soon as it's bottled – yet ages superbly over a dozen years or more – be assured that I have put a great deal of personal effort into reaching that conclusion. And when I say that its price-quality ratio is one of the best in Bordeaux since the wine is always of Classed Growth standard but the price well below it – well, whenever *I* buy claret to lay down I start with d'Angludet. And in 1983 and '85 I only wish I'd bought twice as much.

ANJOU AC
CENTRAL LOIRE

Cabernet Franc, Cabernet Sauvignon, Gamay

Chenin Blanc, Chardonnay, Sauvignon Blanc

This catch-all AC covers the whole Maine-et-Loire *département*, as well as bits of Deux-Sèvres and Vienne. Anjou is best known for its rosé wine, but increasingly the leading winemakers are turning their hand to red wine-making with considerable success, particularly with Gamay or Cabernet Franc grapes. Gamay is the Beaujolais grape and using the Beaujolais method of vinification – carbonic maceration – the results can be similar, if a bit rougher. Cabernet Franc, however, although thin and grassy in cool years, can be extremely good, attractively earthy with a delightful raw blackcurrant and raspberry fruit and enough tannin to age for six to eight years. Best years: 1988, '85, though '83 and '82 can still be good. Best producers (reds and rosés): Château de Chamboureau, Clos de Coulaine, Colombier, Fougeraies, Richou, Rochettes.

Until recently the Chenin grape dominated the area's white wines, although it hardly ever ripened properly and a succession of seedy merchants and mediocre co-operatives contrived to make the worst of what little there was. But Anjou Blanc has changed! Modern cool-fermentation methods reveal unexpected pleasures in the Chenin grape, and both Sauvignon Blanc and Chardonnay, although legally only allowed to a maximum of 20 per cent, contribute massively to produce dry, surprisingly fruity whites. We see some medium wines and they, too, are increasingly attractive – fresh, slightly honeyed and cheap.

The best whites have their own local ACs, such as Bonnezeaux, Saumur or Coteaux du Layon, but Anjou Blanc is now increasingly a source of good straight French whites, dry or semi-sweet; some of the better ones use the Anjou Coteaux de la Loire label. There is an increasing amount of sparkling Anjou Mousseux. Best years: 1986, '85, '83, '82. Best producer (whites): Ackerman-Laurance.

ANJOU-VILLAGES AC
CENTRAL LOIRE

Cabernet Franc, Cabernet Sauvignon

Since the AC Anjou is such a blanket term, taking in red, white, rosé and fizz – and one with a fairly poor reputation and price tag to boot – the better producers of red wines have been lobbying for years to get their wines upgraded. Well, they've at last managed it. Forty-six villages spread through Anjou can now use the AC Anjou-Villages for red wine only, using Cabernet Franc and Cabernet Sauvignon, and the next couple of years will let us see whether they're worth the extra. My feeling is that they *are* and already some extremely attractive dry, but fruity reds are beginning to surface. The title 'Anjou-Villages Val-de-Loire' is also allowed for those who want to add to their printing costs.

ARBOIS AC
JURA

Trousseau, Pinot Noir, Poulsard

Chardonnay, Savagnin

This is the largest of the specific ACs in the Jura region of eastern France, centred round the busy town of Arbois. Over one million bottles of white are made each year, in several different styles, all unified by the death-defying Savagnin grape. This is the archetypal Jura white grape though there is an increasing amount of very good light Chardonnay. The Savagnin manages, uniquely and disconcertingly, to infect the amiable qualities of mountain vineyard dry white wine with the palate-numbing, sweet-sour properties of a really dry *fino* sherry. In an ordinary Arbois white wine this effect is to make you question whether you should send the wine back as being 'off'.

However, there is a type of white Arbois wine called *vin jaune* (yellow wine), made only from Savagnin, which develops a *flor* yeast growth on its surface similar to that of *fino* sherry. *Vin jaune* is also made in other Jura ACs, at its best in Château-Chalon. The wine is left in barrel with the *flor* for six years, during which time it oxidizes, develops a totally arresting damp sourness like the dark reek of old floorboards, and yet also keeps a full fruit, albeit somewhat decayed. To be honest, I prefer *fino* sherry, partly because it has *less* flavour! But just because *vin jaune* exists, I will support it – even if I don't much want to drink it. It comes in strange 62cl, dumpy *clavelin* bottles – and since they are totally out of step with the dead hand of European bureaucratic standardization, I'll support those too!

There is also a sweet *vin de paille* (straw wine) – from grapes supposedly dried on straw mats – which is hardly made nowadays and is therefore very expensive. A very good Arbois Mousseux is made by the Champagne method and using the Chardonnay grape. The co-operative at Pupillin, just south of Arbois, makes a good example. Best producers (whites): Arlay, Bourdy, Rolet; Arbois and Pupillin co-operatives.

You don't see much red Arbois wine outside France and, to be honest, I'm not surprised: the chief black grape, Trousseau, is a pretty brutish specimen, usually giving hefty thick-edged wines quite unlike what you'd expect from mountainside vineyards. The Poulsard grape is less disturbing, and can produce quite pleasant light reds and good smoky rosés. Pinot Noir gives pale but tasty, perfumed reds. Some of the best come from Pupillin and are called Arbois-Pupillin. Best producers (reds): Bourdy, Henri Maire, Aubin and Pupillin co-operatives.

L'ARROSÉE, CH.
St-Émilion AC, *grand cru classé*
BORDEAUX

Merlot, Cabernet Sauvignon, Cabernet Franc

One of those unknown properties that swept to international prominence so quickly you have to keep checking your tasting notes to see you haven't got the name wrong. But this small property, situated on a good slope just south-west of the town of St-Émilion, really is exciting: it makes a rich, chewy and wonderfully luscious wine, full of that buttery soft ripeness which is St-Émilion at its most sensual and delicious. A real hedonist's wine, even in a poor vintage like 1984, and especially in the big broad years of '88, '85, '83 and '82.

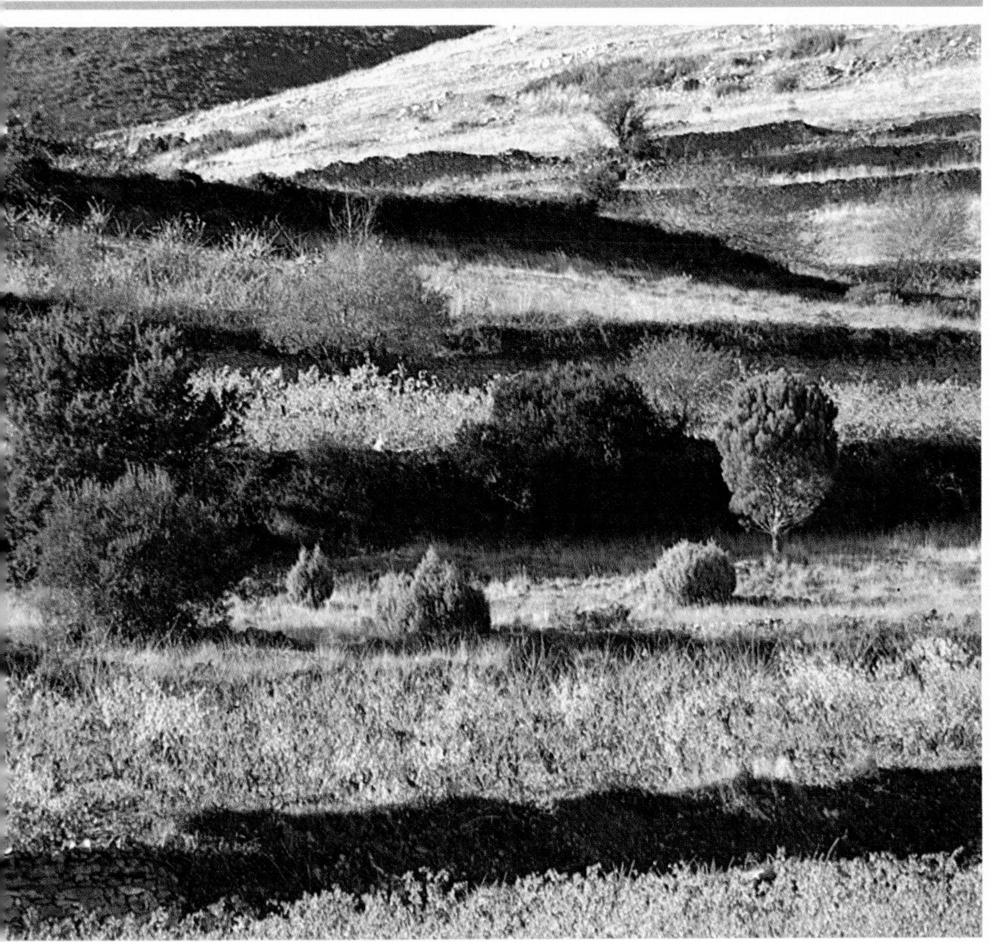

AUDE
LANGUEDOC-ROUSSILLON

▲ In the Aude, vines grow everywhere among the hot, harsh hills. Over half the region's wine is made by co-operatives.

A large *département* which stretches inland from Narbonne on the Mediterranean, up the Aude valley to Carcassonne and the Limoux hills, and more excitingly south-west into the tumbling, tangled mountain wilderness of the Corbières. This area tended to be dismissed with a disdainful sniff and some derogatory remark about wine lakes and oceans of plonk. And that used to be true enough because the Aude *was* a major producer of the *gros rouge* (hefty red) which supposedly slaked the thirst of the French drinking classes in Herculean quantities.

But over the last five years the Aude has emerged as one of the most exciting areas in France. The predominance of mountainous land, particularly in the vast ACs of Corbières and Minervois, and the smaller ones of Fitou and Blanquette de Limoux, means that the potential is enormous, and as estate owners recover their confidence each vintage brings a new crop of exciting wines. Yet they are almost without exception *red*. Gutsy Fitou has become all the rage, and both Corbières and Minervois have been raised to AC status with impressive results.

There is no white Fitou and only a small amount of white Minervois and Corbières. But Blanquette de Limoux in the hills south-west of Carcassonne is a totally white AC for its high-quality Champagne-method sparkling wine and there is a tiny production of sweet Muscat de St-Jean-de-Minervois. Although only a couple of VDQSs now remain, there is a lot of *vin de pays* activity. On average 150 million bottles of *vin*

de pays are produced, almost all red or rosé. About two-thirds go unde the Vin de Pays de l'Aude title, but there are 21 *vins de pays de zon* which include Coteaux de Peyriac with an enormous 35 million bottle the somewhat off-putting Val de Cesse, and the sublimely come-hithe Vallée du Paradis. In that tiny fraction of Aude wine which is white lurk the kernel of great things. Local co-operatives and big companies suc as Chantovent and Nicolas alike have pioneered Chardonnay, Sauvigno Blanc, Sémillon and Chenin Blanc alongside the local varieties – Ugi Blanc, Bourboulenc, Macabeo, Grenache Blanc and their neutra flavoured cronies. The first results show clean, fresh whites of pur varietal character at a low, low price. I think I'm going to keep my eye o Aude whites in the next year or two. Drink as young as possible.

AUSONE, CH.
St-Émilion AC, *premier grand cru classé*
BORDEAUX

Merlot, Cabernet Franc

This elegant property, on what are arguably the best slopes in the whol of St-Émilion, is a success story of the '80s. It has always been judge the potential equal of Médoc First Growths, but all through the '60s an most of the '70s, the wine from this compact 17-acre (7-hectare) site wa wispy and stale. Things changed dramatically in 1975 when a nev hot-shot winemaker, Pascal Delbeck, was appointed. Wine after wine particularly in 1978, '82 and '85, has tasted brilliant from its firs moment, drawn fresh from the barrel in France; actual bottles in th shops, however, have been less reliably memorable. Even so, if curren ownership difficulties are resolved, the 1990s should see Ausone bac on a par with the best of the Médocs.

AUXEY-DURESSES AC
CÔTE DE BEAUNE, BURGUNDY

Pinot Noir

Chardonnay, Pinot Blanc

It was Auxey-Duresses which introduced me to the curious idea th Burgundy undergoes a third fermentation in the bottle. I had th Auxey-Duresses – 1966 of all things – and as I pulled the cork there wa a distinct pop and a fetching little foam formed in the neck. A wise an thirsty friend said not to worry – just decant it into a jug and pour it bac and forth while all the bubbles disperse. Which of course I did, and w had a lovely bottle of red Burgundy for lunch. However, I delved in several respected books and discovered that a 'third fermentation' lik this was by no means uncommon. My wise friend said, 'Rubbish, it jus shows the wine was badly bottled and hadn't finished its *secon* fermentation properly'. Well I believe *him.*

Anyway, by such chances are names engraved indelibly on one mind. Auxey-Duresses is rather a backwater village up in the hills behin the world-famous Meursault. In times of inflated prices, it can be crucial source of supply for those who want to drink top white Burgund yet are damned if they'll pay a loony sum. It makes it all the mor incomprehensible that the standard of Auxey-Duresses wine varies s dramatically though the fact that many of the vines are on north-facin slopes may account for some of the inconsistency. At its best – from producer such as the Duc de Magenta or Roulot – the white is dry, so nutty and hinting at the kind of creaminess which should make a goo Meursault. Too often, though, the wines have ended up rather flabby an flat. Auxey-Duresses *can* produce rather full, round, cherry-an strawberry-fruited reds as well, but too often recently these wines hav been over-sweet and a bit jammy. A pity, because Auxey-Duresses excellent value when it's good. Best years (reds): 1987, '85. Bes producers (reds): Diconne, Duc de Magenta, Leroy, Roland, Thévenin.

The whites make up about 25 per cent of the annual production over 600,000 bottles. They can age but it's best to drink them betwee three and five years old. Best years: 1988, '87, '86, '85, '83, '82. Bes producers: Diconne, Duc de Magenta, Leroy, Prunier, Roulot.

BALESTARD-LA-TONNELLE, CH, St-Émilion AC, *grand cru classé*
BORDEAUX

Merlot, Cabernet Franc, Cabernet Sauvignon, Malbec

I became really keen on this wine in the town of St-Émilion itself. Perusing a seriously overpriced wine list, I saw the 1975 Balestard. Now I don't like many '75s – they're far too tannic and fruitless – but this '75 was excellent, full and sturdy but packed with rather muscle-shouldered fruit. Since then I have frequently sought out the wine and it has always been satisfyingly reliable, full of strong, chewy fruit, and decently priced to boot. Obviously it has been popular for a fair old while, because the label reprints a poem which Villon wrote in the fifteenth century that describes Balestard as 'this divine nectar'. Nothing like an unsolicited testimonial! Best years: 1988, '86, '85, '83, '82, '78, '75.

BANDOL AC
PROVENCE

Mourvèdre, Grenache, Cinsaut, Syrah

Clairette, Ugni Blanc, Sauvignon Blanc, Bourboulenc

There's no doubt that Bandol is a lovely resort town and fishing port, and that many of the vineyards are spectacular, cut high into the cliffs and slopes which tumble down to the Mediterranean beaches. But there is some doubt as to whether Bandol still ranks as Provence's top red wine. As an AC the general standard for reds (and rosés too) is the highest in the French Riviera, though certain properties in Côtes de Provence, Coteaux d'Aix-en-Provence and the Hérault surpass Bandol's best.

The Mourvèdre grape (to a minimum of 50 per cent) is the grape which gives Bandol its character – gentle raisin and honey softness with a slight, tannic, plumskins nip and a tobaccoey, herby fragrance. Other grapes, in particular Grenache, Cinsaut and occasionally Syrah make up the blend. The reds spend at least 18 months in wood. They happily age for ten years, but can be very good at three to four. The rosés, delicious and spicy but really too pricy, should be drunk as young as possible. Best estates for reds and rosés: Cagueloup, Ray Jean, Mas de la Rouvière, Ste-Anne, Tempier, Terrebrune, Vannières.

The AC does make white wine, but Bandol's reputation rests heavily on its ability to make good standard reds, and the whites scarcely pose a challenge, most being made up of the fairly dull Clairette, Ugni Blanc and Bourboulenc. These produce neutral, vaguely nutty but unmemorable wines at horrendous prices. Growers are now allowed to add Sauvignon Blanc to the blend, and there has been a considerable improvement in the freshness of the wines which use it, a green appley fruit balancing a vaguely aniseed perfume, remarkable progress considering the torrid growing conditions. The wines are still for drinking young, but the excessive price tag doesn't hurt quite so much. Out of Bandol's annual production of three million plus bottles, whites account for only about five per cent. Drink these wines as young as possible. Best producers (whites): Bastide Blanche, Laidière, Vannières.

BANYULS AC
LANGUEDOC-ROUSSILLON

Grenache, Cinsaut, Syrah and others

One of those strange, rather heavy, fortified wines – *vins doux naturels* – which the French like well enough but which frankly don't have the style and character of the ones from Spain (sherry, Montilla, Málaga) and Portugal (port, Madeira). The vines are grown on rocky shelves and plateaux strung along the sheer Pyrenean coastline to within spitting distance of the Spanish border. The wine, either red or tawny, must contain at least 50 per cent Grenache Noir.

It is sometimes made fairly dry, but this strong plum and raisin flavour tastes best in a sweet version and it is also best bottled young – a common problem in isolated areas is winemakers' reluctance to draw the wine off from their leaky old casks until it's half-dead. Banyuls *grand cru* is at least 75 per cent Grenache, has 30 months' wood-ageing and is a bit richer as a consequence. *Rancio* means that the wine has been intentionally oxidized and will have a tawny colour. I'd stick to the red. Best producers: Mas Blanc, la Rectorie.

BARSAC AC
BORDEAUX

🍷 Sémillon, Sauvignon Blanc, Muscadelle

Barsac has the dubious distinction of being the only AC in Bordeaux to have suffered the ignominy of having one of its Classed Growths rip up the vines and go back to sheep grazing – within its very boundaries. That's what Château Myrat did in 1976 after the owner gave up the struggle of trying to make ends meet in the face of consumer indifference to his wine. The good news is that a change of heart has led to replanting at the property since those unhappy days.

It is the largest of the five communes entitled to use the Sauternes AC – it comprises about 1750 acres (700 hectares) out of a total for Sauternes of 4905 acres (1985 hectares). The sweet wines of Barsac can also call themselves Barsac AC if they want – and most of the good properties do this. Some even label themselves Sauternes-Barsac.

Barsac is a little village close to the Garonne in the north of the Sauternes AC. Along its eastern boundary runs the diminutive river Ciron – source of the humid autumn mists crucial to the development of noble rot, which intensifies the sweetness in the grapes and without which you can't make truly sweet wine. The important grapes are Sémillon, which can produce syrupy, viscous wines in the best years, and Sauvignon Blanc, which adds fruit and acid balance. There is a little Muscadelle, which is particularly useful for its honeyed spice in less good years. In general, Barsac wines are a little less luscious, less gooily indulgent than other Sauternes but from good properties they should still be marvellously heady, full of the taste of peaches and apricots and creamy nuts. But they're expensive, especially the Classed Growths, of which there are nine in Barsac. Best years: 1988, '86, '83, '81, '80, '76, '75. Best properties: (Classed Growths) Broustet, Climens, Coutet, Doisy-Daëne, Doisy-Dubroca, Doisy-Védrines, Nairac; also Cantegril, Gravas, Guiteronde, Liot, de Menota, Piada.

▼ Château Coutet is the largest estate in Barsac. Its vineyards, 75% Sémillon, produce about 85,000 bottles a year. The château itself is over 700 years old.

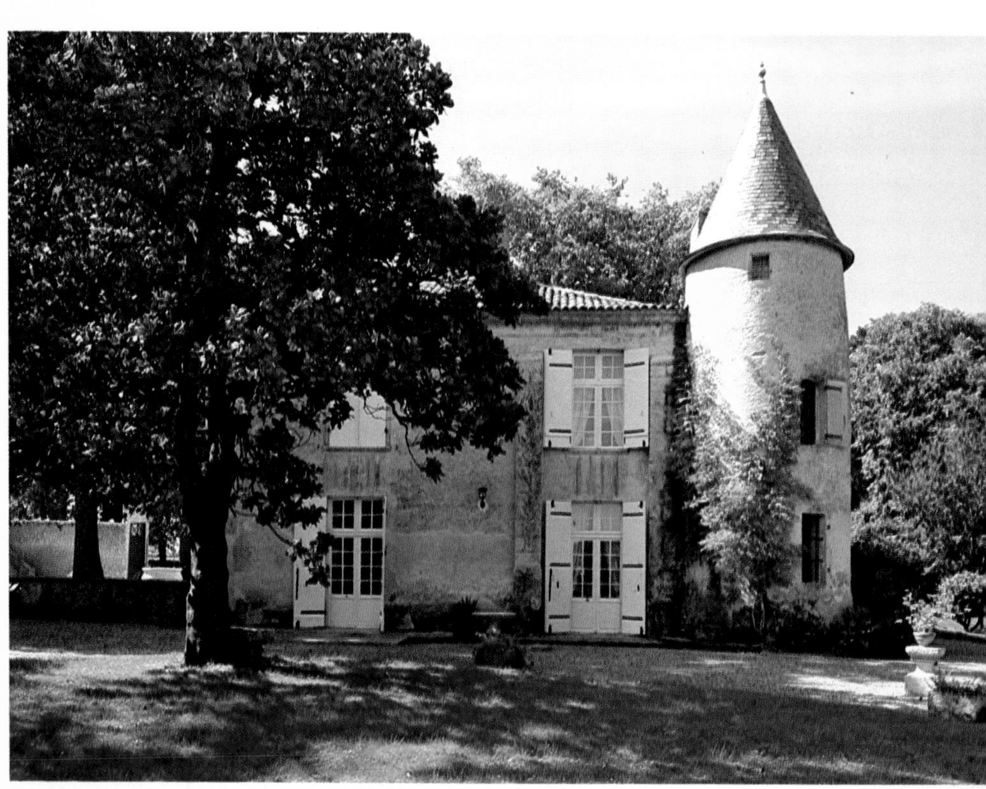

BASTOR-LAMONTAGNE, CH.
Sauternes AC, *cru bourgeois*
BORDEAUX

Sémillon, Sauvignon Blanc, Muscadelle

There's no such thing as a good, cheap Sauternes. Good Sauternes is fiendishly expensive to make, the vineyard yield is low and the incidence of sweetness-inducing noble rot erratic and unpredictable. There is one shining exception – Château Bastor-Lamontagne. Year after year, regardless of the vintage, this Sauternes property on a good site in the commune of Preignac, just north of the great Château Suduiraut, produces luscious, honeyed wine at a price which allows us to wallow in the delights of high-class Sauternes without taking out a second mortgage. This 208-acre (84-hectare) property is actually owned by a bank. I wish I had an account with them. Best years: 1988, '86, '85, '83, '82, '81, '80.

BATAILLEY, CH.
Pauillac AC, *5ème cru classé*
HAUT-MÉDOC, BORDEAUX

Cabernet Sauvignon, Merlot, Cabernet Franc, Petit Verdot

A byword for value-for-money – which, in the rarefied world of Pauillac Classed Growths, is an infrequent accolade indeed. The wine should be a byword for reliability too, because every year since the mid-1970s it has been good, marked by a full, obvious blackcurrant fruit (even when very young), not too much tannin, and a luscious overlay of good creamy oak-barrel vanilla. Lovely to drink at only five years old, the wine nonetheless ages well for 15. Best years: 1988, '86, '85, '83, '82.

BÂTARD-MONTRACHET AC, BIENVENUES-BÂTARD-MONTRACHET AC
grands crus
CÔTE DE BEAUNE, BURGUNDY

Chardonnay

Yes, I'm afraid this means exactly what you think it means. But maybe it's just a rather long, drawn-out French joke in questionable taste, because Bâtard has a near-neighbour vineyard called Chevalier, and lo and behold the Chevalier (French for 'knight') has Les Desmoiselles (French for 'damsels') next-door as well as Les Pucelles (French for . . . oh, perhaps you'd better look it up in the dictionary yourselves!). Right, where were we? Bâtard-Montrachet is a *grand cru* white Burgundy. And it's superb. I've never owned even a tooth mug of it, but this 29-acre (11·8-hectare) vineyard, straddling the border between the villages of Puligny-Montrachet and Chassagne-Montrachet, produces wines of enormous richness and grandeur, which fill your mouth with flavours of freshly roasted coffee, toasted bread still hot from the stove, brazil nuts and spice – and honey which after six to eight years becomes so strong it seems to coat your mouth. Yet despite all this, Bâtard-Montrachet is a dry wine. There is not a hint of sugar, just the alchemy of a great vineyard, a great grape variety – Chardonnay – and the careful, loving vinification and ageing in good oak, which has given *grand cru* white Burgundy its reputation as the world's greatest dry white wine.

There are two other parts of Bâtard – Bienvenues-Bâtard-Montrachet of 5·7 acres (2·3 hectares) just to the north (*bienvenues* means 'welcome') and Criots-Bâtard-Montrachet, 4 acres (1·6 hectares) directly to the south. These are also great wines, although generally a little less overwhelming than straight Bâtard-Montrachet. Best years: 1988, '87, '86, '85, '84, '83, '82, '78. Best producers: Bachelet-Ramonet, Blain-Gagnard, Delagrange-Bachelet, Leflaive, Ramonet-Prudhon, Sauzet.

BÉARN AC
SOUTH-WEST

Tannat, Manseng Noir, Cabernet Sauvignon, Cabernet Franc

Petit Manseng, Gros Manseng, Courbu

While the rest of south-west France has been dusting off its historic reputation for fine wine, and creating shock waves with some highly original flavours, Béarn hasn't managed to cash in. The reason is simple – the wines (750,000 bottles, 90 per cent red and rosé) just aren't special enough, despite some decent grape varieties. The co-operatives which dominate the region have yet to up the quality. If they do, we should see some excellent results. At the moment the juicy rosé is probably best; there are good reds from some Jurançon producers like Domaine Cauhapé. Best of the others: Bellocq co-operative.

BEAUJOLAIS

Of all the recommended soils on which to grow fine red wine, granite must come fairly low on the list. But then, of all the grape varieties you'd choose, the usually dark Gamay would also come fairly near the bottom. But there is a string of magic hills, flowing out of the haunted emptiness of the mountains of the Massif Central into the flat prosperity of the Saône valley above Lyon, which *are* made of granite. And their slopes are covered with the vines of just one red wine variety – and that is the Gamay. The hills are the dreamy, fantastical hills of Beaujolais. And the wine is Beaujolais, perhaps the most famous red wine name in the world!

The Gamay grape's unique characteristic is its youthful fruit, and this is maximized by a special method of making the wine, called carbonic maceration. The grapes are not pressed. They are all piled into the vat still in their bunches. The ones at the bottom burst and the juice begins to ferment. That heats up the vat and the grapes on top actually begin to ferment inside their skins. Since all the perfume and colour is on the inside of the grape's skin and all the acid and tough tannin is on the outside, the result is loads of bright colour and orchard perfumed fruit and hardly any toughness.

The most unmistakable form of this happy juice-type wine is Beaujolais Nouveau, and a great deal of Beaujolais is now drunk a

Nouveau at only a few months old. Certain communes are allowed to use the title Beaujolais-Villages and most of them are in the north of the region. The wine is fuller and riper, but basically it is still the juicy fruit which attracts.

Then there are ten villages with especially good slopes which are called *crus* or 'growths' – Brouilly, Chénas, Chiroubles, Côte de Brouilly, Fleurie, Juliénas, Morgon, Moulin-à-Vent, Regnié and St-Amour. They don't use the name Beaujolais on their labels at all, but most of them are simply that much deeper and juicier than Villages, without being radically different. They should still be drunk within a year or so, except for the occasional wine from Morgon, Chénas and Moulin-à-Vent which can age for a surprisingly long time. A little – very little – Beaujolais Blanc is also made from Chardonnay grapes, the best from old vines towards the south of the region.

WINE ENTRIES
Beaujolais
Beaujolais Nouveau
Beaujolais Supérieur
Beaujolais-Villages
Brouilly
Chénas
Chiroubles
Côte de Brouilly
Fleurie
Juliénas
Morgon
Moulin-à-Vent
Regnié
St-Amour

GRAPE ENTRIES
Chardonnay
Gamay

◄ Beaujolais – a region of gentle tree-topped hills, green valleys and, everywhere, vineyards. About half the wine made exclusively from the Gamay grape is released as Beaujolais Nouveau – fruity-fresh, very young and very popular.

BEAUJOLAIS AC & BEAUJOLAIS-SUPÉRIEUR AC
BEAUJOLAIS, BURGUNDY

🍷 Gamay

🍷 Chardonnay

Most of the Beaujolais drunk nowadays goes under the label Beaujolais Nouveau or Beaujolais Primeur. But that's exactly how it should be. The word Nouveau (new) or Primeur (first) on the label shows that the wine is as young as it can be, and youthful effervescence is precisely what makes Beaujolais such fun – it gushes from the bottle into the glass and down your throat with a whoosh of banana, peach and pepper fruit. It sounds like a white wine, even tastes a bit like it, but Beaujolais is actually France's gluggiest red.

The Beaujolais AC is the basic *appellation* covering 54,000 acres (22,000 hectares) of vineyards between Mâcon and Lyon. Almost all the production is red, though there is some rosé and a little white is made. In the north, towards Mâcon, most of the reds qualify either as Beaujolais-Villages or as a single *cru* (ten villages which definitely *do* produce superior – and more expensive wine: Brouilly, Chénas, Chiroubles, Côte de Brouilly, Fleurie, Juliénas, Morgon, Moulin-à-Vent, Regnié, St-Amour). In the south, towards Lyon, the wide field of vines produces simple AC Beaujolais, a lovely light red wine to be drunk without more ado within months of the vintage.

Statistics differ as to how much white Beaujolais there is, some claiming that five per cent of all Beaujolais is white, others claiming less than one per cent. Well, with 98 per cent of the vineyards planted with the red Gamay grape, that leaves two per cent to divide between Chardonnay and Pinot Noir. Let's say one per cent of the vineyards are Chardonnay – that's *not* going to produce five per cent of the total, is it?

Until recently I wasn't much of a fan of white Beaujolais, finding it rather hard and fruitless. But as the white wines from the neighbouring Mâconnais just to the north have become increasingly shapeless and musky-fruited I've begun to appreciate the dry, stony charms of Beaujolais a bit more. There used to be quite a bit of Beaujolais Blanc made in the far north of the Beaujolais AC, near St-Amour and Leynes, but this is now usually sold as St-Véran AC. The best white Beaujolais now comes from old Chardonnay plantations in the southern part of the region, down towards Lyon. Village names to look for are Theizé, Le Breuil, Châtillon-d'Azergues. Best years: 1988, '87, '86, '85. Best producers (whites): Charmet (the best; lovely, peachy wine), Dalissieux, Jadot, Mathelin.

Beaujolais-Supérieur is an AC occasionally seen in France, but it merely implies a wine with an alcoholic strength one degree higher than straight red Beaujolais. Since freshness is everything, extra strength isn't really the point. Best producers (reds): Carron, Charmet, Château de la Plume, Garlon, Jambon, Labruyère, Mathelin, Texier.

▼ Cellar-worker in Juliénas in Beaujolais – one of the *cru* villages.

BEAUJOLAIS NOUVEAU
Beaujolais AC
BEAUJOLAIS, BURGUNDY

🍷 Gamay

The wine they all love to hate. Well, I love to love it! This is the first release of bouncy, fruity, happy-fresh Beaujolais wine on the third Thursday of November following the harvest. So the wine will normally be between seven and nine weeks old, depending on the date of the vintage – the earlier the better. What started out simply as the celebration of the new vintage in the Beaujolais villages and the nearby metropolis of Lyon has now become a much-hyped beano worldwide. And I'm glad! November's a rotten month. I need a party and Beaujolais Nouveau day is always a good party. And it's affordable!

Also, it is worth defending Nouveau by saying that the quality is usually extremely good, since many of the best selections in the Beaujolais AC are used for Nouveau. And another thing. It usually improves by Christmas and New Year and *good* ones are perfect for Easter and the first picnics of summer! Best producers: Bouchard Père & Fils, la Chevalière, Drouhin, Duboeuf, Ferraud, Jaffelin, Loron, Sarrau.

BEAUJOLAIS-VILLAGES AC
BEAUJOLAIS, BURGUNDY

Gamay

A grouping of 39 communes with superior vineyard sites. When carefully made from ripe grapes, Beaujolais-Villages can represent all the gurgling excitement of the Gamay at its best. Some Villages is made into Nouveau and is often worth keeping six months to drink at its gluggy peak. The best year recently has been 1988, but '87 isn't at all bad. Many Beaujolais-Villages are now bottled under a 'domaine' name; the labels tell you which village produced the wine. The best are Beaujeu, Lancié, Lantignié, Leynes, Quincié, St-Étienne des Ouillières, St-Jean d'Ardières. Best producers: Aucoeur, Crot, Dalicieux, Depardon, Duboeuf, de Flammerécourt, Jaffre, Large, Pivot, Tissier, Verger.

BEAUMES-DE-VENISE
Côtes du Rhône-Villages AC
SOUTHERN RHÔNE

Grenache, Syrah, Mourvèdre, Cinsaut

This sunbaked village has become a household name because of the sweet Muscat de Beaumes-de-Venise which workers used to swig in the vineyards, never dreaming that it would become a highly-priced social necessity for after-dinner-party drinking. Even so the red wine is very good, one of the meatier Côtes du Rhône-Villages, with a ripe plummy fruit in warm years, and an exciting myrtle and musk perfume in cooler ones. The local co-operative is a highly efficient producer.

BEAUNE AC
CÔTE DE BEAUNE, BURGUNDY

Pinot Noir

Chardonnay, Aligoté

Beaune is the capital of the whole Côte d'Or and gives its name to the southern section, the Côte de Beaune. It is also one of Burgundy's most important wine villages and frequently the most consistent. Almost all the wines are red, with a delicious, soft red-fruits ripeness to them, no great tannin, and not much obvious acidity, plus a slight minerally element which is unique and very enjoyable.

Beaunes age well, gaining a savoury yet toffee-rich flavour over five to ten years, but they are also among the easiest of Burgundies to drink young. There are no *grands crus* but many excellent *premiers crus*, especially Boucherottes, Bressandes, Cent Vignes, Grèves, Marconnets, Teurons, Vignes Franches. Best years (reds): 1988, '87, '83, '82 and '81. Merchants dominate the vineyard holdings but there are some independent proprietors – such as Besancenot-Mathouillet, Jacques Germain, Lafarge, Morot, Tollot-Beaut. Best merchants: Chanson, Drouhin, Jadot, Jaffelin, Leroy, Moillard.

Although most people think of Beaune as a 100 per cent red wine commune, five per cent of the 1330 acres (538 hectares) of vines are planted with white grapes, usually on the higher sections of vineyards where outcrops of limestone create good conditions for Chardonnay. Bouchard Père & Fils make a rather erratic Beaune du Château – a blend of white wine from several *premiers crus* – and Drouhin make Clos des Mouches; outstandingly good creamy, nutty wine, similar to a Puligny-Montrachet in style and only just lacking the extra complexity of the very best white Burgundies. Beaune whites age well, particularly the oaky Clos des Mouches, but are also delicious at only two years old. Best years (whites): 1988, '87, '86, '85, '83, '82.

BELAIR CH.
St-Émilion AC, *premier grand cru classé*
BORDEAUX

Merlot, Cabernet Franc

Belair is Château Ausone's neighbour on the steep, south- and south-east-facing slopes just below the town. The properties share the same owner and the same winemaker. Since the late 1970s they have also shared in a spectacular revival of fortunes: during the 1960s Belair was not a wine I'd have dug deep into my pocket to buy, but it is now increasingly good and, of course, expensive. Last century it was regarded as even better than Ausone; now, the position is reversed – just – with Belair giving a lighter but still firmly-textured, rich-fruited wine – at half the price. Best years: 1988, '86, '85, '83, '82.

BELLET AC
PROVENCE

Folle Noire, Braquet, Cinsaut, Grenache

Rolle, Chardonnay

I'm usually a great fan of little, half-forgotten *appellations* which, one suspects, have only avoided oblivion after an against-the-odds struggle by one or two obstinate growers wedded to tradition. Bellet seems to fit this category. It *is* a tiny grouping of small vineyards – only 125 acres (50 hectares) of mostly white vines in the hills behind Nice – whose existence was so precarious that the authorities almost withdrew its AC status in 1947 – they probably couldn't find enough wine to submit to a tasting panel. And there *is* a local hero – the Bagnis family, whose Château de Crémat is the only substantial producer. Most Bellet whites are Rolle-dominated, but theirs has some Chardonnay and it makes a difference. However, Bellet has Nice as its home market, and people on the razzle after a day on the beach don't seem to care much what their wine tastes like so long as it is supposedly rare and too expensive. I can't really recommend it outside France and when I'm in Nice I drink Côtes de Provence – or gin and tonic.

BERGERAC AC, BERGERAC SEC AC
SOUTH-WEST

Cabernet Sauvignon, Cabernet Franc, Merlot

Sémillon, Sauvignon Blanc, Muscadelle and others

Bergerac is the main town of the Dordogne and the overall AC for this underrated area east of Bordeaux; the region might consider itself unlucky to be denied the more prestigious Bordeaux AC, since its vineyards abut those of St-Émilion and Bordeaux Supérieur Côtes de Castillon, and the grape varieties are the same as those of Bordeaux. For centuries Bergerac wines *were* sold as Bordeaux. The production is pretty sizable – 15 million bottles a year, of which about half is red, and the rest rosé and white. The red is generally like a light, fresh claret, a bit grassy but with a good raw blackcurrant fruit. A few producers make a more substantial version with the Côtes de Bergerac AC, which stipulates a higher minimum alcohol level. Bergerac rosés can be exciting too. In general drink the most recent vintage, though a few estate reds can age three to five years (1988 and '85 are particularly good). Best producers (reds): le Barradis, Court-les-Mûts, la Jaubertie, Lestignac, la Raye, Treuil-de-Nailhac.

Production of white Bergerac Sec is dominated by the functional and fairly efficient co-op, whose wines are mostly clean and slightly grassy. However, good Bergerac Sec can have a very tasty strong nettles and green grass tang to it, with a little more weight than an equivalent Bordeaux Blanc. Best years: 1988, '87, '86. Best producers (whites): Belingard, Court-les-Mûts, Gouyat, la Jaubertie, Panisseau.

BEYCHEVELLE, CH.
St-Julien AC, *4ème cru classé*
HAUT-MÉDOC, BORDEAUX

Cabernet Sauvignon, Merlot, Cabernet Franc, Petit Verdot

This beautiful seventeenth-century château overlooking the Gironde graciously announces your arrival in St-Julien – the most concentrated stretch of top quality vineyards in all Bordeaux, with 95 per cent of the land occupied by great Classed Growths. Its name comes from *baisse les voiles* – lower the sails – since the Admiral of France once lived there and every passing ship was expected to strike its sails in respect.

Although it is ranked as a Fourth Growth, its quality is leading Second – and its price too. The wine has a beautiful softness even when very young, but takes at least a decade to mature into the fragrant cedarwood and blackcurrant flavour for which St-Julien is famous. When this occurs, Beychevelle is a sublime claret, always expensive, frequently worth the price. Best years: 1988, '86, '85, '83, '82.

BLAGNY AC
CÔTE DE BEAUNE, BURGUNDY

Pinot Noir

A tiny hamlet straddling the boundary of Puligny-Montrachet and Meursault. Its red, sold as Blagny, can be fair value if you like a rough rustic Burgundy. Matrot is the best producer in this style. Leflaive, on the Puligny side, produces a lighter, more typically fragrant wine.

BLANQUETTE DE LIMOUX AC
LANGUEDOC-ROUSSILLON

Mauzac, Clairette, Chenin Blanc, Chardonnay

The publicity people for Blanquette de Limoux have made great play of the claim that their product is the oldest sparkling wine in the world and that Dom Pérignon and his chums, who are supposed to have 'invented' Champagne in the Champagne region of northern France, pinched the idea on their way back from a pilgrimage to Spain. These wine legends are good fun, impossible to prove or disprove, and totally irrelevant to the quality of the drink, which in this case is pretty high.

Blanquette de Limoux is from a hilly region south-west of Carcassonne in the Aude *département*, a surprising place to find a sharp, refreshing white wine, since most southern whites are singularly flat and dull. The secret lies in the Mauzac grape, which makes up over 80 per cent of the wine and gives it its striking 'green apple skin' flavour. The Champagne method of re-fermentation inside the bottle is used to create the sparkle, although the more rustic *méthode rurale*, finishing off the original fermentation inside the bottle, is also used.

For some time this very dry, lemon and apple-flavoured wine was accorded second place after Champagne among France's sparkling wines, but improved quality in the Loire, Burgundy and Alsace means this position is now hotly disputed. A certain amount of Chardonnay, as well as Clairette and Chenin Blanc, has been planted to give a rounder, deeper flavour – less individual a taste, but certainly more like Champagne. Best producers: the co-operative at Limoux (making the bulk of the six million bottles produced annually); also Froin, Martinolles.

BOLLINGER
Champagne AC
CHAMPAGNE

Pinot Noir, Chardonnay, Pinot Meunier

Far too much Bollinger gets drunk in the wrong way. I don't mean to be stuffy, but Bollinger has long been the preferred tipple of the English upper classes baying for the sound of broken glass, and their more recent imitations, the new wave of financial whizz-kids with more money than manners. 'More Bolly, more Boll', has long been the cry to send shivers down the spines of right-thinking citizens and make them shut up their houses, rein in their daughters and hope they are spared the fizz-fuelled rampage. Which is *very* unfair on poor old Bollinger, which is just about the most *serious* Champagne company imaginable.

The non-vintage is the best-known wine, but the company does a unique range of vintage wines too. As well as a normal vintage release, they do a Vintage RD. RD stands for *récemment dégorgé* – recently disgorged – showing that the wine has been lying in bottle on its yeast for longer than usual, picking up loads of flavour on the way. They also produce Vintage Année Rare – an RD which has spent even longer on its lees, and Vieilles Vignes Françaises Blanc de Noirs – from a single vineyard of incredibly ancient, ungrafted vines in Ay. Impressive stuff – but, as I said, *serious*. If I were celebrating with Bollinger, I'd only use it for something really momentous, like becoming a bishop.

BONNES-MARES AC
grand cru
CÔTE DE NUITS, BURGUNDY

Pinot Noir

A large *grand cru* for red Burgundy of 38 acres (15 hectares), of which 88 per cent is in Chambolle-Musigny and the rest in Morey-St-Denis. This is one of the few Burgundian great names which seems to have preserved its character through the turmoils of the last few decades – the introduction of strict *appellation contrôlée* laws for the export trade, the see-saw of the American market, changing fashions in vineyard and cellar – which produced wild inconsistencies in much top Burgundy. Bonnes-Mares managed to keep its deep, ripe, smoky plum fruit, which starts rich and chewy and gradually matures over 10–20 years into a flavour full of chocolate, smoke again, and pruny depth. 1988 and '85 are the best recent years, but '87, '80 and '78 are also good. Best producers: Drouhin, Dujac, Groffier, Jadot, Roumier, de Vogüé.

BORDEAUX RED WINES

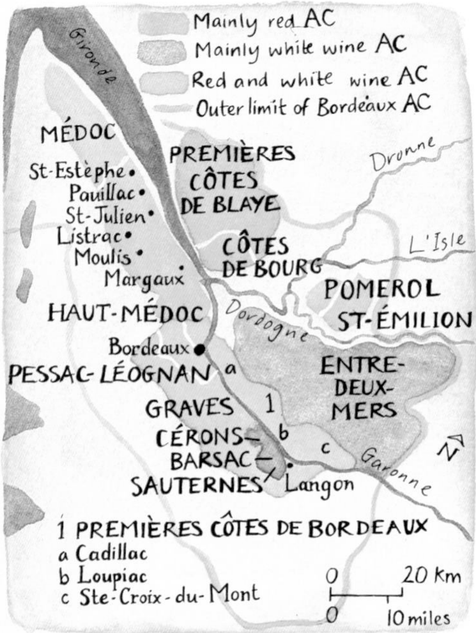

Bordeaux carries a heavy responsibility, because just about every wine book describes it as the greatest wine region in the world. Is it? Yes, I have to admit that it is! And how does it do? Well, it shoulders that responsibility pretty impressively.

The remarkable thing about Bordeaux is that not only does it make what are quite possibly the world's greatest red wines, it also makes what are probably the world's greatest sweet white wines! There isn't much rosé, but what there is can be sublime, and it's really only in fortified wines and sparklers that Bordeaux fails to make the top rank.

Which leads on to the next thing. There's no doubt that some Burgundies are at least as great as top Bordeaux. But they are produced in minute quantities. All the *grands crus* of, say, Burgundy's Vosne-Romanée, only produce about 20,000 cases of wine a year. A single one of Pauillac's First Growths, Château Mouton-Rothschild, produces more than that – 25,000 cases per vintage!

But it isn't only the top wines. Red Bordeaux has been the staple red wine of the northern Europeans for centuries, and the British love affair with it (they've even given it a special name, claret) is explained by the fact that the English owned Bordeaux from 1152 to 1453. It isn't the ritzy Classed Growths that have slaked half a continent's thirst – it's straightforward Bordeaux Rouge and Bordeaux Blanc. And to provide that, alongside the superstars in this vineland on the banks of the Dordogne and Garonne rivers and the Gironde estuary in the south-west of France, there are over 20,000 growers, working to produce about 500 million bottles of wine. *Every year.*

◀ A patchwork panorama of vineyards and villages bordering the Dordogne river in Fronsac – one of the smallest red-wine ACs in the Bordeaux region.

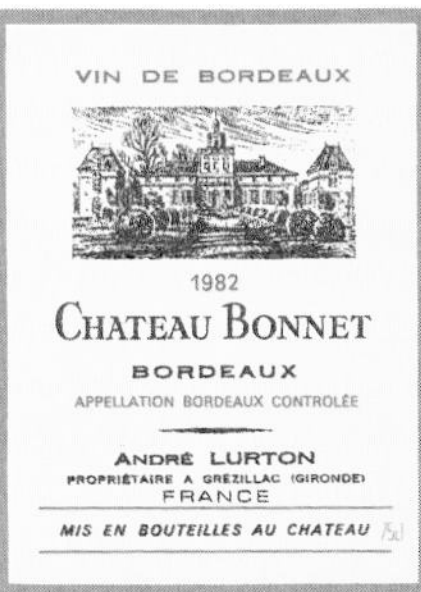

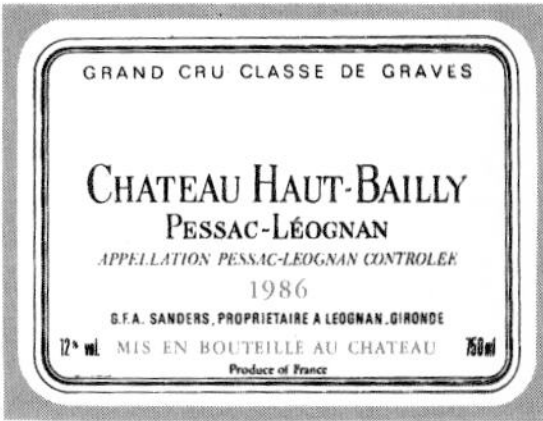

AC ENTRIES

- Bordeaux
- Bordeaux Clairet
- Bordeaux Supérieur
- Canon-Fronsac
- Côtes de Bourg
- Côtes de Castillon
- Côtes de Francs
- Fronsac
- Graves
- Graves de Vayres
- Haut-Médoc
- Lalande-de-Pomerol
- Listrac
- Margaux
- Médoc
- Moulis
- Pauillac
- Pessac-Léognan
- Pomerol
- Premières Côtes de Blaye
- Premières Côtes de Bordeaux
- St-Émilion
- St-Estèphe
- St-Julien

GRAPE ENTRIES

- Cabernet Franc
- Cabernet Sauvignon
- Merlot

See also *Médoc*, pages 146–147, and *St-Émilion*, pages 190–191.

Bordeaux White Wines

On any wine list the biggest section is likely to be Bordeaux. Different vintages abound. Long lists of properties under the title 'Château this' or 'Domaine that' fill the pages. Yet these will almost all be red wines, and it is easy to forget that Bordeaux is a major producer of white wines as well. In fact, some of the greatest whites in the world – the unctuously sweet wines of Sauternes and Barsac, and the spicy dry whites of Graves and Pessac-Léognan – are grown in the Bordeaux area.

Bordeaux is situated way down in the south-west of France. As the river Dordogne flows in from the east and the Garonne from the south-east, the climate becomes mild and the fierce heat of the south is tempered by the influence of the sea. To make great white wine you must avoid the extremes of heat which affect most of southern France throughout the summer because an element of fruit acid is crucial in the grapes if the wine is to be refreshing – one of the chief objectives in a white wine. But here there is an ever-present hint of moisture in the air, even as the August sun beats down. And the landscape – even when thick with vines – always imparts a sense of cool greenness.

North of the city of Bordeaux lie the great vineyards of the Médoc where only a tiny proportion of wines are white, and on the right bank of the Garonne and the Gironde estuary, there are just a few whites in the Bourg and Blaye areas.

To the south of the Garonne, however, are the white wine ACs of Sauternes, Barsac and Cérons, and the Graves where both red and white wines are made. The very best dry whites made in Bordeaux come from the northern end of the Graves, in the zone now allowed its own AC, Pessac-Léognan. The top estates use new oak for the wines which start out with a blast of apricot, peach and cream ripeness and slowly mature to a superb, nutty richness.

Between the Garonne and the Dordogne is the large Entre-Deux-Mers *appellation* (the name means 'between two seas'). This is where much of the good light dry Bordeaux white comes from today. And in the south of the Entre-Deux-Mers, facing Sauternes across the river, are the vineyards of Cadillac, Loupiac and Ste-Croix-du-Mont, which make sweet wine in the Sauternes style, but without quite the richness.

The Sémillon grape is the most important variety for white Bordeaux and it gives a round, rather full bodied wine, which can be a little too fat to be refreshing by itself, and so the Sauvignon Blanc is usually blended in to provide a sharper, green acid tang. Sauvignon Blanc is also frequently made into a dry wine on its own, and there are a few Muscadelle vines here and there in the vineyards which can give an attractive honeyed softness to the wine, dry, medium or sweet.

► Some of the freshest dry white in Bordeaux now comes from Entre-Deux-Mers where vines share the lush landscape with shading trees and grassy meadows.

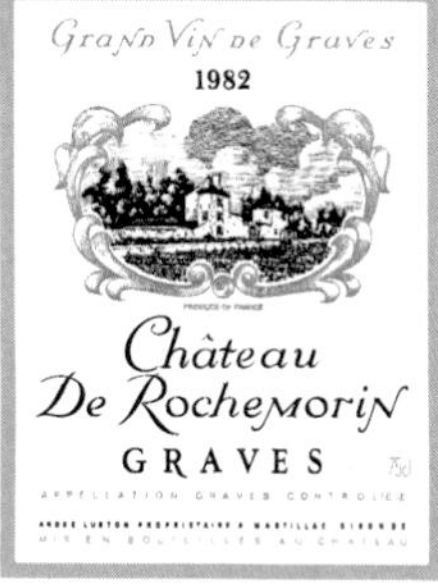

AC ENTRIES

Barsac
Bordeaux
Cadillac
Cérons
Côtes de Blaye
Côtes de Bourg
Côtes de Francs
Entre-Deux-Mers
Graves
Loupiac
Pessac-Léognan
Premières Côtes de Blaye
Premières Côtes de Bordeaux
Sauternes
Ste-Croix-du-Mont

GRAPE ENTRIES

Sauvignon Blanc
Sémillon

See also *Graves and Pessac-Léognan*, pages 120–121, and *Sauternes*, pages 200–201.

BONNEZEAUX AC
grand cru
CENTRAL LOIRE

Chenin Blanc

You pronounce it 'Bonzo' and for years I wanted to try the wine simply to check its canine credentials. Luckily, nowadays most people have stopped calling their dogs Bonzo, and a wise and prudent few are at last taking an interest in the great sweet whites of the Loire. Because Bonnezeaux *is* one of the two greatest Loire dessert wines, a *grand cru* covering about 125 acres (50 hectares) inside the larger Coteaux du Layon AC, on gentle slopes between the villages of Bonnezeaux and Thouarcé. The whole Layon valley, which extends south-east from the Loire near Angers, makes sweet wines, but Bonnezeaux and Quarts de Chaume, the other *grand cru*, are by far the best. They have the lowest yields – Bonnezeaux is allowed just 25 hectolitres per hectare and often achieves only 15 hectolitres per hectare – and because they can request a higher price than their neighbours, the growers generally wait for noble rot to affect their grapes in late October, or even November. The best growers then make several trips through the vines, picking only the most shrivelled, raisiny grapes. These tiny amounts of ultra-sweet juice will then ferment slowly, sometimes on into the New Year. The fermentation stops between about 13·5 and 14·5 degrees of alcohol and the remaining grape sugar gives the wine its sweetness.

This is the same wine-making method as that used in Sauternes, but the flavours are different. In the Layon valley only the Chenin Blanc grape is used, with its very high natural acidity and a sugar content rather lower than Sauternes' Sémillon. Consequently Bonnezeaux can seem surprisingly dry at first, because the acidity is masking the sweetness. But give it 10, 20 or even 40 years, and the colour deepens to an orange gold, and the sweetness builds to an intense, yet always acid-freshened, peach and apricots richness, scraped by a slight bitterness of peach kernels. Never quite as luscious as Sauternes, it is nonetheless unique sweet wine, best drunk by itself, or perhaps with some of those peaches and apricots. Best years: 1988, '85, '83, '82, '78, '76, '70, '64, '59, '47. Best producers: Fesles, Petit Val, Renou.

BORDEAUX AC
BORDEAUX

Merlot, Cabernet Franc, Cabernet Sauvignon and others

Sémillon, Sauvignon Blanc, Muscadelle

The simple Bordeaux AC is one of the most important French ACs and, at the same time, one of the most abused. Its importance lies in the fact that it can apply to the red wines and the dry, medium and sweet white wines of the entire wine-producing area of the Gironde, the largest fine wine vineyard area in the world. Most of the best wines are allowed more specific geographical ACs, such as Sauternes or Margaux, but a vast amount of unambitious but potentially enjoyable wine is sold as Bordeaux AC. Indeed, straight red Bordeaux – often seen labelled as 'claret' outside France – is one of the most reliable of all 'generic' labels and often has a fresh, grassy fruit and attractive, earthy edge. However standards can vary: some Bordeaux Rouge is pretty raw stuff.

Bordeaux Blanc, on the other hand, had until recently become a byword for flabby, fruitless, over-sulphured brews. But as prices of white Burgundies and the Sauvignons of the Loire valley have risen year by year, demand for decent white Bordeaux has picked up, and there is now an increasing number of pleasant, clean wines, frequently under a merchant's rather than a château label, which make refreshing drinking. Cool fermentation in stainless steel tanks, to preserve the fruit aromas of the grapes, and occasional steeping of the juice and grape skins together after crushing but before fermentation (a process which dramatically increases fruit flavours), are the keys to improved quality.

There is a subdivision of the AC for white wines with less than 4g of sugar per litre. These are labelled Bordeaux Sec or Vin Sec de Bordeaux. Since many of these are 100 per cent Sauvignon wines, the grape name may also be used on the label.

The Bordeaux AC also applies to wines made in superior *appellations*, but in the wrong style. White wine made in the red wine ACs of the Médoc can only be AC Bordeaux, and red, rosé or dry white wines made in the sweet wine ACs of Sauternes and Barsac are also only allowed the Bordeaux AC (or Bordeaux Supérieur for reds). With rare exceptions (like Ygrec from Château d'Yquem, and Pavillon Blanc du Château Margaux), all AC Bordeaux Blanc wines should be drunk as young as possible; good Bordeaux Rouge may cope with a year or so of ageing.

ORDEAUX CLAIRET AC
ORDEAUX

Cabernet Sauvignon, Cabernet ranc, Merlot

A very pale red wine, almost rosé in fact, which isn't much seen around Bordeaux any more. But it was once. The name 'claret', which we now apply to *any* red wine from the Bordeaux region, derives from *clairet*. What this means is that a few hundred years ago *all* Bordeaux reds were made in a light, quick-drinking style. As wine-making knowledge improved, the reds became darker and stronger, and Bordeaux Clairet almost faded away. Interestingly, a few very ritzy Classed Growth properties in the Médoc still make a little to have with their lunch. Quinsac, just south of Bordeaux in the Premières Côtes, specializes in Clairet. There are rumours that it is becoming fashionable again.

ORDEAUX SUPÉRIEUR AC
ORDEAUX

Cabernet Sauvignon, Cabernet ranc, Merlot, Malbec

This *appellation* covers the whole Bordeaux region, as does Bordeaux AC. The difference between them is that Supérieur must have an extra half a degree of alcohol for red and rosé and a lower yield from the vines – 40 hectolitres per hectare as against 50. This makes a considerable difference, because the riper fruit which gives the higher alcohol has more taste, and vines which are cropping 20 per cent less give a greater concentration of flavours. Almost all of the *petits châteaux* which represent the best value drinking in Bordeaux will be Bordeaux Supérieur. There are two areas – Côtes de Castillon and Côtes de Francs – which may tack on their own names after Bordeaux Supérieur. Their quality is generally far finer than their low price would suggest.

BOURGOGNE AC
URGUNDY

Pinot Noir, Gamay, Tressot, ésar

Chardonnay, Pinot Blanc, Pinot ris

Bourgogne is the French name we have anglicized as 'Burgundy'. As a generic *appellation*, from Chablis in the north way down to Beaujolais some 180 miles (290km) to the south, it mops up all the wine with no specific AC of its own. This means there are massive differences in style and quality. Pinot Noir is thought of as the red Burgundy grape, and is used for the vast majority of Bourgogne Rouge. Yet around Chablis the local varieties César and Tressot occur (though very rarely), and in the Mâconnais and Beaujolais, Gamay can be used. As for quality, well, some of the less reputable Burgundy merchants buy wine from any source so long as the price is low. On the other hand, some unlucky but dedicated growers possess land only entitled to the simple Bourgogne AC yet lavish on it the same care and devotion as on a *grand cru*.

Bourgogne Blanc may be either an elegant, classy, dry white of marvellous, nutty character or an overpriced washout, depending entirely on how the *appellation* has been interpreted. In general, the Chardonnay grape is used, but there is some Pinot Blanc and Pinot Beurot, as the Pinot Gris is known here, which is often thrown in for good measure.

Here's what you *should* find. Red Bourgogne is usually light, overtly fruity in a breezy, strawberry and cherry way, all up-front, but if the perfume is there, no one minds if the flavour is a bit simple. It should be drunk young – two to three years' ageing is quite enough – and it shouldn't be fussed over too much; just enjoy it. The better merchants'

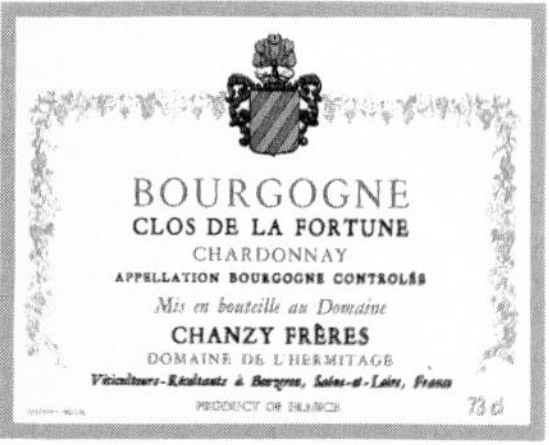

blends usually come into this category. Sometimes, however, Bourgogne Rouge can be much more than this, the cherry and strawberry fruit deeper, thickened into a plummy richness, and perhaps with the creamy softness of some oak-barrel ageing added in.

Usually Bourgogne Blanc will be a bone dry wine from vineyards not considered quite good enough for a classier *appellation*, but vaguely in the same style. So a Bourgogne Blanc from the Yonne region round Chablis will usually be light, slightly tart and refreshing, one from the Côte d'Or might have some of the nutty fullness of nearby Meursault, while one from the Mâconnais will probably be fatter and rather appley. If the wine is from a grower the flavours will follow regional style. However, if the address on the label is of a Côte d'Or merchant, the wine could be from anywhere in Burgundy.

The best wines will usually come from a single grower who has excluded some of his wine from the top label, either because it lacked the necessary concentration, or because the vines are just outside the specific *appellation* boundaries. Some good growers declassify some of their Chardonnay which isn't quite good enough for their top labels, but still age it in newish oak barrels. Such wines can be absolutely superb and far superior to many Meursaults and Puligny-Montrachets from the less reputable merchants. Reds made with care can be almost as exciting as the proprietor's full-blown Pommard, Gevrey-Chambertin or whatever – and half the price. In today's world of overblown prices they may be the only way we can afford the joys of fine Burgundy. Both the Caves Co-opératives of Buxy and of the Hautes-Côtes now mature some of their wine in oak. Best growers (reds): Chanson, Coche-Dury, Germain, d'Heuilly-Huberdeau, Henri Jayer, Moillard, Morey, Parent, Rion, Rossignol. Best merchants: Drouhin, Jadot, Labouré-Roi, Leroy, Vallet and co-operatives at Buxy and Hautes-Côtes.

Most Bourgogne Blanc should be drunk within two years, but those matured in oak (sometimes labelled *vieilli en fûts de chêne*) can age well. Best years: 1988, '87, '85. Best producers: Boisson-Morey, Boisson-Vadot, Boyer-Martenot, Buxy co-operative, Henri Clerc, Coche-Dury, Drouhin, Faiveley, Jadot, Jaffelin, Javillier, Jobard, Labouré-Roi, René Manuel, Millau-Battault.

BOURGOGNE ALIGOTÉ AC, BOURGOGNE ALIGOTÉ DE BOUZERON AC

BURGUNDY

Aligoté

This used to be a byword for sharp, sour wine, and the Burgundians themselves could be seen in the region's cafés, lacing it liberally with blackcurrant liqueur to hide the flavour. But the wine is not as bad as that. The marked lemon acidity and the almost neutral fruit do make it an excellent base for *kir* – just add a dash of blackcurrant liqueur. Yet Aligoté is a vine which benefits enormously from maturity and those growers who possess old vines can make delicious, full, almost Chardonnay-type wines, with a smell of buttermilk and a nuttiness coating the striking lemon acidity. The wine is never complex but can be pretty good. The best examples come from Côte d'Or growers with old vines like Rion, Coche-Dury, Jobard and Confuron.

Bourgogne Aligoté de Bouzeron is a separate AC for one village at the northern end of the Côte Chalonnaise – the only village producing Aligoté that is allowed to use its own name. This is generally reckoned to be the finest Aligoté, and certainly that buttermilk soap nose can be quite marked, and the lemony flavour can have a peppery bite as well. Aligoté is supposed to be the perfect accompaniment for snails (the growers of Aligoté in the Hautes-Côtes have even started a snail brotherhood – the Confrérie de l'Escargot). Bouzeron's best producers are Bouchard Père & Fils, Chanzy, de Villaine. Other Aligoté producers: Coche-Dury, Cogny, Confuron, Dupard, Jobard, Rion.

BOURGOGNE GRAND ORDINAIRE AC
BURGUNDY

Gamay, Pinot Noir, César, Tressot

Chardonnay, Aligoté, Pinot Blanc and others

You hardly ever see this – 'BGO' as they call it. I haven't tried a bottle, except in Burgundy itself, for years. It is almost impossible to know what you're getting because this is the Burgundian catch-all to end all catch-alls. Just about any grape which will grow can be included in the blending cauldron.

Chardonnay (though anyone who uses this for 'BGO', the cheapest AC, must be nuts), Aligoté, Pinot Blanc, Pinot Beurot, Sacy, and Melon de Bourgogne (the Muscadet grape which was supposedly banished from Burgundy generations ago for being too boring) can be used for whites, and Gamay, Pinot Noir, César and Tressot for reds. You won't find the wine abroad and even in Burgundy it's mostly sold as quaffing wine for the bars – for which it can be perfectly suitable, so long as there is a bottle of *crème de cassis* close to hand if it's white, in case the first mouthful explains with awful clarity that epithet 'Ordinaire' – the only French AC to admit in writing that the wine in the bottle may actually be pretty duff stuff.

BOURGOGNE PASSE-TOUT-GRAIN AC
BURGUNDY

Gamay, Pinot Noir

Almost always red (with just a little rosé) this *appellation* is for a mixture of up to two-thirds Gamay with the rest Pinot Noir. In the Côte Chalonnaise and Côte d'Or, as vineyards are replanted, the percentage of Pinot Noir is increasing, which means here that the quality has improved in recent years and should now show a good sturdy, cherry fruit when very young, offset by a raspingly attractive, herby acidity from the Gamay, but softening over three to four years to a gentle, round-edged wine. Best growers: Chaley, Cornu, Rion, Thomas. Best merchants: Chanson, Leroy.

BOURGOGNE ROSÉ AC
BURGUNDY

Pinot Noir

Not much is made, but in overcropping years like 1982 many growers will try to give more concentration to their reds by drawing off some of the rosé wine before it has absorbed very much colour from the skins, and it can make a very pleasant pink.

BOURGUEIL AC
CENTRAL LOIRE

Cabernet Franc, Cabernet Sauvignon

Bourgueil is a village just north of the Loire between Angers and Tours. The area is unusually dry for the Loire valley, favouring the ripening of red grape varieties, which explains why, in a region known for its white wines, Bourgueil is famous for red. Cabernet Franc is the main grape, topped up with a little Cabernet Sauvignon, and in hot years the results can be superb.

Although the wines can be rather peppery and vegetal at first, if you give them time – at least five years, preferably ten – they develop a wonderful fragrance which is like essences of blackcurrant and raspberry combined, with just enough earthiness to keep their feet firmly on the ground. Best years: 1988, '86, '85, '83, '82, '78, '76. Best producers: Audebert (estate wines), Caslot-Galbrun, Caslot-Jamet, Couly-Dutheil, Domaine des Raguenières, Druet, Lamé-Delille-Boucard.

BOUZY
Coteaux Champenois AC
CHAMPAGNE

Pinot Noir

A leading Champagne village on the Montagne de Reims growing the region's best Pinot Noir, usually made into *white* Champagne. However, in outstanding years, a little still red wine is made from Pinot Noir. It is light, high-acid, and often with a cutting, herby edge. But now and then, a waif-like perfume of raspberry and strawberry is just strong enough to provide a fleeting pleasure before the chalky tannins take over again. Best years: 1985, '83, '82. Don't age it on purpose, although it can keep for several years. Best producers: Bara, Georges Vesselle, Jean Vesselle.

BURGUNDY RED WINES

► Gevrey-Chambertin is one of the most famous villages in Burgundy's most celebrated wine region, the Côte d'Or, where what we generally think of as the finest red Burgundy is made. Like many of the best villages, Gevrey-Chambertin possesses a number of particularly good vineyards, classified as *grand cru* – here there are eight.

Burgundy isn't just a wine name or even a wine region. It is a great sweep of eastern France which at one time was a Grand Duchy reaching right up to the North Sea, way down to below Lyon and across to the mountains guarding Switzerland and Italy. At the height of its influence Burgundy was as powerful and as wealthy as the Kingdom of France which eyed it fearfully from the west. What is now left of this grandeur is some inspiring architecture – and a tradition of eating and drinking which still makes gourmets the world over describe Burgundy greedily as the belly of France.

If Burgundy is indeed 'the belly of France', we'd better be a little more specific, because I don't think the Belgians, whose country once was part of Burgundy, will take too kindly to being described as Burgundian, although they're great eaters, and still purchase much of the best Burgundy wine. No, modern Burgundy is a rather slimmed down version – if that's the word.

It begins south of Paris near Auxerre where a few pleasant reds and some sparkling rosés are made, but doesn't really get into gear until the great Côte d'Or rises to the south of Dijon. The Côte d'Or – or Golden Slope – is incredibly small – a single sliver of south- to east-facing land running from Dijon to Chagny, which is in places only a few hundred yards wide. Yet many of the most famous wines in the world are from these barely adequate acres.

The Côte d'Or is divided into two – the Côte de Nuits in the north, and the Côte de Beaune in the south. The Côte de Nuits is almost entirely red wine country. Gevrey-Chambertin, with its great vineyard Chambertin – Napoleon's favourite wine – is the first famous village, followed to the south by Morey-St-Denis, Chambolle-Musigny, Vougeot with its famous Clos de Vougeot, Vosne-Romanée, home of Romanée-Conti, the rarest and most expensive of Burgundies – and finally Nuits St-Georges. The Côte de Beaune grows a considerable amount of white, but also produces wonderful reds in Aloxe-Corton, Beaune, Pommard and Volnay.

The Côte Chalonnaise lacks the cohesion of the Côte d'Or – no great long carpet of vines but rather vineyards taking their place on the best south- and east-facing slopes. It's a relaxing area, and the wines, while good, rarely set out to scale the heights.

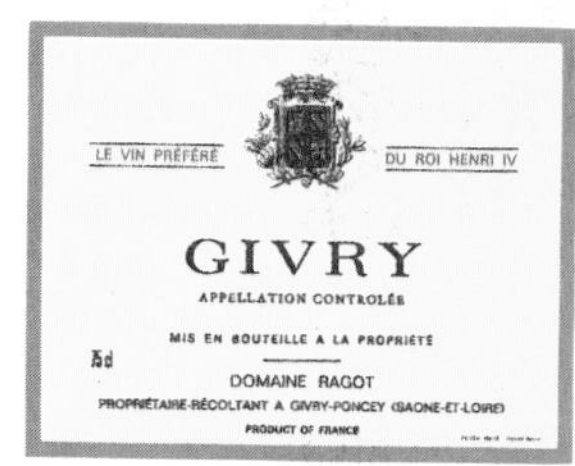

WINE ENTRIES

- Bourgogne
- Bourgogne Grand Ordinaire
- Bourgogne-Passe-Tout-Grain
- Bourgogne Rosé
- Côte de Beaune ACs
- Côte de Nuits ACs
- Givry
- Mâcon
- Mâcon Supérieur
- Mercurey
- Rully

GRAPE ENTRIES

- Gamay
- Pinot Noir

See also *Côte d'Or*, pages 92–93.

Burgundy White Wines

▶ The tiny village of Aloxe-Corton is famous for the magnificent gilded roof of its château and for its two great *grand cru* wines: the red Corton and the white Corton-Charlemagne.

The name Burgundy always seems to be more suitable for red wine than white. BUR-GUN-DY. It sort of booms: it's a rich, weighty sound, purple rather than pale, haunches of venison and flagons of plum-ripe red rather than a half-dozen oysters and Chablis.

Yet white Burgundy is nowadays at least as important as red Burgundy, possibly more so, since the term Burgundy applies to a large swathe of eastern France starting only a few miles from the chilly vineyards of Champagne, at Chablis in the north (which has its own map on page 58) and stretching down through the Côte d'Or south of Dijon, the Côte Chalonnaise and on to the Mâconnais, where France seems to change from being a cold northern nation to a warm, Mediterranean one. In all of these areas, white wine is of crucial importance, and in two – Chablis and the Mâconnais – red wine is something of an irrelevance!

The most important grape right through Burgundy is the Chardonnay, and it is because of the tremendous renown of the white wines of Chablis and the Côte d'Or that Chardonnay became planted worldwide as winegrowers everywhere sought to emulate the flavour of Meursault, Puligny-Montrachet and Chablis. It is now thought of as the world's greatest white wine grape and its birthplace is Burgundy. Aligoté is the second-line grape and rarely sets the world on fire, but can produce some decent tangy whites and can also add a useful acid nip to sparkling Crémant de Bourgogne.

Between Dijon and Chagny lies the long thin sliver of land called the Côte d'Or – the Golden Slope. The northern section, the Côte de Nuits, is almost entirely given over to red wines, but the Côte de Beaune to the south produces fabulously rich, compellingly powerful white wines – from the villages of Aloxe-Corton, Meursault, Puligny-Montrachet and Chassagne-Montrachet.

The Côte Chalonnaise is a small area whose whites were mostly made into sparkling wine, but both Rully and Montagny are now showing they can produce lovely white wines without the help of bubbles. And the Mâconnais is the broadest expanse of white Chardonnay vines in Burgundy. Most of the wine is simple and refreshing, but in the ACs of Pouilly-Fuissé and St-Véran, a few producers are creating some of Burgundy's finest wines.

WINE ENTRIES

GRAPE ENTRIES

See also *Chablis*, pages 58–59, and *Côte d'Or*, pages 94–95.

BROUILLY AC
BEAUJOLAIS, BURGUNDY

Gamay

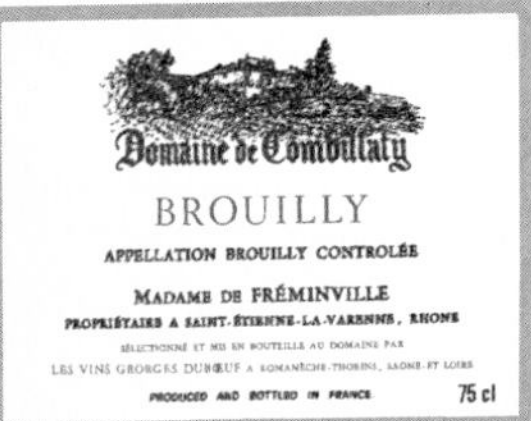

'A bottle of Brooey' doesn't sound quite serious, does it? Well, why should it? Brouilly (which is pronounced approximately as above) is the largest of the Beaujolais *crus* (or special communes allowed to use their own name on their wine), which makes it a top rank Beaujolais. But it's still Beaujolais: it's still made from the juicy-fruity Gamay grape; it's still supposed to make you laugh and smile – not get serious; and you're still supposed to drink it in draughts not dainty sips.

What makes Brouilly special is that it is the closest of the *crus* to the Beaujolais-Villages style (a lot of growers make both). It is the most southerly of the *crus*: south of Brouilly the 'Villages' and the simple 'Beaujolais' vineyards stretch away towards Lyon. The wine is very fruity and can make a delicious Nouveau (several local restaurants use it in this way). There is rarely much point in ageing it. Interestingly, 1985, '86, '87 and '88 have all made some single-estate Brouilly which has improved with ageing, but this is the exception. Best producers: la Chaize, Duboeuf (Garranches, Combillaty), Fouilloux, Hospices de Beaujeu (especially Pissevieille Cuvée), Pierreux, Ruet, Tours.

BROUSTET, CH.
Barsac AC, *2ème cru classé*
BORDEAUX

Sémillon, Sauvignon Blanc, Muscadelle

This is good wine, and so it should be, because this Second Growth Barsac is owned by Eric Fournier, who creates wonderful reds at hi First Growth St-Émilion property, Château Canon. Monsieur Fournier i extremely strict about selecting only the best barrels for bottling unde the Broustet label (the rest goes under the label Château de Ségur) an this results in a very small production – the 40 acres (16 hectares) onl produce around 2000 cases of Broustet. The wine doesn't have grea fruit but does have thick, lanolin-like richness coating your mouth, whic is pretty satisfying. Best years: 1986, '83, '81, '80, '75, '71.

BUGEY VDQS
SAVOIE

Gamay, Pinot Noir, Mondeuse, Poulsard

Jacquère, Chardonnay, Altesse

A few years ago you could have said 'Bugey? Don't waste space on sour little country wine most people will never have heard of, and they've got any sense, won't waste time searching for'. And I'd hav agreed. These straggly little vineyards covering 625 acres (25 hectares) halfway between Savoie and Lyon in the *département* of Ai made thin, lifeless whites from the Savoie grapes Altesse and Jacquèr hindered even further now and then by Aligoté. Red varieties rarely ripe and have a distinct flavour of damp vineyards and vegetable patche But a couple of summers back I stayed at the local hotel in the litt town of Belley. Bugey was the house wine and, having sniffed the re and found it distinctly reminiscent of a turnip field, I had a jug (small) the white. It was fantastic. Another jug (larger) later, I discovered I wa drinking one of the trendiest white wines in France – Chardonnay c Bugey. It's light, wonderfully creamy and fresh as mountain pasture ar one of the crispest Chardonnays in France. Rumour has it they make decent fizz too. Best producers: Cellier de Bel-Air, Crussy, Monin.

BUZET AC
SOUTH-WEST

Cabernet Sauvignon, Cabernet Franc, Merlot, Malbec

Sémillon, Sauvignon Blanc, Muscadelle

From being an obscure south-western *appellation* squashed into th edge of Armagnac, south of the river Garonne, Buzet has recent achieved a most welcome notoriety simply by offering the public what wants! They use the Bordeaux mix of grapes, and so decided to mal Bordeaux look-alike wines. As the prices of Bordeaux rose in the ea 1980s, Buzet produced a string of delicious, grassy-fresh, blackcurran reds – sharp enough to be reviving, soft enough to drink as soon as th were released – and at a lower price than Bordeaux. This kind of mov into a market vacuum was facilitated by the fact that 95 per cent of t production is controlled by the co-operative which, luckily, knows what is doing. Its Cuvée Napoléon, aged in oak, is extremely good to drink at five to ten years. There is very little rosé. Since this area nudges Armagnac, which relies on white wine for distilling brandy, you'd expect Buzet to turn over some decent whites as well, but they aren't terribly exciting – dry, rather full-feeling, but short on freshness and perfume. Best producer: Buzet-sur-Baïse co-operative. Château de Padère is the only major independent property.

CABERNET FRANC

Cabernet Franc is often dismissed as a kind of 'minor' Cabernet Sauvignon, but this is grossly unfair. Where Cabernet Sauvignon ripens effectively – particularly in Bordeaux's Médoc and Graves – there is no doubt that the lighter, less intense character of the Cabernet Franc is overshadowed. But in cooler areas, or in areas where the soil is damper and heavier, Cabernet Sauvignon cannot ripen properly, and here Cabernet Franc comes triumphantly into its own. The Loire is the best example. In Anjou and Touraine, not only do all the best rosés (especially Cabernet d'Anjou) come from Cabernet Franc, but all the best reds as well. The finest Anjou, Saumur and Touraine reds are likely to be Cabernet Franc (although Gamay can be used) and have a strong, grassy freshness linked to a raw but tasty blackcurrant fruit. The best examples come from Saumur-Champigny, Bourgueil and Chinon, where, in a hot vintage, the intensity of orchard-fresh, sharp but juicy, raspberry and blackcurrant fruit is absolutely delicious – and so refreshing – a quality rarely associated with fine red wine.

In the Bordeaux region, St-Émilion and Pomerol growers prefer Cabernet Franc to Cabernet Sauvignon, blending it with Merlot to add toughness and backbone to the luscious, fat Merlot fruit. Many properties have 30 per cent Cabernet Franc; two of the greatest, Ausone and Cheval-Blanc, have 50 per cent and 66 per cent respectively. In the Médoc, vineyards are more likely to have 10–20 per cent. Here the soft, yet slightly grassy flavour of the grape calms down the proud, aggressive Cabernet Sauvignon, and makes it more supple and rounded.

CABERNET SAUVIGNON

The king of red wine grapes – not just in France, but worldwide. Yet it is to France that all other countries look to understand the variety's full glory – and in particular to Bordeaux, where many of the vineyards are regarded as perfect for Cabernet Sauvignon. The heartland of Cabernet Sauvignon is the Médoc, where it can make up as much as 85 per cent of the plantings in a single property, and usually provides at least 60 per cent in the top properties. On the gravel slopes of St-Estèphe, Pauillac, St-Julien and Margaux it ripens late and produces a small yield. This restrained but concentrated harvest of loose-bunched, thick-skinned grapes gives a wine dark in colour, strong in mouth-puckering tannin, yet potentially rich in the heady flavour of pure blackcurrant with a fragrance veering between cedarwood, cigar boxes and the shavings of a newly-sharpened pencil.

This transformation from tough, broody palate-scourer to something of incomparable delicacy may take up to 20 years or more to achieve, and would take even longer if Merlot and Cabernet Franc grapes were not also used to soften and broaden the flavour. Although Cabernet Sauvignon is often grown elsewhere in the world to produce a 100 per cent varietal wine, Bordeaux winemakers always blend it, and they're right: it can be too aggressive in feel and flavour by itself.

In the Graves it is still the dominant grape, but plays a minor role in St-Émilion and Pomerol since it needs warmer, drier soil to ripen well.

Similarly, it is not much planted in the Loire region because the ripening season is too cool. Most of the other red wines of the south-west use Cabernet Sauvignon in varying proportions. And in Languedoc-Roussillon it is used to 'improve' the traditional varieties. As little as ten per cent makes a major difference to a blend. However, it is on the sun-baked hillsides of Provence that many growers are trying to emulate the supreme qualities of the Médoc by planting vineyards mostly in Cabernet Sauvignon; in Baux-en-Provence they even mix it with Syrah – to memorable, juicy-rich effect!

CADILLAC AC
BORDEAUX

Sémillon, Sauvignon Blanc, Muscadelle

This is a rather forlorn little AC, bordering the Garonne, in the southern part of the Premières Côtes de Bordeaux AC. It covers a mere 200 acres (80 hectares), and even this paltry acreage seems to be dwindling. The AC was only created in 1981, with the aim of giving the best wines in the southern Premières Côtes their own AC to help boost sales. This was fair enough, except that the AC specifies the wines must be semi-sweet or sweet and the market is moving fast and furiously towards dry whites – which, of course, the area around Cadillac could produce very well. Cadillac does get affected by noble rot – the fungus which, across the Garonne, intensifies the sweetness of Sauternes – but since it is extremely expensive to separate out the nobly-rotted grapes and since Cadillac has no reputation which might allow it to charge higher prices, most of the wines are merely sweetish with no real lusciousness. Château Fayau is the one exception. The allowed yield is 40 hectolitres per hectare as against 25 hectolitres per hectare for Sauternes – another reason why Cadillac is rarely special.

CAHORS AC
SOUTH-WEST FRANCE

Malbec, Merlot, Tannat

After Bordeaux Cahors is the leading red wine of the south-west, if only because it makes no attempt to ape Bordeaux and its flavours. But then why should it? Cahors has been famous since Roman times, and indeed was often used by Bordeaux winemakers to provide colour and fruit for what (two centuries ago) was nearer Bordeaux rosé than red. The vineyards are on both sides of the river Lot, and the whole region is about as far from hustle-bustle as can be. Only red wine is produced, with Auxerrois as the main grape (70 per cent). This is called Malbec in Bordeaux, where they don't think much of it, but in Cahors it produces dark, tannic wine which has an unforgettable flavour of plummy richness, streaked with apple acidity. As it ages, it takes on a gorgeous tangle of tastes dominated quite superbly by tobacco spice and blackberry and sweet prunes! The vineyards are on slopes, where the toughest wines come from, but also on the valley floor which produces lighter, more mainstream flavours. There is a fast-improving co-operative, but otherwise single estates are best. I recommend the following: Cayrou, Clos la Coutale, Clos de Gamot, Clos Triguedina, Gaudou, Haute-Serre, Quattre, Treilles.

CAIRANNE
Côtes du Rhône-Villages AC
SOUTHERN RHÔNE

Grenache, Syrah, Cinsaut, Mourvèdre

Many Côtes du Rhône-Villages wines have early drinkability as their only virtue, but Cairanne makes full use of the stony *garrigue* soil behind the village to produce dark-coloured, richly juicy wines which can certainly be drunk young because of their sheer burst of spicy up-front fruit, but which normally have a slug of tannic toughness at the back showing they will age well. I haven't finished my 1978 yet and it seems to get better by the bottle. The co-operative is very good, making juicy but fairly formidable reds and a bright, fruity rosé. Best producers: Ameillaud, Grand-Jas, Rabasse-Charavin.

CALON-SÉGUR, CH.
St-Estèphe AC, *3ème cru classé*
MÉDOC, BORDEAUX

Cabernet Sauvignon, Cabernet Franc, Merlot

The most northerly of all the Medoc's Classed Growths and the lowest in altitude, averaging less than 30 feet (10 metres) above sea level. What gives it Classed Growth quality is a spur of chalky, gravelly soil – usually found on higher ground. None of the neighbouring properties – struggling along on heavier clay soils – can produce wine which remotely matches Calon-Ségur. It used to be thought of as St-Estèphe's leading château, along with Montrose, but both have now been overtaken by Cos d'Estournel. Until the last few vintages, Calon-Ségur's problem was that its wine, though quite impressive, has been ever so slightly dull and, at the high prices demanded by Médoc Classed Growths, dullness isn't really on. Best vintages: 1986, '85, '82. Second wine: Marquis de Ségur.

CANON, CH.
St-Émilion AC, *premier grand cru classé*
BORDEAUX

Merlot, Cabernet Franc, Cabernet Sauvignon, Malbec

If I had to plump for the most perfect, most recognizable, most reliably luscious St-Émilion – reeking of that toffee-butter-and-raisins mellow ripeness which only Merlot can impart – I'd go for Canon. This 'buttery' sweetness can seem a little shallow and one-dimensional, but not at Canon, because the wine is also deep, with a rich plummy fruit, and in good vintages is impressively tannic to start with. The vineyard is just west of the town of St-Émilion and completely surrounded by other First Growths. Its young owner is such a perfectionist that in the last few vintages Canon has been as good as any wine in St-Émilion – in fact as good as almost any in all Bordeaux. It is possible to get great pleasure from it at only a few years old, but in good vintages keep the bottle for a dozen years or more. Best vintages: 1988, '86, '85, '83, '82, '79.

CANON-FRONSAC AC
BORDEAUX

Merlot, Cabernet Franc, Cabernet Sauvignon, Malbec

The heart of the Fronsac region, covering 750 acres (300 hectares) of hilly vineyard between the villages of Fronsac and St-Michel de Fronsac, just set back from the flat banks of the Dordogne river. The wines have a minimum of 11 degrees alcohol as against 10·5 degrees for Fronsac, and this means they can be quite strong and beefy when young. But they do age well and, after going through a rather gamy period at a few years old, usually emerge at ten years plus with a lovely, soft Merlot-dominated flavour and a good mineral tang sometimes a little reminiscent of Pomerol. Best years: 1988, '85, '83, '82, '79, '78. Best producers: Canon (there are two, both good), Canon-de-Brem, Haut-Mazeris, Moulin-Pey-Labrie, Vrai-Canon-Bouché, Vrai-Canon-Boyer.

CANTEMERLE, CH.
Haut-Médoc AC, *5ème cru classé*
BORDEAUX

Cabernet Sauvignon, Merlot, Cabernet Franc, Petit Verdot

You head out of Bordeaux on the D2, through suburbs, shrubland, damp meadows, and the occasional vineyard, and you begin to wonder if you're on the wrong road for the great wineland of the Médoc. Then the forests fall away and the land is thick with rows of neatly trained vines. There, on the right, is Château la Lagune then, on the left, Château Cantemerle, a jewel set inside its own little woodland glade. Drive up the long avenue shrouded over with age-old trees and stand in front of the turretted castle. Silence. Stillness. Fairyland? Not far off.

Cantemerle was placed last in the 1855 Classification – perhaps because of its sheltered, unnoticed forest existence. But the wine has always been better than that, and since Cordier, the large merchant house, took over in 1980, it has improved by leaps and bounds. In general, Cantemerle is almost muskily perfumed and relatively delicate, but the 1983 is a whopper – rich, concentrated and dark, yet already showing an exotic fragrance. Apart from the '83, which will benefit from 15 or more years' ageing, you don't have to age Cantemerle more than seven to ten years. Best years: 1988, '85, '83, '82, '81, '78.

CARBONNIEUX, CH.
Pessac-Léognan AC, *cru classé de Graves*
BORDEAUX

🍷 Cabernet Sauvignon, Merlot, Cabernet Franc and others

🍷 Sauvignon Blanc, Sémillon, Muscadelle

▼ Carbonnieux has been making wine since the 12th century. The present château dates from the 1300s.

This is the largest of the Graves Classed Growth properties which now lie within the new Pessac-Léognan AC. Its 175 acres (70 hectares) are divided equally between red and white grape varieties. Sauvignon Blanc dominates the white vineyard at 65 per cent, with 30 per cent Sémillon and 5 per cent Muscadelle, which might explain why the wine is bright and breezy when it's very young. However, it isn't cheap and a Classed Growth white has to mature and develop extra nuances of personality to be worth the money. I haven't had any mature white Carbonnieux which roused the tastebuds from their slumbers. There is now evidence of a little new wood being used – I'd like more.

The red Carbonnieux always seems to lack a bit of stuffing. That might not matter if the objective was to make a fruity, quick-drinking style, but the style is quite 'serious' – dry, rather reserved and closed when young, promising to open up with some maturity. There just isn't the weight or the concentration to achieve it. A pity.

CARIGNAN

I *like* Carignan. But I seem to be in a tiny minority. It's the dominant red grape in the south of France and forms the backbone for most anonymous French *vin de table*. Yet Carignan is ideally suited to modern wine-making. Traditionally, it produced a gigantic amount of tough fruitless wine in many of the Midi's less favoured vineyards, and its sprawling stranglehold over much of the south was a major reason for the paucity of ACs between Provence and the Pyrenees. However, there is potential for a delicious spicy fruit in the Carignan, especially when the Beaujolais method of carbonic maceration is used. This, combined with lower yields and better ripeness levels, means that the Carignan can at least achieve respectability in the sunny south, if not exactly nobility. But who wants nobility in a bottle of cheap, juicy Mediterranean red? My sentiments exactly.

CASSIS AC
PROVENCE

Grenache, Cinsaut, Mourvèdre

Ugni Blanc, Clairette, Marsanne and others

This is really a white wine town. Rosé and red don't figure much on the quality stakes, although they represent almost half the production. The red is dull at best; the rosé can be lovely and can age for a surprisingly long time – but only from a single estate such as Clos Ste-Magdeleine or Mas Calendal. White Cassis is the most well-known and most overpriced white wine of the French Riviera. I can't help wondering whether the stunning views of the vineyards rising up towards the steep cliffs, the port's daily catch of the Mediterranean's freshest fish, and the cavalcade of quayside restaurants crushed tight with trendies from nearby Marseille and Toulouse don't have something to do with it. The wine isn't *that* special – I mean, it really *isn't*. Based on Ugni Blanc and Clairette, sometimes with Marsanne, Sauvignon Blanc and Bourboulenc to help out, the one thing in its favour is freshness. Best producers: Clos Ste-Magdeleine, Ferme Blanche, Paternel.

CÉRONS AC
BORDEAUX

Sémillon, Sauvignon Blanc, Muscadelle

Cérons is an enclave in the Graves region of Bordeaux, on the northern boundary of Sauternes-Barsac. The AC is for sweet white wine; not quite so sweet as Sauternes, and for that reason not so well known, nor so highly priced. Throughout the 1960s and '70s the interest in sweet white wine waned and hard times hit Cérons and Sauternes alike. The only solution was to use the grapes to make dry wine and these, with Graves AC on the label, are now more important in Cérons than 'sweeties'. A few producers still make gently sweet, rather soft, mildly honeyed wines, with the restrained sweetness of a ripe apple rather than syrupy richness. Best years: 1986, '83. Best producers: Château de Cérons, Grand Enclos du Château de Cérons, Haura, Mayne-Binet.

CHABLIS AC
BURGUNDY

Chardonnay

Fact: Chablis wine can only come from 4620 acres (1870 hectares) of vineyards clustered round the town of Chablis in the Serein valley between Dijon and Paris, in France. But you try telling that to a wine producer who happily produces his 'Chablis' in South Australia or California. Fact: Chablis wine can only come from the Chardonnay grape. Nonsense, the New Zealanders call their Chardonnay Chardonnay and sell it at a fair price. They use Müller-Thurgau and Chasselas for their 'Chablis' – it helps to keep the price down. Fact: Chablis is a still dry white wine. Not at all. An Argentinian producer may find that the sweeter style of 'Chablis' sells best, and he has a surplus of red grapes. So he thinks he'll make his 'Chablis' pink this year – or why not sparkling? Sure, sparkling wines are popular; let's have pink sparkling 'Chablis'.

Chablis' trouble is that it has become synonymous in many parts of the world with dry-to-medium, white-to-off-white wine from any available grape and with a low, low price. Real Chablis couldn't be more different. It is always white and dry, often bone dry, so green-edged, so flinty that the taste reminds me of the click of dry stones knocked together. Sometimes the dryness opens out into a broader taste, nutty, honeyed even, yet never rich, a Puritan's view of honey spice, not a Cavalier's.

The Serein river valley is Burgundy's northernmost outpost. The Chardonnay only ripens with difficulty, and there is a dreadful record of devastation by frost. Consequently the price is high. Too high, because much Chablis can be rather mean and not a lot better than a decent Muscadet. In general, straight Chablis AC is drunk at one to two years old, but the better producers often produce wine which can improve for three to five years. Best years: 1988, '87, '86, '85, '84, '83. Best producers: Brocard, Defaix, Droin, Durup, Fèvre, Laroche, Long-Depaquit, Louis Michel, Pico-Race, Pinson, Raveneau, Régnard, Rottiers-Clotilde, Simmonet-Febvre, Vocoret.

CHABLIS

Chablis has managed to make a virtue out of the fact that in most years it barely manages to ripen its grapes and the resulting wines have long been a byword for green, ultra-dry whites of no discernible richness and little discernible fruit. Yet that just shows how easy it is for a reputation to linger on long after it bears little resemblance to the truth. Chablis is certainly dry, but it is very rarely green or raw nowadays, and although it doesn't have the almost tropical fruit ripeness of some white wines from further south in Burgundy, it does have a gentleness and a light unassertive fruit which can make for delicious drinking.

Also, Chablis does come from one small, decidedly marginal area in the frost-prone, autumn-cool valley of the river Serein between Dijon and Paris – and from there alone. Sadly for Chablis, non-French winemakers and marketing men found the name beguiling to the eye, and extremely easy to pronounce and remember. Consequently all over the world the name Chablis has been adapted to local wines. Spanish 'Chablis' was, for a long time, a common sight on British wine-shop shelves; and today, California, Australia, New Zealand, South Africa and many others all produce their Chablis versions – which are limited by one thing only – not the grape type, not by the wine style, but by the fact that they are *cheap*.

True Chablis comes only from the Chardonnay grape, comes only from the French AC region, and is always white and dry. And it is *never* cheap. It *cannot* be cheap because the vineyards are at the northern limit for fully ripening Chardonnay grapes. The Champagne

WINE ENTRIES
Chablis
Chablis Grand Cru
Chablis Premier Cru
Petit Chablis

GRAPE ENTRY
Chardonnay

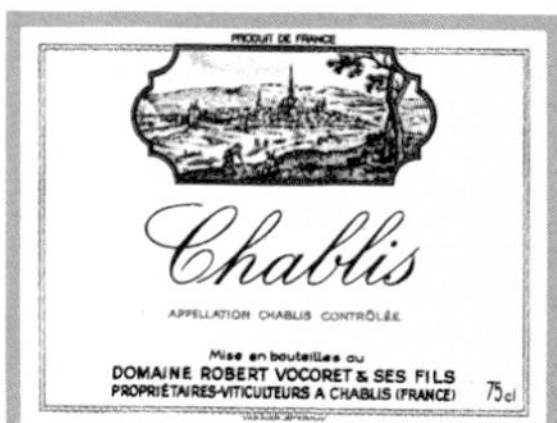

PRODUIT DE FRANCE
Chablis
APPELLATION CHABLIS CONTRÔLÉE
Mise en bouteilles au
DOMAINE ROBERT VOCORET & SES FILS
PROPRIÉTAIRES-VITICULTEURS A CHABLIS (FRANCE)
75cl

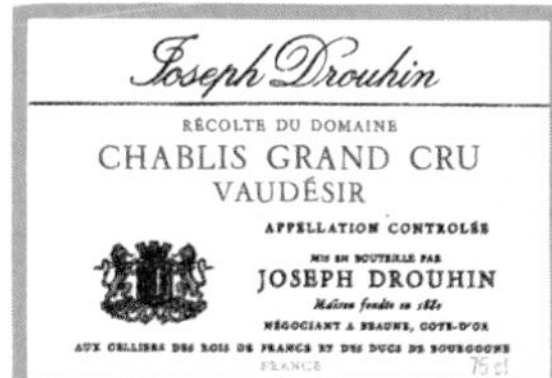

◀ Three of Chablis' top-quality – or *grand cru* vineyards. In the foreground, Vaudésir, with Grenouilles and Valmur behind.

region is a mere 19 miles (30km) to the north, and you only have to taste a still Coteaux Champenois Chardonnay to realize how tart and thin unripe Chardonnay can be. The better Chablis vineyards – especially the seven *grand cru* sites – are all on slopes to catch the maximum heat from the sun, which automatically increases labour costs, and the harvest is notoriously unreliable due to the ever-present risk of spring frosts, the likelihood of bad weather when the vines flower, and the probability of winter setting in early.

All of which might make one wonder if it is worth continuing the effort. Well, it is. New methods of frost prevention are cancelling out the worst effects of a spring-time relapse into winter. A better understanding of the malolactic fermentation (which converts tart malic acid into softer, creamier lactic acid) means that very few wines are now harsh and green, though some may be too creamy and dull. And, despite Chablis' 'bone-dry' reputation, an increasing number of producers are experimenting with oak barrel ageing – resulting in some full, toasty, positively rich dry whites which make me almost prepared to pay the high prices.

CHABLIS GRAND CRU AC
BURGUNDY

Chardonnay

This is the heart of Chablis: the vineyards of Bougros, Preuses, Vaudésir, Grenouilles, Valmur, Les Clos and Blanchots, which comprise a single swathe of vines rising steeply above the little river Serein, facing serenely towards the south-west and able to lap up every last ray of the warm afternoon sun. It is only because of the perfect exposure, the steep elevation and the unique Kimmeridgian limestone that the Chardonnay grapes can fully ripen and gain the fatness and strength which should mark out a *grand cru*. And while the quality of much Chablis has become rather haphazard in recent years, *grand cru* growers, in general, have been making exceptional wines during the 1980s, especially those who have used oak to mature their wines, adding a rich warmth to the taut flavours of the wine.

Prices are high, naturally, because supplies are very limited – especially since the *grands crus* suffer more than the other vineyards from the late frosts which can decimate Chablis' crop in the spring. There is much argument between those who use new oak to age their wines and those who don't. The anti-new wood brigade *do* make the *vrai* Chablis – if you're after a wine which always keeps a firm grip on that lean, streak of self-denial which, even after ten years, stops a *grand cru* ever wallowing in its own deliciousness. If you use new oak barrels, the wine gains a rich, almost tropical, apricotty fruit, nuts and cream flavour and the spicy butter of the oak completes a picture of high-quality, indulgent white. And then, just when you're about to say 'this is as sumptuous as Montrachet' you find that reserved, minerally restraint clambering back to centre stage, admonishing you at the last gasp for forgetting the prim self-restraint that is the key to Chablis' character. Never drink *grand cru* too young – it's a total waste of money. Five to ten years is the normal timescale. Best years: 1988, '87, '86, '85, '84, '83, '82, '81, '78. Best producers: Dauvissat, Defaix, Droin, Fèvre, Long-Depaquit, Louis Michel, Pinson, Raveneau, Régnard, Robin, Servin, Simmonet-Febvre, Vocoret.

CHABLIS PREMIER CRU AC
BURGUNDY

Chardonnay

Of Chablis' 4620 acres (1870 hectares), 1435 are designated *premier cru* or First Growth. In true Burgundian style *premier cru* is the second tier of quality, *grand cru* (Great Growth) being the top. There's no doubt that *some* of these *premiers crus* are on splendid slopes, but Chablis has been the scene of much contentious politicking in recent years as 'interested' parties (those owning the relevant vineyards) have sought to upgrade Petit Chablis land to Chablis AC, and much straight Chablis land to the superior AC, Chablis Premier Cru. There is a good argument for upgrading the majority of Petit Chablis land since it can produce perfectly good wine from the Chardonnay grape. However, there is little evidence yet that the 'new' *premiers crus* are doing anything except lessening the expectations of the consumer when confronted by a *premier cru* label – because *I* can't detect any difference with many of them and I don't expect the consumer can either. But what am I saying? Of *course* I can tell the difference. *Premier cru* prices kick off at up to twice as much as straight Chablis. Once again, is the consumer being taken for a ride? Of those 1435 acres (580 hectares) of *premier cru*, 500 acres (200 hectares) are brand new – and some historically have names like *Verjus* (sour grapes) and *Champs des Raves* (turnip fields).

So what of the good *premiers crus*? The best are Montée de Tonnerre, Vaillons and Mont de Milieu, just south of the *grand cru* slopes, and some examples of Côte de Léchet and Montmains, south-east-facing slopes to the west of the town of Chablis. The flavours are still dry, and are often nutty, fairly full, with a streak of something almost mineral there. They should feel bigger and more intense than straight Chablis AC, and if the winemaker has used wood rather than stainless steel to make his wine, they probably will. But at these prices, satisfaction, I'm afraid, is *not* guaranteed, and the sincerity of the producer is actually more important than the particular vineyard site in the long run. A good *premier cru* may take as much as five years to show its full potential. Best years: 1988, '87, '86, '85, '83, '82, '81. Best producers: La Chablisienne co-operative, Dauvissat, Defaix, Droin, Drouhin, Fèvre, Laroche, Louis Michel, Pinson, Raveneau, Régnard, Rottiers-Clotilde, Simmonet-Febvre, Testut, Tour Vaubourg, Vocoret.

HAMBERTIN AC
rand cru
ÔTE DE NUITS, BURGUNDY

Pinot Noir

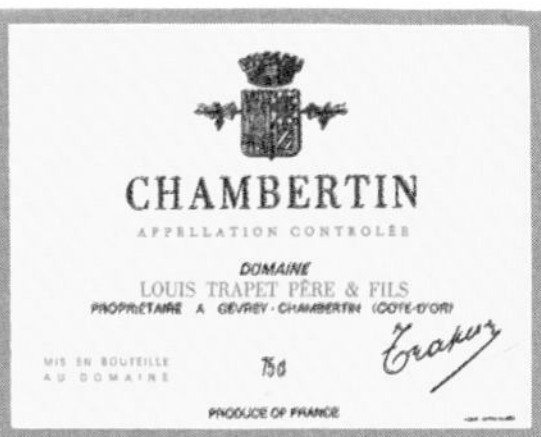

'Chambertin, King of Wines!' is how the old-timers described this powerful *grand cru* from Gevrey-Chambertin. 'Emperor of Wines' might have been more apt since this was Napoleon's favourite tipple. They say he drank it wherever he went – Russia, Egypt, Italy . . . Waterloo? Perhaps 1815 was a bad vintage? Well, maybe, but this can be a hell of a wine, the biggest, most brooding of all.

In a good year the wine starts off positively rasping with power, the fruit all chewy damson skins and tarry tannin. But give it time, five years, maybe ten, or even 20, and Chambertin transforms itself. The scent is exotic and rich, fleetingly floral, but more likely to envelop you with the powerful warmth of choice damsons and plums so ripe they would long have fallen from the tree – add to this the strange brilliance of black chocolate, prunes, and the delicious decay of well-hung game – and you have one of the most remarkable flavours red wine can create. Best years: 1988, '87, '85, '83, '80, '78, '76. Best producers: Camus, Damoy, Drouhin, Ponsot, Rebourseau, Armand Rousseau, Tortochot, Trapet.

HAMBERTIN CLOS-DE-ÈZE AC
rand cru
ÔTE DE NUITS, BURGUNDY

Pinot Noir

Chambertin and Chambertin Clos-de-Bèze are neighbours on the stretch of slope at just below 1000 feet (300 metres), running from Gevrey-Chambertin south to Vosne-Romanée, which produces the greatest reds in Burgundy. The wines are basically the same, and Clos-de-Bèze can simply call itself 'Chambertin' if it wants to. There is, however, a great difference in the quality of the different producers. Both wines are relentlessly popular, and overproduction is a recurrent problem, but good Chambertin or Clos-de-Bèze can be so good it is worth persevering. Best years: 1988, '87, '85, '83, '80, '78, '76. Best producers: Camus, Damoy, Drouhin, Ponsot, Rebourseau, Armand Rousseau, Tortochot, Trapet.

HAMBOLLE-MUSIGNY AC
ÔTE DE NUITS, BURGUNDY

Pinot Noir

Chambolle-Musigny is supposed to produce the most fragrant, perfumed red wines in all Burgundy. Well, yes and no. A few bottles of Chambolle-Musigny Les Amoureuses or Les Charmes have really set my heart fluttering. Les Amoureuses and Les Charmes are two of the village's leading vineyards, and their suggestion of coy, flirtatious femininity – all rustling silks and fans – is what many writers claim as the character of Chambolle-Musigny wines. The fact that 'Charmes' probably derives from the French for 'straw' or 'hornbeam' takes a bit of the romance out of it. The fact that most modern Chambolle-Musigny suffers from the Burgundian disease of over-cropping and over-sugaring the grape juice doesn't help much either.

The potential for beautiful wines is there. The vineyards are excellently situated just south of Morey-St-Denis, between 800 and 1000 feet (250 and 300 metres) up. Best years: 1988, '87, '85, '83, '78. Best producers: Drouhin, Dujac, Grivot, Hudelot-Noëllat, Jadot, Mugnier, Roumier, Serveau, de Vogüé.

CHAMPAGNE

The Champagne region of France has given its name to the whole concept of sparkling wine. Fizz is thought of and described as 'Champagne' even when it's made thousands of miles away from this chilly, windswept northern area. And although the hordes of imitations throughout the world relentlessly pursue a style as close as possible to that of true Champagne, they never achieve it – for one simple reason. No-one in their right mind in a country like Spain, Italy, Australia, America or Argentina – where sunshine to ripen the grapes is taken for granted – would ever risk planting vines in such an unfriendly, hostile environment as the stark chalklands of France's far north, where it never gets warm enough for a grape to ripen totally, where the acidity stays toothachingly high and where the thin, meagre flavour of the young still wine makes it virtually undrinkable on its own.

But I've just described the perfect base wine for great bubbly. If you make sure this workhouse gruel of a wine is made from top quality grape varieties like the white Chardonnay and the black Pinot Noir and Pinot Meunier (rosé Champagne is made by blending a little red wine with the white – the only French AC to allow this), then you can't go wrong. It's a good thing though that the Romans decided to plant grapes in the region. It must have been warmer then, and I doubt if anyone would do it now.

'La Champagne' – the only place in the world real Champagne can come from – is mostly a charmless, treeless, bitingly cold prairie land to the east of Paris. Yet centred on the towns of Reims and Épernay, and stretching down towards the northern tip of Burgundy at Chablis, there are five areas where the combination of chalk soil and well-drained, protected microclimates allows the grapes to ripen. The Montagne de Reims is a low, wide hill south of Reims where Pinot Noir excels. Côte des Blancs is a long east-facing slope, south of Épernay, almost exclusively planted with Chardonnay. Vallée de la Marne runs east-west through Épernay and grows good Pinot Meunier and Pinot Noir. There are two less important areas to the south – the Aube and the Côtes de Sézanne. There are a very few still wines made in the region, labelled AC Coteaux Champenois.

► The characteristic chalk of Champagne. True Champagne can only come from this region and must have got its bubbles through a second fermentation in the bottle.

AC ENTRIES
Champagne
Coteaux Champenois
Rosé des Riceys

CHAMPAGNE HOUSE ENTRIES
Bollinger
Alfred Gratien
Krug
Moët & Chandon
Pol Roger
Louis Roederer
Taittinger
Veuve Clicquot

GRAPE ENTRIES
Chardonnay
Pinot Noir

CHAMPAGNE AC
CHAMPAGNE

🍷 🍷 Pinot Noir, Chardonnay, Pinot Meunier

The renown of Champagne is such that it is the only *appellation contrôlée* wine which does not have to bear the words *appellation contrôlée* on its label. Yet Champagne *is* an AC – very definitely so – and one more tightly controlled than most because of the insatiable thirst of the world for this most exciting of sparkling wines.

Champagne is thought of as a general term for sparkling wine, and there are countries – mostly in the New World – which still use it to describe their sparkling wines, but in fact the AC applies only to sparkling wines (mostly white but occasionally rosé), which have gained their effervescence by undergoing a second fermentation in the actual bottle from which they will eventually be served (called the 'Champagne method') and which come from one precise geographical location centred on Épernay and Reims, to the east of Paris. Nothing else, coming from anywhere else in the world, can be true Champagne.

The northerly origin of Champagne means that the grape varieties rarely ripen fully, and the result is a light wine of very high acid. This isn't much fun by itself, but is perfect for making sparkling wine, so long as the wine comes from good grape varieties. In Champagne it does. The Chardonnay is the world's greatest white grape and here produces lovely, fragrant wines which become surprisingly creamy with a little maturity. Pinot Noir and Pinot Meunier are both high quality *black* grapes. This far north, their skins never develop much colour and careful pressing can remove the juice with virtually no coloration.

Although some Champagne is made only from a single grape variety – Blanc de Blancs from Chardonnay, or Blanc de Noirs from Pinot Noir – most is the result of blending the three grape varieties. Blending of the produce of different villages is also crucial, and most Champagnes will blend wines from perhaps a dozen throughout the region. The villages are classified according to quality. There are 17 *grand cru* villages at the top followed by 38 *premier cru* villages.

A small amount of Champagne is made by the vine-grower himself – this is usually unblended, and is only exciting when it comes from a *premier cru* or *grand cru* village. This will be clearly marked on the label. However, most Champagne is made by large merchant houses. It comes in sweet, medium, medium dry, very dry (brut) and very, very dry (ultra-brut) styles. It is usually a blend of two or more years, labelled 'non-vintage', but when the vintage is good, a 'vintage' cuvée is released of wine from a single year's harvest. There are also 'de luxe' cuvées, normally (but not always) vintage and supposedly the *crème de la crème* of Champagne. Frequently, they are more remarkable for the weirdness of their bottles and absurdity of their price, than the perfection of their flavours. Best years: 1988, '85, '83, '82, '81, '79, '78, '76, '75. Best producers: Billecart-Salmon, Bollinger, Deutz, Duval-Leroy, Gosset, Alfred Gratien, Henriot, Jacquesson, Krug, Lanson, Laurent-Perrier, Moët & Chandon, Paillard, Perrier-Jouët, Piper-Heidsieck, Pol Roger, Pommery & Greno, Roederer, Taittinger, Veuve Clicquot.

CHAMPAGNE ROSÉ AC
CHAMPAGNE

🍷 Pinot Noir, Pinot Meunier, Chardonnay

Quite the most chic of fizz a year or two ago, but the demand has cooled off a bit. Good pink Champagne has a delicious fragrance of cherries and raspberries to go with the foaming froth and is a gorgeous tongue-tingler – usually to be drunk as young as possible, though a few wines, like Pommery and Taittinger, age really well over two to three years. It's usually made by taking an ordinary white Champagne and mixing in a little still red wine – the only time that practice isn't frowned on in AC-conscious France. Best years: 1988, '85, '83, '82. Best producers: Charbaut, Krug, Laurent-Perrier, Moët & Chandon, Pommery, Roederer, Taittinger Comtes de Champagne.

CHAPELLE-CHAMBERTIN AC
grand cru
CÔTE DE NUITS, BURGUNDY

Pinot Noir

A small *grand cru* on the slopes just below Chambertin Clos-de-Bèze, which owes its name to the monks of Bèze building a chapel there in 1155. It's one of the marvellous things about Burgundy that you can stand among the vines of La Chapelle or Clos-de-Bèze knowing that this little field has been producing great wines without a break for 800 years or more. It makes sense of the rigid and seemingly nit-picking regulations regarding which plots of land – or even strips of vine – are *grand cru*, or *premier cru*, or simple village wines: they've been working out which soil is best for over 20 generations! La Chapelle is not the most impressive *grand cru*. The wines are lighter than the others, although they can have a lovely perfume. This is partly due to a difference in soil type, but it's also that La Chapelle produces more wine per acre than any of its neighbours – the old problem. Best years: 1988, '85, '83, '80, '78. Best producers: Damoy, Trapet.

CHARDONNAY

A thin, rasping white, all raw edges and streaked with enough acidity to make an unripe cooking apple blush – that's Chardonnay-Coteaux Champenois from northernmost France. A rich and buttery wine, so heady with spice, honey and cream that you think it must be sweet, yet it isn't; that's Chardonnay too, a single-vineyard Meursault from Burgundy's Côte d'Or. Chardonnay is chalk-dry but nutty in Chablis, lemony and racily tasty as a Vin de Pays from the Muscadet region, as fleeting but thrilling as melting mountain snow in Bugey, but packed with the flavours of peaches, melons, apricots and cream in Pouilly-Fuissé. Clean, round and simple like a fat apple in a Vin de Pays de l'Aude, it froths with cream, honey and excitement as a Blanc de Blancs sparkler from Champagne. This wonderfully adaptable grape is now the white wine star worldwide.

It is a less recognizable grape than varieties like Sauvignon Blanc, Riesling or Gewürztraminer, whose basic personality shouts at you from the glass. But the full yet unassertive flavour is what attracts winemakers. Chardonnay is the canvas on which they can test all kinds of styles. The most famous of these is the use of oak barrels. Chardonnay extracts a delicious spicy, creamy fullness from new oak barrels, and in Burgundy's Côte d'Or a mixture of Chardonnay, ideal soil and oak barrels is reckoned to produce the greatest white wine of all.

Chardonnay plantings are taking place at a hectic pace all over France, and figures become out of date as soon as they are published – yet there are certainly over 37,000 acres (15,000 hectares) already in production. The Côte des Blancs in Champagne is virtually all Chardonnay, and Burgundy – from Chablis in the north, through the heartland of the Côte d'Or, and on to the Côte Chalonnaise, the Mâconnais and even, to a slight degree, the Beaujolais – has Chardonnay as its focal white grape. The Loire is not reckoned to be Chardonnay land, but many producers in Touraine, Anjou and the Muscadet region are planting it – either to release on its own, or else to soften up the Chenin Blanc. The VDQS regions in the centre of France make lean, slightly tart wines from it, while Jura, Savoie and Bugey to the far east have considerable success with it. Although Château Rayas in Châteauneuf-du-Pape makes a remarkable mouthful from Chardonnay, in the south it generally appears in the *vin de pays*, not the AC, wines, because it isn't traditional to the area. Even so, it is having a massively positive effect upon the flavour of southern whites. Chardonnay from the Coteaux de l'Ardèche is already making waves worldwide, and Provence, the Gard, Hérault and Aude are producing delicious flavours at low, low prices. Just a splash can make a surprising difference to an otherwise dull blend.

CHARENTAIS, VIN DE PAYS
SOUTH-WEST

Merlot, Cabernet Sauvignon, Cabernet Franc, Gamay

Ugni Blanc, Folle Blanche, Colombard

The Charentais, between La Rochelle on the Atlantic coast and th upper reaches of the Charente river beyond Angoulême, is the Cogna region, and the best wines for distilling have traditionally been bot neutral and acid. Since the Ugni Blanc is the chief brandy grape variet here grown at the northern limits of its ability to ripen at all, neutrali and acidity aren't a problem. However, with the decline in Cogna production there has been an increasing surplus of both white and re grapes and thin wine, and many growers now allow some of the harvest to ripen as fully as possible and make Vin de Pays Charentais light, lemony, sharp whites, and reasonably refreshing, if a little acidi reds.

CHARMES-CHAMBERTIN AC
grand cru
CÔTE DE NUITS, BURGUNDY

Pinot Noir

We see more of this *grand cru* than any of the others based Gevrey-Chambertin, because this large vineyard is, at 78 acres (31 hectares), more than twice the size of any of the others. The wine can b superb – not quite so startlingly grand as Chambertin, but big and broa developing more quickly to a full, soft, chocolate and raspber sweetness. Lovely wine, but it doesn't often make your spine tingle wi excitement. Also, because the name Charmes-Chambertin is beguiling come-hither, there are a fair few producers who decide to let the vin rip and produce all that they can. Result? Not charming that's for sur Best years: 1988, '85, '83, '80, '78, '76. Best producers: Bachele Leflaive, Rebourseau, Roty, Armand Rousseau, Taupenot, Tortochot.

CHASSAGNE-MONTRACHET AC
CÔTE DE BEAUNE, BURGUNDY

Pinot Noir

Chardonnay

This is the least fashionable of the great Côte de Beaune white wi villages. One explanation might be that over half the production of th supposedly white wine village is in fact *red*. Another explanation is th Chassagne has no restaurant, no café – not even a bar! You have to wa across the dangerously busy Route Nationale 6, past Pulign Montrachet, to Meursault to find somewhere to relax.

Well, that can be turned to our advantage, because the general pric level in Chassagne is lower than in Puligny or Meursault and the quali of the whites right now is increasingly good. There are 880 acres (35 hectares) of vines in this AC between Puligny and Santenay, at th southern end of the Côte de Beaune. Only 40 per cent of these vines a for white grapes, but they include 8½ acres (3·5 hectares) of the gre Montrachet *grand cru* as well as 15 acres (6 hectares) of Bâtar Montrachet and the entire 4 acres (1·6 hectares) of the smallest whi *grand cru* – Criots-Bâtard-Montrachet.

I have never quite understood why so many red vines are plante here, since the wine is frequently rather jammy and uncouth, while eve the simplest Chassagne white can be exquisite – and far mo expensive. I can only assume that once a Burgundian grower h planted a vineyard in one grape variety, he's blowed if he'll switch un he's got his money's worth from what he's planted. Red Chassagne always a little earthy, peppery perhaps and plummy, but there a relatively few examples when these three are all in balance. Best yea (reds): 1988, '86, '85, '83, '82. Best producers: Bachelet-Ramone Carillon, Clerget, Duc de Magenta, Gagnard-Delagrange, Lequin-Roussc Albert Morey, Ramonet-Prudhon.

The white Chassagne *premiers crus* are not well-known, but can off big, nutty, toasty wines with more traditional savoury richness, and le of the currently fashionable exotic fruits taste which is increasing occurring in Meursault and Puligny-Montrachet. En Cailleret, L Ruchottes, La Romanée, Morgeot and Les Embrazées can be exciti wines – especially if aged for four to eight years. Ordinary whi

Chassagne-Montrachet may lack the complexity of the *premier cru* wine, but since the village is not that 'chic', there is less temptation to 'stretch' and it is usually a thoroughly enjoyable high-quality Burgundy. Best years (whites): 1988, '87, '86, '85, '84, '83, '82. Best producers: Bachelet-Ramonet, Blain-Gagnard, Colin, Delagrange-Bachelet, Duc de Magenta, Fontaine-Gagnard, Gagnard-Delagrange, Lamy, Albert Morey, Marc Morey, Pillot, Ramonet-Prudhon.

CHASSELAS

The Swiss drink copious amounts of Chasselas under the names Fendant, or Dorin or even Perlan. But if you're looking for it in France, you won't find the name Chasselas on a label, since it is very definitely a variety on the way out. I can see why. The wine it produces is about as neutral as wine can get, and although it might be pleasant enough as a thirst-quencher during an alpine hike, it doesn't have enough personality to survive a few months in bottle. There is a little planted in Savoie, and also at Pouilly on the Loire where it confusingly makes the AC Pouilly-sur-Loire in the same area as the far more exciting Sauvignon-based Pouilly Blanc Fumé. However, the main plantations, still about 1000 acres (400 hectares), are in Alsace, where it is turned into simple jug wine, or occasionally, if spiced up with Pinot Blanc or Gewürztraminer, it can be part of the blend for Edelzwicker.

CHASSE-SPLEEN, CH.

Moulis AC, *cru grand bourgeois exceptionnel*
HAUT-MÉDOC, BORDEAUX

Cabernet Sauvignon, Merlot, Cabernet Franc, Petit Verdot

All owners of lesser Bordeaux properties who gaze wistfully at the Classed Growths and sulk in silent envy at the prices they can charge should look at the example of Chasse-Spleen. Since the mid 1970s, this property (whose name is supposed to come from Lord Byron's claim that the wine chased away his attacks of spleen) has backed up vigorous quality control with an astute marketing strategy. The result is that this rich, round, grandly textured wine is now more expensive than many of the lesser Classed Growths, and yet everyone thinks it is splendid value for money. I agree! Second wine: l'Ermitage de Chasse-Spleen.

CHÂTEAU-CHALON AC

JURA

Savagnin

This tiny AC covering 86 acres (35 hectares) in the centre of the mountainous Jura vineyard applies to one of the most daunting wine types yet invented, *vin jaune* or yellow wine, which offers the same kind of experience as potholing, hang-gliding or taking an afternoon nap on a bed of nails. Yet for a brave, indeed demented few, the eventual pleasures far outweigh the initial torments. Only the Savagnin grape is used to make *vin jaune*. It produces a fierce, farmyardy white, blending oily thickness with a raw volatile acidity and a strong whiff of damp straw. It can develop a raging, sour, woody brilliance that only the very best sherries ever get. You can see I'm a fan!

Well, in a funny way, I *am* a fan because there is nothing like it in the world of wine. Its nearest equivalent would be an old *fino* sherry – and the reason is that they both grow a *flor* yeast on their surface as they age in barrel, which imparts this strange sweet/sour intensity. *Vin jaune* lies in barrel for six years; during this time the wine evaporates by perhaps one-third, but is protected from oxidation by the *flor*. The painfully concentrated liquid is put in dumpy 62cl *clavelin* bottles, and you can age it for, well, certainly up to 100 years. The intense flavour – a surge of stale, nutty richness, slapped about by a cruel searing sourness – makes this monstrous beauty a wine to be approached with trepidation and a good life assurance policy, but I've survived it, and in a helpless sort of way I'm rather looking forward to my next glass – just so long as it's a small one. Best producers: Bourdy, Courbet, Macle, Perron.

CHÂTEAU GRILLET AC
NORTHERN RHÔNE

🍷 Viognier

A single estate renowned as the smallest AC in France at 6½ acres (2· hectares) – but actually there are several *grands crus* in Burgundy wit their own AC which are even smaller! This rare Rhône white from th village of Vérin, south of Vienne, is remarkable stuff. The Viognier, th only permitted grape variety, produces a most exciting dry wine – a apricots and slightly soured cream, spring blossom floating on the win and honey tinged with tangerine spice. It is *very* expensive – but the there's very little of it – the allocation for the British market last yea was only 60 bottles! Would I buy it? At approaching £50 a bottle? No, wouldn't. I'd save myself at least £30 and buy Condrieu – same grape same taste and no feeling that perhaps you're being taken for a bit of ride. Best years: 1988, '86, '85, '83.

CHÂTEAUMEILLANT VDQS
UPPER LOIRE

🍷 🍷 Gamay

If you can find a bottle of this outside the immediate locality, you're better man than I am. Well, that's not quite fair (on me, that is) because have cast a rather unenthusiastic palate over the odd bottle of red an rosé and found them rooty, vegetal and one of the least appealin manifestations of Gamay wine I can think of. If you're lost about 37 mile (60km) south of Bourges and in severe need of a thirstquencher, yo could give it a go, but I think I'd have a beer.

CHÂTEAUNEUF-DU-PAPE AC
SOUTHERN RHÔNE

🍷 Grenache, Syrah, Mourvèdre and others

🍷 Grenache Blanc, Clairette, Bourboulenc and others

Châteauneuf-du-Pape is a name we all know, but I wonder how many o us have ever tried a good bottle? It isn't that the wine is scarce: thi large vineyard area, between Orange and Avignon, covers 7400 acre (3000 hectares) and produces about one million cases every year – 9 per cent of them red. It's just that Châteauneuf-du-Pape ('the pope' new castle') used to be one of the most abused of all wine names low-priced bottles appeared on every wine list, tasting thick, muddy an coarse. Now, much Châteauneuf comes from single estates – it's n longer cheap, and deservedly ranks as one of France's top wines.

Châteauneuf now has very strict AC regulations – which is apt because it was here, in 1923, that Baron Le Roy of Château Fortia firs formulated the rules which became the basis of all French AC laws. remarkable 13 grape varieties are permitted for the red – eight red an five white – though most growers only use half-a-dozen or so. Five pe cent of the crop must be left on the vine at harvest – thus reducing th use of poor grapes. And the minimum alcohol level is the highest i France – 12·5 degrees. This is rarely a problem because the broad fla stones which cover the vineyard soak up the sun's heat during the da and release it at night – so the Grenache (the chief grape) often make 14 degrees! Yield is low at 35 hectolitres per hectare.

There are two styles of red Châteauneuf: a light Beaujolais-type whic nonetheless has a delicious dusty warmth, juicy spice and raspberr fruit, and the big traditional style, which may need ageing for five year or more and can last for 20. It is fat, weighty, and piled high with fruit raspberry, blackcurrant, plums – plus a chocolate-coffee-cinnamo richness and the tang of southern herbs. Acidity is low, tannin usuall overwhelmed by fruit and the whole effect is a richly satisfying re especially good with winter meals. It is always worth getting an estat wine, and these are now distinguished by a coat of arms embossed o the bottle above the label. Best years (reds): 1988, '86, '85, '83, '81, '7 (though '84 and '80 are also very good, if lighter). Best producer (traditional, to age), Beaucastel, Bosquet des Papes, Chante-Cigale Chante-Perdrix, Clos des Papes, Fortia, la Nerte, Rayas; (moderr fruitier), Brunel, Clos du Mont Olivet, Font de Michelle, Font du Lou Grand Tinel, Quiot, Roger Sabon; also good, Guigal, Jaboulet.

Only three per cent of Châteauneuf production is white, although white grapes are quite often used for softening the red wines. The vast vineyards of bleached earth don't look as though they could possibly produce a decent, refreshing white wine – but they can. The main grapes are the Grenache Blanc and Clairette, helped along by Bourboulenc, Picpoul and Roussanne. None of these are exciting, aromatic grapes and yet, with modern cool-fermentation methods, the wines can be brilliant – exciting liquorice and peach fruit, freshened up with mountain herbs and the snappy acidity of a lime. The wines are good when very young, between one and two years old. Best years (whites): the most recent. Best producers: Beaucastel, Bérard, Font de Michelle, Fortia, Mont-Redon, Nalys, La Nerte, Vieux Télégraphe (the very best).

▼ Harvest-time on a Châteauneuf-du-Pape estate. The AC regulations for red allow 13 grape varieties, including five white ones for blending.

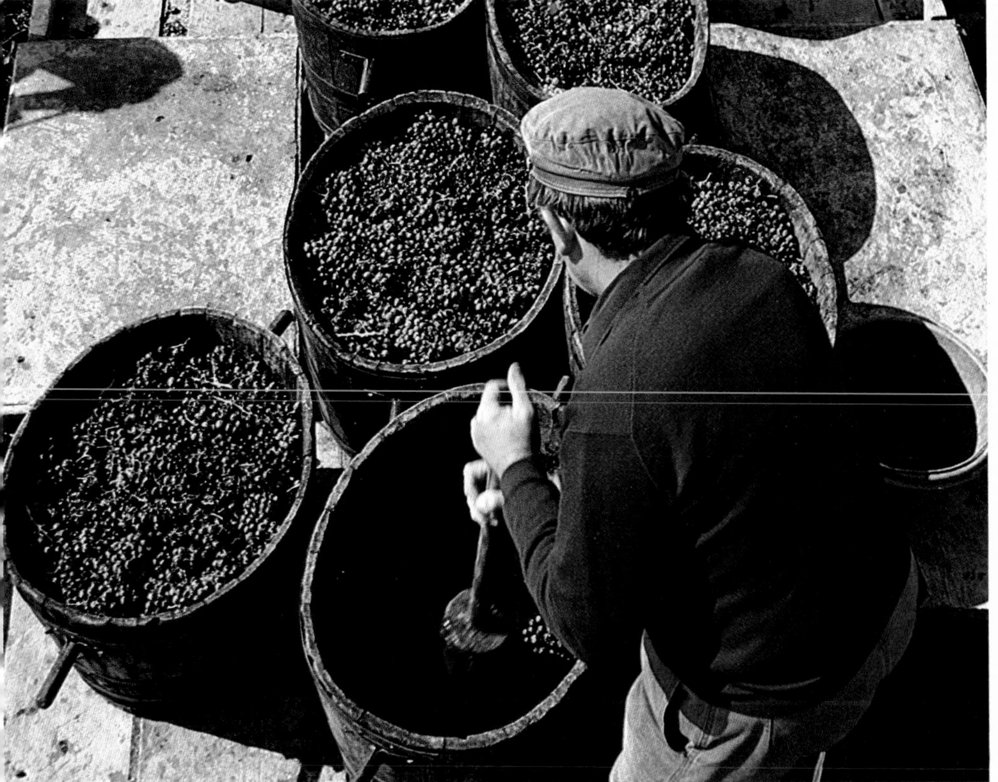

CHÂTILLON-EN-DIOIS AC
CENTRAL RHÔNE

🍷🍷 Gamay, Syrah, Pinot Noir

🍷 Chardonnay, Aligoté

One of the all-time obscure French ACs – not only because the wines rarely surface, but also because they grow in a beautiful, isolated outpost on the river Drôme, tucked into the foothills of the Alps and on the road to absolutely nowhere. All the best wines are sparkling and the village of Die is best known for its excellent Clairette de Die, a Muscat-based fizz. A few vineyards are planted with Aligoté and Chardonnay, and this is one of those rare times when the Aligoté seems to perform as well as Chardonnay. Neither is memorable, but both do just enough to explain why the AC was created back in 1974. The reds and rosés of Châtillon-en-Diois, grown south and east of Die, are something of an afterthought. Gamay does quite well here, and is often blended with Syrah or Pinot Noir to give a fairly dark, quite fruity wine.

CHÉNAS AC
BEAUJOLAIS, BURGUNDY

🍷 Gamay

A few years ago a leading Beaujolais merchant stated that the Chéna AC should be merged with its neighbour Moulin-à-Vent since the wine were similar and they'd be easier to sell under that label. What cheek! we pushed that train of thought, all Loire wines would be Sancerre o Muscadet, all Rhône wines would be Châteauneuf-du-Pape – and fo that matter his beloved Moulin-à-Vent would disappear, becaus adjacent Fleurie is better known, sounds nicer and sells for more money!

Chénas is the smallest of the Beaujolais crus and its wines, like those of Moulin-à-Vent, are usually quite tough when young, benefit enormous ly from two years' ageing and reach their peak after five years or more They only rarely have the gorgeous juicy fruit of young Beaujolais, bu can make up for this with a deep, gently Burgundian flavour whe mature – less peaches and redcurrants, more chocolate and strawber ries with a lean, dry streak of earthy reserve. Best producers Champagnon, Château de Chénas, Lapierre, Émile Robin.

CHENIN BLANC

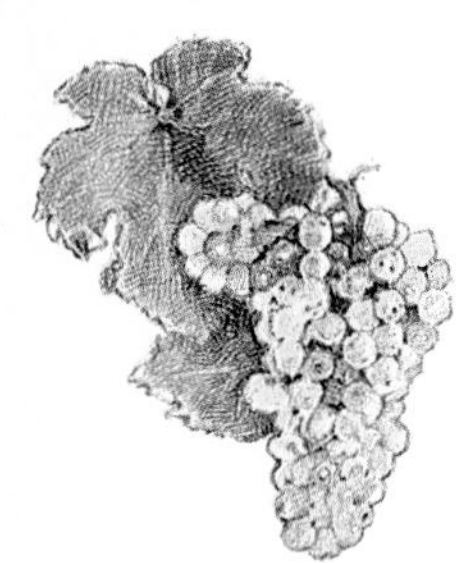

My goodness, you have to be a good winemaker to coax anythin enjoyable out of the thin-lipped Chenin grape. Much of the nastiest sourest, dry and medium white wine of the Loire valley comes from thi late-ripening, high-acid variety. But, like all the best things in life, yo must take up the challenge, and then there is great wine to be had fron the Chenin grape. In fact, the Chenin could lay claim to being the mos underrated great white wine grape in the world. Although there is a littl in the Aude at Limoux and in the Bouches-du-Rhône at the giant Liste winery, all the rest of France's Chenin is grown in the Loire valley, where it is also known as Pineau de la Loire. It provides the base for the Loire's sparkling wine industry, centred on Saumur, but is also evident a Vouvray and elsewhere in Anjou and Touraine. All the best sparklers nov have some Chardonnay or Cabernet Franc included as softener.

Chenin Blanc makes dry or off-dry wines in Anjou and Touraine. I poor years these can be raspingly austere, but increasingly the bette winemakers are creating dry, appley wines very like good Sauvignon The co-operative at Saumur is a leader here. Dry Vouvray and Jasnières can be remarkably nutty – if you allow them the five to ten years they need to soften. Some growers – like Monsieur Girault in Touraine Mesland – are producing marvellous apricot-scented fruity wines by steeping the skins with the juice before fermentation starts.

Sweet wines are the speciality of Anjou – though in sunny years there are some from Vouvray and Montlouis. The Coteaux de l'Aubance makes mildly sweet whites, whereas the Coteaux du Layon produces quite rich nuts-and-honey flavour. However, the stars are two tiny areas in the Layon valley, Quarts de Chaume and Bonnezeaux, where the Chenin is attacked by noble rot, giving tiny amounts of intensely sweet juice Because the acidity is so high these wines seem dull and indistinct whe young, but the best age brilliantly, building up to a most exciting peach apricot and quince flavour at anything between 10 and 30 years of age

CHEVAL-BLANC, CH.
St-Émilion AC, *premier grand cru classé*
BORDEAUX

🍷 Cabernet Franc, Merlot

Although Ausone (since 1978) and, to a lesser extent, Figeac contest the position, Cheval-Blanc is the leading property in St-Émilion, and likely to remain so for the foreseeable future. It is a large property, right on the border of Pomerol, at the end of a billowing row of gravel humps whic run north from Figeac. Cheval-Blanc derives much of its backbone which allows it to mature for longer than most St-Émilions, from this gravelly land; but up by the Pomerol border there are rich veins of clay mixed with sand and iron, and these give the wine its phenomena richness and sumptuous fruit. Strangely for St-Émilion, Merlot is the minor grape, occupying only 33 per cent as against 66 per cent for Cabernet Franc. You might expect the wine therefore to lack some of the luscious Merlot fruit, but on the contrary, Cheval-Blanc is one of the grandest, most voluptuous, perfumed St-Émilions. Yet its legendary longevity may well be due to the Cabernet Franc – and those precious hillocks of gravelly soil. Even lesser years like 1980 and 1987 can be great successes, and only 1984 hasn't worked here among recent vintages. Best years: 1988, '87, '86, '85, '83, 82, '81, '80, '79, '78, '75.

CHEVALIER-MONTRACHET AC
grand cru
CÔTE DE BEAUNE, BURGUNDY

🍷 Chardonnay

They say that after Le Montrachet, Chevalier's next-door neighbour, this is the greatest white wine in the world. Well, never having possessed enough money to indulge in a bottle – its price is astronomical – I can't really . . . But hang on . . . Chevalier-Montrachet . . . Think, think. The palate memory stirs. A limpid golden colour, a heavenly aroma of roasted hazelnuts and fresh-ground coffee and new bread new-toasted from the grate. And a flavour of honey and of cream, of nuts now smoking from the fire, and the waft of coffee just brewed late on a Sunday morning. So rich, coating my mouth with ripeness, luscious enough to be sweet as syrup, yet dry – amazingly, totally, dry. And I was in a garden in Hampshire, many summers ago, with my closest friends. And it was *my* bottle. Part of my first-ever wine-tasting prize. Yes. That summer's day at least, the greatest, the happiest bottle of white wine in the world. And what else? It's an 18-acre (7-hectare) *grand cru* in Puligny-Montrachet, just above Le Montrachet on the south-east facing slope. The higher elevation yields a slightly leaner wine, but good examples will last 20 years. Best years: 1988, '86, '85, '84, '83, '82. Best producers: Leflaive, followed by Bouchard Père & Fils, Jadot, Latour.

CHEVERNY VDQS
CENTRAL LOIRE

🍷🍷 Gamay, Cabernet Franc, Cabernet Sauvignon and others

🍷 Sauvignon Blanc, Romorantin, Chenin Blanc, Chardonnay

Cheverny – a little-known area south-west of Blois covering 1250 acres (500 hectares) – has an absolutely splendid seventeenth-century château with a collection of 2000 antlers on display – implying that they're always roasting great haunches of venison and downing great draughts of ruddy-flavoured red wine as they warm themselves by the roaring log fire. Well, if they are, the wine won't be from Cheverny. Although they grow Gamay, Cabernet Franc, Cabernet Sauvignon and Pinot Noir in this northerly loop of the Loire, the wines never perform as well here as they do in warmer areas. They can smell rather good – sharp and distinct – but they usually taste raw and acid, better suited to marinating the venison than accompanying it. The rosés are a slight improvement.

Cheverny whites are more of a mixed bag, depending on the vines used. Grapes like the Romorantin must survive simply because of the locals' stubbornness in preserving their traditions – it *can't* be because of the nice flavour of the wine. The Romorantin grows *only* in Cheverny and gives an unremittingly harsh wine, bone dry, almost bitter in its acidity, and smelling like a farmyard in need of a good hose down. It's another occasion when I say – yes, I support this wine's existence, but I hope to goodness I never have to drink the stuff. Cheverny *can* make some very attractive light, nutty Chardonnay, and the fizz they create using the Champagne method is sharp, clean and 'bracing'. I wish I could bring myself to say – forget that old Romorantin rubbish and let's have another supply of good Chardonnay and decent fizz. But I can't. So I'll just say – let's see more of their Chenin, Sauvignon and Chardonnay as well. Best producers: Cheverny co-operative, Gendrier, Gueritte, Puzelat, Tessier.

CHINON AC
CENTRAL LOIRE

Cabernet Franc, Cabernet Sauvignon

Chenin Blanc

The best red wine of the Loire valley. The growers of Bourgueil might dispute that, but the wonderful thing about Chinon is that it is so good so young, yet can improve for five, ten, 15, even 20 years to a fragrant, ethereal shadow of the great châteaux of the Médoc, and as such is a rare and precious delight. Good Chinon is doubly precious because the Cabernet Franc, which normally makes up all, or almost all, of the wine achieves a pure, startling intensity of fruit – the piercing acid/sweetness of blackcurrant juice pressed straight from the bush, sweetened and perfumed with a few drops of juice from ripe raspberries. I've several times bought some to age, only to try a bottle – you know, just to check how it's getting on – and end up slurping the lot because it was irresistibly delicious. Chenin wines only account for about one per cent of Chinon production. Best recent years: 1988, '85, '83, '82, '78, '76. It's always worth buying a single-estate wine. Best producers: Couly-Dutheil, Gouron, Joguet, Plouzeau, Olga and Jean-Maurice Raffault.

▼ The historic town of Chinon is noted for its hilltop castle and its fruity red wine – one of the top ACs in Touraine.

CHIROUBLES AC
BEAUJOLAIS, BURGUNDY

Gamay

The lightest, most delicately fragrant of the Beaujolais *crus*, often littl[e] more than deep pink in colour with a perfume full of strawberries an[d] flowers with just a whisper of cherries. There are only two things wron[g] with Chiroubles; there isn't much of it and it costs too much. At 69[…] acres (280 hectares) it is one of the smallest *crus*. It's expensiv[e] because the Parisians go batty about it; restaurants queue up for it, an[d] allow their customers to pay too much for what is often only marginally superior Beaujolais-Villages. Best producers: Domaine de l[a] Grosse Pierre, Duboeuf, Javernand, Georges Passot.

CHOREY-LÈS-BEAUNE AC
CÔTE DE BEAUNE, BURGUNDY

Pinot Noir

One of those forgotten little Burgundian villages we should be thankful for, because they mean that we can still experience the flavour of good, if not great, Burgundy, without having to take out a second mortgage. The wine should not by rights be very special, as the village, with its 300 acres (120 hectares) of vineyard, is almost entirely on the flat valley land, just north of Beaune and east of the main N74 road. The general rule in the Côte d'Or is that decent wine only grows west of the N74, but Chorey is lucky in having several very committed property owners based there, who, although they also own much more classic land elsewhere, use their considerable skills on their local wine. Without them, Chorey-lès-Beaune wine would merely be sold as Côte de Beaune-Villages and never heard of again. Which would be a pity. Best producers: Drouhin, Jacques Germain, Goud de Beaupuis, Tollot-Beaut.

CINSAUT

A useful rather than exciting grape, Cinsaut (also spelt Cinsault) is grown all over the southern Rhône, Provence and the Midi. By itself, it gives light-coloured wine even at the best of times, with a fresh, but rather fleeting, neutral fruit. However, the one thing Cinsaut does have is good acidity and since Grenache acidity is low, it can act as a life-support system to the richer, spicier Grenache fruit, allowing rosés and light reds to age longer than any pure Grenache wine could manage. If it allows the delicious fruit of the Grenache to flower – I'm all for it. But by itself, except for a 'young vines' *vin de table* from Vieux Télégraphe – no thanks!

CISSAC, CH.
Haut-Médoc AC, *cru grand bourgeois exceptionnel*
BORDEAUX

Cabernet Sauvignon, Merlot, Petit Verdot

Sometimes, tasting Cissac, you feel as if you are in a time warp. The tannin is uncompromising, the fruit dark and stubbornly withheld for many years, the flavour of wood more like the rough, resinous edge of hand-hewn pine than the soothing vanilla creaminess now fashionable. Well, it is something of an anachronism. Although not included in the 1855 Classification, it nonetheless doggedly refuses to accept the situation, and makes high quality wines for the long haul by proudly traditional methods: old vines, lots of wood everywhere, and meticulous exclusion of below par wine from the final blend. The wines of the '80s are nowhere near ready yet, the decade of the '70s are hitting their peak – while '64 and '61 are wonderful, dry, cedary claret.

CLAIRETTE DE BELLEGARDE AC
LANGUEDOC-ROUSSILLON

Clairette

This is one of those dull workhorse whites you try out as you swelter in the Mediterranean sun, but is so unrefreshing you end up having a beer. Maybe that's unfair, but whenever *I* try the wine it's July or August and the stuff's been around for nearly a year, and that's well past retirement age for most Clairette. At a few months old it is supposed to have a lovely floral aroma of violets and honeysuckle and if I'm ever between Arles and Nîmes in the *département* of the Gard – where the half million or so bottles of this wine are made – around Christmas and New Year, I'll check that theory out on the new vintage and let you know.

CLAIRETTE DE DIE TRADITION AC
CENTRAL RHÔNE

Muscat, Clairette

Thinking man's Asti Spumante! This is one of the most deliciously enjoyable sparkling wines in the world. It's made from at least 50 per cent Muscat mixed in with Clairette and the result is a relatively dry, light wine with a lovely creamy bubble and the most orchard-fresh fragrance of ripe grapes and springtime flowers. In fact, why am I saying it's 'thinking man's Asti Spumante'? That sounds like an apology and this mouth-watering delight needs no apology from me.

Die is one of those lost areas of France on the road to nowhere and ringed round with hills. It's a very relaxing place to visit, with the river Drôme meandering through its centre. The 'Tradition' wine is made to sparkle by the *méthode Dioise*. This involves fermentation in bottle, but the process (unlike in Champagne) is arrested before all the grape sugar has been used up, and the wine is then filtered and re-bottled under pressure. As a result, the wine retains the flavour of the grape sugars and that heavenly Muscat scent. There is a Clairette de Die (*not* Tradition) from 100 per cent Clairette grapes and made by the Champagne method – but it isn't as good. Best producers: Clairette de Die co-operative; also Achard-Vincent, Andrieux, Magord, Raspail.

CLAIRETTE DU LANGUEDOC AC
LANGUEDOC-ROUSSILLON

Clairette

What you want in the searing heat of the Languedoc is cooling draughts of fresh, dry, white wine – exactly the kind the locals find most difficult to make. I can only presume that the very fact that 11 communes between Montpellier and Béziers made white wine at all was enough to earn them their AC, until 1985 the only all-white AC in the Hérault *département*. But you're never going to make anything exciting out of the Clairette grape; much of the local white used to go to the vermouth factories. The 1·2 million bottles can be dry or semi-sweet – but either way the result is usually heavy and dull. Catch it as young as possible and drink it ice cold on the spot – but I'd drink rosé if I had a choice. Best producers: Condamine Bertrand, St-André.

LA CLAPE
Coteaux du Languedoc AC
LANGUEDOC-ROUSSILLON

Carignan, Cinsaut, Grenache and others

Bourboulenc, Clairette, Grenache Blanc and others

The mountain of La Clape can appear as a bit of a shock. It rears quite unexpectedly from the flat coastal fields to the south-east of Narbonne, like the snout of a great whale leaping from a lifeless sea. Its novelty has been recognized by the French government who have made it a protected site. The mountain or *massif* of La Clape has created a rare microclimate too, with a fair amount of chalk in the soil, uncommon for the Midi, and more breezes than usual to take the burn out of the relentless Midi sun.

The result – excellent whites from Bourboulenc and Clairette plus good reds and rosés with the Carignan often dominant, but a fair amount of Grenache, and also Cinsaut to ease back the throttle. The high proportion of Bourboulenc in the white (the best of all are in fact 100 per cent Bourboulenc), combined with the microclimate, makes La Clape the most interesting white wine in the Aude *département*, often developing quite a nutty, honeyed character at two to three years old. La Clape, a designated *cru* within the AC, is now allowed to use its name along with the Coteaux du Languedoc AC on the label. Although the whites do age, reds and rosés are usually best young. Best producers: Boscary, Hue, Pech-Redon, de St-Exupéry, Ségura.

CLARKE, CH.
Listrac AC, *cru bourgeois Listrac*
HAUT-MÉDOC, BORDEAUX

Cabernet Sauvignon, Merlot, Cabernet Franc, Petit Verdot

I couldn't exactly leave this one out, could I? Still, only ten years ago I'd have had to, because Château Clarke was just a wistful Anglo-Saxon footnote in the more scholarly books on Bordeaux, and the vineyard looked more like a bomb site. OK, I'll explain. In 1973 one of the numerous Rothschilds (a certain Baron Edmond) decided to recreate from scratch this derelict has-been. He spent millions on it, totally re-doing the vineyards and their drainage, and building imposing new installations. It was a stunning sight – sparkling new masonry, gleaming steel and reassuring piles of new oak barrels. It reeked of money and commitment, and since the 1983 vintage it shows in the wines, which have a delicious blackcurrant fruit and a warm oaky richness.

CLIMENS, CH.
Barsac AC, *premier cru classé*
BORDEAUX

Sémillon, Sauvignon Blanc

This is Barsac's leading property, a position which used to be shared with Château Coutet, but in recent vintages Climens has pulled away from its rival in the quality stakes. The 75-acre (30-hectare) vineyard lies on the highest ground in the AC to the south-west of the village of Barsac, its vines coming to rather an abrupt end when they meet the A62 autoroute that runs between Bordeaux and Toulouse. This height gives Climens a particularly well-drained vineyard and helps to account for its reputation as the most elegant and refined of all Barsac properties. It is a deserved reputation, as I have never had a Climens which was sticky or cloying. But it's also only half the story, because these wines are rich, luscious and exotic, not bursting with the peach and pineapple fruit of some 'sweeties', but having an exciting syrupy sweetness, a most appetizing, toasty, nutty, dry edge and a light, clear streak of lemon acidity to keep the wine fresh and long-lasting. Easy to drink at five years old, a good vintage will be richer and more satisfying after 10 to 15 years. Best years: 1988, '86, '83, '81, '80, '76, '75. There's a lovely second wine called Les Cèdres.

CLOS DE LA ROCHE AC, CLOS DE TART AC, CLOS DES LAMBRAYS AC & CLOS ST-DENIS AC
grands crus
CÔTE DE NUITS, BURGUNDY

Pinot Noir

It is strange that the little-known village of Morey-St-Denis has five *grands crus* (the four named here and a sliver of Bonnes-Mares), when far better-known villages like Nuits-St-Georges don't have any at all.

Clos de la Roche is the best and biggest. The wine has a lovely, bright, red-fruits flavour when young which, from a grower like Dujac or Ponsot, may get chocolaty or gamy as it ages. Clos de Tart is unusual in that it is entirely owned by one firm – Mommessin, of Beaujolais fame. The wine, light and dry at first, can build up an unexpected but delicious savoury richness over the years. Clos des Lambrays was made a *grand cru* only in 1981. New owners took it over and began renovating it in 1979, but it'll be a few years before the exact style of the wine becomes clear. Clos St-Denis is well-made by producers like Lignier and Dujac – red fruit browning gracefully with age – but is rarely seen. Best producers: Dujac, Lignier, Ponsot, Armand Rousseau.

CLOS DE VOUGEOT AC
grand cru
CÔTE DE NUITS, BURGUNDY

Pinot Noir

Clos in Burgundy means a vineyard enclosed by a wall, hence Clos de Vougeot is the 'walled vineyard in the village of Vougeot'. Founded by Cistercian monks in the fourteenth century, it had reached 125 acres (50 hectares) by the time they put a wall round with due proprietorial pride and for more than 600 years this original boundary has stayed intact.

But the French revolution put paid to single ownership. The vineyard was confiscated and sold first to a wool merchant, then to a gunsmith, and gradually it became fragmented until it now has over 80 owners. This multiplicity of ownership has turned it into one of the most unreliable *grand cru* Burgundies. And there's another reason. The Clos runs from the top of the Côte d'Or slope, next to the *grand cru* vineyards of Grands-Échézeaux and Le Musigny, right down to the flat, clay soil on the N74 road – only two cars' width away from dead-end land relegated to the basic appellation Bourgogne. Yet it is all *grand cru*. A good owner should be able to make great wine on the upper slopes, but these heavy, muddy lower vineyards can never produce wine of the fragrance and beauty a *grand cru* label demands.

However, when it's good it is wonderfully soft, fleshy wine, coating your mouth with ripeness, the fruit like perfumed plums backed up by a smoky chocolate richness turning dark and exotic with age – when it's good. Best years: 1988, '85, '83, '80, '78. Best producers: Arnoux, Confuron, Drouhin, Grivot, Gros, Jayer, Lamarche, Rebourseau.

CLOS RENÉ
Pomerol AC
BORDEAUX

Merlot, Cabernet Franc, Malbec

If there's one wine I'd choose to convert a white-wine drinker to Bordeaux, I think it would be Clos René. This 27-acre (11-hectare) estate is on sandy soil in the less fashionable western side of the AC. The result is wonderfully plummy, juicy, fleshy wine – fleshy like the flesh of peaches or pears or lychees – oozing fruit, and slipping down hardly touching the sides. You think it's sweet almost, and as it ages it acquires a kind of chocolaty, creamy consistency. It is also sometimes sold under the label Moulinet-Lasserre.

You can drink Clos René at any age but it ages well for at least ten years. Best years: 1988, '85, '83, '82, '81.

COLLIOURE AC
LANGUEDOC-ROUSSILLON

Grenache, Mourvèdre, Carignan and others

This tiny AC is well into the Pyrenean foothills only a few miles from Spanish Catalonia, and well worth visiting, if only for the thrill of the mountain peaks tagged at their ankles with straggly vines, and for the peaceful, historic calm of the little towns-cum-fishing-ports of Collioure and Port-Vendres. The wine, based on Grenache with some Cinsaut, Mourvèdre and Carignan, is throat-warming, head-spinning stuff – capable of ageing a decade but marvellously, gooily aggressive when young. Hardly seen outside the region. Best producer: Mas Blanc.

CONDRIEU AC
NORTHERN RHÔNE

Viognier

I made a little pilgrimage in 1986. Although I was racing down the Rhône valley to keep an appointment at Avignon, I turned off the motorway at Vienne, and drove six miles along the river's precipitous right bank to the village of Condrieu. It's not a pretty place: the houses are modern and functional, and the busy road barely squeezes through, but it is the unlikely birthplace of one of the world's great white wines.

To the west of the town, stark, forbidding cliffs rear towards the clouds; from the road you can see rows of vineyard terraces – many abandoned and rotting – and, on the first plateau, the roofs of modern villas poking above the ridge. Where are all the vines then? Well, there are *very* few and, since you can make more money by selling your Rhône-side plot to a property-developer than you can by growing grapes, the rest of the vines are mostly in the nooks and crannies with less good vistas. Under 50 acres (20 hectares) of vineyard cling to the daunting rockface, although the AC covers a protected 500 acres (200 hectares).

But what a wine these straggly patches of struggling vines produce! The Viognier is the grape variety – a disease-prone, shy-yielding vine found only here, at neighbouring Château Grillet, at Côte-Rôtie (where it can be mixed with the red Syrah) and, in minute amounts, in the southern Rhône. A grand total of 75 acres (30 hectares) for one of France's greatest grapes! A pathetic yield – rarely more than 20 hectolitres per hectare – and a proneness to rot and 'floral abortion' (when no grapes develop from the flowers) are the reasons for this scarcity: an entire Condrieu vintage has been known to give only 19 hectolitres!

But the flavour. Mmm! A fragrance of ripe apricots and juicy Williams pears floods the room, freshened by spicy flower perfumes. Yet the wine is dry. Full in your mouth, yes, almost thick and viscous – juicy apricot skins and ripe golden peaches, coated with a perilous richness like double cream about to turn sour. These remarkable wines fade with age and are horrifyingly expensive – as expensive as a top white Burgundy – but at one to three years old they are a sensation everyone should try just once.

Best producers: Delas, Dezormeaux, Dumazet, Guigal, Jurie des Camiers, Pinchon, Rozay, Vernay.

CORBIÈRES AC
LANGUEDOC-ROUSSILLON

Carignan, Cinsaut, Grenache and others

Bourboulenc, Clairette, Grenache Blanc and others

The Corbières region is one of the most captivating in France. It is a wild, wind-swept, sun-drenched marvel of stubborn hills and delving valleys, tossed beneath a wide, burning sky and framed to the far south by the snowy majesty of the Pyrenees. It's hardly surprising that consistency was never the watchword in the wines squeezed from these turbulent hillsides and, even though AC status was granted in 1985, a certain amount of the production was still excluded from it.

The Carignan grape dominates, aided largely by Grenache, Cinsaut, Mourvèdre and Syrah. Carbonic maceration is on the increase, producing big beefy reds, dusty to the taste but roaring with a sturdy juicy fruit, a whiff of spice and a slap of herbs. Excellent quality at an excellent price to drink young. The old Corbières, heavy, thick and cloddish in a burnt-jam kind of way, is less and less seen. Some producers are ageing wines in wood and these can be excellent and worth keeping for a few years. Production is around 75 million bottles. Best producers: numerous co-operatives, especially Cascastel, Embres-et-Castelmaure, Mont Tauch; also Fontsainte, les Palais, Surbézy-Cartier (Ollieux), Voulte-Gasparets.

White Corbières is very much the minor partner. About seven million bottles are normally produced, mostly using Clairette and Bourboulenc. Few of these are more than adequate; most producers of Corbières concentrate on their gutsy reds. However, there is now a move towards producing *vin vert* or green wine. The grapes are picked early, before they have ripened fully, then they are fermented cold to a strength of only 10 degrees or so. The effect is a wine that is light, sharp, lemony and, yes, green! Ice cold it's a pretty decent thirst-quencher, especially welcome after a dusty hike in the hills. Drink as young as possible; and don't think about it too hard.

Best producers: Baronne, Bouïs, Étang des Colombes, Lastours; also Camplong d'Aude, Embres-et-Castelmaure, Mont Tauch co-operatives.

CORNAS AC
NORTHERN RHÔNE

Syrah

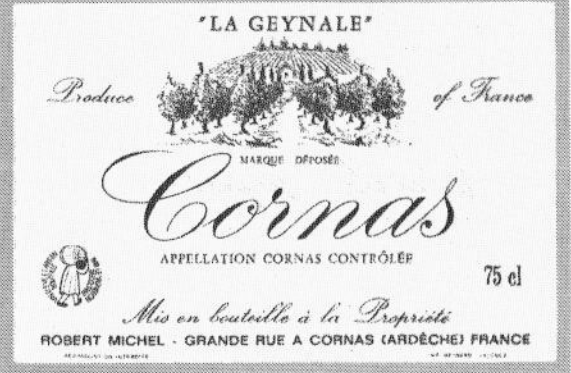

The Northern Rhône's up-and-coming star. Ten years ago the Northern Rhône didn't really have any star, though Hermitage and Côte-Rôtie were both making splendid wine. But the ballooning prices of Burgundy and Bordeaux made wine-lovers look elsewhere for excellence. Côte-Rôtie and Hermitage are now very expensive, so the spotlight turned to the very south of this northern section, where the valley spreads out at Valence, and the western crags return to their natural, uncultivated state.

Cornas is the last roar from the great Syrah grape. The thin terraces clinging doggedly to these granite cliffs can make the most massive of all Rhône reds. People used to say it was too coarse, but I don't agree. Certainly you must be *brave* to drink Cornas, but what's wrong with that? The colour when young is thick, impenetrable red, almost black in the ripest years. It is tough and chunky, pummelling your mouth with tannin and sheer force of personality.

So you wait, five years at least – more like ten. The colour is still deep, but tingling with life; the smell is rich and opulent, blackcurrants and raspberries, heady and exotic; the taste is almost sweet, with the fruit bursting through its tannic chains; and *there's* the roar – pure, sensuous fruit, coating your mouth, tannin too, and herbs, and deep chocolaty warmth to sear the flavour into your memory. Cornas means 'burnt earth', and blame suggestion if you like, but I'd say a charred intensity marks the best wines. Prices have risen in recent years, but then so has quality; so it doesn't hurt too much. So far anyway. Best years: 1988, '85, '83, '80, '78. Best producers: de Barjac, Auguste Clape, Jaboulet, Juge, Michel, Verset, Voge.

CORTON AC
grand cru
CÔTE DE BEAUNE, BURGUNDY

Pinot Noir

Chardonnay, Pinot Blanc, Pinot Gris

Vines have been grown on this flat-topped hill at the northern end of the Côte de Beaune for over a thousand years. The Corton vineyard, occupying the sections of the hill mostly facing south and east on red iron-rich soil are the only red *grand cru* in the Côte de Beaune. In a typically quirky example of Burgundy's *appellation* intricacies, there is an AC for white *grand cru* Corton too, but whereas *red* Corton is the greatest red wine from these vineyards, *white* Corton is not – the Corton-Charlemagne *grand cru* has that distinction. Corton now has 2 sub-divisions spanning the villages of Ladoix-Serrigny to the east, Aloxe-Corton to the south (the most important section) and Pernand-Vergelesses to the west; all can label their red wine Corton. I think that's spreading the great name too thin and the taste of the wine bears this out. Ideally the wine has the burliness and savoury power of the top Côte de Nuits wines, combined with the more seductive perfumed fruit of Côte de Beaune, but a surprising number of examples are rather light and insipid – which is very sad. Red Corton should take ten years to mature; many modern examples never make it. Best years: 1988, '87, '85, '83, '80, '78. Best producers: Chandon de Briailles, Chevalier, Dubreuil-Fontaine, Gaunoux, Rapet, Senard, Tollot-Beaut, Voarick.

Very little white Corton is grown, some in the commune of Aloxe-Corton but more in Ladoix-Serrigny, at the north-east end of the hill. The best example is from the Vergennes vineyard. The Domaine Chandon de Briailles also make white Corton in their Bressandes vineyard (a tip-top red site) from half-and-half Chardonnay and Pinot Blanc. There is even some Pinot Beurot (Alsace's Pinot Gris) grown!

CORTON-CHARLEMAGNE AC
grand cru
CÔTE DE BEAUNE, BURGUNDY

Chardonnay

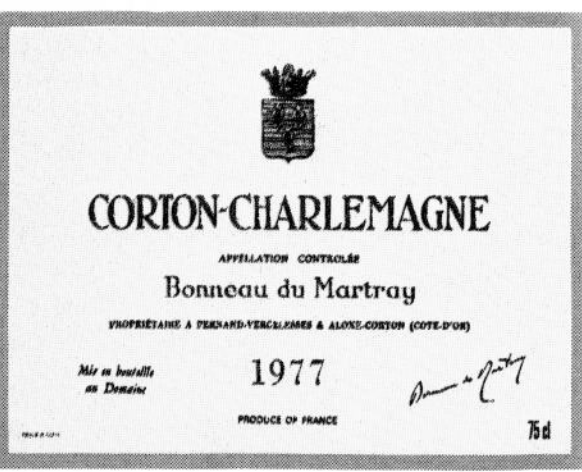

Perhaps it's because I've always drunk these wines young, and have never possessed a bottle on which I could lavish care and attention for the ten years or more Burgundy buffs say is necessary. Perhaps it's because most of the examples I've had have been bottled by merchants and individuality has been lost. Or is the wine just not what it was?

In the early '70s I enjoyed young bottles of '71, '70 and '68 – yes, *'68* a horrid year. They were inspiring and memorable. But then in the early '70s *red* Burgundy was the more sought-after, more expensive wine. There was no great pressure on white production and there were no Burgundy-starved buyers intent on lapping up the great labels regardless of the wine's actual flavour. In these white-crazy days there certainly *is* pressure, but Corton-Charlemagne, the largest of the white *grands crus* with a production of about 150,000 bottles, should be able to produce enough to cope. Ah well.

So, where is it? And why Charlemagne? It is a wide strip of vineyard at the top of the hill of Corton, part south-facing in the commune of Aloxe-Corton, but veering round to the west in Pernand-Vergelesses. And the name? Well it really does stem from the Emperor Charlemagne whose favourite vineyard this was – though in those days, the wine was red, which left an awful mess on his flowing white beard. After a fair bit of nagging from his wife, he ripped up the red wines and planted white – the inferior Aligoté, not the delicious Chardonnay.

Nowadays it's all Chardonnay and *can* produce the most bluntly impressive of all white Burgundies – rich, buttery, nutty, a blast of splendid golden flavours, not as perfumed or thrilling as Montrachet – more like a kind of super-Meursault. Yet it is more than that, because if it does only show its true splendour at ten years old and more, which I can well believe, that slow revelation of unsuspected depths and nuances is the mark of a great wine. Best years: 1988, '87, '86, '85, '83, '82. Best producers: Bonneau du Martray, Bouchard Père & Fils, Dubreuil-Fontaine, Hospices de Beaune, Jadot, Laleure-Piot, Latour, Rapet.

► Wicker harvesting baskets, traditional to Burgundy, piled high with Chardonnay grapes in Corton-Charlemagne.

COS D'ESTOURNEL, CH.
St-Estèphe AC, *2ème cru classé*
HAUT-MÉDOC, BORDEAUX

Cabernet Sauvignon, Merlot

Cos d'Estournel bears more than a passing resemblance to a Chinese temple complete with pagodas and bells. Well, that's just what Monsieur d'Estournel intended. He was a horse dealer in the early nineteenth century who traded extensively with the east, and discovered his wine improved enormously if he took it on the journey with him. So he went 'oriental' in a grand manner as a way of promoting his wine.

Cos d'Estournel is the best wine in St-Estèphe, and one of the best in all Bordeaux. Although St-Estèphe wines are generally less perfumed than those of neighbouring Pauillac because of the heavier clay soil, Cos d'Estournel makes up for this by having a high proportion of Merlot (40 per cent) and by extensive use of new oak barrels. The result is rich, powerful flavours – cherries, blackcurrants and a rather roasted vanilla softness. The wines usually need ten years to show really well, but then build up to a strong, concentrated mouthful, edged by tannin. Best years: 1988, '86, '85, '83, '82, '81, '79, '76. Second wine: Marbuzet.

COSTIÈRES DU GARD AC
LANGUEDOC-ROUSSILLON

🍷🍷 Carignan, Grenache, Syrah and others

🍷 Clairette, Bourboulenc, Grenache Blanc and others

This large AC of 10,000 acres (4000 hectares) lies between Nîmes and Arles, close to the Rhône delta in the *département* of the Gard. I find the reds usually have too much of a meaty, earthy flavour to be that enjoyable, and prefer the rosés – which, if you get them really young can have more spice and style than many of the Mediterranean pinks.

There are 20 million bottles of Costières du Gard produced annually, only one million of these are white, although the trend is towards a higher white production. At present Clairette, Ugni Blanc and Bourboulenc are used – and at best they can produce light, appley, quick-drinking wines from careful cool fermentation. But the Grenache Blanc, which can add an attractive *anis* freshness, is also widely planted in the area, as well as Sémillon, Sauvignon Blanc, Marsanne and Chardonnay which, if allowed in the AC, would dramatically improve the quality of the wines.

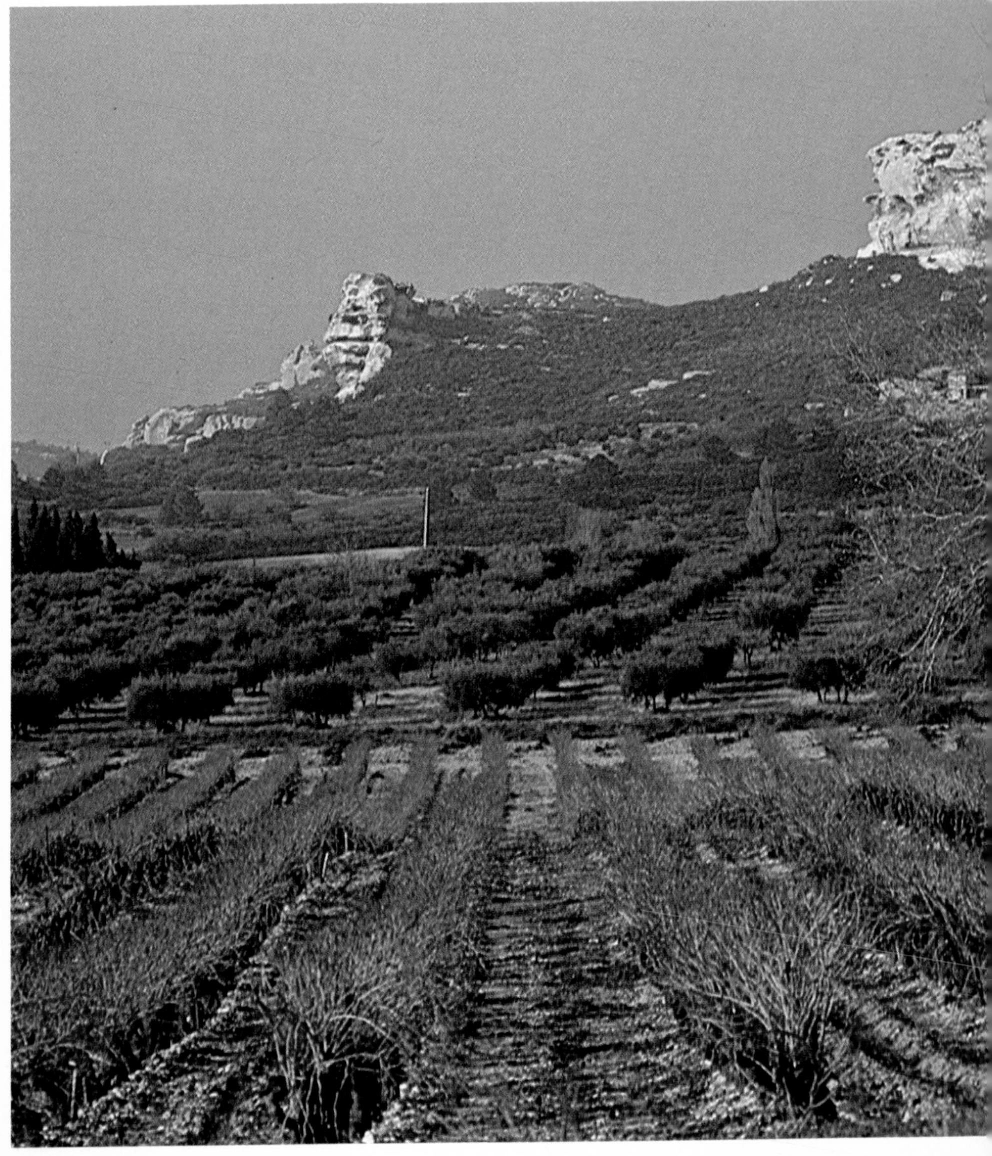

:OTEAUX CHAMPENOIS AC
HAMPAGNE

Pinot Noir, Pinot Meunier

Chardonnay

I don't know what possessed me, but I drank white Coteaux Champenois on Easter Day last year. Strange choice? You're telling me! But I *thought* I'd be getting a really nutty mature Chardonnay because it was a 1976 – a really hot year – from the good firm of Chaudron. I'd bought this wine in 1978. Then, it was tart, lemony, raspingly chalky and dry. Ten years on, had it changed? Not a bit. Pale gold, shockingly dry and with that chalky austerity like the lick of a cat's tongue on your cheek.

Made from black grapes, Coteaux Champenois can be either red or rosé, but usually pretends to be red. The trouble is, even when fully ripe, these Champagne grapes don't have a lot of colour or sugar, so with few exceptions (usually from the villages of Bouzy or Ay) the wine is pale and rather harsh, though it often has a fresh strawberry or cherry scent. No wonder they turn 99 per cent of the region's wine into fizz.

This AC, which covers still wines from the whole Champagne area, was only granted in 1974. Before then the wines could only be *vin de table*. I'm terribly tempted to say, repeal the AC, but I mustn't must I? After all, somebody, somewhere quite likes these lean, overpriced, ultra-dry wines. Best years: 1988, '86, '85, '83, '82. Best producers: Château de Saran (Moët & Chandon), Laurent-Perrier, Ruinart.

'OTEAUX D'AIX-EN-ROVENCE AC
ROVENCE

Grenache, Cabernet auvignon, Syrah and others

Ugni Blanc, Grenache Blanc, émillon, Sauvignon Blanc

Coteaux d'Aix-en-Provence, covering a large area around Aix-en-Provence in the Bouches-du-Rhône *département*, was only made AC in 1985 – long overdue when one considers that the sprawling Côtes de Provence region next door had been granted AC in 1977 despite a pretty frightful track record on quality. Prejudice against Cabernet Sauvignon was the cause of the delay; 95 per cent of the AC's production of 14 million bottles is red or rosé and it was the first area to acknowledge that Cabernet can enormously enhance the local varieties of Grenache, Cinsaut, Mourvèdre and Carignan.

Some quite good fresh rosé is made, but the best wines are red, and they can have a maximum of 60 per cent Cabernet Sauvignon. The wines are good but could do better, because some enterprising Côtes de Provence estates, as well as many in Coteaux des Baux-en-Provence, achieve richer, more succulent fruit flavours in their wines. The wines can age, but it's better to catch them quite young with their fruit intact.

Traditionally-made whites, based on Ugni Blanc, are pretty flabby mouthfuls. But cool fermentation in, where possible, stainless-steel tanks, early bottling and, very importantly, an increased use of Grenache Blanc, Sémillon and especially Sauvignon Blanc are now producing some pleasant, but hardly rivetting, dry whites – to knock back sharpish. Best producers (reds): Bas, Beaupré, Fonscolombe, Seuil, Vignelaure. Best producers (whites): Beaupré, Fonscolombe, Seuil.

:OTEAUX D'ANCENIS VDQS
'ESTERN LOIRE

Gamay, Cabernet Franc

Chenin Blanc, Pinot Gris

The old fortress town of Ancenis, guarding the Loire upstream from Nantes, is most famous now for its pig market and giant food-processing plant. A good deal of unmemorable Muscadet is made in the surrounding vineyards, but Ancenis itself has kept alive a non-Muscadet tradition – Coteaux d'Ancenis VDQS. The 750 acres (300 hectares) of vines are more than 80 per cent Gamay and Cabernet Franc making fairly raw red and rosé, and there is also a fair amount of Chenin. This too, I'm afraid, is pretty sharp stuff. The one joy of white Ancenis is the Malvoisie – alias Pinot Gris of Alsace. Only three growers even attempt it, but the wine has a delicious, gently honeyed, rather smoky flavour, vaguely sweet – and just right for a welcome draught of fruit after wading through the ocean of bone-dry Muscadet and Gros Plant which otherwise dominates the Pays Nantais. Best producer: Guindon.

COTEAUX DE L'ARDÈCHE, VIN DE PAYS
SOUTHERN RHÔNE

🍷🍷 Gamay, Syrah, Cabernet Sauvignon and others

🍷 Chardonnay, Aligoté, Sauvignon Blanc, Ugni Blanc

► The Ardèche, with its rugged rockscapes, is producing good country wines, helped by classic varieties Gamay, Syrah, Merlot.

I can't be sure whether my enthusiasm for the Ardèche was kindled by the fact that a steam railway runs from Tournon up to the heavenly hill town of Lamastre, or by the fact that in the value-for-money stakes the region is just about unbeatable. Add to all this the fact that the Ardèche is a wild mountainous paradise, west of the seething Rhône valley, and you have my idea of the perfect place to get away from it all.

The wines come under the general title of Vin de Pays des Coteaux de l'Ardèche. This applies primarily to the area south of Privas where the large co-operative groups are models of how such organizations should operate. Instead of sticking to lacklustre local grapes, they have planted top varieties like Syrah, Gamay, Cabernet Sauvignon and Chardonnay and have succeeded in producing some of France's best-priced and most delicious country wines. In 1984 I wrote that the best 'Beaujolais Nouveau' I'd tasted all year was a Gamay de l'Ardèche!

White wines only account for about three per cent of the 20 million bottles the Coteaux de l'Ardèche produced annually, yet it was white wine which first drew attention to this wild, upland area. Louis Latour, a leading Burgundy merchant, saw that the world was developing a thirst for dry white wine from the Chardonnay grape (responsible for white Burgundy). Yet he also saw that there was no room for expansion in Burgundy itself. So he looked south and found these unexploited, disorganized backwoods and in the jumble of gorges and hillsides he saw tremendous potential for good vineyards.

Luckily, the co-operative movement there also saw that 'quality first' was the only route out of the poverty trap and they made an arrangement to produce Chardonnay for Louis Latour. When the foreseen world shortage of Chardonnay did develop, Louis Latour wheeled out his new baby, Chardonnay *vin de pays* from Ardèche. It was delicious!

There are now several Chardonnays produced here, and Sauvignon, Aligoté and, unfortunately, the boring Ugni Blanc make up the rest of the white plantings. Best producers: Latour, Ucova.

COTEAUX DE L'AUBANCE AC
CENTRAL LOIRE

🍷 Chenin Blanc

Gentle, charming, mildly sweet white wine from a wide area centred on the Aubance river south of Angers. However, it isn't a popular AC probably because it is neither fish nor fowl – neither sweet nor dry – in a wine world which likes to define flavours more exactly. So although ten different communes each produce a little Aubance, the total crop rarely amounts to more than 250,000 bottles. Many vineyards which could make Coteaux de l'Aubance prefer to produce red, rosé or dry white Anjou AC – easier to sell, though at a lower price. Best years: 1988, '86, '85, '83. Best producers: Chauvin, Richou.

COTEAUX DE PEYRIAC, VIN DE PAYS
LANGUEDOC-ROUSSILLON

🍷🍷 Grenache, Carignan, Syrah and others

🍷 Ugni Blanc, Clairette, Macabeo and others

The most prolific French *vin de pays* covering roughly the same area as Minervois, east of Carcassonne, and producing as much as 35 million bottles of wine a year, 99 per cent of which is red or rosé. Although the traditional red grapes of the region are widely grown, this *vin de pays* has been one of the leaders in adopting more northern 'classic' grapes: Cabernet Sauvignon, Cabernet Franc and Merlot, in particular, have been planted, primarily at the insistence of the giant Chantovent group.

Only one per cent of those millions of bottles is white. The bad news is that so far the wines aren't very good, based largely on the dreaded Ugni Blanc, Clairette and Macabeo grapes – just about the most neutral trio it is possible to imagine. There are now some plantings of Sémillon, Sauvignon Blanc and Chardonnay, so things should start looking up in the future.

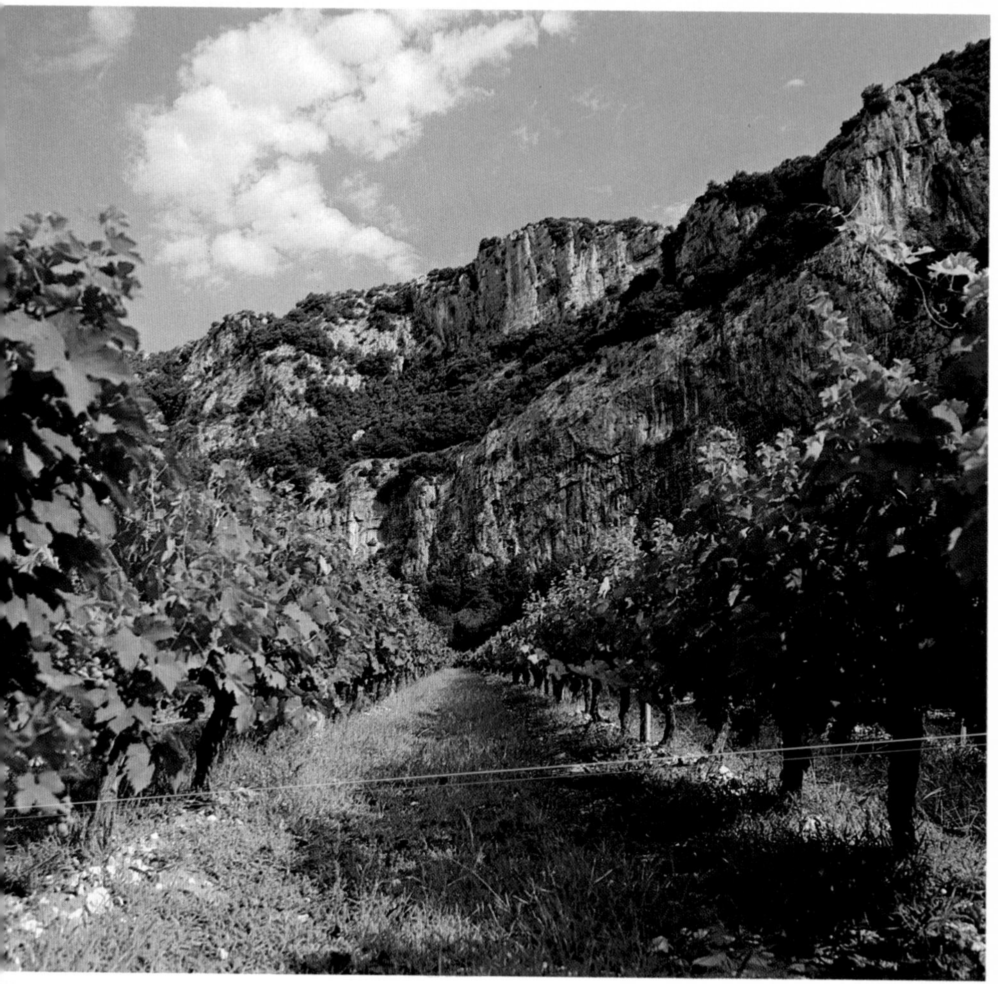

COTEAUX DES BAUX-EN-PROVENCE Coteaux d'Aix-en-Provence AC
PROVENCE

Grenache, Syrah, Cabernet Sauvignon

Ugni Blanc, Clairette, Grenache Blanc, Sauvignon Blanc

Technically part of the Coteaux d'Aix-en-Provence AC, this is the most exciting new area in the south of France, in particular showing that organic farming methods can produce spectacular results. It's a weird place, though – a desolate moonscape of tumbled rocks and gaunt, skull-like cliffs dominating the scenery between Cavaillon and Arles in the foothills of the Alpilles in the Bouches-du-Rhône. Still, the welcome is in the wines, which can be the best reds and rosés in the south. Fruit is what marks them out, and incredible softness – incredible because the wines are well-structured, full and balanced, and are ideally suited to ageing for several years; yet even when young they seem to soothe your palate and calm your thoughts. The most important grape is the Syrah, which here gets into its joyous, fruit-first mood. The leading estate, Domaine de Trévallon, mixes Syrah with Cabernet Sauvignon – to sensational effect. The AC authorities have decided in their 'wisdom' to down-grade Trévallon, the area's one world-class wine, to *vin de pays* for this heretical improvement with Cabernet. I need hardly add my views on bureaucratic airheads like these.

Virtually all of the wine so far is red, but the quality of the fruit – and the inspiration displayed in the wine-making – is so good here, that we are sure to see some good whites soon, so watch this space. Estates like Mas de Gourgonnier, using 40 per cent Sauvignon Blanc in its fresh snappy white, and Terres Blanches are among those showing the way. Best producers: Mas de la Dame, Mas de Gourgonnier, Mas de Ste-Berthe, Terres Blanches, Trévallon.

COTEAUX DU GIENNOIS VDQS
UPPER LOIRE

🍷🍷 Gamay, Pinot Noir

🍷 Sauvignon Blanc, Chenin Blanc

This little VDQS's claim to be one of France's most obscure wines is considerably enhanced by the fact that you turn up at Gien, a little town on the Loire about 30 miles (50km) to the north of Sancerre, and no-one seems to know anything about it. So you retrace your steps back south and arrive at Cosne with your thoughts already firmly fixed on a nice cool glass of Sancerre – but alas, you'll have to wait. There's a sign in the town which declaims, 'Taste here the *excellent* wine of Cosne, Coteaux du Giennois'. Your eyes spy the odd scattered vine, and your unenthusiastic inquiries elicit the fact the these are the vineyards of Coteaux du Giennois. In fact, there are a couple of vines at Gien, but most are at Cosne – white Sauvignon, and red Gamay and Pinot Noir, producing about 500,000 bottles of entirely forgettable wine. Well, *almost* entirely forgettable. I've had one bottle of rosé from the Pouilly-sur-Loire co-operative which was absolutely delicious. I wonder if they remember how they did it.

COTEAUX DU LANGUEDOC AC
LANGUEDOC-ROUSSILLON

🍷🍷 Carignan, Cinsaut, Grenache and others

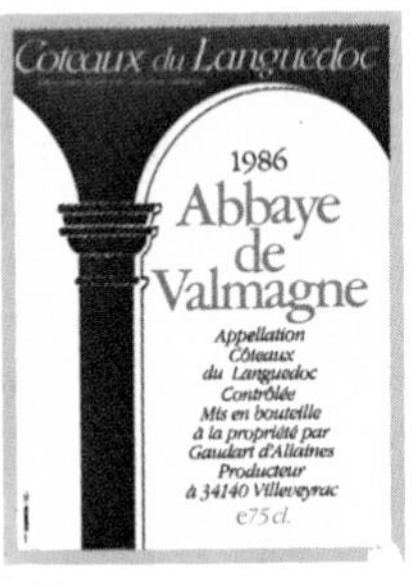

A recent, but large and increasingly successful AC running across the south of France – approximately from Montpellier to Narbonne. There are 121 villages in the *appellation*, producing about 12 million bottles of red and rosé. (White wines are not permitted the Coteaux du Languedoc AC, although a number of producers make whites from Clairette, Bourboulenc and Picpoul.) Although the wines used to have, at best, a rather solid, sturdy kind of fruit, things are now on the move, and it is this area which some experts reckon could be the French California of the 1990s. They look forward to a flood of fresh, fruity, well-made wines at affordable prices as bad vineyards disappear, better grape varieties are planted, and up-to-date wine-making techniques are adopted.

I agree, and think the wines will actually be a good deal better than those of California's Central Valley, more closely resembling the highly drinkable bulk wines of Australia. In a new 'incentive and reward' approach to improving quality, 11 leading villages can now add their own names to Coteaux du Languedoc. Best of these are Cabrières, La Clape, Montpeyroux, Pic St-Loup, St-Drézéry and St-Georges-d'Orques. Some of these villages now use oak barrels to mature the best reds, and these can age for several years, though most reds and rosés are best drunk young.

COTEAUX DU LAYON AC
CENTRAL LOIRE

🍷 Chenin Blanc

It's a mixed blessing being a wine-grower in one of those rare micro-climates where the noble rot fungus strikes. This rot clings to the grape skins in warm, moist autumns and sucks out the water, leaving the sugar and acids to concentrate almost to treacle. If the rot claims all your vines and you carefully pick only the most syrupy, mushy grapes, then you have the chance of making great, intensely sweet, luscious white wines.

Well, the Layon valley, running south of the Loire just west of Angers, does get noble rot – and the Chenin grape reacts well to it in the 3200 acres (1300 hectares) out of a possible 7400 acres (3000 hectares) which are planted. But it is incredibly expensive and risky to wait way into the autumn for the fungus to develop – some years it never does –

and then to make several sorties through your vines selecting only the most-rotted grapes. If you get Sauternes' prices, maybe it's worth it, but, except for its two *grands crus* – Quarts de Chaume and Bonnezeaux – prices for Coteaux du Layon are not high enough. Each bottle of Coteaux du Layon is certainly going to be sweet, perhaps with a very attractive peach or apricot flavour developing after three to five years, but it is unlikely to be intensely rich – though it isn't going to be very expensive either. A Coteaux du Layon makes a lovely, fresh, sweetish aperitif at a very fair price. If we want it to be a rich and rare dessert wine – we'll have to pay more for it to encourage the producers to risk all in those swirling late autumn mists. Best years: 1988, '85, '83, '82, '76, '75. Best producers: Fresne, Rochettes, Soucherie.

COTEAUX DU LAYON-VILLAGES AC
CENTRAL LOIRE

Chenin Blanc

Seven villages in the Coteaux du Layon AC have, since 1955, been allowed to use their own name on their labels. These are Beaulieu-sur-Layon, Chaume, Faye-d'Anjou, Rablay-sur-Layon, Rochefort-sur-Loire, St-Aubin-de-Luigné and St-Lambert-du-Lattay. To qualify for this superior AC the wines must have at least one degree more alcohol than straight Coteaux du Layon – 12 degrees rather than 11. These wines can be extremely attractive – peachy-sweet after five to six years' ageing – and they are definitely underpriced for the quality. The village of Chaume can only call its wines Coteaux du Layon-Chaume if it reduces its yield to 25 hectolitres per hectare as against the general 'Villages' level of 30 hl/ha, pretty low by any standards. Best years: 1988, '85, '83, '82, '76, '75. Best producers: Breuil, Clos de Ste-Catherine, Guimonière, la Motte, Rochettes, Soucherie.

COTEAUX DU LYONNAIS VDQS
NORTHERN RHÔNE

Gamay

Chardonnay, Aligoté, Muscadet

Good light reds and a few whites and rosés from somewhat haphazard vineyards in the area between Villefranche and Lyon. It became an AC in 1984 and, although pretty large, it produces only a million or so bottles annually. A first cousin to simple Beaujolais, the red wine is light, quite fruity and very pleasant chilled young, but not too demanding on the old grey matter. There's a little white too, from Chardonnay, Aligoté or Melon de Bourgogne (the Muscadet of the Loire), mostly fresh and snappy, to be drunk at six months rather than a year.

COTEAUX DU TRICASTIN AC
SOUTHERN RHÔNE

Grenache, Syrah, Cinsaut and others

Marsanne, Bourboulenc

You have to approve of a wine region which shares its promotional headquarters with a truffle-hunters' organization – the 'House of the Truffle and of Tricastin' – it even has a truffle exhibition! This large and fast-growing vineyard area was only created in the 1960s to cater for a flood of displaced wine-growers fleeing from North Africa after Morocco, Tunisia and Algeria gained independence from France, the first two in 1956 and Algeria in 1962. The available area for the AC is pretty spread out in the southern part of the Drôme – between Montélimar, the nougat capital of France, and Bollène. The zone became VDQS in 1964, and AC in 1974. Right from the start the wines have been good because the new settlers introduced modern methods – formulated to cope with the desert conditions in Africa – on to good virgin vineyard land. Reds and rosés are often quite light, but very fresh, having an attractive juicy fruit livened up with some peppery spice – and rarely marred by excess of tannin or acid.

Only a tiny amount of white wine is made, but if you do see some, it's worth trying for a fairly good, nutty, but fresh drink, ideally to consume within the year. Best producers: Grangeneuve, Lônes, Tour d'Elyssas (especially a pure Syrah Cuvée).

COTEAUX DU VENDÔMOIS VDQS
CENTRAL LOIRE

🍷🍷 Pineau d'Aunis, Gamay, Pinot Noir and others

🍷 Chenin Blanc, Chardonnay

One of those minuscule Loire country wines that one is glad to see surviving at all, but which doesn't exactly cause one to dash down to the shops in feverish anticipation when the whisper goes round they've got a bottle in. Well, the whisper wouldn't go round when Coteaux du Vendômois hit the shelves. The 50 acres (20 hectares) of vines near the Loir (no 'e') river 25 miles (40km) north of Tours produce hardly enough red, rosé or white for the locals, let alone export. By the time you get to Vendôme, wine-growing is becoming a fairly marginal occupation. When the red Pineau d'Aunis grape predominates the resulting wine can be light, dry and refreshing. Too much Gamay, or indeed Pinot Noir, Cabernet Franc and Cabernet Sauvignon – the other permitted grape varieties – rather spoils it.

Whites account for barely a tenth of the annual production, and have to cope with the late-ripening Chenin as the main white grape, but at least the rules do allow 20 per cent Chardonnay in the blend – so there is a little softness in what is otherwise an extremely dry white. Neither reds nor whites here benefit much from ageing. Best producer: Minier.

COTEAUX VAROIS VDQS
PROVENCE

🍷🍷 Grenache, Cinsaut, Mourvèdre and others

🍷 Grenache Blanc, Ugni Blanc, Clairette and others

A large area to the north of Toulon, and nudging Côtes de Provence to the east, Coteaux Varois in the Var *département* was promoted to VDQS in 1985. This was largely because a lot of growers were making great efforts, especially with new plantings of classic grapes Cabernet Sauvignon and Syrah, to upgrade their quality. Good for them! Otherwise the grapes are much the same as for Côtes de Provence; our old friends Grenache, Cinsaut and Mourvèdre. A splash of Malvoisie assists greatly in making the whites more interesting. Best estates: Clos de la Truffière, Deffends, St-Estève, St-Jean.

CÔTE CHALONNAISE
URGUNDY

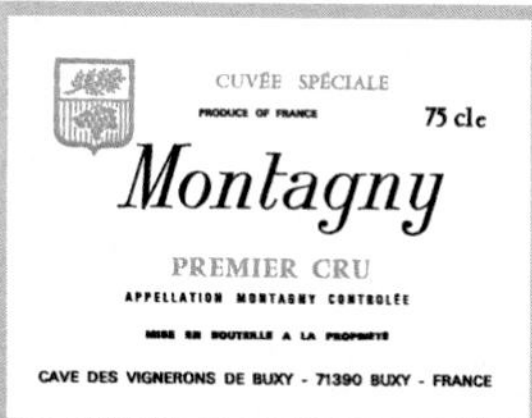

◀ Provence – a characteristic vista of vines and olives and cypresses that has changed little since Roman times.

It's easy to see why the Côte Chalonnaise is the least known of the Burgundy regions. All the other regions have their names enshrined at very least in their overall ACs – Chablis, Côte de Nuits, Côte de Beaune, Mâcon and Beaujolais – but did you ever see AC Côte Chalonnaise? No. There isn't one. Add to that the fact that the region doesn't have any world-famous wines, whereas all the others are thick with them, and the fact that the area considers itself unfairly excluded from the renowned Côte de Beaune. You can almost understand the growers feeling miffed but, frankly, the Côte de Beaune does apply to a single swathe of vines along one single slope of land and the Chalonnaise vineyards are on a different slope. In fact, there isn't a single slope at all here; the hills twist and turn, valleys form and peter out, forests crowd the meadows and vineyards fight for space. It's a different, more traditionally rural world where the vine is merely one part of the texture of rustic life. Despite the lack of renown, the vineyards of the Côte Chalonnaise have gained enormously in importance in the last few years, as a result of the spiralling price of white Burgundy from famous villages like Meursault and Puligny-Montrachet in the Côte d'Or. The Côte Chalonnaise vineyards could almost be thought of as an extension of the Côte d'Or, since they are directly to the south, but they are far less cohesive.

Altogether there are five villages with their own ACs in the 15 miles (24km) running south from Chagny, with the best white wine vineyards lying in the north. Most northerly is Bouzeron, with its own AC for Aligoté wine since 1979. Over the Montagne de la Folie is Rully, originally known for its sparkling wine but now producing light yet very attractive reds and very fine Chardonnay whites with excellent fruit and a hint of oak – Meursault flavours at half the price. A run through the woods then takes you to Mercurey, the biggest AC with over 1500 acres (600 hectares). Famous for red wines, its whites are now increasingly good. Four miles (6km) south is Givry, again a red wine village, although bottles of white Givry occasionally surface. There are only 300 acres (120 hectares) of vines here, but it's the only Chalonnaise wine to bask in notoriety as yet – Henri IV drank a particularly 'enthusiastic' amount of it and many labels still commemorate this fact. And in the south is Montagny, an all white AC – which is a pity because the neighbouring village of Buxy makes very good red which for some reason only qualifies as simple AC Bourgogne. Montagny's Chardonnays can seem a little lean and chalky, though there are now signs of improvement. The growers are lobbying for a more specific AC and they deserve to succeed.

CÔTE DE BEAUNE AC
CÔTE D'OR, BURGUNDY

Pinot Noir

The Côte de Beaune AC covers a couple of vineyard sites around the town of Beaune and is very rare. The wine is usually very dry to start, but has a good lean fruit which can be delicious at two to three years old. Certainly worth trying if you come across one. Best producers: Bouchard Père & Fils, Chantal Lescure, Labouré-Roi.

CÔTE DE BEAUNE-VILLAGES AC
CÔTE D'OR, BURGUNDY

Pinot Noir

The general *appellation* covering wine from 16 villages on the Côte de Beaune. These villages have the right to use their own names, but, since some of them are not well-known, merchants may prefer to blend several wines together to sell under the Côte de Beaune-Villages label. This used to be one of the commonest Burgundy *appellations* in the export market, but nowadays, even villages like Pernand-Vergelesses, Monthélie and Auxey-Duresses confidently sell wine under their own name and, to be honest, what's left over for Côte de Beaune-Villages usually tastes as though they really had to scrape the barrel to make up the blend.

CÔTE DE BROUILLY AC
BEAUJOLAIS, BURGUNDY

🍷 Gamay

One of the Beaujolais '*crus*' we see least of – perhaps because we see great deal of Brouilly. Well, that's a pity; the Côte de Brouilly is a volcani mound rising to 1650 feet (500 metres) in the middle of the Brouilly A and, because of its steep slopes, the sun ripens the grapes more full than on the flatter vineyards.

This extra ripeness is reflected by the fact that the minimum alcoh requirement for Côte de Brouilly is higher than for any other *cru*. An that extra sun produces a full, juicy, strawberry-and-peach ripeness – sort of 'super-Brouilly', which is good young, but can age beautifully fo several years. Best years: 1988, '87, '86, '86, '83. Best producer Conroy, Geoffray, Ravier, Thivin, Verger.

CÔTE DE NUITS
CÔTE D'OR, BURGUNDY

This is the geographical description of the northern part of Burgundy' great Côte d'Or. It is *not* an AC. Nuits-St-Georges is the main town of th narrow stretch of east- and south-east-facing vineyards which starts i the southern suburbs of Dijon and ends just below the 'pink marbl quarries of Corgoloin and Comblanchien. Between these two points ar villages with some of the greatest wine names of France – Gevrey Chambertin, Vougeot, Chambolle-Musigny, Vosne-Romanée, Nuits-S Georges itself. I still get a thrill driving down the N74 to see these name slapped on an ordinary signpost without the slightest romance, ye every time I read the names, see the huddled houses surrounded b their sweep of vineyards, and hear the rustle of vine leaves playing in th breeze, my heart beats just a little faster. The Côte de Nuits is almos entirely red wine country, although a little rosé is made at Marsannay i the north, and there are minuscule amounts of white in several villages

CÔTE DE NUITS-VILLAGES AC
CÔTE DE NUITS, BURGUNDY

🍷 Pinot Noir

🍷 Chardonnay, Pinot Blanc

An *appellation* specific to Corgoloin, Comblanchien and Prissey in th south of the Côte de Nuits, and Brochon and Fixin in the north. Fixi wines may also be sold under their own name. The 750 acres (30 hectares) of vines usually produce almost one million bottle overwhelmingly red. Although not much seen, the wines are often goo not very deep, but with a good cherry fruit, and an attractive resin-bitte edge which can go smooth and chocolaty with age. Grand Côte de Nuit flavours in miniature. Best years: 1988, '85, '83, '80, '78. Best producer (reds): Durand, Julien, Rion, Rossignol, Tollot-Voarick.

Out of the total Côte de Nuits-Villages AC production, which veer between 400,000 and one million bottles depending on the vintag there are up to 25,000 bottles of white. Do I think they're worth seekin out? Well, no, not really. You'll be better off with the reds.

CÔTE ROANNAISE VDQS
UPPER LOIRE

🍷🍷 Gamay, Pinot Noir

The Côte Roannaise straddles the upper reaches of the Loire river, bu the nearest large town is Lyon, capital of Beaujolais, and Roanne doe lean towards Beaujolais rather than the Loire. The principal grape is th Gamay, and almost all the wine is red, going from the wispy, but fres and fruity, to big chocolaty numbers which quite resemble Morgon on good day. In general, drink them very young, though the Domain Lapandéry will age for some time. Best producers: Chaucesse, Chargro Lapandéry, Lutz.

CÔTE-RÔTIE AC
NORTHERN RHÔNE

🍷 Syrah, Viognier

Côte-Rôtie – the 'roasted slope' – is the most northerly Rhône vineya and definitely one of the oldest – there have been vines on these slope for 24 centuries! Yet it is only recently that wine-drinkers have becom aware that this is one of France's greatest red wines – the Syrah grap

bakes itself to super-ripeness on these steep south-east-facing slopes. What marks Côte-Rôtie out from the heftier Rhône reds like Hermitage is its exotic fragrance, quite unexpected in a red wine. This is because a little of the heavenly-scented white Viognier grape is allowed in the vineyard (up to 20 per cent, though 5–10 per cent is more likely). The result is damson-juicy, raspberry-sweet, sometimes with a hint of apricot skins and pepper. Lovely young, it is much better aged for ten years. The two best slopes are called Côte Brune and Côte Blonde; they are usually blended but you *may* see the name on a label. Best years: 1988, '85, '83, '82, '80, '78. Best producers: Champet, Dervieux-Thaize, Gentaz-Dervieux, Guigal, Jaboulet, Jasmin, Rostaing, Vidal-Fleury.

CÔTES D'AUVERGNE VDQS
UPPER LOIRE

Gamay, Pinot Noir

Based on the Gamay, with a little Pinot Noir, the red is usually bright, cherry-flavoured and very easy to drink nice and young; the rosé (about 25 per cent of production) is extremely pale, slightly sharp but very refreshing when drunk cool. There are 54 villages making the wine, totalling about 2·5 million bottles, and some, making slightly fuller wines, can add their own name.

CÔTES DE BERGERAC AC, CÔTES DE BERGERAC MOELLEUX AC
SOUTH-WEST

Cabernet Sauvignon, Cabernet Franc, Merlot and others

Sémillon, Sauvignon Blanc, Muscadelle

The straight AC Côtes de Bergerac is for good quality reds, made from the same grapes as Bergerac AC, but achieving a higher minimum alcohol level. There are also subdivisions which apply to whites. Côtes de Bergerac–Côtes de Saussignac is a superior *appellation* for dry Bergerac whites, using Sauvignon, Sémillon and sometimes Muscadelle. The minimum alcohol is 12·5 degrees as against the usual 11 degrees for Bergerac Sec, and consequently the wine is fairly big and broad, rather than the usual sharp, zesty Sauvignon-style now popular in Bergerac. Côtes de Bergerac Moelleux is the AC for sweet wines from the whole Bergerac region. It can cover a multitude of sins, but the wines should be pleasant, fruity, easily sweet but not exactly rich.

CÔTES DE BLAYE AC
BORDEAUX

Sémillon, Sauvignon Blanc, Colombard

The AC for whites from the Côtes de Blaye vineyards on the right bank of the Gironde. Almost all of the best whites of the area are now dry. A few sweetish wines remain, none very good, and these may be seen under the Premières Côtes de Blaye label. The most interesting wines include a fair percentage of the Colombard grape, which has far more character here than the more renowned Sauvignon and Sémillon.

CÔTES DE BOURG AC
BORDEAUX

Merlot, Cabernet Franc, Cabernet Sauvignon, Malbec

Sémillon, Sauvignon Blanc, Muscadelle and others

Château Margaux, Château Palmer, and all the other luminaries of the Médoc big-time are just a tantalizing mile or two away on the other side of the Gironde, yet Bourg shares none of their glory. These seemingly perfectly placed vineyard slopes are one of Bordeaux's forgotten areas, struggling to regain a place in the sun. Côtes de Bourg is very much a red wine district, an enclave inside the larger Blaye area; its sloping vineyards are mostly clay, but there is enough gravel to suit the Cabernet Sauvignon, and the good local co-operative at Tauriac and leading properties are beginning to use new oak as they strive to upgrade their wine. They deserve to succeed. The red wines are quite full, fairly dry, but with a pleasant blackcurrant fruit which ensures the earthy quality doesn't dominate; when they are splashed with the spice of new oak, they can age to a delicious maturity at six to ten years old. Best years (reds): 1988, '85, '83, '82. Best producers: de Barbe, du Bousquet, Haut-Guiraud, Haut-Rousset, la Croix-Millorit, Tauriac co-operative. Only three per cent of the production is white wines. Mostly made from Sémillon with a little Sauvignon Blanc, they are bone dry rather lifeless and flat. If you find one with a bit of fruit and zip th grower has probably sneaked in some Colombard – an underrate grape quite widely grown in the northern reaches of the region.

CÔTES DE CASTILLON AC
BORDEAUX

Cabernet Sauvignon, Cabernet Franc, Merlot, Malbec

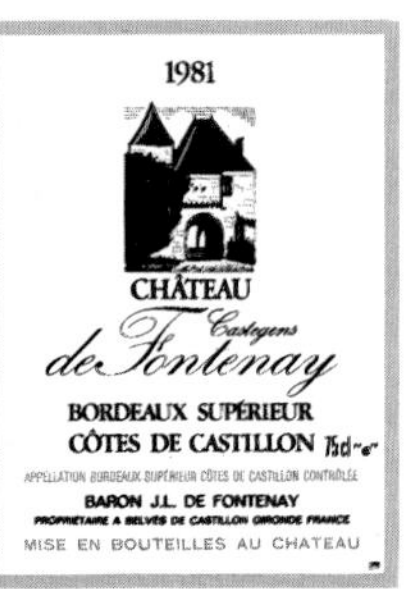

On the Dordogne to the east of St-Émilion is the little town c Castillon-la-Bataille, where defeat at a crucial battle in 1453 lost th English control of Aquitaine – and their supply of Bordeaux wine. W didn't hear much about Castillon after that until the 1980s, when th prices of decent red Bordeaux became so loony that we began castin about for a few understudies while we waited for the primadonnas of th Médoc to calm down. Well, they still haven't calmed down, and th 'replacement' wines consolidate their reputation with every vintage.

Côtes de Castillon is one of two red Bordeaux Supérieurs (the other i Côtes de Francs) allowed to add its own name on the label. It manage to be more special than simple Bordeaux Rouge, because the vineyard impart flavours of mint, blackcurrant and cedar to the wine – i miniature maybe, but these are the flavours which made the Médo famous. They use a high proportion of Merlot – which makes wine mor immediately attractive – and some estates now use new oak barrels t age the wine; it is never expensive, but delicious at three to ten year old – depending on the vintage. One feature of Côtes de Castillon wine is that they can be especially good in less ripe vintages. Best years 1988, '86, '85, '83, '82, '81. Best châteaux: Belcier, Fonds-Rondes, le Hauts de Granges, Moulin-Rouge, Parenchère, Pitray.

CÔTES DE DURAS AC
SOUTH-WEST

Cabernet Franc, Cabernet Sauvignon, Merlot, Malbec

Sauvignon Blanc, Sémillon, Muscadelle

The growers of Côtes de Duras could justifiably feel aggrieved at th legislation fixing AC boundaries. Bordeaux AC covers wines in th Gironde *département*. Côtes de Duras is in Lot-et-Garonne, and so i excluded – despite the fact that only a chartered surveyor could te where one stops and the other starts. The Côtes de Duras has spawne a very active co-operative movement, which offers extremely goo fresh, grassy reds and whites from traditional Bordeaux grapes, a distinctly lower prices. The Duras vineyards are north of the Dropt rive between Entre-Deux-Mers and Bergerac, and produce up to seve million bottles a year; 4½ million of them are white. There is som sweet white but it's the dry, often labelled Sauvignon Blanc, which i now far more important – it has a strong, grassy green fruit, but surprisingly soft, gentle texture. So you can drink fashionably dry, yet doesn't feel too much of an ordeal. Best producers (reds): Conti, Cours Ferrant, Laulan, co-operatives at Duras and Landerrouat. Drink th wines (of either colour), young, preferably at around a year old. Bes producers (whites): Duras and Landerrouat co-operatives.

CÔTES DE FRANCS
Bordeaux Supérieur Côtes de Francs AC
BORDEAUX

Merlot, Cabernet Sauvignon, Cabernet Franc, Malbec

Sémillon, Sauvignon Blanc, Muscadelle

Côtes de Francs, a tiny area on the eastern fringe of St-Émilion wit good clay and limestone soil, often on fairly steep slopes, has th warmest and driest micro-climate in Bordeaux. Its potential is immens – at the best properties, closely controlled yields plus the use of nev oak barrels give the wines a remarkable concentration of fruit; dee plum and blackberry flavours, strengthened by tannin and oak spice Investment by families from St-Émilion and Pomerol, who hav ambitions to produce Classed Growth standard reds should assure th AC's future. As the vineyards mature the wines will improve with ever vintage. Best vintages: 1988, '86, '85, '83. Best producers: la Claverie de Francs, Puyguéraud.

About ten per cent of the million or so bottles a year is white. Most of it is dry, though sweet is permitted under the Côtes de Francs Liquoreux AC. Quality so far is less than memorable – and the leading estates are sticking to reds. Best years: 1988, '87, '86.

CÔTES DE GASCOGNE, VIN DE PAYS
SOUTH-WEST

Tannat, Merlot, Cabernet Sauvignon, Cabernet Franc

Ugni Blanc, Colombard, Gros Manseng, Sauvignon Blanc

We have the decline in Armagnac production to thank for a most unlikely superstar of the '80s. The white wine that out-Sauvignons Sauvignon, out-Bordeauxs Bordeaux, yet is made from two grapes generally dismissed with contempt as inferior and gutless.

Côtes de Gascogne covers the Armagnac region in the Gers *département* and the best whites come from the chalky soils of Haut-Armagnac to the north and south of the town of Auch. The wines are fabulous, usually very dry (though sometimes quite unnecessarily sweetened a bit for export), with high acidity, but a startling array of flavours – peach, pear, apple slashed with the tang of lemon and a whiff of liquorice and tobacco – and they're tremendous value. If growers here can do such exciting things with the supposedly unexciting Ugni Blanc and Colombard – why on earth can't their counterparts in Entre-Deux-Mers and Bordeaux do twice as well with their supposedly superior grapes?

There is also a certain amount of rather sharp red – initially exclusively from the east of the Armagnac region but increasingly now coming from the better vineyards in the centre and to the south. Best producers: Cassagnoles, Grassa, Jalousie, Meste Duran, Plaimont co-operative, Planterieu, Tariquet.

▼ Sunflowers and vines colour the Armagnac landscape. The *vin de pays* of Côtes de Gascogne covers all of the Gers *département*.

CÔTE D'OR RED WINES

The Côte d'Or is Europe's northernmost great red wine area. The name, meaning 'Golden Slope', refers to one single stretch of vines in Burgundy, starting just south of Dijon, and fading out 30 miles (48km) later west of Chagny. It is divided into two sections. The Côte de Nuits in the north encompasses little more than 3460 acres (1400 hectares) of vines, since the slope is often only a few hundred yards wide, and at the Clos Arlots in Nuits-St-Georges it measures less than 70 yards (64 metres) in width!

The Côte de Beaune is the southern section. Beginning at the hill of Corton, it twists and turns a little more than the Côte de Nuits. Beaune is the main town, and as the Côte progresses southwards past Volnay, white takes over from red as the most exciting wine style, until red briefly reasserts itself at Santenay. The less abrupt slopes of the Côte de Beaune possess 7410 acres (3000 hectares) of vines, but again, that isn't a lot of vineyard.

The soil of the Côte d'Or is a mix of clay, marl and limestone. Where the marl is dominant red wines are produced from the Pinot Noir; where the limestone takes over white wines from Chardonnay are best. In the Côte de Nuits where the marl is more prevalent, the slopes are steepest, so the richness of the soil is offset by particularly efficient drainage. In the Côte de Beaune the slopes are gentler, which is fine because in all the best sites, easy-draining limestone is much in evidence.

Over the centuries grapes growing on the best sites have consistently ripened earlier than those too high up the slope or on flatter ground at the bottom. So a minutely accurate system of vineyard classification has evolved. Top of the pile are the *grands crus*, which are allowed to use only the vineyard name. These are almost always at between 250 and 300 metres in elevation, and facing between south and east. Slightly less well-situated vineyards are accorded *premier cru* status. Their wines should still be excellent, if a little lighter than those of the *grands crus*. Vineyards on the bottom of the slope are less favoured and will usually carry just the village name.

WINE ENTRIES

- Aloxe-Corton
- Auxey-Duresses
- Beaune
- Blagny
- Bonnes-Mares
- Chambertin
- Chambolle-Musigny
- Chapelle-Chambertin
- Charmes-Chambertin
- Chassagne-Montrachet
- Chorey-lès-Beaune
- Clos de la Roche
- Clos de Vougeot
- Corton
- Côte de Beaune
- Côte de Beaune-Villages
- Côte de Nuits
- Côte de Nuits-Villages
- Échézeaux
- Fixin
- Gevrey-Chambertin
- Grands-Échézeaux
- Griotte-Chambertin
- Hautes-Côtes de Beaune
- Hautes-Côtes de Nuits
- Ladoix-Serrigny
- Latricières-Chambertin
- Maranges
- Marsannay
- Mazis-Chambertin
- Meursault
- Monthélie
- Morey-St-Denis
- Musigny
- Nuits-St-Georges
- Pernand-Vergelesses
- Pommard
- Richebourg
- la Romanée-Conti
- Ruchottes-Chambertin
- St-Aubin
- St-Romain
- Santenay
- Savigny-lès-Beaune
- la Tâche
- Volnay
- Volnay-Santenots
- Vosne-Romanée
- Vougeot

GRAPE ENTRY

- Pinot Noir

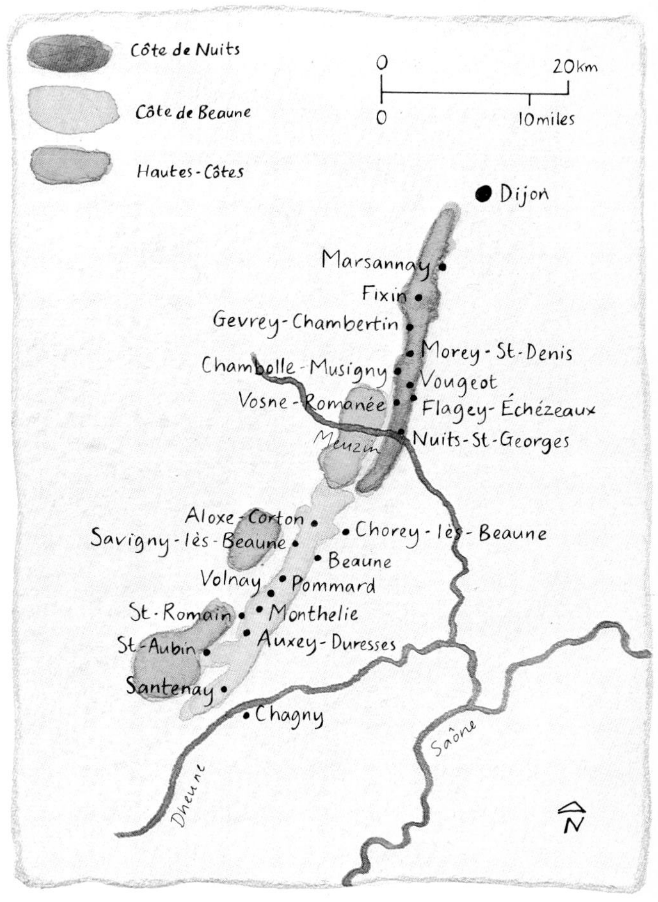

◀ Winter vines on the Côte de Nuits at Clos de Vougeot, one of Burgundy's best-known *grands crus*.

Côte d'Or White Wines

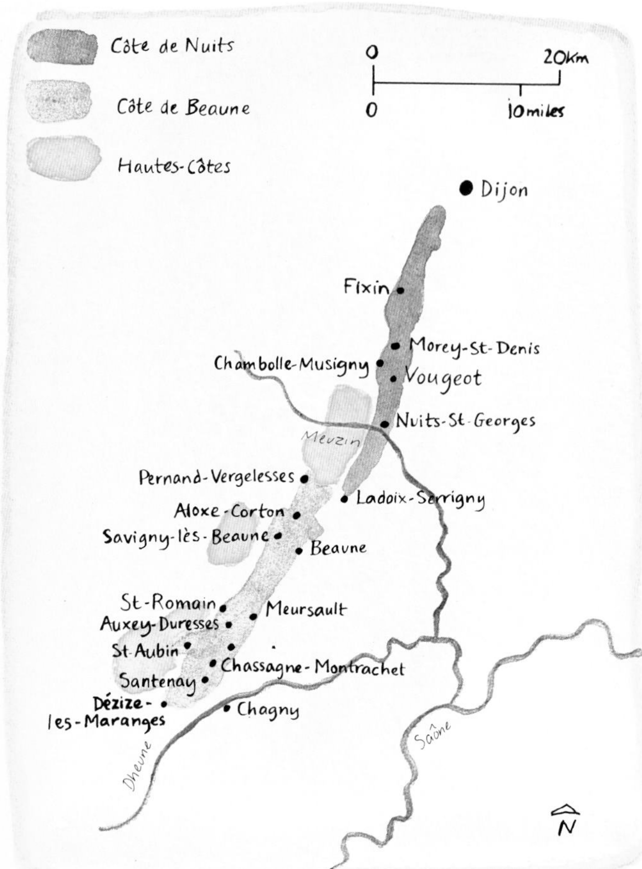

The Côte d'Or – one tiny little sliver of land, never so wide that you can't easily see the other side, and sometimes so narrow that it wouldn't take you more than a couple of minutes to walk across it.

The suitability of land for vineyards is one of the frustrations yet fascinations of wine. Why can't there be more Côte d'Or wine made when there is so much demand? What's wrong with all those vineless acres, on the other side of the road, stretching out towards the Saône? Well, they *do* grow some vines there, and the wine is *never* anything like as good as even the most basic wine of Puligny-Montrachet. The soil is wrong – damp and clay-heavy – making it difficult for Chardonnay to ripen. And the aspect to the sun is wrong. Burgundy is a northerly wine-growing region, and every ray of sunligh and warmth counts. The best vineyards ar gently angled towards the south-east and sout on quick-draining limestone slopes. You on have to experience a Montrachet or Corto Charlemagne at its brilliant best to realize ther is a logic behind the laws which, for instanc restrict the perfectly-sited Montrachet vineyar to precisely 18½ acres (7·5 hectares). There a difference; those 18½ acres hold a mag something that no other vineyard does.

The Côte d'Or divides into two halves. Th Côte de Nuits, south of Dijon, and extending below Nuits-St-Georges is almost entirely re wine country. There are, literally, the occasion single hectares of white in villages like Fixi Chambolle-Musigny, Vougeot, Morey-St-Den and Nuits-St-Georges, but the wines have an almost red wine power to them, and are often made from Pinot Blanc rather than Chardonnay.

The Côte de Beaune – although white wines comprise a mere 25 per cent of the crop – shows the true brilliance of which Chardonnay is capable. Ladoix-Serrigny grows attractive white, but this is immediately superseded by Corton-Charlemagne, one of the majestic *grands crus* which have made white Burgundy famous worldwide. Pernand-Vergelesses, Savigny and Beaune produce a little delicious white but the world's greatest concentration of top quality dry white wine is found in the villages of Meursault, Puligny-Montrachet and Chassagne-Montrachet. The wines are never cheap – but they are unforgettable.

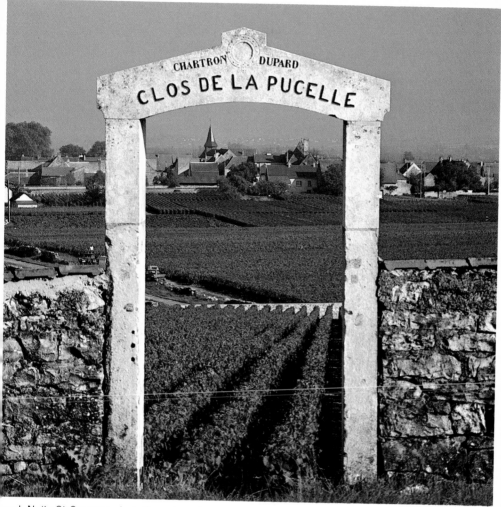

▲ The Côte de Beaune village of Puligny-Montrachet has several *premiers crus*, including Clos de la Pucelle.

CÔTES DE PROVENCE AC
PROVENCE

Mourvèdre, Grenache, Syrah and others

Ugni Blanc, Rolle, Sémillon, Clairette

A few years ago I would have agreed wholeheartedly with th traditionalists who grumbled that Côtes de Provence was grossl overpriced *vin ordinaire*, and deemed Hugh Johnson's verdict – that th reds were like 'tarpaulin edged with lace' – quite brilliant in its horri accuracy. The reds were fruitless and cloddish and the whites . . .

Thank goodness things are changing, because Provence is such hauntingly beautiful region I feel deprived when the wine doesn't com up to scratch. As far as we can tell the wine was up to scratch in Roma times, and an increasing number of growers are now rediscovering th magic in this soil. Rosés are becoming fruitier, and reds are emergin which, along with the powerful pine, thyme and rosemary perfumes o the rugged sun-soaked hillsides, are now displaying other scents (myrtl is one) as well as the one component previously lacking – fruit.

New plantations of Cabernet Sauvignon, Syrah and Mourvèdre ar primarily responsible, as are cooler fermentations and restricted yields This is good news because, though the wines from this larg 45,000-acre (18,000-hectare) vineyard have never been cheap, Pro vence's romantic overtones have 'seduced' people into buying them There are three main vineyard areas: the coastal strip betwee Ste-Maxime and Toulon, providing most of the quaffing wine for th fashionable watering holes of the Riviera; the coastal vineyards betwee Toulon and Marseille, where most of the best sites qualify for the Bando or Cassis ACs; and the vast sprawl north of the Massif des Maures where quality is rarely even considered, and only the most committe winemaker is going to rise above the stewpot of fruitless hooch.

I suppose it's too much to hope that Provence – the area of Franc most capable of besotting and beguiling normally level-headed people should have the perfect white wine to sip on the perfect beach, th perfect terrace or the perfect hill top. Over 90 per cent of the enormou production here is red or rosé, and most of the whites suffer from th usual southern French grape varieties of Ugni Blanc and Clairette though these can be improved by Sémillon or, unofficially, by Sauvigno Blanc. Domaine Gavoty is creating waves by using the Rolle grape t make a delicious fruity wine – and a few producers are following sui But in general, unless you pick white grapes early, ferment them cold and drink the wines as young as possible, they really don't have a lot t say for themselves. It doesn't always matter in good company, with a that clear warm air and wafting scents of Mediterranean thyme. But I' drink ice-cold rosé on *my* terrace. Drink both reds and rosés very young Best producers (reds): Barbeyrolles, Berne, Commanderie de Peyrasso Féraud, Gavoty, les Maîtres Vignerons de St-Tropez, Minuty, Ott Pampelonne, Rimauresq, St-Maur.

Some properties use the title *grand cru classé*. This is an old, informa grouping of the self-styled leading properties and is largely irrelevan nowadays. Best producers (whites): Commanderie de Peyrasso Curebéasse, l'Estandon (a surprisingly good branded wine), Férauc Gavoty, Hauts de St-Jean, Ott (de Selle and Clos Mireille), les Maître Vignerons de St-Tropez, Richeaume.

CÔTES DE ST-MONT VDQS
SOUTH-WEST

Tannat, Cabernet Sauvignon, Cabernet Franc, Merlot

Meslier and others

An increasingly good producer of quite sharp but intensely fruity red and some fair rosé, from a hilly region just to the south of Armagnac an bordering Madiran. If anything the reds are like a lighter version o Madiran, easier to drink young and less tannic. Small amounts of dr white Côtes de St-Mont are made from Meslier, Jurançon, Picpoul an Sauvignon grapes. Best producer: the go-ahead co-op group, the Unio de Producteurs Plaimont, whose St-Mont wine is now clearly of A quality.

ÔTES DE TOUL VDQS
LSACE

Gamay, Pinot Noir, Pinot Ieunier

Côtes de Toul almost doesn't merit a mention, but I have twice turned off the autoroute in north-east France and scoured the windswept landscape for a vineyard or two – and discovered a sweet little wine route through just 160 acres (65 hectares) of vines. When I finally tasted a few examples of the very pale rosé, *vin gris*, made from Gamay, I actually liked its sharp, lean, but refreshing style. So if you're passing the town of Nancy around lunchtime, the *vin gris*, or even the pale, wispy red Pinot Noir, can make a very pleasant picnic diversion.

ÔTES DU FRONTONNAIS C
OUTH-WEST

Négrette, Cabernet auvignon, Cabernet Franc and thers

One of the most original red wine flavours in south-west France. The vineyard area isn't very big, clustered round Toulouse on dry, sun-soaked slopes. Négrette is the chief grape and the wine can be superb, positively silky in texture – very rare in a red wine – and combining a juicy fruit like raspberry or strawberry, coated in cream, with a lick of anise. They drink almost all of it in Toulouse but a little is exported and is well worth seeking out. It can age, but I prefer it in its full flush of youth. There's a little rosé – good but not *so* good. Best producers: Baudare, Bellevue-la-Forêt, la Colombière, Flotis, Laurou, Montauriol, la Palme.

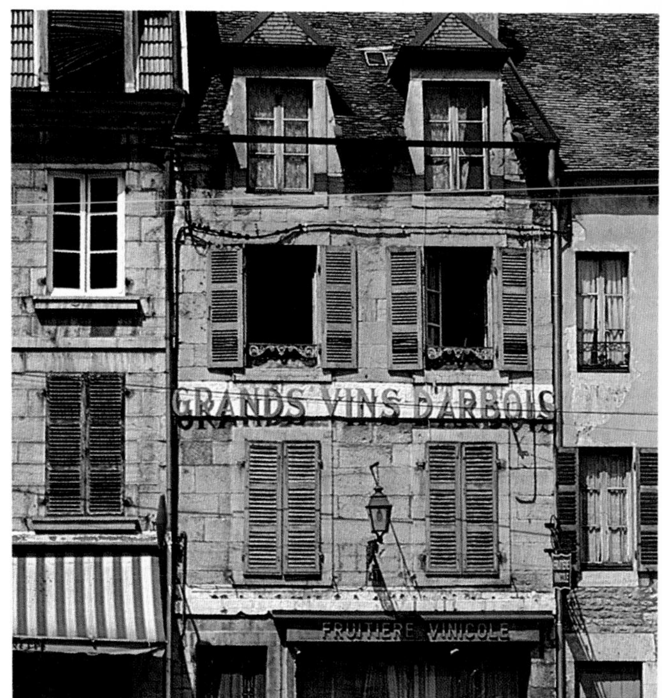

Arbois in the Jura makes a range of vines, mostly based on indigenous rapes. Fruitière Vinicole is the largest roducer.

CÔTES DU JURA AC
URA

Poulsard, Trousseau, Pinot Noir

Chardonnay, Savagnin, Pinot Blanc

The regional AC for Jura covers a wide variety of wines, including still dry white, Champagne-method sparklers, reds, rosés, *vins jaunes* and *vins de paille*. Most of the vineyards lie in the south of the region between Poligny and Lons-le-Saunier, where they spread up the mountain sides or nuzzle into thickly forested slopes. The area is wonderfully relaxing, often hemmed in by trees, always shadowed by the Jura mountain range, and sometimes affording spectacular vistas across the Saône valley to Burgundy. But I'm afraid the flavours of the wines, especially the whites, aren't of the delicate sylvan sort at all. The reason for this is

the white Savagnin grape – a strange, sour creature – which admitted
does come into its own with the dark yellow, sherry-like *vin jaune*.

However, there is respite in the friendly form of the Chardonnay an more rarely, the Pinot Blanc, which both perform well in the Jura. Som unblended Chardonnay is now coming on to the market. It can still b infected with the strange, resiny Savagnin character, especially whe not vinified in a separate cellar; but at its best, especially from th vineyards betwen Poligny and Arbois, it is a particularly thirst-quenchin mountain-fresh Chardonnay. There is a little Champagne-method Côte du Jura *mousseux* made from Chardonnay and Pinot Blanc; the or from the co-operative at Pupillin is outstanding. Drink Côtes du Jura one to two years old, although the Chardonnay and the fizz can age.

It would be nice to report that such a mountain paradise ha nectar-like red wines too, but both reds and rosés are rarely special and often aggressively weird. The southern part of the vineyard regic can produce some lighter red and rosé from the Trousseau ar Poulsard grapes which are not too savage, while the Pinot Noir can yie rather good light, perfumed reds. Poulsard also produces a very pa pink, *vin gris*. Only 20 per cent of Côtes du Jura AC is red or rosé. Be producers (reds): Arlay, Bourdy, Gréa. Best producers (whites): Arla Bourdy, Gréa, Pupillin co-operative.

CÔTES DU LUBÉRON AC
SOUTHERN RHÔNE

Grenache, Syrah, Cinsaut and others

Ugni Blanc, Clairette, Bourboulenc

A lovely lost area to the east of Avignon and north of Aix, running alor the Durance valley and sharing the land with the asparagus crops. Th landscape is dominated by the Montagne du Lubéron and the region wine production is dominated by co-operatives. Until recently, wh struck me most often about the Côtes du Lubéron was that, strange the white was always offered for sale a year older than the red. Sinc the white is at best a light, fresh-faced quaffer whose only virtue is i youth, I stuck to the red. But things are changing as the co-operative react to the consumer's wishes rather than to their members' indolenc and the area was promoted to AC in 1988.

The vines are mostly spread along the north banks of the Durance the Vaucluse *département*, and yield light, easy wines for early drinkin They are not exactly long on complexity and perfume, but between s and nine months old they are bright, refreshing and very enjoyable. Th one exception to this rule is Domaine Val Joanis – a vast new plantatic wrested from the wild scrubland whose white, though still at its be within the year, can develop a full, soft peachy warmth, spiced with hint of aniseed, if you leave it for longer. First results with reds a proving very tasty too, though still for young drinking. Château c l'Isolette red is absolutely delicious. Best producers: Canorgue, Châtea de l'Isolette, Mille, Val Joanis, the co-operative at La Tour-d'Aigues.

CÔTES DU MARMANDAIS VDQS
SOUTH-WEST

Abouriou, Fer, Cabernet Sauvignon and others

Sémillon, Sauvignon Blanc, Muscadelle, Ugni Blanc

Another 'me-too' Bordeaux look-alike close to the Entre-Deux-Me region, but in the Lot-et-Garonne département. The Marmanda producers have always set out to make red Bordeaux look-alikes – wi a fair amount of success. However, the potential is for a red with definably *non*-Bordeaux flavour because Bordeaux varieties make only half or less of the grape mix. Ninety-five per cent of Côtes Marmandais wine comes from two co-ops, of which the Cocumo examples are the better. The prices are low, and, so far, the wines a pleasant and light with a Cabernet-influenced flavour.

You need to have the nose of a bloodhound to track down whi Marmandais – there is very little of it and what there is won't get mo than a mile or two from the winery before it is hijacked by locals a consumed. I don't know why they guard it so jealously because it isn't actually terribly exciting. The wine *ought* to be a cheaper version of Bordeaux Blanc – it's produced a little way up the Garonne from Entre-Deux-Mers. But it is hampered by including the desperately feeble Ugni Blanc in the brew. Best white producer: Cocumont co-operative.

CÔTES DU RHÔNE AC
SOUTHERN RHÔNE

🍷🍷 Grenache, Cinsaut, Syrah and others

🍷 Clairette, Roussanne, Marsanne and others

Although this general AC covers the whole viticultural Rhône valley – from just south of Lyon at Vienne all the way down to below Avignon – most of the wine comes from the broad southern section between Montélimar and Avignon, the Côtes du Rhône Méridionale, which is one of the great grape baskets of France. Côtes du Rhône AC applies to over 80 per cent of the Rhône valley's wines; over 90 per cent of these are red and rosé. The chief red grape is the Grenache, followed by Cinsaut, Syrah, Carignan and Mourvèdre; the last three in particular have lots of warm spicy southern personality to offer to the rich, heady flavours of Grenache.

Côtes du Rhône reds used to be marked by a rather heavy, jammy fruit and a rough, herby perfume. Modern techniques – temperature control, stainless steel installations, some carbonic maceration – have revolutionized the style, and today's red Côtes du Rhône should be juicy, spicy, raspberry-fruited, sometimes almost light as Beaujolais, sometimes juicier and rounder, but as a rule mouth-filling and very easy to drink, ideally within two years of the harvest. Single-estate wines can age considerably longer. Best years: 1988, '86, '85, '84. Best producers (reds): Aussellons, Cantharide, Cru de Coudoulet, Duboeuf, Fonsalette, les Goubert, Grand Moulas, Guigal, Jaboulet, Mont-Redon, Mousset, Pascal, de Ruth, St-Estève.

Some of the best white Côtes du Rhône AC comes, incongruously, from a Beaujolais producer – Georges Duboeuf. He makes it taste like a white Burgundy! Duboeuf created his 'Rhône-Mâcon-Villages' flavour by getting hold of early-picked grapes and then fermenting them really cool in stainless steel tanks. The result? Fresh, appley, dry whites, lovely to quaff and, yes, distinctly Burgundian. They almost taste as though they are made from Chardonnay – yet that grape's not allowed in the AC. Instead, there's the fairly interesting Marsanne and Roussanne, and the less electrifying Clairette, Bourboulenc, Grenache Blanc and sometimes Ugni Blanc. Most white Côtes du Rhône – about three million bottles out of a total of 200 million – is made in co-ops and sold under various merchants' labels. But as the price of white Burgundy shoots up, white Côtes du Rhône (and Côtes du Rhône-Villages) is sure to be more in demand. Drink as young as possible. Best producers (whites): Bruthel, Chambovet, Duboeuf, Garrigon, Pelaquié, Rabasse-Charavin, Ste-Anne; co-operatives at Chusclan and Laudun.

CÔTES DU RHÔNE-VILLAGES AC
SOUTHERN RHÔNE

🍷🍷 Grenache, Syrah, Mourvèdre and others

🍷 Clairette, Roussanne, Bourboulenc

In general the addition of the word 'Villages' to a French appellation means that the wine, red or white, comes from a grouping of villages with better vineyard sites. Côtes du Rhône-Villages is allowed only for 17 villages which have historically made superior wine. The wine may be labelled Côtes du Rhône-Villages indicating that it is a blend from any or all of these villages, or it may be labelled with its own village name – as in Côtes du Rhône-Cairanne. Normally the best wines will carry a single village name. There is a move afoot to expand the 'Villages' category and up to 65 different villages are under consideration. I hope the authorities think carefully, because the original 17 villages really do produce finer wine.

Almost all the best wines are red. Only Chusclan and Laudun have

any reputation for white. The reds have a higher minimum alcohol 12·5 per cent, as against 11 per cent for ordinary Côtes du Rhône. Th yield is strictly restricted to 35 hectolitres per hectare as against 50, th Grenache is limited to 65 per cent and the Carignan to ten per cer while the classier Syrah, Mourvèdre and Cinsaut must make up 25 pe cent. The result is splendid wine. For rosé a simple Côtes du Rhôn often suffices, but for red with a marvellous, dusty, blackcurrant an spicy raspberry flavour and tannin to support the wine as it matures fc up to ten years – you must go to a Côtes du Rhône-Villages. Best year 1988, '85, '84, '83, '80, '78. Best villages: red – Cairanne, Vacqueyras Beaumes-de-Venise, Séguret, Valréas, Sablet, Visan; rosé – Chusclar Laudun, Visan; white – Chusclan, Laudun. Best producers: Ameillau Boisson, Brusset, Cartier, Combe, Grangeneuve, l'Oratoire St-Marti Pelaquie, Présidente, Rabasse-Charavin, St-Antoine, Ste-Anne, Trignor Verquière.

CÔTES DU ROUSSILLON AC
LANGUEDOC-ROUSSILLON

Carignan, Cinsaut, Grenache and others

Macabeo, Malvoisie

Roussillon is the frontier area where France melts imperceptibly int Catalonia and Spain, somewhere high among the Pyrenean peaks. Mos people only know the region as the last fractious stretch of autorout before the Pyrenees and the Costa Brava. But drive up the Tech, the Té or the Agly valleys to the west and the furious whine of holiday traff fades blissfully into the sharp, sunny mountain air; you stop at one of th hill-villages, and the chatter of the menfolk breaks into your noon-da thoughts – and it's not French at all, but the strange rasping, convolute clamour of Catalan. The wine you drink is Côtes du Roussillon – re dusty as a mountain track, but juicy as fresh orchard fruit – based on th Carignan, but increasingly helped by Cinsaut, Grenache and Mourvèdre

Roussillon was one of the first areas of France where th co-operative movement geared itself towards quality, and although th has stamped the wines with a certain uniformity, it is a small price to pa for consistency and an immediately attractive wine style based solely c current drinkability rather than on traditional preferences. As usual the far south, the Côtes du Roussillon AC – which spreads south c Perpignan to the foothills of the Pyrenees, as well as taking in a goo deal of the flatter land to the north along the Agly river valley, and th most suitable vineyard sites to the west – is primarily red wine land. Th co-operatives dominate the production – and for once this is a goo thing, because they have an enlightened leadership which managed t gain an AC for the region in 1977, almost a decade before neighbourin Corbières.

The winemakers emphasize the carbonic maceration method, whic draws out the juicy flavours of red grapes and is crucial when th potentially rough Carignan makes up the majority of the blend. Th production is now 25 million bottles, 95 per cent of it red or rosé. Th price is never high and so long as the wine is young, both red and ros provide some of southern France's best-value drinking. Best producer (reds): Cazes Frères, Corneilla, Jau, Jaubert et Noury, Rey; th Rasiguères co-op makes excellent rosé.

Out of the millions of bottles produced annually, only about four pe cent are white. These come from the Macabeo grape, a variety whic rivals Ugni Blanc for being unmemorable; but – in the hands of th modern co-operatives – if picked very early (almost unripe in fact) an fermented at low temperature, it makes bone-dry, lemon and *ani* scented white wine for very early drinking, which isn't half bad at *les* than a year old. Taichat is the brand name for a heavier, deeper sty which I find just a bit solid. Best producers (whites): Cazes Frère Jaubert et Noury, Sarda-Malet, Vignerons Catalans.

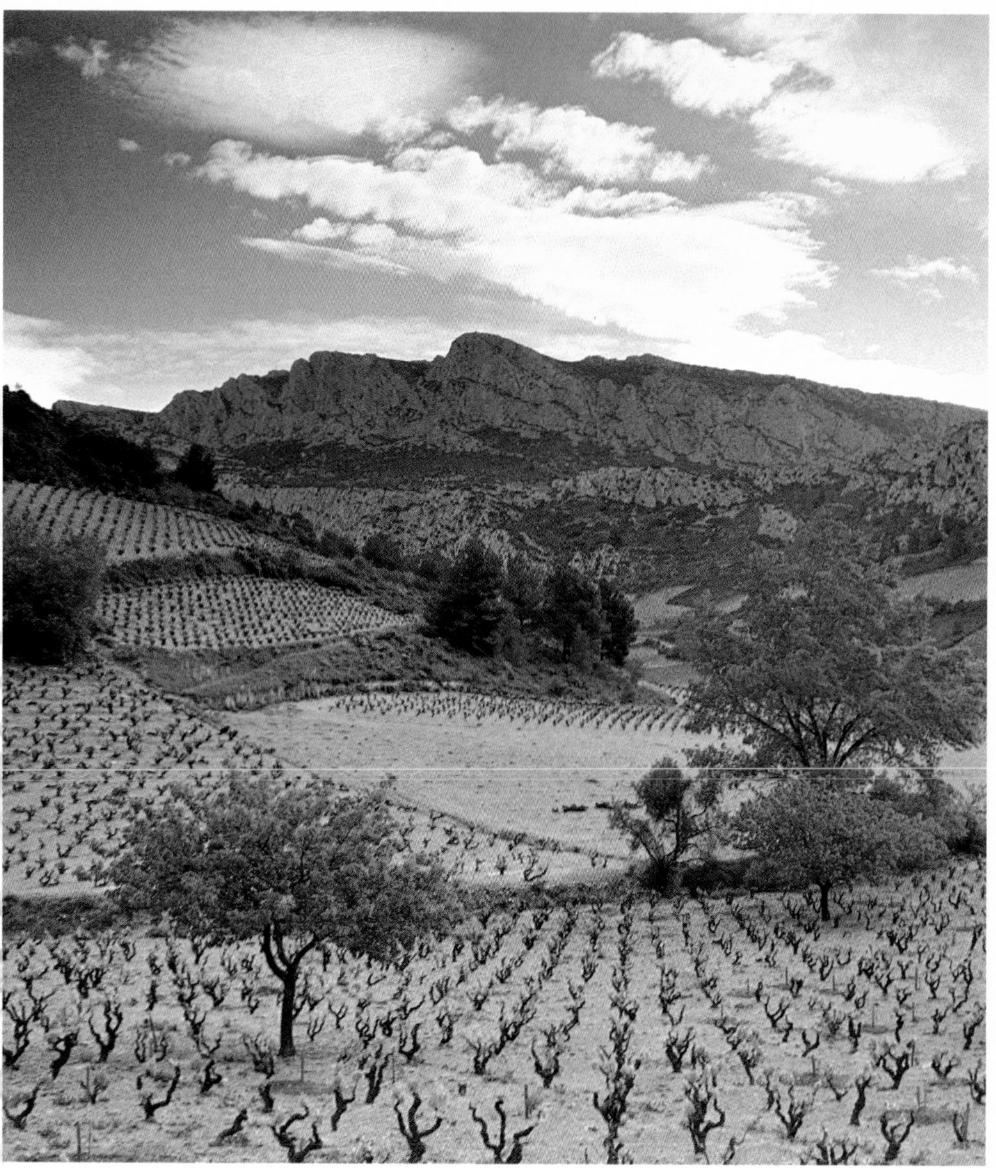

CÔTES DU ROUSSILLON-VILLAGES AC
LANGUEDOC-ROUSSILLON

🍷 Carignan, Grenache, Mourvèdre and others

▲ Spring in a Roussillon vineyard: the vines are bursting back to life, sprouting leaves, tendrils and then flower buds.

The northern part of the Côtes du Roussillon, centred on the Agly river, which runs east from the Mediterranean just above Perpignan. The vineyards on the valley sides are especially good, and the Côtes du Roussillon-Villages AC is applicable only to red wines from the best sites. They have a higher minimum alcohol (12 degrees) and a lower yield (45 hectolitres per hectare) than straight Côtes du Roussillon, and the wine, especially from the villages of Caramany and Latour-de-France (which are allowed to add their names to the AC), is full, ripe, wonderfully juicy when young – though still keeping that soft, dusty grain – and capable of maturing for several years. There are a few wines now aged in new oak, and these too are impressive – drinkable young or at five years old. Best producers: Cap de Fouste, St-Martin; Agly, Bélesta, Latour-de-France, Vignerons Catalans co-operatives.

CÔTES DU VENTOUX AC
SOUTHERN RHÔNE

Grenache, Syrah, Mourvèdre and others

Clairette, Bourboulenc, Grenache Blanc and others

Côtes du Ventoux, away to the east of Châteauneuf-du-Pape and Gigondas, is one of those ACs which has still not found its own identity. It quite surprised me to realize that these lovely vineyards, tumbling down the sides of the magnificent 6000 feet (1830 metres) Mont Ventoux, towering above the eastern side of the Rhône valley, had enjoyed their own AC since 1973, because I had become so used to seeing them listed next to the cheaper Côtes du Rhône as a kind of innocuous Rhône substitute. With the exception of a couple of single estates making good reds they still fill this role, and 99 per cent of the 18 million bottles produced annually are made by the local co-operatives and sold off anonymously to merchants. When well-made, the reds have a lovely fresh juicy fruit – tasting of raspberry and spice – which is bright and breezy and undemanding. There are some fuller reds now made, but the best still keep this lovely simple flavour – they just have a bit more of it per bottle! The white production is insignificant but, interestingly, the area was making fresh, breezy whites *before* Big Brother Côtes du Rhône cottoned on to the fact and I wish more were made. Best producers: Anges, Jaboulet, Pascal, la Vieille Ferme.

CÔTES DU VIVARAIS VDQS
SOUTHERN RHÔNE

Grenache, Syrah, Mourvèdre and others

Clairette, Marsanne, Bourboulenc and others

These VDQS wines could either be seen as junior Côtes du Rhône or senior Vin de Pays des Coteaux de l'Ardèche. The vineyards are spread along the west bank of the Rhône where the river Ardèche joins at Pont-St-Esprit, in the Ardèche and northern Gard *départements*. As with most southern French wine areas, this is predominantly a red wine zone. When they use the typical southern Rhône varieties – Grenache, Cinsaut, Carignan – the result is light, fresh red and rosé, for drinking as young as possible without further thought. But plantings of grapes such as Cabernet Sauvignon, Syrah and Gamay are producing exciting, deep-flavoured, rich, fruity wines of quite surprising quality and irresistible price.

As I search both my mind and my tasting files for the slightest sign that I've ever experienced the rarefied joys of Vivarais *white* wines, the one thing that spurs me on is that as the quality of the *reds* is modern, enjoyable and cheap – then hopefully the whites can start on that same path, even if they're not there yet. The basic grape varieties are the same as those used for Côtes du Rhône whites – Clairette, Marsanne, Bourboulenc – but as in the Vin de Pays de Coteaux de l'Ardèche, with which it shares common boundaries, there are signs of classier grapes such as Sauvignon Blanc and Chardonnay creeping in. If the success of the Ardèche wines is anything to go by, the results could be exciting – but as currently only 30,000 bottles out of the three million annual production are white, I just hope I'm lucky enough to find a bottle to witness the improvements. A good co-op movement controls most of the production from the Côtes du Vivarais.

COUTET, CH.
Barsac AC, *premier cru classé*
BORDEAUX

Sémillon, Sauvignon Blanc, Muscadelle

I thought I should check – and anyway, I felt in need of a bit of a treat – so I opened a half bottle of Coutet 1979 to write this entry. I was checking out the rumours that Coutet, Barsac's largest Classed Growth property at 100 acres (40 hectares), was no longer making the quality of wine which had traditionally linked it with Climens as the co-leaders of the Barsac AC. Coutet and Climens are the only two Barsac First Growths and are equally famous.

Well, was my 'treat' a treat? Only sort of – the wine was quite rich, vaguely unctuous, or sumptuous, or one of those other words which are all suggestion, yet have no real meaning. But was it First Growth Barsac? No, not really, and looking back at my tasting notes I find I haven't really got excited about Château Coutet since 1971. Well, that's not quite true. In exceptional years a wine called Cuvée Madame is made from the sweetest grapes on the oldest vines. I've managed to taste it a couple of times and it is stupendously rich and, well, sumptuous. But only a few barrels are made and I've never seen it in a shop. And I do think the wine that we can actually buy is the important one for judging the property. Best years: 1986, '83, '76, '75, '71.

CRÉMANT D'ALSACE AC
ALSACE

🍷 Pinot Blanc, Auxerrois Blanc, Riesling and others

▲ The grey skies are misleading. Alsace, protected by the Vosges mountains, has a warm, dry climate ideal for grape-growing.

This Champagne-method sparkling wine from Alsace shot to fame a few years ago. An AC had been granted in 1976, but nothing much happened until the price of Champagne rocketed in the early 1980s. From a pretty docile start, with only eight registered producers, the numbers went up to 200! Five per cent of the Alsace crop was being processed as Crémant. All looked set fair – until Champagne had two whopping harvests in 1982 and '83. The price of Alsace Crémant plummeted and the producers were left with large amounts of froth on their faces.

Enthusiasm has since waned for this pretty tasty sparkler, but, paradoxically, the quality is better now that the opportunists have departed the fray, and someone must be drinking it, because production has gone from half a million bottles to 13 million in the last ten years. The only trouble is the price – higher than sparkling Saumur, Blanquette de Limoux and Crémant de Bourgogne – and not that much cheaper than Champagne. Best producers: Cattin, Dopff au Moulin, Dopff & Irion, Ginglinger, Willy Gisselbrecht, Kuentz-Bas, Muré, Ostertag, Willm, Wolfberger from the Éguisheim co-operative.

CRÉMANT DE BOURGOGNE AC
BURGUNDY

🍷🍷 Chardonnay, Aligoté, Pinot Blanc, Pinot Noir

I don't go out on a limb and state categorically in my pre-Christma newspaper articles, 'Forget cheap Champagne this year, Crémant d Bourgogne is better – and less pricy,' unless I really believe what I'r saying. Well, a few years ago Crémant de Bourgogne – then calle Bourgogne Mousseux – was dismissed as raw and reedy fizz, only fit fc the desperate. And I sort of agreed. To be honest, I could neve understand why it was such a feeble fizz – after all didn't it come fron Burgundy and have a good dose of Chardonnay in it? Well, I rather thin that then, any left-over grapes from anywhere between Chablis an Beaujolais were pressed into service, but in the '80s things have taken dramatic turn for the better.

Most Burgundian Crémant is white and contains Chardonnay sometimes up to 100 per cent – and in the 1985, '86 and '88 vintage the full, soft, almost honeyed flavour of ripe Chardonnay grapes mad far more attractive drinking than the green, tart, bargain-basemer Champagne produced further north. Cheap Champagne is now back o track, but I have to admit – I'm still buying Crémant de Bourgogne. ages well for two to three years, but is usually good to drink whe released. There is a growing amount of pink being made in response t the fad for pink fizz which Champagne has enjoyed. The best ros Crémant de Bourgogne is made in the Chablis and Auxerre regions a the northern tip of Burgundy, where pale, creamy wines of considerabl class and fruit are made. Best producers: Delorme, Lucius-Gregoire Simmonet-Febvre; co-operatives at Bailly (the best for rosé), Lugny St-Gengoux-de-Scissé and Viré.

CRÉMANT DE LOIRE AC
CENTRAL LOIRE

🍷 Cabernet Franc, Gamay, Pineau d'Aunis and others

🍷 Chenin Blanc, Chardonnay, Cabernet Franc

If there is a way forward for sparkling Loire wines, Crémant de Loi should provide it. The problem with most Loire sparklers, and especial Saumurs, is a rasping, rather fruitless acidity and an explosive bubbl The Crémant de Loire AC was created in 1975 in an effort to up th quality of sparkling wines made in the Loire by lowering yields – 5 hectolitres per hectare instead of the 60 allowed for Saumur – an requiring that 330lb (150kg) of grapes are used to produce on hectolitre of juice rather than the 287lb (130kg) allowed for Saumu Grapes may come from anywhere in Anjou or Touraine, but th proportion of free-run juice is much higher with Crémant, producin fruitier, less harsh, base wine. The wine must then lie on its yeast depos after second fermentation for at least a year, instead of the nine montl required for Saumur. All this produces a much more attractive win with more fruit, more yeast character and a more caressing mouss Crémant de Loire is always made by the Champagne method.

However, all the major producers have created brands based on th Saumur name so there is little incentive to use a more expensiv process which you then sell under a less specific name. Althoug Crémant actually outclasses supposedly superior sparkling Saumur an Vouvray, so far the designation hasn't taken off. Since Crémant de Loir is generally a softer wine than Saumur, it is usually good to drink as soo as it is released. Best producers: Ackerman-Laurance, Berger, Gabillièr Vincent Girault, Gratien & Meyer, Liards.

CRÉPY AC
SAVOIE

🍷 Chasselas

I'm always reminded of lace curtains when I think of Crépy. That, an streamers at Christmas time. Which is just as well, because there's not lot else to remember about Crépy – definitely a front-runner for the titl 'white AC with the least discernible taste'. The problem is its grape, th Chasselas, which is fine for eating but produces wines which a water-white and water-light. It has a low alcoholic strength – only nin degrees – with a relatively noticeable acidity of the 'neutral lemon' sort. The only examples with any zip are those bottled off their own lees (*sur lie*, like the best Muscadets). This traps a little carbon dioxide in the wine and may also leave the slightest hint of yeast. The AC's 800,000 bottles are grown on 200 acres (80 hectares) of hillside vineyard just south of Lake Geneva. Some people age them, but I've never seen the point and would drink them as young as possible. Best producers: Goy, Mercier.

CRIOTS-BÂTARD-MONTRACHET AC
grand cru
CÔTE DE BEAUNE, BURGUNDY

Chardonnay

Criots-Bâtard-Montrachet is the only white *grand cru* entirely in the Chassagne-Montrachet commune. It occupies just 4 acres (1·6 hectares) of stony slope (*criots* is dialect for pebbles), facing due south towards the N6 road. To all intents and purposes the wine is the same as that of its neighbour Bâtard-Montrachet – rich, savoury, full of nuts and honey and spice – but since there is so little of it and it is fiendishly expensive, such a direct comparison is not easily made! There are only about 7000 bottles produced in an average year. Best years: 1988, '86, '85, '84, '83, '82. Best producers: Bachelet, Blain-Gagnard, Delagrange, Marcilly.

CROZES-HERMITAGE AC
NORTHERN RHÔNE

Syrah

Marsanne, Roussanne

Crozes-Hermitage is the largest of the northern Rhône ACs, with 2000 acres (800 hectares) of vines spreading over the hillocks and plains behind the great hill of Hermitage. The last few years of Rhône wine history have been notable for the succession of rising stars, particularly in the small but high quality northern section. Hermitage and Côte-Rôtie, Cornas and St-Joseph have all been getting the showbiz treatment. Well, there's only one AC for red wine left, and that's Crozes-Hermitage, traditionally thought of as a rather common, unsubtle poor relation. With the finite amounts of wine available from the terraced hill slopes of the other ACs, people are suddenly discovering that red Crozes-Hermitage is rather better than they thought.

Ideally, Crozes-Hermitage should have a full red colour, a rich blackcurrants, raspberries and earth smell, and a strong, meaty but rich flavour. As so often with Syrah, the delicious fruit flavours have to mingle in with strange tastes of vegetables, damped-out bonfires, well-hung meat and herbs. You can drink it young especially if the grapes were grown on flat land, but in ripe years, from a hillside site, it improves greatly for three to six years. Best years: 1988, '85, '83, '82. Best producers (reds): Bégot, Delas, Desmeure, Fayolle, Jaboulet (Thalabert), Michelas, Tain co-operative, Tardy & Ange.

Crozes-Hermitage whites are almost never as exciting as Hermitage whites, even though the same grapes are used – the Marsanne and the Roussanne. This is because, except on the hilly slopes at Mercurol, most of the wine is grown on fairly flat, productive land and so the fruit lacks the astonishing concentration which marks out Hermitage.

There is another reason – modern wine-making techniques! While most white Hermitage is still produced in the traditional manner, which results in thick, gluey wines which may take ten years to open out properly, Crozes-Hermitage is almost always now made by cool fermentation to draw out the fruit and perfume at the expense of the weight. Although Desmeure still makes a highly successful old-style Crozes – thick with the flavour of buttered almonds and bruised apples – the best modern Crozes is now extremely fresh, with a lovely flavour of raw nuts and apple blossom, sometimes licked with aniseed and smartened up by a gentle but clean acidity. In general, drink white Crozes young, since the floral perfume will go. Best years: 1988, '85, '83. Best producers (whites): Desmeure, Fayolle, Jaboulet, Pradelle.

DE LA DAUPHINE, CH.
Fronsac AC
BORDEAUX

🍷 Merlot, Cabernet Franc

Fronsac wines have been regarded as the next hot property in Bordeau for almost as long as I've been out of short trousers. And they *sti* haven't managed to progress beyond the 'heir apparent' state. Howeve Château de la Dauphine is just the kind of property which may give th area the push it needs. The Moueix family, who run many of Pomerol' greatest properties (including Château Pétrus, the world's mos expensive red wine) have begun to invest in Fronsac and de la Dauphin is their flagship property. The wine is already changing for the bette with a proportion of new oak barrels being used for ageing. The result are still a little chunky and the flavour's slightly gamy, but the 1985 an '86 vintages showed that this château will quickly become one c Fronsac's leading properties.

DAUZAC, CH.
Margaux AC, *5ème cru classé*
HAUT-MÉDOC, BORDEAUX

🍷 Cabernet Sauvignon, Merlot, Cabernet Franc, Petit Verdot

A problematical Margaux Classed Growth, from the village of Labarde o the Bordeaux side of the *appellation*. It was made Fifth Growth in th 1855 Classification, and that seemed about right – good but no memorable wine. I first tasted it in the 1961 vintage, bottled in Englanc and the wine was rich and juicy – and cheap. But it faded from th scene until the end of the 1970s when a new owner lavished attentio and money on it, and re-launched in the mid-1980s with a blaze c publicity. But I'm afraid this only proved that money alone isn't enough In spite of new winemakers and new oak barrels, this rather lear charmless wine still falls short of other Margaux Classed Growths. Th 1980 is the most enjoyable of recent vintages – which isn't saying much

DOISY-DAËNE, Ch.
Barsac AC, *2ème cru classé*
BORDEAUX

🍷 Sémillon, Sauvignon Blanc

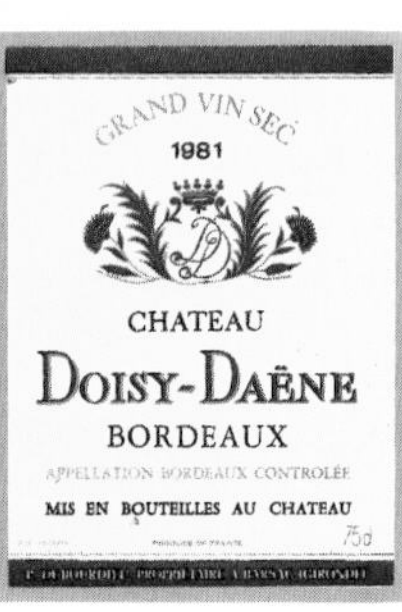

This is a consistently good Barsac property and unusual in that th sweet wine is made from 100 per cent Sémillon. Since Sémillo provides the fatness in Sauternes and Barsac wines this would lead m to expect Doisy-Daëne, a 35-acre (14-hectare) vineyard next to Châtea Climens, to be one of the richest examples around, but Pierr Dubourdieu ferments his wine in stainless steel and ages it for only on year in new oak barrels (as against two or three years in many othe properties). The result is a wine which is certainly extremely sweet, bu which has an almost lemony acidity clinging to the richness that not onl stops it from cloying, but allows it to age well for ten years and more Best (sweet) years: 1988, '86, '83, '82, '80, '79.

There is also a highly successful Doisy-Daëne Sec, sold under th Graves AC, which is full of perfume and fruit, far in excess of tha achieved by any other Barsac property. How? Well, by not taking to much notice of the local AC laws, that's how. Monsieur Dubourdieu use Sauvignon Blanc, Sémillon and Muscadelle for his dry white wine, whic is fair enough – but then adds in both Chardonnay and Riesling, tw grapes which *definitely* don't figure in the Bordeaux regulations. Th wine is so good I suspect no-one has ever dared question the Bordeau AC he sticks on the label! Best (dry) years: 1988, '87, '86.

DOISY-VÉDRINES, CH.
Barsac AC, *2ème cru classé*
BORDEAUX

🍷 Sémillon, Sauvignon Blanc

This is a completely different style of wine from its neighbou Doisy-Daëne (they used to be the same estate until split in th nineteenth century). The wine is both fermented and aged in barrel an the result is *very* rich wine, fatter and stronger, more syrupy even tha most Barsacs, but at the same time lacking a little of the perfume charm of Climens or Doisy-Daëne which is such a mark of the bes Barsac wines. Even so, I must say that if I'm paying high prices for m Barsac I do want it to be *sweet* – so I'll stick by Doisy-Védrines withou complaint.

Although 50 acres (20 hectares) of vineyard are planted with white grapes – 80 per cent Sémillon and 20 per cent Sauvignon Blanc – the total production of Barsac wine on the property is only 30,000 bottles (as against 48,000 from the smaller Doisy-Daëne). This is because much of the production is vinified dry and sold as Bordeaux AC. There are, in fact, a further 25 acres (10 hectares) of vineyard in *red* grapes – simply because during the 1960s no-one wanted to buy sweet wines and the owners had to develop a red and dry white wine brand in order to survive. Now most Sauternes and Barsac châteaux make some dry white, though not many also make red! Best years: 1988, '86, '85, '83, '82, '80, '76, '75.

DOMAINE DE CHEVALIER
Pessac-Léognan AC, *cru classé de Graves*
BORDEAUX

Cabernet Sauvignon, Merlot, Cabernet Franc

Sauvignon Blanc, Sémillon

In years when the sun is hot, but not too hot, when the weather is dry, but not too dry, and when the grapes ripen gently as the autumn evenings close in, rather than race to maturity in the blaze of a late summer heat wave, Domaine de Chevalier can produce Bordeaux's finest wines. The white is frequently the best dry white in Bordeaux. The red faces far stiffer competition, but always ends up at least in the winning frame. Yet when you finally reach the property after nonchalantly wandering through the woodland and intermittent agriculture of the Pessac-Léognan region, you could be excused for exclaiming, 'Is that all?'.

There's no elegant château, no sense of sombre superiority, just a clearing cut in the forest – covering a mere 45 acres (18 hectares) – and a placid, low, white homestead surrounded by vines. From this unprepossessing source flows a series of red wines which always start out rather dry and tannic but over 10–20 years gain that piercing, fragrant cedar, tobacco and blackcurrant flavour which can leave you breathless with pleasure, and Domaine de Chevalier also adds a slight earthy rub to the taste – just to keep your feet on the ground. Best years (red): all since 1978, with '78, '81, '83, '85 and '88 excelling.

The white grapes occupy just 5 acres (2 hectares), producing at best 7000 bottles as against 60,000 bottles of red. The wine is both fermented and aged in oak barrels. At first the Sauvignon greenness is very marked, but after three to four years this fades and an increasingly creamy, nutty warmth takes over, building at ten years old to a deep, honeyed, smoky richness, just touched with resin. At the VinExpo world wine fair in Bordeaux one of Burgundy's most famous winemakers was offered a glass of white Domaine de Chevalier to taste blind. 'Mmm, lovely, nutty, intense, exciting *grand cru* Burgundy,' he thought. He said he liked it very much indeed and probably thought he'd made it. 'But it's a Bordeaux,' his host finally blurted out. The Burgundian's eyes narrowed, his lips pursed, and suddenly this 'nectar' was merely 'curious', the glass was set down and we heard no more from him for quite a while. In the best vintages the wine will still be improving at 15–20 years old. Only 7000 bottles are made each year. Best years (white): 1988, '86, '85, '84, '83, '82, '81, '79, '78, '75.

LA DOMINIQUE, CH.
St-Émilion AC, *grand cru classé St-Émilion*
BORDEAUX

Merlot, Cabernet Franc, Cabernet Sauvignon, Malbec

A superbly situated St-Émilion property next to the great Château Cheval-Blanc. Although not a *premier grand cru classé*, its wine achieves that quality, and is marked by a delicious, rich, almost overripe fruit which piles into your mouth and coaxes a smile out of the most cool-blooded taster. Strangely, neither the 1985 nor the '86 vintages match up to this standard, being unbalanced and stand-offish. Let's hope it's just a passing phase, because La Dominique on form is a real delight.

DUCRU-BEAUCAILLOU, CH.
St-Julien AC, ***2ème cru classé***
HAUT-MÉDOC, BORDEAUX

Cabernet Sauvignon, Cabernet Franc, Merlot, Petit Verdot

You really do get a feeling of quiet opulence and self-assure confidence as you gaze at the imposing Victorian solidity of thi château. If this image also conjures up reliability, then it is accurat enough. I can't think of a single bad wine made at this property in mor than 20 years, and in the late 1970s this fact was recognized when th wine consistently sold for higher prices than any other Second Growt We called it a 'super-second' – and though the more showy, extrove wines of Léoville-Las-Cases and Pichon-Lalande now also rank a super-seconds, many people still prefer the fragrant cedar perfume, th soft, gently blackcurranty fruit and the satisfying round sensation of th Ducru-Beaucaillou. If you wanted to seek out the epitome of St-Julie mixing charm and austerity, fruit and firmness, this is where you'd find i Best years: 1988, '86, '85, '83, '82, '81, '78.

ÉCHÉZEAUX AC, *grand cru*
CÔTE DE NUITS, BURGUNDY

Pinot Noir

Of all the *grands crus* in the Côte de Nuits this is the one with the leas reputation. Consequently it is also the least expensive (except from th Domaine de la Romanée-Conti). It is a big vineyard – 76 acres (30· hectares), spread between Clos de Vougeot and Vosne-Romanée – an few of the growers have made a name for themselves, preferring t harvest as many grapes as possible and sell them or their wine withou any fuss. However, there is some good Échézeaux. It can be a subt powerful wine, developing an attractive raspberry and chocolat perfume as it ages. It is rarely a hefty style of Burgundy. Best year 1985, '83, '80, '78, '76. Best producers: Domaine de la Romanée-Cont Drouhin, Grivot, Jayer, Lamarche, Mongeard-Mugneret.

NTRE-DEUX-MERS AC
ORDEAUX

Sémillon, Sauvignon Blanc, Iuscadelle

◀ The clay-gravel soil of Entre-Deux-Iers in the Château Thieuley ineyards.

The phoenix rises from the ashes. Ten years ago Entre-Deux-Mers was a byword for boring, fruitless, vaguely sweet white wines of the sort that could put you off drinking for life. But in the 1980s there has been a dramatic about-turn, and Entre-Deux-Mers is increasingly coming to stand for some of the freshest, brightest, snappiest dry white wine in the whole of France.

The name means 'between two seas' – in this case the Garonne and the Dordogne rivers, which form a triangular wedge until they converge just north of the city of Bordeaux. It contains over 6250 acres (2500 hectares) of vines – intensively cultivated in the north-west of the region, but becoming interspersed with other crops as you head east. The AC only covers dry white wines, on average 13 million bottles annually. Red wines are produced extensively but they can only use the Bordeaux or Bordeaux Supérieur AC.

The technique behind the Entre-Deux-Mers revival is cold fermentation, and the flavours are totally dry, grassy, appley, often with a little more weight than straight Bordeaux Blanc AC. A few properties use new wooden barrels for ageing and this adds a creamy, apricotty flavour which can be delicious. Although there are still some dull, stale-nutty tasting wines, they are being squeezed out by the good guys. In general, drink the wine of the latest vintage, though the better wines will last a year or two.

Much of the wine is made by modern co-operatives, but there are some excellent private producers emerging too. Best producers: Bonnet, Canet, les Gauthiers, Launay, Laurétan, Moulin-de-Launay, Thieuley, Toutigeac.

'ÉTOILE AC
URA

Savagnin, Chardonnay, Poulsard

L'Étoile – the star – is a lovely name for a tiny little area in the centre of the Côtes du Jura which has its own AC for white wines and *vin jaune* only. The Savagnin grape is much in evidence, though less violently so than further north in the region, and there is a good deal of Chardonnay, either unblended – when it is light and fresh, but creamy – or blended with Savagnin, when it does succeed in soothing the savage character of the grape and dissuading it from its worst excesses. The red Poulsard variety can also be part of the white wine blend.

In general the wines are cleaner and fruitier than most Côtes du Jura or Arbois whites, and Champagne-method fizz can be as good as that of Pupillin in Arbois. There is also the daunting *vin jaune* and even the very rare sweet *vin de paille* (straw wine) – so beware! The best place to taste is the local co-operative in L'Étoile – it's the only place I've found inhabited whenever I've visited – but don't expect some efficient-looking concrete monstrosity – this co-operative is more like the ante-room of some half-forgotten monastery, and even then I met more chickens than humans. Best producers: Château d'Étoile, the l'Étoile co-operative, Domaine de Montbourgeau.

'ÉVANGILE, CH.
omerol AC
ORDEAUX

Merlot, Cabernet Franc

A reasonably large property by Pomerol's Lilliputian standards – 32 acres (13 hectares) – which has shot to prominence in the last few years by making wines which critics have compared to Château Pétrus. Well, the wine isn't *quite* that good, but the vineyard *is* bang next door to Pétrus, and the wine is made by one of Bordeaux's most talented oenologists, Michel Rolland – a man who not only understands the rule book, but who also knows that for a wine to be great it must gladden your heart, not merely impress your mental faculties. L'Évangile is rich, exciting, expensive wine, worth the price. Best years: 1988, '85, '83, '82, '79, '75.

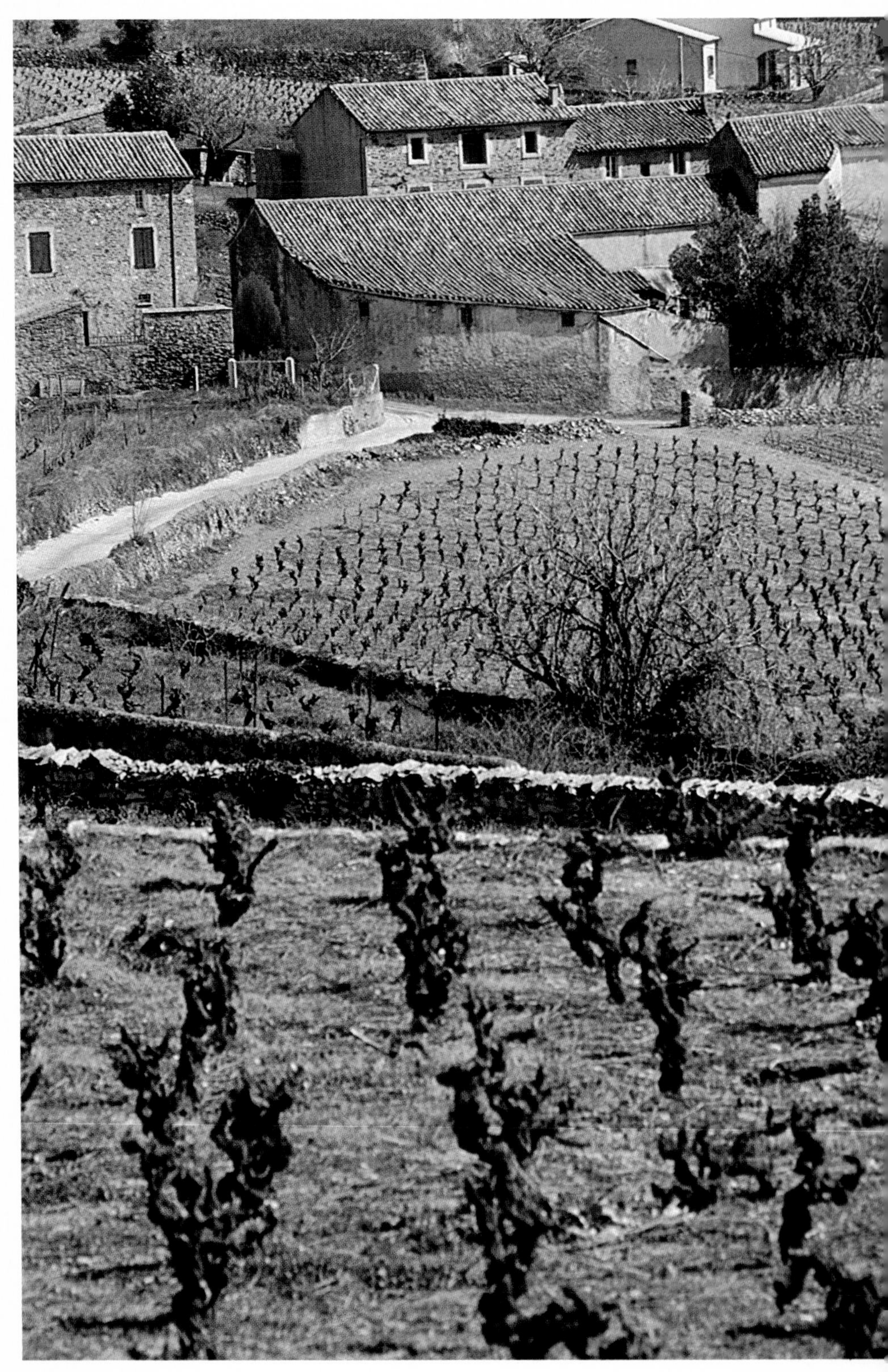

DE FARGUES, CH.
Sauternes AC, *cru bourgeois*
BORDEAUX

Sémillon, Sauvignon Blanc

The most remarkable thing about Château de Fargues is that, even though it is a mere Bourgeois Growth, it regularly sells for more than any other wine in the AC save the great Château d'Yquem. It is owned by the Lur-Saluces family who also own d'Yquem. Indeed they've owned de Fargues for 500 years – 300 years longer than they've owned d'Yquem!

The vineyard – 30 acres (12 hectares) on the edge of the Sauternes AC in the village of Fargues – is by no means ideal, and the quality of the wine is more a tribute to the commitment of the Lur-Saluces family and their winemaker, Pierre Meslier, than to the inherent quality of the estate. The vines ripen around ten days later than at d'Yquem, and the selection of grapes is so strict that each vine only yields two-thirds of a glass of wine! The result is that the total production rarely exceeds 10,000 bottles of rich, reasonably exotic wine, very honeyed, indeed almost syrupy, with something of the taste of pineapples and peaches, and a viscous feel, like lanolin, which coats your mouth. Fine, rich wine, but there are several Classed Growths which are better, and less expensive. Best years: 1988, '86, '83, '81, '80, '76, '75.

FAUGÈRES AC
LANGUEDOC-ROUSSILLON

Carignan, Grenache, Cinsaut, Syrah

Faugères, with its valleys stretching up into the mountains north of Béziers, in the Hérault, away from the suffocating heart of the Mediterranean plains, was the first of the communes in the Languedoc area to make its own reputation. For a year or two at the beginning of the 1980s it was the new 'buzz wine' of the Paris bistros, and duly got its AC in 1982. Then nothing more was heard about it, and Faugères was left to ponder the fickle finger of fashion.

Luckily the wine *is* good and well deserves its AC. It's almost entirely red, and comes from hilly vineyards in seven little villages just north of Béziers. Production is about six million bottles. What marks it out from other Languedoc reds is its ripe, soft, rather plummy flavour, and though it's a little more expensive than neighbouring wines, the extra is well worth it.

Faugères certainly has the terrain to make good white wine too, but so far, while the red wine quality has steamed ahead, nothing much has happened with the white. Of course, if your only white grape is the dullish Clairette there's not an awful lot you can do and the best results so far have come from winemakers who have picked the grapes early, fermented the juice cold and then sold the wines for drinking as young as possible. These show a quite attractive, full, liquorice and apple softness for a few months, but it has long gone by the time they are 12 months old. There is very little white made, but one or two more progressive growers have now planted Bourboulenc, Grenache Blanc and Marsanne, which, while still not the most exciting grapes in the world, should add a bit more character to the wine. Best years: 1988, '86, '85. Best producers: Faugères co-operative, Fraisse, Grézan, Haut-Fabrègues, St-Aimé.

◀ Winter vines, well-pruned, in Faugères. Pruning, controlled by AC regulations, normally takes place between December and February.

DE FIEUZAL, CH.
Pessac-Léognan AC
BORDEAUX

Cabernet Sauvignon, Merlot, Petit Verdot, Malbec

Sauvignon Blanc, Sémillon

An exceptionally good estate, but one which nobody seems to know about. Usually this would result in wines priced well below their real value, the owners pleading for custom. Not at Fieuzal. The owners of this 57-acre (23-hectare) estate, just south of Domaine de Chevalier near Léognan, have invested a lot of money in their property. The first time I ever tasted apricots in a dry white Bordeaux was at Château de Fieuzal. A neighbour nodded sagely as I waxed lyrical about this wonderful discovery, then took me outside and pointed to the right-hand side of the vineyard. 'That used to be an apricot grove,' he said, 'before they extended the vineyard.' Well, I was really chuffed, but for all the wrong

reasons. I hadn't really pulled off some wonderful wine-tasting coup. It was just that de Fieuzal was the first property I had come across which was using cold fermentation, followed by maturation in new oak barrels – and this combined with ripe Sauvignon Blanc and Sémillon grapes does produce a wonderful taste of apricots! Since then I've found it more frequently every year, and I love it – but de Fieuzal led the way, and the wine is still outstandingly good, whether drunk young, or aged.

The property is one of the most up-to-date in the region, and their delicious, ripe, oaky wine sells at a high price. Good luck to them; the wine's worth it. Yet the strange thing is that only the red wine is a Classed Growth (*cru classé de Graves*), to be precise. The little white plot does admittedly produce fewer than 10,000 bottles a year out of a total of over 100,000 bottles, but the quality should put it at the top of the white Classed Growths. Perhaps when the Graves classification was revised in 1959 to include white wines, the patch of white vines was still apricot trees. Best years (reds): 1988, '87, '86, '85 '84, '83, '82, '81, '78; best years (white): 1988, '87, '86, '85, '84, '83, '82, '81.

FIGEAC, CH.
St-Émilion AC, *premier grand cru classé*
BORDEAUX

Cabernet Sauvignon, Cabernet Franc, Merlot

You have hardly finished shaking hands with Thierry Manoncourt, the delightful though zealous owner of Château Figeac, before he has marched you over into the vineyards, and pointed accusingly to the north. Half-a-mile away sit the small, whitewashed buildings of Cheval-Blanc, acknowledged as St-Émilion's greatest wine. This small section of St-Émilion, to the west of the *appellation*, is called 'Graves' St-Émilion – because the gravel soil gives the wine its special quality. Yet who has the most gravel? Not Cheval-Blanc, but Figeac! Indeed you quickly learn that Cheval-Blanc used to be part of Figeac, was only sold as 'Vin de Figeac', and derives its name (meaning 'white horse') from the fact that it was there that Figeac had its stables!

Well, it's all true, but luckily there is a twinkle in Monsieur Manoncourt's eye as he berates his mighty neighbour, and luckily his own wine is superb, but in a different way from Cheval-Blanc. In his 100-acre (40-hectare) vineyard he uses 35 per cent Cabernet Sauvignon (rare in St-Émilion) and 35 per cent Cabernet Franc – both varieties which love gravel – and only 30 per cent of St-Émilion's main variety Merlot. The result is wine of marvellous minty, blackcurranty perfume with some of the cedar and cigar smoke spice of the great Médocs, and a caressing gentleness of texture. Often more 'beautiful' than Cheval Blanc, though rarely so grand. It is lovely young yet ideally should age 10–20 years. Best years: 1986, '85, '83, '82, '78, '76, '75.

FITOU AC
LANGUEDOC-ROUSSILLON

Carignan, Grenache, Cinsaut and others

Fitou has become one of the great unexpected success stories of the 1980s. The small *appellation* is virtually submerged by its neighbour, the giant Corbières; and it's not all that cheap. Yet it obviously struck a good chord, because there now isn't enough to go round. The wine is a good dark red, and has been recognized as special for quite a while, because the AC was granted in 1948, (almost 40 years before Corbières got it AC). The main Fitou area is a pocket of land around the lagoon of Salses on the coast between Perpignan and Narbonne, but there are also som villages, where better, tougher wine is made, in the heart of th Corbières hinterland, of which Tuchan is the most important. Fitou' strong, burly flavour comes from the Carignan grape which mus constitute 70 per cent of the blend. This makes for a pretty stern basi brew, so there is a minimum ageing requirement of 18 months in woo the wine itself then ages well for five or six years at least. Bes producers: Mont Tauch co-operative, Nouvelles, Vignerons Val d'Orbie

IXIN AC
ÔTE DE NUITS, BURGUNDY

Pinot Noir

Pinot Blanc

Fixin would clearly love to be talked of in the same breath as the great villages of the Côte d'Or. There it sits, looking down indulgently on its great neighbour Gevrey-Chambertin, confident in the knowledge that the Grand Dukes of Burgundy used to spend their summers here. But Fixin wines, try as they will, never manage to scale the heights. Worthy wines, usually quite full in the mouth, tannic enough to last well, but – perfume, fragrance, the mysterious mix of flavour and fantasy that marks out the greatest red Burgundies? No, not in my experience. So trust their worthiness not their magic. There are four *premiers crus* among the 370 acres (150 hectares) of vines but, at the other end of the scale, Fixin wine is often sold as Côte de Nuits-Villages.

Surprisingly enough, the AC regulations for this totally red wine area include the permission to make white wine. So you would presume that someone, somewhere, makes a bit of it, wouldn't you? Or would you just presume – as happened at Musigny a few miles further south – that the local grandee's wife was partial to a drop and so allowance was made for white? Well, when I say that Fixin has 370 acres devoted to Pinot Noir red wines, I should really say 369, because I have managed to winkle out *one* grower of white Fixin – Bruno Clair, who has planted a few rows of Pinot Blanc (rather than Burgundy's more normal Chardonnay). So I have discovered white Fixin exists. I haven't yet managed to taste it, but I'll report when I do. Best years (reds): 1987, '86, '85, '83, '80, '78. Best producers: Bordet, Durand-Roblot, Gelin, Joliet.

LEURIE AC
EAUJOLAIS, BURGUNDY

Gamay

If you get me in the right mood – spring flowers bursting free, the bright May-time sun promising an endless summer of warm, dreamy days, the picnic prepared and only ten minutes to go before she arrives – then Fleurie can be my very favourite wine in all the world; flowery, flowing, flirtatious, fun-filled, the most Beaujolais of all Beaujolais! The happy carefree flavours of the Gamay grape at their best, plus heady perfumes and a juicy sweetness which can leave you gasping with delight.

I'm not the only one who loves good Fleurie, because demand has made it the most expensive Beaujolais *cru*. Luckily there's a fair amount of wine as Fleurie, with 1754 acres (710 hectares), is the third biggest *cru* – and the quality in recent years has been outstanding. I only hope it can cope with its new-found popularity. Best years: 1988, '87, '85. Best producers: Bernard, Chignard, Duboeuf (especially from named vineyards), Fleurie co-operative, la Grande Cour, Montgénas, Paul.

OURCAS-HOSTEN, CH.
istrac, *cru grand bourgeois xceptionnel*
ORDEAUX

Cabernet Sauvignon, Merlot, abernet Franc

An important Listrac property of 100 acres (40 hectares), owned by a multinational bunch of Americans, Danes – and French. I used to keep finding stray bottles of this wine in the strangest of places – I had the 1962 and '64 at an abbey lost in a Welsh valley – and they were always dry and cedary, gentle yet austere, in a sort of kind-but-firm-bachelor-uncle way. Nowadays the wines are thoroughly modern, with new wood adding its nuance to the flavour – but recent vintages have lost a little of that pipe and carpet-slipper charm I liked in the older wines. Best years: 1988, '85, '82, '81, '78, '75.

RONSAC AC
ORDEAUX

Cabernet Franc, Cabernet auvignon, Merlot, Malbec

In 1970 people were saying that Fronsac wines would soon be the next star in the Bordeaux constellation. In the late '70s I went to several tastings of Fronsac wines and thought them splendid – full, strong reds, with some of the buttery richness of St-Émilion, the minerally backbone of Pomerol, and more than a whiff of the Médoc's cedar fragrance. But they still didn't appear in the shops.

GARD
LANGUEDOC-ROUSSILLON

Gard could consider itself a bit unlucky, because of all the southern *départements* it has the least coastline and what it has is merely a sliver of unprepossessing marshland just east of Montpellier. It's a little unlucky in its wines, too, because although there is a decent chunk of the Côtes du Rhône in the Gard, with Tavel and Lirac inside its borders, the real Rhône fireworks are to the east and the north. To the south and west of the Gard, the Languedoc is taking off as a wine producer, with increasing amounts of exciting gutsy wines – and yet the Gard can't quite get in on that act either. The reds have a rather meaty, earthy style and, Lirac apart, its only white AC of any renown is the flat, dull Clairette de Bellegarde, although one or two fresh whites are beginning to appear from good, young, Costières du Gard producers. Otherwise, the only bright signs are the experimental plots of Chardonnay and Sauvignon Blanc and the occasional Grenache Blanc.

GEVREY-CHAMBERTIN AC
CÔTE DE NUITS, BURGUNDY

Pinot Noir

Gevrey-Chambertin is an infuriating village. Capable, with its *grands crus* Chambertin and Chambertin Clos de Bèze, of making the most startling intoxicatingly delicious red wines of Burgundy, yet maddeningly liable to produce a succession of pale, lifeless semi-reds which really don't deserve the AC at all.

It's the old Burgundian problem of supply and demand. With its world-famous top vineyard, Chambertin, leading the way, all the wines – *grand cru*, *premier cru* and the village wines – are keenly sought-after. Production increases – Gevrey-Chambertin already has easily the biggest production on the Côte d'Or – less suitable land is planted (some of the Gevrey-Chambertin AC is on the plains side of the N74 road, which is generally seen as the boundary below which good wine cannot be made), and standards slip. So straightforward Gevrey-Chambertin village wine should be approached with circumspection. But good examples are proud, big-tasting Burgundy at its best, usually a bit chewy, jammy even, when young, but gradually getting a fascinating flavour of perfumed plums and dark, smoky chocolates after six to ten years' ageing. Best years: 1988, '87, '85, '83, '80, '78. Best producers: Bachelet, Burguet, Camus, Damoy, Drouhin, Faiveley, Jacquesson, Labouré-Roi, Leclerc, Magnien, Rodet, Rossignol, Rousseau, Varoilles.

GEWÜRZTRAMINER

Although the Gewürztraminer is a popular grape throughout the wine-making world, in France, the country where it most easily reaches its peak, the variety is found in only one place, Alsace. Alsace's proximity to Germany, and its Germanic dialect, explain the long, very German name. *Gewürz* means 'spicy', and *Traminer* means 'from Tramin' – actually a German-speaking town in the Tyrolean region of northern Italy and the presumed birthplace of this variety.

It is the 'spice' which has made Gewürztraminer famous, but the intense, often overpowering smell and taste isn't so much spicy as exotically perfumed, muskily floral and tropically fruity! It's face cream, flowers – full, blowsy roses, just losing their petals but still exuding heady perfumes in a last ditch effort to seduce – and tropical fruits – especially lychees, mangoes and maybe peaches, often flecked with freshly ground black pepper.

Sometimes, on the down side, there's a rather oily tackiness and consequent lack of refreshing acidity – but if the pungency is there I can cope with that. The fact that it covers 6250 acres (2500 hectares) in Alsace, which makes it Alsace's most widely planted grape, does mean that styles can vary considerably, but even the lightest ought to have a few of these marvellous self-indulgent flavours in there somewhere.

GIGONDAS AC
SOUTHERN RHÔNE

Grenache, Syrah, Mourvèdre, Cinsaut

A large village squashed up into the craggy slopes of the Dentelles de Montmirail on the east of the Rhône valley near Orange, with 3000 acres (1200 hectares) of vines, Gigondas used to be a Côte du Rhône-Villages but gained its own AC in 1971, and deservedly so, because, even though I don't like all the wines, they certainly have personality. They're sometimes described as poor man's Châteauneuf-du-Pape, but they have a tougher, chewier, jam-rich fruit which takes longer than Châteauneuf to soften and never quite sets the heart aflutter. Production is mostly red with a little rosé; Grenache is dominant in both. Best years: 1988, '86, '85, '83, '82, '81, '78. Best producers: Beaumet-Bonfils, Faraud, les Gouberts, Guigal, Jaboulet, Longue-Toque, les Pallières, Pascal, Raspail, St-Gayan.

GILETTE, CH.
Sauternes AC
BORDEAUX

Sémillon, Sauvignon Blanc, Muscadelle

A tasting to display the new vintage from Château Gilette was held a couple of years ago. It was delicious wine: deep and honeyed with a fabulous gooey richness, like toffee and butter melted over squashy banana. In fact, it was holding up very well for a 1955. Yes. I really mean it, 1955! This astonishing Sauternes property of a mere 8·6 acres (3·5 hectares), huddled down near the Garonne river in the village of Preignac, releases its vintage wine at anything between 20 and 30 years old – when even the best of its neighbours are beginning to taste distinctly wobbly at the knees. Production is tiny – perhaps 500 cases, sometimes more. Gilette's method is to pick the grapes in their full flood of overripeness, seething with the richness-concentrating noble rot; to ferment the wines very gently, and then to store them in little concrete vats! Whereas wooden barrels add flavour and allow oxygen to speed up the maturation of the wine, concrete is inert. Almost nothing happens for year after year, but the wine imperceptibly deepens and gains character. If I have to be absolutely honest I think the top Sauternes made in the traditional way are a tiny bit more exciting, their intense sweetness a little more unnervingly exotic – but Gilette is a great original and I wouldn't have it exposed to boring things like economic necessity for anything. Best years: 1959, '55, '53, '49.

GISCOURS, CH.
Margaux AC, ***3ème cru classé***
HAUT-MÉDOC, BORDEAUX

Cabernet Sauvignon, Merlot, Cabernet Franc, Petit Verdot

It took me quite a while to come round to Château Giscours. I began tasting it with the vintages of the 1960s, which I found hot and rich, almost as though the barrels had been coated in chocolate. Not at *all* like Margaux. But, beginning with a stunning '75 (a very tricky year in Margaux), Giscours has made a string of fabulous wines which certainly do start off with a rather solid, almost tarry quality, but which also have a heavenly perfume just asking for a few years' maturity, and a fruit which is blackberries, blackcurrants and cherries all at once. Best years: 1987, '83, '82, '81, '80, '79, '78, '75.

GIVRY AC
CÔTE CHALONNAISE, BURGUNDY

Pinot Noir

Chardonnay

An important Côte Chalonnaise village of 300 acres (120 hectares), east of Chalon-sur-Saône. The reds are generally good, not that heavy, but with a full, ripe strawberry perfume and gently plummy flavour. Whites are much rarer – about 65,000 bottles out of 600,000. The number of Burgundy tastings I've been to which featured a white Givry can be counted on the fingers of one hand. They've usually veered towards the sharp and neutral (not at all like Chardonnay should be in Burgundy) but in recent years the wines seem to be a little fuller and nuttier – which is much more attractive. Best years (reds): 1988, '85, '83, '82, '78. Best producers: Chofflet, Derain, Ragot, Thénard. Best years (whites): 1988, '86, 85. Best producers: Derain, Joblot, Ragot, Thénard.

GRAND-PUY-LACOSTE, CH.
Pauillac AC, *5ème cru classé*
HAUT-MÉDOC, BORDEAUX

Cabernet Sauvignon, Merlot, Cabernet Franc

Don't be fooled by this wine only being a Fifth Growth. Because Pauillac dominated the awards of First Growth in the 1855 Classifications, one sometimes gets the feeling that several very exciting properties were rather unceremoniously dumped in the Fifth Growths for appearance's sake. However, this 110-acre (45-hectare) estate makes a classic Pauillac. It isn't as weighty and grand as one or two better-known wines like Latour and Mouton-Rothschild, but the purity of its flavour marks it out as special. Although it begins in a fairly rough, dense way, that's just how a Pauillac should start out; as the years pass the fruit becomes the most piercingly pure blackcurrant and the perfume mingles cedar with lead pencils and the softening sweetness of new oak. Best years: 1988, '86, '85, '83, '82, '79, '78. Second wine: Lacoste-Borie.

GRANDS-ÉCHÉZEAUX AC
grand cru
CÔTE DE NUITS, BURGUNDY

Pinot Noir

Always thought of as a Vosne-Romanée *grand cru* – because that village's greatest property, Domaine de la Romanée-Conti, is a major owner and most of the other proprietors also live in Vosne-Romanée – the 22-acre (9-hectare) Grands-Échézeaux is actually in the parish of Flagey-Échézeaux, a hidden and fairly moribund village in the plain well below the vineyard. The wine has never achieved the fame either of Clos de Vougeot, to the east, or of Vosne-Romanée's leading *crus*. But when it is good, it does have a lovely, smoky, plum richness, and a soft caressing texture that ages well over 10–15 years to a gamy, chocolaty depth. Best years: 1988, '87, '85, '83, '80, '78, '76. Best producers: Domaine de la Romanée-Conti, Drouhin, Engel, Lamarche, Mongeard-Mugneret, Sirugue.

ALFRED GRATIEN
Champagne AC
CHAMPAGNE

Pinot Noir, Chardonnay, Pinot Meunier

If I have to own up to having a favourite Champagne, I must admit it'll have to be Alfred Gratien. Alfred who? Well, this isn't a big company, producing only 200,000 bottles in its backstreet cellars in Épernay (the giant Moët & Chandon, for instance, produces 18 million), but whoever said you had to be big to be good? No, the reason I love Gratien is because in the modern world of Champagne where many companies are more concerned about their international brand image than they are about the quality of their wines, Gratien declares that its image *is* the quality of the wine and nothing else. The wines are made in wooden casks – *very* rare nowadays, only moved by gravity since pumping is thought to bruise the wine, kept on their lees under a real cork – most other houses use crown corks similar to those on a Coca-Cola bottle – and stored appreciably longer than usual before release. The non-vintage blend is usually four years old when sold; many other companies sell their wine aged for little more than two years. The vintage wine is deliciously ripe and toasty when released but can age for another ten years, and is usually in the slightly less fizzy Crémant style.

GRAVES AC
BORDEAUX

Cabernet Sauvignon, Merlot, Cabernet Franc

Sémillon, Sauvignon Blanc

The Graves has always relied for its good reputation on the efforts of a small number of famous properties situated just to the south and west of the city of Bordeaux. Here the soil was extremely gravelly – which is how the area came to be called 'Graves' – and the climate was slightly warmer than the Médoc to the north, excellent conditions for producing high-quality wine. Well, it can't rely on the efforts of these favoured few any longer, because the villages in the north of the Graves region, close to Bordeaux, broke away in 1988 and formed their own AC – Pessac-Léognan – to emphasize what they see, quite rightly, as their historic superiority. So now, although the Graves *region* extends for about 37 miles (60km) from the very gates of Bordeaux down the bank

of the Garonne to south of Langon, the AC will generally be for wine from the less-favoured southern section. This certainly weakens the red wine hall of fame more than the white, because much of the most exciting white is already being created outside the most famous villages.

It is not an AC I would particularly want to be lumbered with anyway, since Graves for too long has been a byword for vaguely medium, fairly fruitless, murky-tasting wine of no style. However, there is a new wave of wine-making sweeping through the Graves which is producing bone-dry white wines, with lots of snappy freshness and a lovely, rather apricotty flavour, as well as some juicy, quick-drinking reds. Add to this a touch of spice from a few new oak barrels, and Graves AC doesn't really have any reason to be sorry for itself at all.

There is no doubt that the soil isn't so gravelly in the south of the Graves, and consequently the ripening of the grapes and drainage of the land is more difficult. The soil is similar in the south towards Langon and there are several villages to the south of the Garonne river, like Portets, Arbanats and Illats (in the sweet white Cérons AC but allowed the Graves AC for its dry wines) which are already making a name for themselves and their fresh, fruity whites. In general, drink these within two years, but the wines which have been given some oak maturity can age much longer. I hope we'll see a resurgence of gluggable, fruity reds and bright, fragrant whites, because the southern Graves does these so well. Best years (reds): 1988, '86, '85, '83, '82. Best years (whites): 1988, '87, '86. Best properties: Cabannieux, Clos Floridène, Constantin, Domaine de la Grave, la Garence, Magence, Rahoul, Respide-Médeville, Roquetaillade-la-Grange, St-Pierre.

GRAVES DE VAYRES AC
BORDEAUX

Cabernet Sauvignon, Cabernet Franc, Merlot

Sémillon, Sauvignon Blanc, Muscadelle

A small enclave in the north of the Entre-Deux-Mers region, running down to the Dordogne river and looking across to Libourne and the red wine paradise of Pomerol and St-Émilion. It's one of those ACs which sounds rather grand, but isn't really; just another obscure Bordeaux mini-*appellation* of no renown, but, I must say, some potential.

The 'Graves' refers to gravel soil and is nothing to do with the famous Graves region south of Bordeaux city. The reds *are* quite good, fruity and soft, but I've never had one which seemed any more than a bumped-up Bordeaux Supérieur. Most of the whites are made dry, to be drunk at one to two years old, and as such they are perfectly pleasant, if unexciting, mainstream white Bordeaux wines. Total production of white is about 19·7 million bottles. Best years: 1988, '87, '86, '85.

GRAVES SUPÉRIEURES AC
BORDEAUX

Sémillon, Sauvignon Blanc, Muscadelle

This is an *appellation* in decline. The intention was to use it for dry, medium and sweet white Graves of at least 12 degrees alcohol, which in the case of the dry wines would ensure only the ripest grapes would be used (straight Graves has a minimum strength of 11 degrees). But the AC never caught on, especially since the producers of dry wines found no benefit at all in tacking Graves Supérieures after their name. Since the most successful producers using the AC come from the southern Graves around the Sauternes area, and *they* apply it to sweet wines, it became positively confusing for the dry producers' customers, so they dropped it altogether. There are some fair wines from the villages of Portets and Langon in the south, and the AC of Cérons can also label its sweet wines Graves Supérieures. The sweet wines can, in decent years, have a good lanolin richness to them and quite a sweet, buttery taste, making not bad Sauternes substitutes – costing a lot less. In general, drink these wines young. Best years: 1988, '86. Best producer: Clos St-Georges.

GRAVES AND PESSAC-LÉOGNAN

The world of Graves was thrown into turmoil in 1987 when the northern part of the area, closest to the city of Bordeaux, and containing all the most famous properties, declared independence, and announced that from henceforth it would be called Pessac-Léognan, after its two leading communes. So now, although the whole region is still known as the Graves, it has two ACs: Pessac-Léognan for the area closest to Bordeaux, and Graves for the rest, primarily to the south and encircling white wine areas Cérons, Sauternes and Barsac.

The name 'Graves' means gravel, and the vineyards which now make up Pessac-Léognan are notable for their gravelly soil. Gravelly soil is heat-retaining and quick-draining, and thi allied to a warmer climate than that of th Médoc further north, and a close proximity t the city of Bordeaux, meant that the 'Graves', a the area became known, was for a long time th leading Bordeaux wine area. And until *ver* recently the bulk of the wine made was whit However, the majority of this was extremel *bad* white wine, so it is hardly surprising t discover that almost two-thirds of the wine no is red.

However, the world is thirsty for good whit wine, and while some proprietors were bus replacing white vines with red, others wer revolutionizing the way white wine was mad and in so doing were creating one of France' most exciting white wine regions. The majc grapes are the Sémillon and the Sauvigno Blanc, abetted by a little Muscadelle for th white wines, and Cabernet Sauvignon an Merlot for the reds.

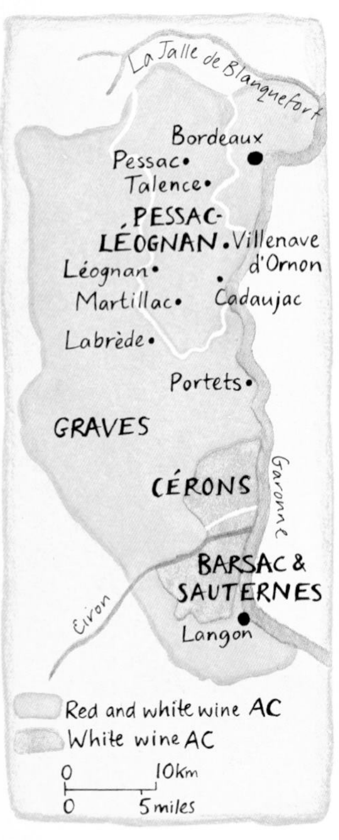

▶ Château la Louvière, a non-classified property near Léognan, is known for particularly distinguished white wines.

Pessac-Léognan encompasses ten communes. The supremely gravelly soil tends to favour red wines over the rest of the Graves, and in fact this *appellation* is home to the only Bordeaux red to be awarded First Growth status which is outside the Médoc – Château Haut-Brion. Still, whites can be grown successfully on the sandier, and less well-exposed areas further south towards Langon. The best estates use new oak to make wines with rich, apricotty fruit and creamy vanilla spice, capable of competing in the top quality league.

The Graves AC only applies to reds and dry whites, but there is a little-known Graves Supérieures AC, which can be applied to sweet white wines, and which sometimes comes up with super sweet wines at a very low price. However, if the Graves is to be encouraged to produce world-class wine, we mustn't try to force the price too low – or it won't be worth the winemakers' while.

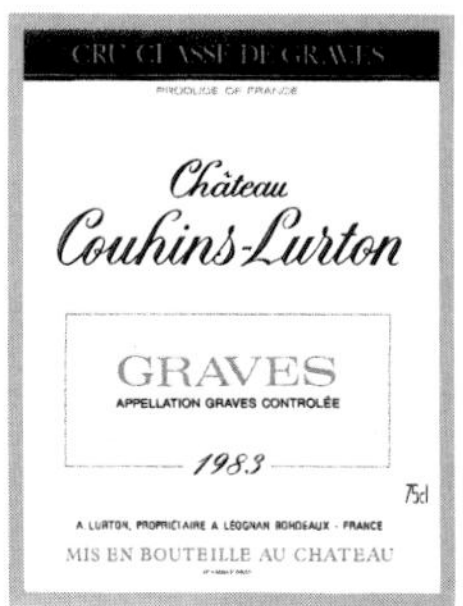

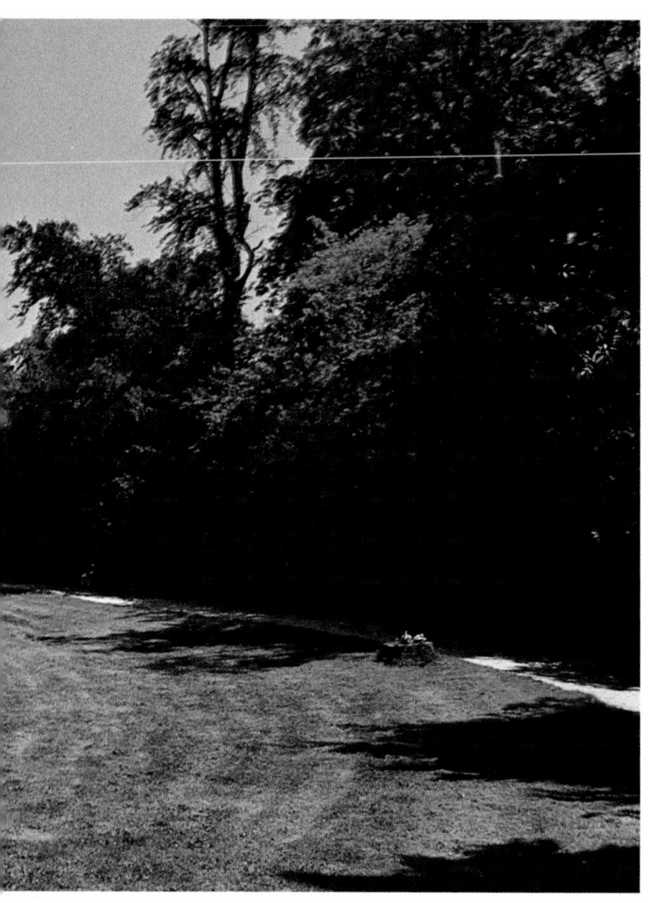

AC ENTRIES
Graves
Graves Supérieures
Pessac-Léognan

CHÂTEAUX ENTRIES
Carbonnieux
Domaine de Chevalier
de Fieuzal
Haut-Bailly
Haut-Brion
Malartic-Lagravière
La Mission-Haut-Brion
Rahoul
Smith-Haut-Lafitte
La Tour-Martillac

GRAPE ENTRIES
Cabernet Franc
Cabernet Sauvignon
Merlot
Sauvignon Blanc
Sémillon

GRENACHE

Grenache can be a brilliant grape or a flabby old plonk-producer depending on what you do with it. It is the world's most widely-planted red variety (the bulk of its acreage is found in Spain under the name Garnacha Tinta). It is a hot country grape: in France, you don't find it north of the central Rhône, but it reaches its zenith in the Southern Rhône round Châteauneuf-du-Pape. Here it is the dominant grape variety in the 13-grape blend allowed for the wine, and in the torrid, pebble-blanketed vineyards it often ripens to 14 degrees of alcohol, resulting in luscious, juicy-rich reds, sometimes almost too voluptuous for their own good and needing to be blended to acquire acidity and tannin.

Indeed, throughout the southern Rhône, Grenache is the most important grape. If overcropped, it produces rather pallid, empty-tasting wines, but from a normal yield the alcohol is high and the fruit strong and spicy. Carignan becomes more important round the Mediterranean basin, but Grenache is very much in evidence right down to the Spanish border and in Corsica. All the best southern rosés, in particular Tavel, Lirac and Côtes de Provence, are based on Grenache, usually blended with Cinsaut. In Rasteau (Côtes du Rhône) and Languedoc-Roussillon (especially Rivesaltes, Maury, Banyuls), Grenache also makes thick sweet, fortified red.

GRIOTTE-CHAMBERTIN AC
grand cru
CÔTE DE NUITS, BURGUNDY

Pinot Noir

A 'griotte' is a little cherry and, fanciful though it may seem, drinkers really do find the taste of cherries in Griotte-Chambertin. Actually, it's not *too* fanciful, because that's why they called this particular vineyard the 'Cherry-Chambertin' in the first place. In fact, if the locals could discern the taste of cherry in a particular wine hundreds of years before the first modern wine writer mewled and puked his way into print it reassures me that we're not all daft for finding flavours other than 'wine' in wine. What does 'wine' taste of? Well, cherries for a start, in some vineyards, and this little *grand cru* of 13·8 acres (5·6 hectares) (the third-smallest *grand cru*, following Ruchottes-Chambertin and Chapelle-Chambertin) in the village of Gevrey-Chambertin is there to prove it. Best years: 1988, '87, '85, '83, '80, '78. Best producers: Drouhin, Pernot-Fourrier, Ponsot, Roty, Thomas-Bassot.

GROS PLANT DU PAYS NANTAIS VDQS
WESTERN LOIRE

Gros Plant

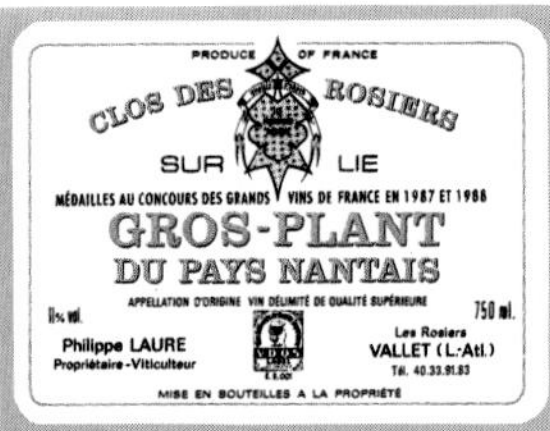

1987 wasn't a vintage which won widespread acclaim in France. But in the damp, marshy, salt-flats around Nantes, at the mouth of the Loire, they were rejoicing: they had finally made wine which a foreigner not brought up on draughts of battery acid and spirit vinegar might possibly enjoy – because the vineyards around Nantes are the home of the Gros Plant du Pays Nantais, one of the fiercest, sourest, most gum-numbing white wines the world has yet invented. And in 1987, somehow, the acid just wasn't there.

But, traditionally, Gros Plant is searing stuff – one of the grape's other names is Picpoul which roughly translates as 'lipstinger' and it is also grown in the Cognac and Armagnac regions, (under the names Folle Blanche or Picpoul) because its searingly high acid wine is perfect for distilling. Yet strangely, if you have a great plateful of seafood plonked down in front of you – wreathed in seaweed and still heaving with the motion of the ocean and the crunching of Atlantic rollers against the battered Brittany coast – you'll find the barefaced, eye-watering tartness of Gros Plant is surprisingly well-suited as a quaffer to cope with oysters mussels, crab and the rest. Since they eat seafood by the bucketful around Nantes I can only presume that explains the survival of Gros Plant as the local white. But, except in reasonably warm years like 1988 and '87, personally I'd pay a few francs more and drink the other equally dry, and – in comparison – positively sumptuous local wine: Muscadet. Best years: 1988, '87. Best producers: Bois-Bruley, Clos des Rosiers, Cuvée du Marquisat, Guindon, Hallereau, Métaireau, Sauvion.

GRUAUD-LAROSE, CH.
St-Julien AC, *2ème cru classé*
HAUT-MÉDOC, BORDEAUX

Cabernet Sauvignon, Merlot, Cabernet Franc, Petit Verdot

Of all the Médoc's great wines, Gruaud-Larose blows its own trumpet most *sotto voce*. In fact, were it not for American wine critics suddenly going weak at the knees over the quality of the last three or four vintages, Gruaud-Larose might still be trundling along, out of sight, quietly going about the business of making brilliant wine at an affordable price. There is a lot of it – at 203 acres (82 hectares), Gruaud is one of the largest St-Julien estates.

With vineyards set a little back from the estuary, Gruaud used to exhibit a softer, more honeyed style when young than, say, the Léoville trio whose vineyards slope down to the Gironde. This didn't stop the wine ageing brilliantly and gaining a piercing, dry, blackcurrant and cedarwood aroma over 20 years or so. The vintages of the 1980s have been made darker, deeper, thick with the flavours of blackberry and plums, sweetened with wood, toughened with tannin. They're not so easy to drink young nowadays, but I think they'll be even more exciting when they're mature. Best years: 1988, '86, '85, '83, '82, '81, '79, '78, '75. Second wine: Sarget de Gruaud-Larose.

GUIRAUD, CH.
Sauternes AC, *premier cru classé*
BORDEAUX

Sémillon, Sauvignon Blanc, Muscadelle

Guiraud was just about the first Sauternes I ever drank. A local off-licence had loads of the stuff on a top shelf; its label was dusty with neglect, but you couldn't help noticing the sultry, burnished gold colour of the wine, challenging the world to get those bottles down and drink up. Goodness only knows what the shopkeeper thought of all these students snapping up hoary has-beens. But that wine was so rich it flowed as slow as honey from the bottle, the colour was turning the unquenchable, raging gold of a dying sun, and the flavour was burnt syrup, nuts boiled in caramel, honey and cream and pineapple chunks.

Well, that was the 1961 and '62. I'd never had anything like it, and once I'd polished off my hoard – that was it. Guiraud went into decline and the property was heading for oblivion until 1981, when it was bought by an obsessively determined Canadian, bent on making great Sauternes. He's managed it. His 1983 was exceptional. His '86 is quite possibly the richest young Sauternes I have ever tasted. The vineyard is a good one, classified as a First Growth, and big – 185 acres (75 hectares) of vines in the south of the AC, just by the village of Sauternes. The owner, Hamilton Narby, ruthlessly selects only the best grapes, uses at least 50 per cent new oak each year to age the wine, and charges a very high price – quite rightly since it is clearly one of Sauternes' most exciting wines. The wine needs at least ten years to reach its peak – and good years may need 15–20. Best years: 1988, '86, '83, '82, '81.

HAUT-BAGES-LIBÉRAL, CH.
Pauillac AC, *5ème cru classé*
HAUT-MÉDOC, BORDEAUX

Cabernet Sauvignon, Merlot, Petit Verdot

This 64-acre (26-hectare) property, up to now relatively obscure and rarely seen, stands a very good chance of becoming one of my favourite Pauillac wines. Not because it is the most classic – it isn't; not because it has the most beguiling subtleties and nuances of perfume – it doesn't; no, it's the fruit that I love. Big, unbridled bucketsful of delicious plum and blackcurrant fruit, wonderfully unsubtle in a way, but exciting and satisfying. Haut-Bages-Libéral changed hands in 1980: only the recent vintages give me such a buzz. They will age, but are already deliciously drinkable at five years. Best years: 1988, '86, '85 '83 '82.

HAUT-BAILLY, CH.
Pessac-Léognan AC, *cru classé de Graves*
BORDEAUX

Cabernet Sauvignon, Merlot, Cabernet Franc

The softest and most invitingly charming of the Graves Classed Growths. The 62 acres (25 hectares) of vines are on gravelly soil with rather more sand than usual, just to the east of Léognan, and this contributes to Haut-Bailly becoming agreeably drinkable very early. However, the wines do age fairly well and what is ready to drink at ten years old often seems magically unchanged at 20. Up till 1970 the wines were consistently fine, but there was then a gap till 1979, when the property returned to the top level. Best years: 1988, '86, '85, '82, '81, '79. Second wine: la Parde-du-Haut-Bailly.

HAUT-BATAILLEY, CH.
Pauillac AC, *5ème cru classé*
HAUT-MÉDOC, BORDEAUX

Cabernet Sauvignon, Merlot, Cabernet Franc

They call this the 'St-Julien' of Pauillac. It's a small property of 49 acres (20 hectares), set back from the melting pot of brilliant wines close to the river, and is in fact owned by one of St-Julien's greatest wine-making families – the Bories of Ducru-Beaucaillou. It gets its 'St-Julien' tag because it doesn't have the concentrated power of a true Classed Growth Pauillac. In recent years, only 1970 and '82 have been 'powerful' wines. This lack of oomph wouldn't matter if the wines had the perfume and cedary excitement of St-Julien, but they rarely do; they're pleasant, a little spicy, but not memorable. Recent vintages have improved, and the style is getting a bit more substantial. Best years: 1988, '85, '83, '82.

HAUT-BRION, CH.
Pessac-Léognan AC, *premier cru classé de Graves*
BORDEAUX

Cabernet Sauvignon, Merlot, Cabernet Franc

Sémillon, Sauvignon Blanc

Haut-Brion has been in the news for longer than any other Bordeaux property. It seems to be the first property that got a write-up in the British press for a start when, in 1663, Samuel Pepys wrote that during a session at the Royal Oak Tavern he 'drank a sort of French wine called Ho Bryan; that hath a good and most particular taste that ever I met with'! It was a good 50 years before other Bordeaux wines began to be known by their own name. One reason for this is that the excellent gravel-based vineyard which constitutes Haut-Brion is actually in the suburbs of the city of Bordeaux and so was readily accessible to visiting merchants. Haut-Brion's continued popularity is shown by the fact that when the local merchants decided to classify the top red wines of Bordeaux in 1855 all the wines they chose were from the Médoc – except one, Haut-Brion from the Graves (now Pessac-Léognan), which was accorded First Growth status – along with Margaux, Lafite and Latour.

There's no doubt the wine is worth its position. It has all the potential longevity and weight of the Médoc First Growths, and starts out tasting very like them because of the 100-acre (40-hectare) vineyard's deep gravel soil. Yet after a few years the flavour changes course; the tough tannins fade away more quickly, a gentle creamy-edged fruit takes their place and a few years' more maturity brings out all the fruit of plums and blackcurrants mingled with a heady scent of unsmoked Havana tobacco. Frequently Haut-Brion is *not* at its best in the greatest years, but that's OK – the lesser years are always cheaper and more fun to drink. Best years (reds): 1988, '86, '85, '84, '83, '81, '79, '78. Second wine: Bahans-Haut-Brion.

There is also a white Château Haut-Brion, and the owners would like to claim the same quality achievement for this – 12,000 bottles a year from 7 acres (3 hectares) – as for their red. But the white can be prone to inconsistency, and since the price of the latter is an arm and both legs I'm not so keen to risk a disappointing bottle. But, at its best Haut-Brion is fabulous wine, which over five to ten years blossoms out into a wonderfully lush flavour of nuts and spice, cream and a hint of apricots, sometimes a hint of pine resin too. Best years (whites): 1988 '87, '86, '85, '83, '82, '81, '79, '76.

HAUTES-CÔTES DE BEAUNE AC
CÔTE D'OR, BURGUNDY

🍷 Pinot Noir

🍷 Chardonnay

These wines come from vineyards set back in the hills behind the great Côte de Beaune slopes. If scenery could influence what went into the bottle, this lost little region of twisting country lanes, ancient trees and purest sylvan peace would surely produce ecstatic wines. As it is, the very beauty of the land is the wine's undoing. For, in this higgledy-piggledy landscape, the aspect of the sun is rarely ideal and the altitude, at 1150–1300 feet (350–400 metres), is also a handicap; all the best vineyard sites on the Côte de Beaune itself are below 1000 feet (300 metres). So don't expect very ripe flavours from the Hautes-Côtes de Beaune. If the price of decent red Burgundy had not been pushed through the roof during the 1970s, we probably wouldn't be hearing too much of the AC at all. As the supply of affordable Burgundy dwindled, the tumbling backwater came under the spotlight. A few growers eked out a living, and the new Caves des Hautes-Côtes was beginning to chivvy them along.

Then, in the 1970s, merchants began to prospect land and replant derelict vineyards. Now, the Hautes-Côtes de Beaune are reasonably prosperous and the wines are fairly good. Only in exceptional years like 1976 and '85 will they attain the quality of Côte de Beaune, but in their light, rather chewy or raspberry-fresh way, they often give a purer view of what Pinot Noir should taste like than many supposedly classier offerings. Best years (reds): 1988, '87, '85, '83, '82.

There's some white Hautes-Côtes de Beaune too, and the 20 villages with the right to AC can produce pleasant, slightly sharp Chardonnay and, under the Bourgogne Aligoté AC, some good, spirited, ultra-dry Aligoté. In really hot years, like 1982, '83 and '85, the Chardonnay can even get a dry, but discernibly nutty, taste after a couple of years in bottle which slightly – ever so slightly – might remind you of a wispy Chassagne-Montrachet. Best years (whites): 1988, '86, '85, '83. Best producers: Caves des Hautes-Côtes, Cornu, Jacob, Joliet, Marcilly, Château de Mercey.

HAUTES-CÔTES DE NUITS AC
CÔTE D'OR, BURGUNDY

🍷 Pinot Noir

🍷 Chardonnay

The relatively compact Hautes-Côtes de Nuits vineyards belong to 14 villages directly behind the Côte de Nuits. Inevitably, altitude, averaging out at 1300 feet (400 metres), is a problem. Frequently the land is just scrub at anything over this height. So ripening is by no means guaranteed. As the vineyards mature this is less serious, and attractive lightweight wines can be made, but so far the best are red. Vine growing here had virtually died out in the first part of the twentieth century, but there has been extensive replanting in recent years. The granting of AC to the Hautes-Côtes de Nuits and Hautes-Côtes de Beaune in 1961 acted as a spur, and several growers, in particular Hudelot and Thévenot, planted large estates. They were followed by the merchant houses, and the establishment of the Caves des Hautes-Côtes co-operative in 1968 gave cohesion to the area.

The wines are never weighty and are, if anything, a little leaner to start with than the Hautes-Côtes de Beaune, but they do have an attractive cherry and plum flavour, sometimes with a pleasing bitter finish. Best years (reds): 1988, '87, '85, '83, '78. Best producers: Caves des Hautes-Côtes, Delauney, Dufouleur, Hudelot, Thévenot-le-Brun.

The whites from Chardonnay and Aligoté (not covered by the Hautes-Côtes AC) tend to be rather dry and flinty. Interestingly, one of the fuller whites I've tried was not Chardonnay at all but its less good look-alike, Pinot Blanc. Production of white is only 50,000 bottles out of a total of over one million. In general drink young – although they will age. Best years (whites): 1986, '85, '83, '82. Best producers: Caves des Hautes-Côtes, Chaley, Dufouleur, Hudelot, Thévenot-le-Brun, Verdet.

HAUT-MARBUZET, CH.
St-Estèphe AC, *cru grand bourgeois exceptionnel*
HAUT-MÉDOC, BORDEAUX

Merlot, Cabernet Sauvignon, Cabernet Franc

I can't believe that Haut-Marbuzet's 94-acre (38-hectare) vineyar between Montrose and Cos d'Estournel is really as good as those of it illustrious neighbours, and yet I freely admit that tasting the wine together I've regularly put Haut-Marbuzet ahead of Montrose and not fa behind the mighty Cos. So maybe the energetic Monsieur Dubosq i right because he treats his wine like a top Classed Growth – right up t using 100 per cent new oak for maturing it – and the great, ricl mouthfilling blast of flavour certainly isn't subtle but certainly impressive. Best years: 1988, '86, '85, '83, '82, '81, '78.

HAUT-MÉDOC AC
BORDEAUX

Cabernet Sauvignon, Cabernet Franc, Merlot and others

Haut-Médoc is a geographical entity *and* an AC. The geographical entit is the southern half of the Médoc peninsula, stretching from Blanquefo in the suburbs of Bordeaux, north to St-Seurin-de-Cadourne. All th finest gravelly soil is situated in this section, and it contains six separat village ACs: Margaux, Listrac, Moulis, St-Julien, Pauillac and St-Estèphe

The *appellation* Haut-Médoc covers all the parts of this geographica area not included in a village *appellation*. There are five Classed Growth within the Haut-Médoc AC, including the excellent La Lagune an Cantemerle in the south, but otherwise the wines vary widely in qualit and style. If anything they are inclined to lack a little fruit, but may ag well in a slightly austere way. Best villages: Ludon, Macau, Lamarque Cussac, St-Laurent, St-Sauveur, Cissac, St-Seurin-de-Cadourne, Vert euil. Best properties: d'Agassac, Camensac, Cantemerle, Castillo Cissac, Coufran, Hanteillan, la Lagune, Lamarque, Lanessan, Larose Trintaudon, Malescasse, Pichon, Ramage-la-Batisse, la Tour-Carnet, l Tour-du-Haut-Moulin.

HAUT-POITOU VDQS
CENTRAL LOIRE

Gamay, Cabernet Franc, Cabernet Sauvignon

Sauvignon Blanc, Chardonnay, Chenin Blanc

◀ Haut-Poitou has evolved from a supplier of Cognac-distilling wine into a producer of light, dry table wines.

Thought of as a Loire area, Haut-Poitou is in fact a little island of vine-growing near Poitiers – which is well on the way south to Bordeaux. Even so, the styles are similar to the Loire. You've got to relish crisp, zingy acidity to like Haut-Poitou whites, because they are austere, squeaky clean demonstrations of the varietal flavour of each grape – the bare essentials, with not an ounce of spare flesh to soften the blow. Your Sauvignon will be as green and nettly and mouthwateringly tart as it knows how to be; your Chardonnay will out-Chablis Chablis – lean, almost lemony, very refreshing but making no attempt to charm. There is also a little Pinot Blanc, and some Chenin is grown. Not surprisingly, with this high acid, but characterful style they're having a go at sparkling wine, and their Champagne-method Diane de Poitiers is a great success.

Red Haut-Poitou, normally made from Gamay, but occasionally from Cabernet, is light and dry, veering towards the raw except in warm years. The rosé, usually Cabernet-based, is also very dry but can be good and refreshing, marked by a nice grassy tang when young. The wines' high-tech taste is matched by the co-operative which completely dominates production; its director, virtually single-handed, restored the vineyard area in the '60s and '70s. In general drink Haut-Poitou wines young for that 'snap you awake' effect. Best producer: the Haut-Poitou co-operative at Neuville.

L'HÉRAULT
LANGUEDOC-ROUSSILLON

The Hérault is the fountainhead of France's infamous contribution to the European wine lake. It is accustomed to producing a positive deluge of rock-bottom gut rot every year. However, things are on the up. This is the heart of the Brave New World of wine-making which could yet transform the Midi into a high-tech, California-style provider of cheap, attractive, everyday table wines. This dull, tired land centred on Béziers and Montpellier is the most densely planted *département* in France – and until recently had the fewest ACs. Fortunately, politicians have realized you can't protect sub-standard producers for ever, and between 1976 and 1984 in Hérault and the neighbouring *département* of Aude, over 74,000 acres (30,000 hectares) of unsuitable vineyards were uprooted. There is now a good deal of interesting wine coming from the hills to the north of Béziers, most of it as yet red, but as methods of cool-fermentation in stainless steel take hold, and as new grape varieties are planted, the whites are improving too.

Until the 1980s, Hérault only had one AC – the dull and insipid white Clairette du Languedoc. Since then Faugères, St-Chinian and the widespread Coteaux du Languedoc (where several villages, notably La Clape and Pinet, now have a good reputation for white) have joined the AC list. The Vin de Pays de l'Hérault – France's most elephantine *vin de pays* at a giant 200 million bottles annually – is doing sterling work in improving the quality of the non-AC vineyards. Here plantings are heavily loaded in favour of red Carignan, which can be coarse and tough but which, when made by carbonic maceration, can be extremely pleasant. Plantings of Syrah, Mourvèdre, Cabernet Sauvignon and Merlot are increasing. There is one super-star property, Mas de Daumas Gassac whose fans liken the wine to Classed Growth Bordeaux.

Languedoc-Roussillon's leading fortified Muscat is made at Frontignan, on the coast near Sète, and the 27 *vins de pays de zone* in the Hérault are encouraging wine merchants to be innovative and to aim for quality. Chardonnay, Sauvignon Blanc, Sémillon and Marsanne are appearing as well as attractively aromatic versions of Grenache Blanc, Bourboulenc, Macabeo and dry Muscat. Some good Vin de Pays de l'Hérault producers are Bosc/Cante Cigale (the best), Lenthéric, Prieuré d'Amilhac.

HERMITAGE AC
NORTHERN RHÔNE

Syrah, Marsanne, Roussanne

Marsanne, Roussanne

There was a time, a century or more ago, when Hermitage was regarded by many as the greatest red wine in France. And there was a time, amid the Bordeaux and Burgundy fever of a decade or so ago, when it was dismissed by almost all as a rough-and-tumble Rhône red. And then there's now. Once again Hermitage is revered – rare, rich red wine, expensive, memorable, classic. But these words are too cold to describe the turbulent excitements of a great Hermitage! The boiling cauldron of flavours – savage pepper, herbs, tar and coalsmoke biting at your tongue, fruit of intense blackcurrant-raspberry-and-bramble sweetness – is intoxicatingly delicious and, as the wine ages, a strange, warm softness of cream and liquorice and well-worn leather blends in to create one of the world's greatest red-wine taste experiences.

Now, not all Hermitage achieves this eccentric but exciting blend of flavours, because the vineyard – flowing down the slopes of this bullish mound above the little town of Tain-l'Hermitage on the banks of the Rhône – only covers 310 acres (125 hectares) and a lot of merchants will take any grapes just to have Hermitage on their list. But the best growers – using the red Syrah, with sometimes a little white Marsanne and Roussanne, and carefully blending the wines from different plots of the 'hill' (which do give *very* different flavours) – can make superbly original wine, needing five to ten years' ageing even in a light year; but for the full-blown roar of flavours which a hot, ripe vintage brings, then 15 years is hardly enough for the tip-top wines. Best years (reds): 1988, '85, '83, '82, '80, '78. Best producers: Chave, Delas, Desmeure, Faurie, Fayolle, Ferraton, Guigal, Grippat, Jaboulet, Sorrel, Vidal-Fleury.

White Hermitage is rather less famous – but the best can actually out-live the reds! I did a tasting of Hermitage reds and whites from Gérard Chave (reckoned by many Hermitage fans to be the best producer). The reds were tremendous, though they were clearly getting tired at the 20-year-old mark and distinctly fading long before they hit

▼ Dawn light over Tain l'Hermitage picks out the chapel which give Hermitage hill and its vineyards their name. Below, in the morning mist, lies the river Rhône.

40. But those whites! I mean, for the first five or ten years I thought – what's so special about these dull, heavy, lumpish things? And then they just got better and better. They had to drag me away from the simply sensational 1929 *white*!

Later I went round to Chapoutier's, one of the most important Hermitage merchants. I wasn't enjoying the reds that much, and I think Monsieur Chapoutier noticed because he disappeared for a moment and came bouncing back with – a 1942 white. Fantastic stuff. Unbelievably deep and rich, alive and kicking long after the reds had given up the ghost. Yet it is *red* Hermitage which has the reputation for ageing. Well! Some winemakers, like Jaboulet, are making modern, fruity, fragrant whites – with an exciting floral, lemon peel, liquorice and apple flavour. They are lovely at one to two years old but I can't see how they'll improve.

But there are others – from grisly-minded traditionalists who won't be swayed by fashion and the chance of an easy sale. They've been growing the Marsanne and Roussanne grapes on the dizzy slopes of the giant hill of Hermitage for generations, and they don't care if their wine then takes generations to mature so long as it is the 'real thing'.

The flavour of white Hermitage from someone like Gray, Chave, Grippat or Chapoutier will seem fat and oily at first, reeking of bruised apples, soured peaches and unswept farmyard rubbish; but if you give it ten years, 20, maybe twice as long, then a remarkable transformation will take place – apples and pears blend with fresh-roasted nuts, toffee, liquorice, pine resin, herbs from the wild Rhône hills, mint and peaches and cream. From such sullen beginnings the glory of white Hermitage finally blazes forth – for you if you can wait, for your children if you can't. About 30 per cent of the vineyard is white, producing some 200,000 bottles a year. Best years (whites): 1988, '87, '85, '83, '82, '78, '76, '71, '70, '69. Best producers: Chapoutier, Chave, Desmeure, Gray, Grippat, Guigal, Jaboulet.

ÎLE DE BEAUTÉ, VIN DE AYS
ORSICA

🍷 Nielluccio, Sciacarello, arignan and others

Vermentino, Ugni Blanc

The *vin de pays* for Corsica. If you don't like the rather warm, vaguely tanniny, vaguely resiny flavours of most mainstream Corsican reds and rosés, you may find a bit of relief here. As is frequently the case in the south of France, the more flexible *vin de pays* regulations allow experimentation with non-traditional grapes, and so far there are encouraging signs from reds based on Syrah and Cabernet and rosés based on Grenache and Pinot Noir. Altogether about 15 million bottles are produced, 95 per cent of them red and rosé. Modern methods are helping to improve the standard of the whites, but few are seen away from the island.

RANCY AC
URGUNDY

🍷 Pinot Noir, César, Tressot

This northern outpost of vineyards, just south-west of Chablis, is an unlikely champion of the clear, pure flavours of Pinot Noir. In the compact south-facing amphitheatre of 155 acres (63 hectares) which makes up the vineyard of Irancy, the sun gives just enough encouragement to the vines to produce a delicate, clean red wine, lightly touched by the ripeness of plums and strawberries.

The wines will also age well, especially if they have an addition of César and Tressot, two local grapes of diminishing importance. There is a little rosé which can also catch a fleeting glimpse of Pinot Noir fruit. Two other local reds are Bourgogne-Coulanges-la-Vineuse – rougher than Irancy, with a disconcerting rooty taste – and Bourgogne-Épineuil – frail, rare, but a delightful summer red. Best years: 1988, '85, '83, '82. Best producers: Bienvenue, Cantin, Delaloges, Simmonet-Febvre.

IROULÉGUY AC
SOUTH-WEST

🍷🍷 Tannat, Cabernet Franc, Cabernet Sauvignon

🍷 Petit Manseng, Gros Manseng, Courbu and others

Yes, I think this gets my vote as the most obscure French AC Geographically obscure anyway. I eventually found my way to the winer by asking the Spanish customs officer – I'd already crossed into Spai without noticing – but that's what life's like way up in the Pyrenea mountain valleys where they make Irouléguy. The wine's not as good a the setting but the red is fairly full and peppery with a nice acid streak The rosé is, well, rosé. The whites are virtually non-existent. Drink thes wines young – preferably in the meadows by the St-Étienne-de-Baigorr winery, just below the snow line! The co-operative dominates productio for the 370 acres (150 hectares).

D'ISSAN, CH.
Margaux AC, *3ème cru classé*
HAUT-MÉDOC, BORDEAUX

🍷 Cabernet Sauvignon, Merlot

I've always had a vaguely covetous feeling about d'Issan, because it ha an outrageously sumptuous-looking gold label. I had a bottle of 196 once, and spent so much time drooling over the label that the wine wa exhausted by the time I finally pulled the cork. Still, I'm *told* the 196 was extremely good! We didn't see much of d'Issan during the 1970s bu the last few vintages have been some of the most scented and deliciou in the whole Margaux commune. The property is a reasonable size at 7 acres (32 hectares), and is unusual for not having any Cabernet Franc i the vineyard, plantings being 75 per cent Cabernet Sauvignon and 2 per cent Merlot. As the deliciously rich vintages of 1982, '83, '85 an '86 mature, the gold label will seem increasingly apt. Best years: 198 '87, '86, '85, '83, '82, '81, '78.

JASNIÈRES AC
CENTRAL LOIRE

🍷 Chenin Blanc

I didn't think I'd ever be able to look a Jasnières producer in the eye an say, 'I would like to try your wine'. All my attempts to enjoy it have foun me reeling and gasping for breath as it confirmed its reputation as th Loire's most uncompromising, bone-dry Chenin wine. But one Decem ber at a Wine Fair in Paris I got caught by a most disarmin unthreatening lady who, I discovered too late, owned a largish vineyar – in Jasnières. Without breaching the most basic rules of good manner I didn't have a lot of choice really, so there I was, shifting from foot t foot and wondering if my travel insurance covered dissolved teeth a she wrested the cork from the bottle with some difficulty (if I'd been th cork I'd have been out quicker than a rat up a drain-pipe).

Well, it was delicious. This young, 1986, Domaine de la Chaniè white Jasnières was very dry but full of lovely apricot, honey and eve sultana overtones which were already attractive but would be fabulou in five years' time. It was simply a case of modern wine-making. Th skins of the grapes were steeped in the juice before fermentation t extract the perfume which the skins possess – but which is usually lo in the crushing and running-off of juice. And the fermentation had bee careful, clean and cold. So this tiny, 47-acre (19-hectare) AC, 25 mil (40km) north of Tours on the little Loir river (Tours is on the big Loi river) still makes bone-dry Chenin white – but it *can* be delicious rath than a heavy-duty gum scourer. Best years: 1988, '86, '85, '83, '82. Be producers: Chanière, Fresneau, Pinon.

JULIÉNAS AC
BEAUJOLAIS, BURGUNDY

🍷 Gamay

A friend of mine once told me that the problem with Juliénas was tha lacked 'humour'. I know what he means. Juliénas. It's rather a seric name; the school prefect rather than the tearaway among the Beaujol *crus*. The flavour often reflects that too. It frequently lacks t happy-fruit style which we think of as Beaujolais' calling-card. But wha does have is the weight and strength to develop in the bottle: Julién *may* have a little too much tannin and acid to be as immediat enjoyable as the others, but in years like 1985 and '88 there is a solid juiciness of peaches and cherry and strawberry which may not make great glugging, but which makes delicious, if slightly more 'serious', drinking. There are 1380 acres (560 hectares), producing about four million bottles. Best years: 1988, '87, '85, '83. Best producers: Duboeuf, Château de Juliénas, Gonon, Juliénas co-opérative, Pelletier.

JURANÇON AC
SOUTH-WEST

Petit Manseng, Gros Manseng, Courbu

'I was a girl when I met this prince; aroused, imperious, treacherous as all great seducers are – Jurançon.' It's not my quote, but I wish it were (though I'd have to do something about the 'girl' bit). It's the great French novelist Colette, and the confident power of suggestion – unhindered by the requirements of accurate description, or grape types, or even taste – puts us wine-writers to shame. Jurançon is the historic white wine of the western Pyrenees. It's made mostly from the excellent Petit Manseng and the not quite so good Gros Manseng, and is dry or sweet. Dry, it is rather dull and flat – especially as made by the rather too-powerful local co-operative, though a new oenologist is rapidly raising standards. But sweet, from one of the few independent growers, it can be heavenly. They let the grapes hang late into November – shrivelled and thick with sugar – then slowly ferment the juice and leave the wine for a couple of years, till it develops a lusciousness of honey, nuts and mangoes, strongly spiced with cinnamon, cloves and ginger, cut by a pure laser streak of lemon acidity. Best producers: Cauhapé, Clos Cancaillaü, Clos Uroulat, Cru Lamouroux, Guirouilh.

KRUG
Champagne AC
CHAMPAGNE

Pinot Noir, Chardonnay, Pinot Meunier

If Bollinger has cornered the image of high society's favourite fizz for whooping it up, Krug has always had a much more demure reputation, partly because the cheapest bottle of Krug costs more than most companies' most expensive cuvées. The Krug non-vintage is called Grande Cuvée and knocks spots off the general run of De Luxe brands which one sometimes suspects were merely developed for the night club trade. It comes in a supremely elegant wide-based bottle and although splendid on release, gets much more exciting with a year or two's extra ageing. The blend is made up of as many as 50 different wines from up to 25 different villages and utilizing perhaps eight different vintages going back ten years or more. Krug also do an excellent vintage wine, a rosé and a single vineyard Clos du Mesnil Blanc de Blancs.

In Champagne, the stark-white chalk soil is crucially important: it provides ideal drainage, aids ripening by reflecting back the sun's heat, and produces grapes with high acidity – vital for good Champagne.

LADOIX-SERRIGNY AC
CÔTE DE BEAUNE, BURGUNDY

🍷 Pinot Noir

🍷 Chardonnay

The most northern village in the Côte de Beaune, and one of the least known since its best wines are usually sold as Corton or Aloxe-Corton *premier cru* and its less good ones as Côte de Beaune-Villages. Even so, wine with a Ladoix label does occasionally surface and can be worth a try – there are several good growers in the village and it is likely to be reasonably priced. The output is overwhelmingly red, quite light in colour and a little lean in style, but after a few years the rough edges slip away and a rather attractive soft, savoury style emerges. I have actually got a bottle of Ladoix white. It was given to me by a contralto who had it given to her by a bass. I'm a baritone, waiting for a soprano to share it with, perhaps. White wine from Ladoix-Serrigny is very rare – they only produce 15,000 bottles each year. And the wine *is* good – a light, clean Chardonnay flavour, softened to nuttiness with a little oak ageing and two or three years' maturity. Best years (reds): 1988, '87, '85, '83, '82, '78. Best producers: Capitain-Gagnerot, Chevalier, Cornu, Florent de Mérode. Best years (whites): 1988, '85, '83, '82. Best producer: Cornu.

LAFAURIE-PEYRAGUEY, CH.
Sauternes AC, *premier cru classé*
BORDEAUX

🍷 Sémillon, Sauvignon Blanc, Muscadelle

It's fashionable to criticize the detrimental effect on quality following the takeover of a property by a large merchant. Often the criticism is justified, as organization becomes centralized in some distant head office, traditions are lost and loyalty undermined – but the large Cordier company has always taken great care of its properties (they bought this one in 1913). In the 1980s their investment and commitment in this 50-acre (20-hectare) *premier cru* have made Lafaurie-Peyraguey one of the most improved Sauternes properties. They made outstanding wines in the great '86 and '83 vintages, but also were very successful in lesser years like '85, '84 and '82. Lafaurie-Peyraguey has a deep apricot and pineapple syrup sweetness, a cream and nuts softness and a good clear, lemony acidity which give it wonderful balance for long ageing. Best years: 1988, '86, '85, '83, '82, '81, '80, '79.

LAFITE-ROTHSCHILD, CH.
Pauillac AC, *premier cru classé*
HAUT-MÉDOC, BORDEAUX

🍷 Cabernet Sauvignon, Merlot, Cabernet Franc, Petit Verdot

Possibly, even probably, the most famous red wine in the world. This First Growth Pauillac of 222 acres (90 hectares), is quoted more often than any other red wine as being the height of elegance, indulgence and expense. I wish I could draw near in humble mood to worship at this shrine of perfection but I can't, and the reason is simply that the wine is so wretchedly inconsistent. I *have* had some wonderful bottles – a cedarwood scent and fragrant blackcurrant, mingled with tobacco and kitchen spice – unnervingly light in the mouth yet entrancingly persistent in their beauty long after the last lingering sip has drained the glass. Yet in great years like 1970, '66, '62 and '61 I feel let down because the expectation was so great and the experience so limp and timid. There does seem to be a new mood in Lafite as far as more serious wine-making in the 1980s goes, but I still find the château and the wine rather distant and aloof. Since Lafite often takes 15 years to weave its subtle strands into cloth of gold, and *can* need 30 years or more to come finally into balance, we won't know for a while yet quite how good the 'new' Lafites are going to be. Even so – these look to be the best years: 1988, '86, '84, '82, '81, '79, '76.

LAFLEUR, CH.
Pomerol AC
BORDEAUX

🍷 Merlot, Cabernet Franc

This tiny vineyard of only 9 acres (3·6 hectares) has some of Pomerol's oldest vines, some of Pomerol's most traditional wine-making, and the potential to equal Pétrus for sheer power and flavour. In fact Christian Moueix of Pétrus recognizes the quality of his rival, and now takes charge of operations here. The best of Lafleur is to come, because

Moueix only took over in 1981, but vintages like '82, '83 and '85 already exhibit a massive, old-fashioned, unsubtle brute strength loaded with the fatness of oak and soaked in the sweet fruit of plums – unforgettable mouthfuls which will need years to evolve into memorable wines, but I'm confident they'll get there in the end.

LAFON-ROCHET, CH.
St-Estèphe AC, *4ème cru classé*
HAUT-MÉDOC, BORDEAUX

Cabernet Sauvignon, Merlot

I have been a fan of Lafon-Rochet ever since the 1970 vintage, not only for the full, almost honey-edged, dark fruit which usually finds it easy to keep the St-Estèphe earthiness well in check, but also because I can afford it. There weren't many wines I could afford when I bought the 1970 so I was extremely grateful to Lafon-Rochet – and still am – for the chance to possess a case of Classed Growth claret. That said, the owner has been 'improving' Lafon-Rochet since 1960 and nearly 30 years of investment and effort should be showing more regular results than Lafon-Rochet has yet achieved. The vineyard is a good one – 110 acres (45 hectares) at the western end of the slopes which Cos d'Estournel also occupies – but perhaps there is just a little too much Cabernet Sauvignon (80 per cent with 20 per cent Merlot) for these heavy clay soils; Merlot ripens more easily on clay and adds crucial richness to otherwise rather austere wines. Best years: 1988, '87, '86, '85, '83, '82, '79.

LAGRANGE, CH.
St-Julien AC, *3ème cru classé*
HAUT-MÉDOC, BORDEAUX

Cabernet Sauvignon, Merlot

Bruno Prats of Cos d'Estournel, one of Bordeaux red's high-flier properties, looked out into the backwoods of St-Julien and told me that Lagrange had potentially one of the finest vineyards in the whole Médoc. He should know, I thought, but I must say that this ramshackle, lumbering estate – 120 acres (50 hectares) of vines at the very western borders of St-Julien – didn't seem a likely candidate for super-stardom. However Monsieur Prats knew that land and knew the quality; and since Lagrange was bought by the Japanese Suntory company in 1983 the leap in quality has been astonishing. No longer an amiable, shambling St-Julien, but instead a clear-eyed, single-minded wine of tremendous fruit, meticulous wine-making and superb quality. Best years: 1988, '86, '85, '83, '82. Second wine: les Fiefs de Lagrange.

LA LAGUNE, CH.
Haut-Médoc AC, *3ème cru classé*
HAUT-MÉDOC, BORDEAUX

Cabernet Sauvignon, Cabernet Franc, Merlot, Petit Verdot

La Lagune has given me more pleasure than any other single wine. A chap who worked for a brewery, Reg was his name, sidled up to me one day and intimated that he might be possessed of something I could find to my liking. Château La Lagune 1961. Thirty bob a bottle. 'Er, how many bottles?' 'One hundred and two,' came the reply. Eight and a half cases of 1961 claret? Well, out came the life savings – and I got them. The lot!

Now, the experts say that 1961 wasn't a success at La Lagune, but I can only say that no wine has ever tasted of purer, sweeter, more luscious essence of blackcurrants than that wine did. It's fading now, and I've only a bottle or two left, but if you ever pass by my flat and hear Thomas Beecham's recording of La Bohème blasting at full tilt into the cold night air, you'll know I'm up there with a few of my friends singing, laughing and swigging back the last of my La Lagune '61!

So you can see I find it difficult to think of La Lagune in brass-tack terms – but here are a few facts. It's a Third Growth, Haut-Médoc AC, just to the south of Margaux, and the closest Classed Growth to Bordeaux. The wine is consistently excellent, richer, spicier now than my 1961 was, but full of the charry chestnut sweetness of good oak and a deep, cherry-blackcurrant-and-plums sweetness to the fruit which, after ten years or more, is outstanding Bordeaux, always accessible, yet perfect for the long haul. Best years: 1988, '86, '85, '83, '82, '78, '76, '75.

LALANDE-DE-POMEROL AC
BORDEAUX

Merlot, Cabernet Franc, Cabernet Sauvignon, Malbec

Although Lalande-de-Pomerol is regarded as a Pomerol satellite, with nearly 2500 acres (1000 hectares) of vines it is actually bigger than Pomerol at 1800 acres (725 hectares). The wines are usually full, soft, plummy and even chocolaty, very attractive to drink at only three to four years old, but ageing reasonably well. They lack the mineral edge and the concentration of top Pomerols, but are nonetheless extremely attractive, full, ripe wines. They're not cheap, but then nothing with the name Pomerol included in it *is* cheap these days. Best years: 1988, '87, '85, '83, '82. Best properties: Annereaux, Bel-Air, Belles-Graves, Bertineau, Clos des Templiers, Grand-Ormeau, Hautes-Tuileries, Lavaud-la-Maréchaude, St-Vincent, Siaurac, Tournefeuille.

LARMANDE, CH.
St-Émilion AC, *grand cru classé*
BORDEAUX

Merlot, Cabernet Franc, Cabernet Sauvignon

One of those wines which is so creamy, so juicy, so full of coconut spice and gooey fruit that you can't quite take it seriously. But why not? If drinking wine is supposed to be about pleasure, having fun, then Larmande is a very 'serious' wine indeed! The estate is 46 acres (18·5 hectares) situated directly north of the town of St-Émilion, and is a rising star. No-one had heard of Larmande till 1975 when the owners decided to invest and improve. Since then the rich, heady flavours of Larmande have stood out in tastings whenever the wine is shown. Best years: 1988, '85, '83, '82, '81.

LAROSE-TRINTAUDON, CH.
Haut-Médoc AC, *cru grand bourgeois*
HAUT-MÉDOC, BORDEAUX

Cabernet Sauvignon, Cabernet Franc, Merlot

The largest property in the Médoc – 425 acres (172 hectares) in St-Laurent, producing some 65,000 cases of wine! It's a real success story because the Forner brothers who owned it until 1986 had to plant this massive vineyard from scratch in 1966. They aimed to produce large amounts of good quality, affordable, red Bordeaux. Direct easy flavours at a decent price is what they were after – and they achieved it almost every year. Rumour has it it's the most popular red Bordeaux in the United States. The wines are made to drink at about five years old but can age for ten. Best years: 1988, '86, '85, '84, '83, '82, '81, '78.

LASCOMBES, CH.
Margaux AC, *2ème cru classé*
HAUT-MÉDOC, BORDEAUX

Cabernet Sauvignon, Merlot, Cabernet Franc, Petit Verdot

A large and important Second Growth which hasn't really managed to match the efforts of its peers for some time. This could be because the remarkable achievement of properties like Léoville-Las-Cases and Pichon-Lalande are due to the dedication of a single owner, whereas Lascombes is owned by the massive Bass-Charrington brewing combine. However, Rausan-Ségla, one of the most rapidly improving Second Growths, is owned by a large multi-national, as is Latour, the most consistent of the First Growths. No, it's a case of the will to excel not being very evident. Hopefully the most recent vintages – promising some of the tantalizing fresh flowers and blackcurrant perfume of which Lascombes is capable – will mark a permanent improvement. If not, we shall have to go on drinking the Chevalier de Lascombes rosé which is rather good. Best years: 1988, '87, '86, '85, '83, '82.

LATOUR, CH.
Pauillac AC, *premier cru classé*
HAUT-MÉDOC, BORDEAUX

Cabernet Sauvignon, Cabernet Franc, Merlot, Petit Verdot

The first bottle of Château Latour I ever had was the 1954. Or was it '56? It doesn't matter really: both years were truly lousy vintages in Bordeaux and mercifully few bottles ever surfaced. Lousy vintages? Yes. Although not as lousy as the next two vintages – '63 and '65. Hang on. Why am I talking about what is undoubtedly one of Bordeaux's greatest properties in these terms? Simple. Firstly, I could actually afford to buy the '54 and the '56 Latour. Secondly, they were absolutely and characteristically delicious. *That's* why.

In years when the rest of Bordeaux might as well have packed up and gone home without pressing a grape, Latour stuck to it and produced good wine. All through the 1950s, '60s and '70s Latour stood for integrity, consistency and refusal to compromise in the face of considerable financial pressure. The result was that in poor years the wine was good; in merely adequate years – like 1960, '67, '74, the wine was excellent. In great years like 1966, '70, '75 and '82, Latour's personality – the sheer power of blackcurrant fruit, the temple columns of tannin daring anyone to broach a bottle before its twentieth year, the full-tilt charge of cedar-dry flavours, rich, expensive, but as unconcerned with fashion and fawning as a fifteenth-generation duke – marks it as the most imperious of Pauillac's three First Growths.

Interestingly, the 150-acre (60-hectare) vineyard is on the southern side of the AC, bordering St-Julien. This might lead one to expect a lighter style of wine, but the vineyard, with 75 per cent Cabernet Sauvignon, ten per cent Cabernet Franc, five per cent Petit Verdot and only ten per cent Merlot, gives as big and proudly impressive a wine as any in Bordeaux.

Strangely, in the '80s, there has been an attempt to make lighter wines. It is by no means a total success – and in any case completely unnecessary because Latour's reputation is built on power and longevity. And although the '82 is a classic, I haven't been impressed by '83 and '81. I (and all Latour's other fans) hope this is only a temporary aberration; '86 and '88 brought a return to classic Latour. Best years: 1988, '86, '82, '81, '79, '78, '75, '70. Second wine: les Forts de Latour.

LATOUR-À-POMEROL, CH.
Pomerol AC
BORDEAUX

Merlot, Cabernet Franc

I first got to like Latour-à-Pomerol because it made an absolutely fabulous 1973, gorgeously soft and ripe with a delicious hint of mint. This luscious, almost juicy fruit, soft and *very* easy to drink, has been a mark of Latour-à-Pomerol, but the wines do age well. Recent vintages, now directed by Christian Moueix of Pétrus, show a beefier, brawnier style, but the super-ripe softness of fruit is still there, so I'm not worried. The vineyard covers 20 acres (8 hectares). Best years: 1988, '85, '83, '82, '81, '79.

LATRICIÈRES-CHAMBERTIN AC
grand cru
CÔTE DE NUITS, BURGUNDY

Pinot Noir

Yet another of the *grands crus* of Gevrey-Chambertin, this time a 17-acre (7-hectare) stretch of vines at the southern boundary of the commune. Only about 2500 cases are produced and the wine can be very fragrant although not, as some people claim, almost the equal of the best wines in Chambertin – it rarely has the intensity or the rich swathe of perfume which suffuses the best Chambertins from the best growers. Best years: 1988, '87, '85, '83, '80. Best producers: Camus, Rémy, Trapet.

LAUDUN
Côtes du Rhône-Villages AC
SOUTHERN RHÔNE

Grenache, Syrah, Cinsaut

Clairette, Roussanne, Bourboulenc

One of the best Côtes du Rhône-Villages, and one with a particular reputation for whites and rosés. Situated on the flatter land to the west of the Rhône river, and without the concentrated power which comes from the villages at the steeper slopes to the east, the reds are best when they emphasize the gentle, spicy fruit of the Grenache. The wines are fresher and fruitier than any other Côtes du Rhône-Villages except those of Chusclan. Rosé and red are for drinking young. The whites, from Clairette, Roussanne and Bourboulenc, tend to be more aromatic than most whites made around here, without losing that vital, freshening acidity. Best years: 1988, '85, '83. Best producers: Laudun co-operative, Pelaquie, Vignerons des Quatres Chemins.

LÉOVILLE-BARTON, CH.
St-Julien AC, *2ème cru classé*
HAUT-MÉDOC, BORDEAUX

Cabernet Sauvignon, Merlot, Petit Verdot, Cabernet Franc

Anthony Barton, whose family has run this Second Growth St-Julien since 1821, has resolutely refused to profiteer in spite of considerable pressure for him to do so, especially in the early to mid-1980s, when every vintage was released at a substantially higher price than the last regardless of actual worth. But Anthony Barton refused to raise prices above a level he considered fair. By 1986 he was charging only half what one or two of his more ambitious neighbours thought reasonable. Yet as he freely declares, he runs a profitable business with Léoville-Barton. He knows what it costs to make fine wine, he never stints on quality, and he certainly doesn't intend to make a less than satisfactory profit. So thank you, Mr Barton. And your wine? Old-fashioned, classically proportioned, excellent. This 100-acre (40-hectare) estate – with 70 per cent Cabernet Sauvignon, seven per cent Cabernet Franc, eight per cent Petit Verdot and only 15 per cent Merlot – makes dark, dry, tannic wines, difficult to taste young and therefore frequently underestimated at the outset, but over 10–15 years achieving a lean yet beautifully proportioned quality, the blackcurrants and cedarwood very dry, but pungent enough to fill the room with their scent. A traditionalist's delight. All the vintages in the '80s have been attractive, and the '88 is one of the best wines of the Médoc. Best years: 1988, '87, '86, '85, '83, '82, '80, '78, '75.

LÉOVILLE-LAS-CASES, CH.
St-Julien AC, *2ème cru classé*
HAUT-MÉDOC, BORDEAUX

Cabernet Sauvignon, Merlot, Cabernet Franc, Petit Verdot

St-Julien wasn't accorded a First Growth in the 1855 Classification. Any re-evaluation would change all that, because in Léoville-Las-Cases, St-Julien has a property and an owner whose total dedication to quality, whose ruthless, even dour, pursuit of perfection would put most First Growths to shame. Going to meet Monsieur Delon who runs Léoville-Las-Cases is rather like having an audience with your headmaster at school, but I've undergone a couple of these challenging, uncompromising tasting sessions in his cellars, and I can only say, with gratitude, that they've given me more understanding about the passion that is great Bordeaux than any amount of money could buy.

The Léoville-Las-Cases vineyard, at 210 acres (85 hectares), is the biggest of the three Léovilles, and a direct neighbour of the great Latour. There are similarities in the wine because Las-Cases, since 1975, has been making wines of startling, dark, deep concentration. Yet there is also something sweeter, something more enticing right from the start – the fumes of new oak spice linger over the glass even in the wine's most stubborn adolescent sulks, and the tannins, strong though they are, have a habit of dissolving into smiles in your mouth exactly at the moment you've decided that they're just too much. I reckon that, along with Ducru-Beaucaillou, this is the most exciting of all the St-Juliens. Las-Cases from a good year really needs 15 years and should happily last for 30. Best years: 1988, '86, '85, '83, '82, '81, '79, '78, '75. Second wine: Clos du Marquis.

LÉOVILLE-POYFERRÉ, CH.
St-Julien AC, *2ème cru classé*
HAUT-MÉDOC, BORDEAUX

Cabernet Sauvignon, Merlot

A glittering name from the distant past, and I mean *distant*. I haven't had a single exciting bottle from this faded famous name, although I was once offered some '66 bottled in England which seemed to have improved with the journey and the '67 I got hold of in Welwyn Garden City wasn't too bad except for a slightly disturbing tarmac smell which may have come from the nearby roadworks . . . It's a big vineyard of 156 acres (63 hectares), bang in the middle of the best part of St-Julien, but you'd never know, and if it weren't for hopeful signs of effort and investment since the 1982 vintage, I don't think I'd have included it in this book at all.

LIRAC AC
SOUTHERN RHÔNE

Grenache, Cinsaut, Syrah, Mourvèdre

Clairette, Bourboulenc, Picpoul and others

An excellent, but underrated AC between Tavel and Châteauneuf-du-Pape in the southern Rhône, making wines which resemble both its more famous neighbours. There are 1630 acres (660 hectares) of vines producing 2·5 million bottles, more than 95 per cent of it red and rosé, though production of white is increasing. The red has the dusty, spicy fruit of Châteauneuf-du-Pape, without achieving the intensity of the best examples, plus an attractive metallic streak which is unusual but good. Rosés are breezier, more refreshing than Tavel, and can have a lovely strawberry fruit. Reds age very well but are always delicious young. Rosés should be drunk sharpish. Best years (reds): 1988, '86, '85, '83. Best producers (reds): Assémat (Causses et St-Eymes and Garrigues), Devoy, Fermade, St-Roch, Ségriès, la Tour.

Only a tiny proportion of Lirac product is white, but I wish there were more bottles around because white Lirac can be as good as white Châteauneuf-du-Pape when it's on form. Clairette is the chief grape, with other local varieties like Bourboulenc and Picpoul added. You must drink it young though, because the perfume goes and what's left is nice, soft Rhône white – which tastes OK, but not a patch on what was there before. Best producer (whites): Maby.

▼ At work in the Lirac vineyards. This small AC makes reds and rosés; the best reds in the style of Châteauneuf-du-Pape.

LISTRAC AC
HAUT-MÉDOC, BORDEAUX

Cabernet Sauvignon, Cabernet Franc, Merlot and others

One of the six specific ACs inside the Haut-Médoc area, but not possessing any Classed Growths. All the best Haut-Médoc vineyards are on gravel soil and the majority of them on ridges and plateaux within sight of the Gironde estuary. Listrac is set several miles back from the Gironde, its 1410 acres (570 hectares) of vineyards fashioned on outcrops of partially gravelled heavy soil, encircled by forest. Even so, the wine can be good, although the relative lack of gravel means few of its vines have the tantalizing fragrance of top Margaux or St-Julien wines, being nearer to St-Estèphe in style. Solid fruit, a lightly coarse tannin and an earthy flavour are the marks of most Listracs. Château Clarke is the classiest property. Best years: 1988, '86, '85, 83, '82, '78. Best properties: la Bécade, Cap-Léon-Veyrin, Clarke, Fonréaud, Fourcas-Dupré, Fourcas-Hosten, Grand Listrac co-operative, Lestage.

LOIRE

The Loire river cuts right through the heart of France, east to west. It rises at a mere 30 miles (50km) from the Rhône valley and, after surging northwards, executes a graceful arc up to Orléans and then sets off for the sea.

Along the way the Loire manages to encompass some of France's best-known wines – Sancerre, Anjou, Muscadet – with some of its most obscure – Jasnières, Bonnezeaux, Vin de l'Orléanais. Altogether there are about a hundred different wines made in the Loire valley – reds, rosés, sparkling, and the entire gamut of whites from searingly dry to unctuously sweet.

The upper reaches of the Loire don't produce a great quantity of wine, but what there is has become world-famous, because this is the home of Sancerre and Pouilly-Fumé.

The province of Touraine is a positive market garden, with vines taking their place alongside a host of other crops, but the Sauvignon grape excels here too, and at Vouvray and Montlouis, the Chenin makes pretty good fizz and still whites ranging from sweet to very dry. The Loire's best reds are made here at Chinon and Bourgueil from Cabernet Franc. Anjou is most famous for rosé, though there are some decent reds, but the best wines are white, either sweet from the Layon valley or very dry Chenin from Savennières. Saumur's sparklers are well-known and reasonably good.

Finally, in the low flatland around Nantes they grow that uncomplicated white, Muscadet.

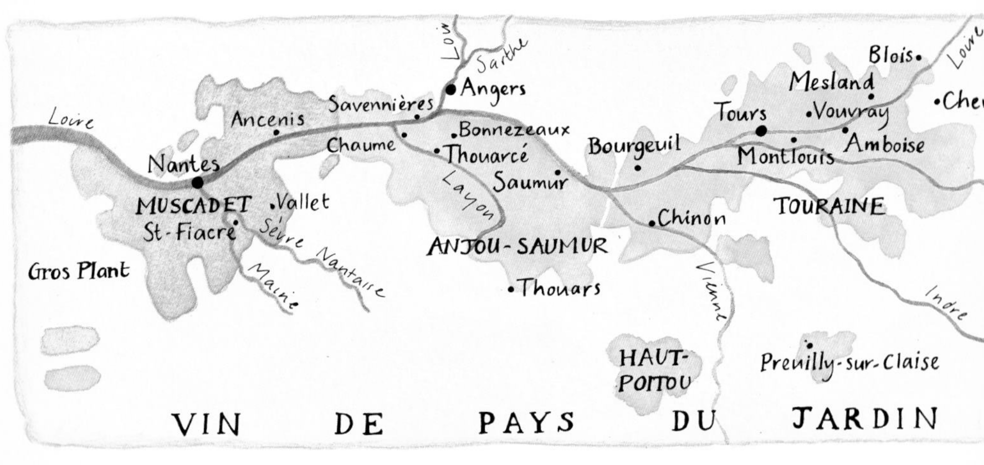

WINE ENTRIES

- Anjou
- Anjou-Villages
- Bonnezeaux
- Bourgueil
- Cabernet d'Anjou
- Châteaumeillant
- Cheverny
- Chinon
- Coteaux d'Ancenis
- Coteaux de l'Aubance
- Coteaux du Giennois
- Coteaux du Layon
- Coteaux du Layon-Villages
- Coteaux du Vendômois
- Côte Roannaise
- Côtes d'Auvergne
- Crémant de Loire
- Gros Plant du Pays Nantais
- Haut-Poitou
- Jasnières
- Menetou-Salon
- Montlouis
- Muscadet
- Muscadet de Sèvre-et-Maine
- Muscadet des Coteaux de la Loire
- Pouilly-Fumé
- Pouilly-sur-Loire
- Quarts de Chaume
- Quincy
- Reuilly
- Rosé d'Anjou
- Rosé de Loire
- St-Nicolas-de Bourgueil
- St-Pourçain-sur-Sioule
- Sancerre
- Saumur
- Saumur-Champigny
- Saumur Mousseux
- Savennières
- Touraine
- Vin de l'Orléanais
- Vin de Pays du Jardin de la France
- Vouvray

GRAPE ENTRIES

- Cabernet Franc
- Cabernet Sauvignon
- Chardonnay
- Chenin Blanc
- Gamay
- Pinot Noir
- Sauvignon Blanc

◀ Sancerre, in the Upper Loire, produces one of France's trendiest white wines – from the super-tangy Sauvignon Blanc – and a less exciting red, from Pinot Noir. Someone likes the red though – plantings are on the increase.

LOUDENNE, CH.
Médoc AC, *cru grand bourgeois*
BORDEAUX

Red: Cabernet Sauvignon, Merlot, Cabernet Franc

White: Sauvignon Blanc

In a way, I'd rather write about the *place* Château Loudenne than the wine. It is a lovely, warm-welcome, pink château set on the banks of the Gironde – fields and vines to the back, paths and croquet lawn to the front. Sounds a bit English? Well, it is. The property was bought by the Gilbeys of London in 1875 and ever since has been a little outpost of mild-mannered English hospitality in the northern Médoc. The wine is mild-mannered too. More so than I'd like, really, because the red is often so gentle and buttery that there seems to be no acid and tannin at all which doesn't make for exciting drinking. Gentle about describes the white too. Best years: 1988, '86, '85, '83, '82.

LOUPIAC AC
BORDEAUX

White: Sémillon, Muscadelle, Sauvignon Blanc

A sweet wine area directly across the Garonne from Barsac. But the Loupiac growers, despite using the same grapes, can't persuade noble rot to affect their vines nearly so frequently as it does in Barsac, and they do have a far higher permitted yield – 40 hectolitres per hectare as against Barsac's 25 hectolitres per hectare. Despite this, there are some good estates producing wine which is attractively sweet, if not really gooey. Drink young, though it can age. Best years: 1988, '86, '85, '83. Best producers: du Cros, Loupiac-Gaudiet, Mazarin, de Ricaud.

LUSSAC-ST-ÉMILION AC
BORDEAUX

Red: Merlot, Cabernet Franc, Cabernet Sauvignon, Malbec

There are 2700 acres (1100 hectares) of vines in Lussac, a few miles to the north of St-Émilion town; much of the wine is made by the co-operative at neighbouring Puisseguin, and we see few single-estate wines on the export market. Properties like Lyonnat make mouthfillers for a ten-year haul. Best years: 1988, '85, '83, '82. Best properties: Barbe-Blanche, Cap de Merle, Courlat, Lyonnat, Villadière.

LYNCH-BAGES, CH.
Pauillac AC, *5ème cru classé*
HAUT-MÉDOC, BORDEAUX

Red: Cabernet Sauvignon, Merlot, Cabernet Franc, Petit Verdot

Sometimes, tasting this wonderful wine with its almost succulent richness, its gentle texture and its starburst of flavours all butter and blackcurrants and mint, I find myself reflecting that its comparatively lowly position as a Fifth Growth Pauillac can only be because the chaps who devised the 1855 Classification were basically puritans. They couldn't bear to admit that a wine as open-heartedly lovely as Lynch-Bages could really be as important as other less generous Growths. Well, it is. Wine is about pleasure. Great wine is about great pleasure and there are few wines in the world which will so regularly give you such great pleasure as Lynch-Bages. The 175 acres (70 hectares) of vines in the middle of the AC, near the town of Pauillac, are planted in the traditional Pauillac mix, with a lot of Cabernet Sauvignon – 70 per cent – a certain amount of Cabernet Franc and Petit Verdot totalling 15 per cent, and only 15 per cent Merlot. This sounds like a tough wine taking a long time to mature – but that's the magic of Lynch-Bages – beautiful at ten years old, even more beautiful at 20. Best years: 1988, '87, '86, '85, '83, '82, '81, '79, '78. Second wine: Haut-Bages-Avérous.

MÂCON AC & MÂCON SUPÉRIEUR AC
MÂCONNAIS, BURGUNDY

Red, Rosé: Pinot Noir, Gamay

White: Chardonnay

The Mâconnais region produces either Mâcon or Mâcon Supérieur. Supérieur is rarely a quality indicator, merely a sign that the wine has reached a minimum alcohol level one degree higher than straight Mâcon. That means 11 degrees instead of 10 for the white, 10 instead of 9 for the red. Whatever the rules, these figures are almost always exceeded. This is the most basic AC in the Mâconnais, accounting for three million of the 14 million bottles produced. It is increasingly used for red wines, but has been usurped by the superior Mâcon-Villages for whites. Whatever the colour, the flavours are rarely exciting: the re usually has a 'rooty', vegetal rasp, and the rosé lacks the fresh, breezy perfume which can make pink wine such fun. Mâcon Blanc used to be a cheap, bland quaffer. Now it is a rather expensive basic quaffer, since the magic name Chardonnay has allowed prices to boom. Quality has rarely kept pace with prices, and it is generally worth moving up to Mâcon-Villages if you want more than simple lemony zing. Occasionally, good wines will appear from quality-conscious shippers like Duboeuf, but in any case the wine should be drunk as young as possible. Best year: 1988.

MÂCON-VILLAGES AC
MÂCONNAIS, BURGUNDY

Chardonnay

I used to wax and wane, enthusiastic or despairing, about Mâcon-Villages in fairly equal proportions, but I must admit that recently there's been a lot more waning than waxing. The period 1981–87 saw a series of good to excellent vintages. There was no excuse whatsoever for us not to see a steady stream of enjoyable, fruity, fresh, creamy Mâcon-Villages Chardonnay wines flowing out of the region at a fair price. However, this same period has seen the revival of Bordeaux as a producer of attractive whites, and we've also been regaled and seduced by the Chardonnays of Australia and New Zealand – twice the flavour and cheaper every time.

Chardonnay can be a blessing and a curse. It is a marvellous, easy-growing grape producing lots of good wine at not too great a cost – that's the blessing. The curse is the name: 'Chardonnay' has a magic ring, and white Burgundy is Chardonnay's most sought-after manifestation, so Mâconnais wine is ripe for exploitation. Mâcon-Villages can be very attractive, direct wine – appley, with a touch of honey warmth – and as such it deserves a fair price, not a grand one. At the moment, it can be more expensive than a Sancerre or a Graves.

Altogether there are 43 villages which can either call their wine Mâcon-Villages or else append their own name – as in Mâcon-Viré for the village of Viré. The bulk of the best 'Villages' wine comes from the northern Mâconnais; Mâcon-Lugny, Mâcon-Viré and Mâcon-Clessé are the most frequently seen labels. Other good villages include Uchizy, Chardonnay (probable birthplace of the vine), Igé, St-Gengoux-de-Scissé and, in the south, Prissé and Charnay. Eighty-five per cent of Mâconnais wines are made by co-ops who are as strong here as anywhere in France. Best years: 1988. Best producers: Bonhomme, de Chervin, Domaine de la Condemine, Guichard, Pierre Mahuet, Manciat-Poncet, de Roally, Jean Thévenet, Tissier, co-operatives at Chardonnay, Clessé, Lugny, Prissé, St-Gengoux-de-Scissé, Viré.

MÂCONNAIS
BURGUNDY

The Mâconnais is the large, 14,825-acre (6000-hectare) vineyard area based on the town of Mâcon, south of the Côte Chalonnaise and directly north of Beaujolais. Two-thirds of it is planted with Chardonnay, and all of the most interesting Mâconnais wines are white. Gamay accounts for a further 25 per cent of the vineyard, and Pinot Noir makes up the remaining 7·5 per cent. However, the reds have failed to make a name for themselves. Lack of perfume, dominant earthy tastes, and a fairly high acid/tannin level are the main problems. Gamay reds are normally sold as Mâcon and Mâcon Supérieur; Pinot reds are sold as Bourgogne and, from a good producer, can have a pleasant light strawberry taste. A blend of both grapes, with at least one-third Pinot Noir, is sold as Bourgogne Passe-Tout-Grain. The rosés should be drunk very young, and the reds within a couple of years, because the fruit fades before the toughness softens. The co-operatives at Buxy (in the Chalonnaise), Igé and Mancey make reasonable wines.

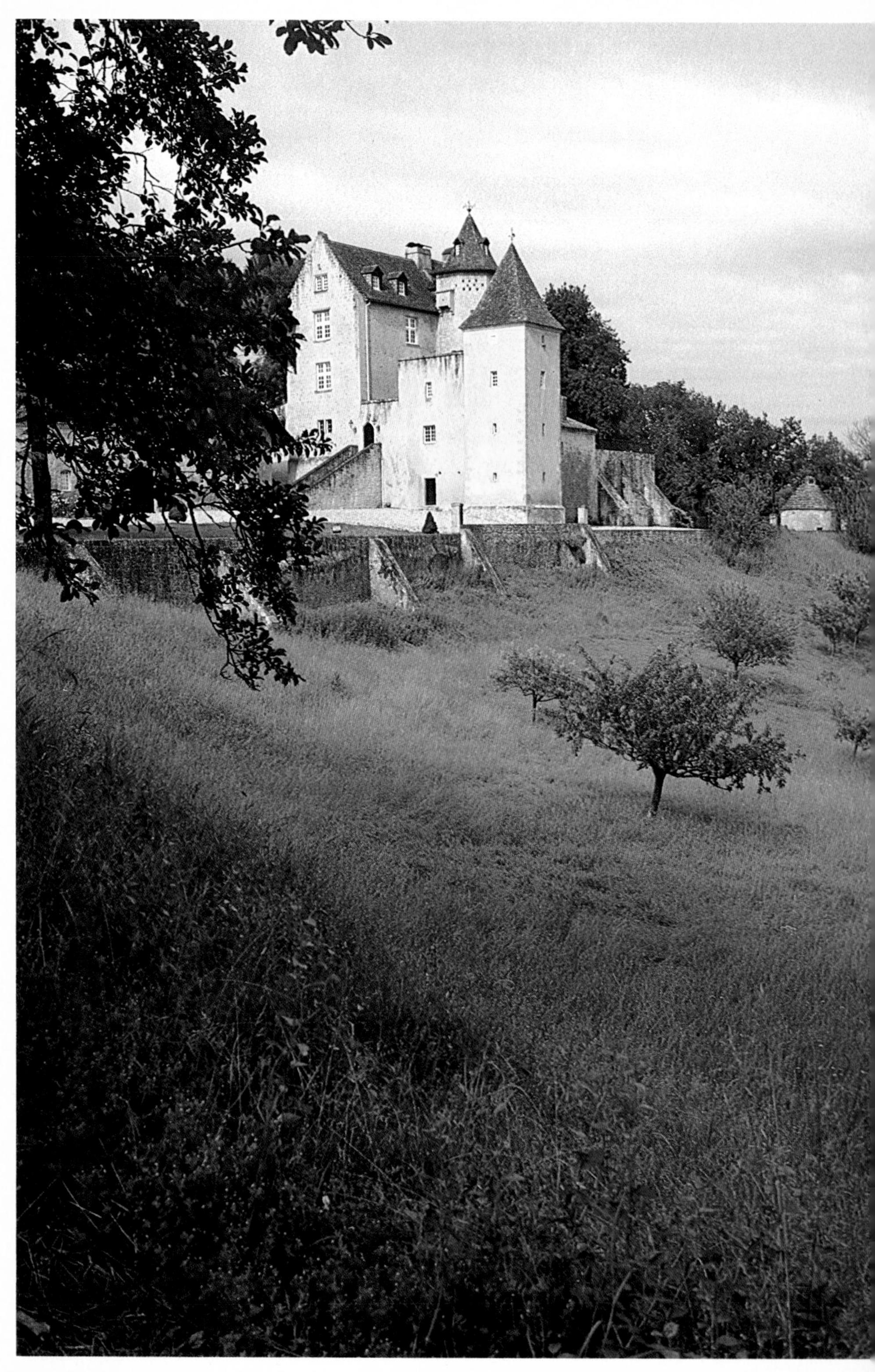

MADIRAN AC
SOUTH-WEST

Tannat, Cabernet Sauvignon, Cabernet Franc

◀ The medieval château of Arricau-Bordes makes its Madiran wine from 50% Tannat and 50% Cabernet Sauvignon/Franc.

I am not one of Madiran's greatest fans. With few exceptions, I find the wine heavy, aggressive and short on personality. It often has the weight of a Médoc or a Graves but never has the complex excitement of flavour and perfume. Too much tannin is the problem. The tannic Tannat grape is the main variety up to a maximum of 60 per cent; Fer, Cabernet Sauvignon and Cabernet Franc make up the difference. Fans of Madiran will say I haven't waited long enough, that the wine becomes soft and limpid with age. Well, if it does, it will be an amazing transformation.

The vineyards are in the wonderfully relaxing Vic Bilh hills just south of Armagnac; they had virtually died out after World War Two, being down to 15 acres (6 hectares). The Tannat grape had become too degenerate to cultivate, but modern botanical science found a way, and now there are 2000 acres (800 hectares). One thing that does help Madiran achieve a more attractive style is new oak and several of the best producers (like Château Montus) are now using it. Best years: 1988, '85, '83, '82, '81, '78. Best producers: Arricau-Bordes, Aydie, Boucassé, Cru du Paradis, Montus, Peyros, Union des Producteurs de Plaimont.

MAGDELAINE, CH.
St-Émilion AC, *premier grand cru classé*
BORDEAUX

🍷 Merlot, Cabernet Franc

Very much a wine of two personalities. In lighter years – because of its tremendously high percentage of Merlot (80 per cent) – the wine has a gushing, tender juicy fruit, easy to drink at only four to five years old, which seems to epitomize the indulgent softness of St-Émilion. However, in the grand vintages, Magdelaine changes gear. Those 27 acres (11 hectares) of Merlot-dominated vineyard sit on the steep slopes just south-west of the town of St-Émilion – a plum position for super-ripeness. Because the property is owned by the quality-obsessed J-P Moueix company in Libourne, the grapes are left to hang until the last possible moment, then an army of pickers swoops in. This gives grapes with a significantly higher ripeness than in neighbouring vineyards. Then the wine is fermented long and slow, stalks are added in to impart tannin and structure, and the wine is then aged in predominantly new barrels for a year-and-a-half. The result? Dark, rich, aggressive wines, yet behind the tough exterior there is a whole pile of luscious fruit and oaky spice waiting for release. Lighter vintages such as 1981 and '79 can be enjoyed at five to ten years old; bigger years like '85, '83 and '82 will take 15. Best years: 1988, '87, '85, '83, '82, '81, '75.

MALARTIC-LAGRAVIÈRE, CH.
Pessac-Léognan AC, *cru classé de Graves*
BORDEAUX

🍷 Cabernet Sauvignon, Cabernet Franc, Merlot

🍸 Sauvignon Blanc

One of the few Pessac-Léognan Classed Growths whose reputation has been upheld by its white rather than its red wine (though the red is also good). It is a strange property, set in 35 acres (14 hectares) near the woods just south of Léognan, and is a neighbour of de Fieuzal. The vineyard is atypical with only 44 per cent Cabernet Sauvignon, 31 per cent Cabernet Franc and 25 per cent Merlot for the reds. The little block of white vines – just under 5 acres (2 hectares) – is all Sauvignon Blanc, with no Sémillon at all. White Malartic-Lagravière is given new oak ageing, but still has a startling nettle green fruit at first, which then softens over three to four years into a really lovely nutty Graves.

Malartic-Lagravière produces more red wine per hectare than any other *cru classé*, frequently having to declassify some of the crop. These factors should lead to a light, easy-drinking style. Well, they don't. The owner is adamant that heavy cropping suits his wine, and I can only say that, although Malartic-Lagravière does often start out a little lean and dry, it ages brilliantly. The 1955 is only now fading; the '70 is nowhere near ready. I can't explain it, and, frankly, nor can the owner. But it's a fact! Best years (reds): 1988, '87, '85, '83, '82, '81. Best years (whites): 1988, '87, '86, '85, '84, '83, '82, '81.

MALBEC

Malbec only really produces exciting wine in Cahors (where it is known as Auxerrois), although it is also planted in the Loire where they call it Cot, as well as in Bordeaux (where the St-Émilion growers call it Pressac!).

Its contribution in Bordeaux is to give a slightly squashy softness to reds in areas like Bourg and Blaye, while in the Loire region it can also have a soothing effect when Cabernet Franc is cutting up rough. However, in the warmer climate of Cahors it steps up to centre stage, making up a minimum of 70 per cent of the *appellation*'s historic red wine and producing deep, chewy plum-and-tobacco-flavoured wine quite unlike any other in France. Total plantings are about 12,350 acres (5000 hectares).

DE MALLE, CH.

Sauternes AC, *2ème cru classé*
BORDEAUX

Sémillon, Sauvignon Blanc, Muscadelle

Even if you don't taste the wine, Château de Malle is one of Bordeaux's loveliest estates. The de Bournazel family have owned it for more than 500 years, and the present château – shown on the label of the wine, with the wrought iron gates making an elegant frame – was designed in the seventeenth century and set in the midst of lawns and an Italian garden. That all this survives – and didn't go under the hammer during the Sauternes slump of the '50s to '70s – is because Comte de Bournazel was one of the first to see the slackening demand for fine sweet wine and to diversify into dry red and dry white. The wine itself is more like a Barsac than a Sauternes, with a soft, brazil-nuts-in-caramel sweetness and light, lemon peel acidity. You can drink it at five years old but good vintages will be better at ten. Best years: 1988, '86, '83, '80.

MARANGES AC

CÔTE DE BEAUNE, BURGUNDY

Pinot Noir

In 1989 this single AC was created to represent ACs Cheilly-lès Maranges, Dezize-lès-Maranges and Sampigny-lès-Maranges. The wines rarely have much excitement about them, being rather thin and shallow even in the best vintages, although they can sometimes have a pleasant strawberry perfume. In practice, most of the growers declare their wine as Côte de Beaune-Villages – a 'catch-all' *appellation* applying to 16 different Côte de Beaune communes – and that is probably the best fate for most of it.

MARCILLAC VDQS

SOUTH-WEST

Fer, Gamay, Jurançon Noir

Well at least I *have* tasted Marcillac red (though not the rosé), which is more than most people can say because the Aveyron *département* where it comes from, is an almost totally wineless area and the locals lap up the lot. In fact, there are 275 acres (110 hectares) of Marcillac – though you'd never notice it – and the Fer, at 80 per cent and often more, is the main grape type. The wine is strong and dry, rasping with herbs, grassy freshness and a slightly metallic zing. That may sound a bit off-putting, but you find me another red wine that can cope with the local Roquefort cheese! Best producer: Marcillac-Vallon co-operative.

MARGAUX AC

HAUT-MÉDOC, BORDEAUX

Cabernet Sauvignon, Cabernet Franc, Merlot and others

Margaux is the most sprawling of the six specific ACs in the Haut-Médoc. It covers 2850 acres (1150 hectares), just a little more than the more compact St-Estèphe's 2700 acres (1100 hectares) in the north. The vineyard is centred in the village of Margaux but also takes in the wine of Soussans to the north, and southwards, Cantenac, Labarde and Arsac. The key to Margaux's style is the pale gravel banks which cleave their way through the vineyards, giving little by way of nutrition but providing perfect drainage so that the wines are rarely heavy and should have a quite divine perfume when they mature at 7–12 years old.

The best examples of this style are La Gurgue, d'Issan, Labégorce-Zédé, Margaux, Palmer, Rausan-Ségla. A fuller, rounder but still perfumed style comes from the southern part of the AC, and is at its best from d'Angludet, Giscours, Siran, du Tertre. Altogether there are 21 Classed Growths in Margaux AC but many of these were underachieving in the '60s and '70s. Several, like Rausan-Ségla, Brane-Cantenac and Kirwan are only now waking up after a long sleep. There are a large number of non-classified properties – some regularly making Classed Growth quality wine. Most important is d'Angludet, followed by Siran, La Gurgue, Labégorce-Zédé and La Tour-de-Mons. Bottles labelled 'Margaux' shouldn't be taken too seriously since almost all the decent stuff sports a property's name. Best years: 1988, '86, '85, '83, '82, '81, '79, '78.

ARGAUX, CH.

argaux AC, *premier cru lassé*

AUT-MÉDOC, BORDEAUX

Cabernet Sauvignon, Merlot, etit Verdot, Cabernet Franc

Sauvignon Blanc

I first came across Château Margaux in a car park in the Rhône valley. It was lunchtime. I swigged it down with the *charcuterie*, and thought it uncommonly good. It was the 1961! Then a chap turned up one morning at my place for breakfast. He brought some Margaux to wet our whistles; the fruit and perfume in the wine swept aside the Weetabix and Cooper's Oxford marmalade with an imperious toss of the mane. That was the 1962. Then there was . . . in fact I realize I've only once sat down to a sensible dinner in a sensible place and drunk Château Margaux in a vaguely normal way. Even then I ended up having the 1961 poured over my strawberries with a twist of black pepper. Despite all this I think it is the greatest wine in the whole Médoc.

This large 210-acre (87-hectare) property, set back in the trees just outside the village of Margaux, gives a new meaning to the words perfume and fragrance in a red wine, as though an inspired *parfumeur* had somehow managed to combine a sweet essence of blackcurrants with oil from crushed violets and the haunting scent of cedarwood, then swirled them together with more earthy pleasures like vanilla, roasted nuts and plums, and spirited all these into the bottle. Between 1967 and 1977 the property was in decline, but since 1978 the Mentzelopoulos family, who bought it in 1977, have produced a flawless series of wines which are as great as any Margaux ever created. At one time everyone was saying that Margaux wasn't worth a place among the First Growths, but it's pistols at dawn for anyone who suggests that to me now. Best years (reds): 1988, '87, '86, '85, '83, '82, '81, '80, '79, '78. Second wine: Pavillon Rouge du Château Margaux.

Château Margaux also makes some white wine. The grapes don't come from the precious Margaux vineyards, but from an entirely separate holding in Soussans, outside the best red wine area. There are 25 acres (10 hectares) planted exclusively with Sauvignon Blanc, which is vinified at the château, but in a separate cellar so that the great red wine is not in any way affected. The result is delicious, but Pavillon Blanc du Château Margaux must be the most expensive Bordeaux AC by a mile. Best years (whites): 1988, '86, '85, '83.

ARSANNAY AC

ÔTE DE NUITS, BURGUNDY

Pinot Noir

Chardonnay

Marsannay is north of Fixin, with some if its vineyards virtually touching the suburbs of Dijon. Until 1987 it was famous only for its rosé which was Bourgogne AC but was allowed to include the Marsannay name on the label. Since 1987 Marsannay has been an AC in its own right for reds, whites and rosés. The rosé can be quite pleasant but nowadays is made too dry and austere. The red is a little rough-hewn, and lacks fruit, but can give a reasonable drink at three to four years old. Best years: 1987, '86, 85, '83, '82. Best producers: Clair, Fougeray, Huguenot, Quillardet.

MÉDOC

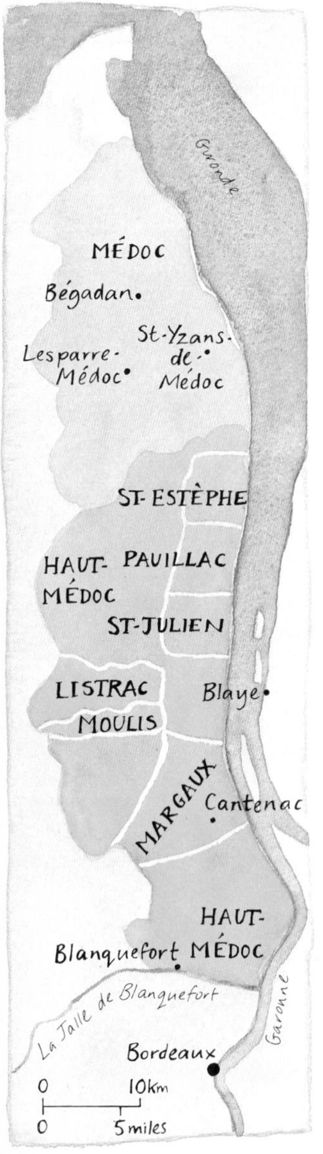

The Médoc produces a good fistful of the world's most renowned red wines, but it was a bit late in getting going, because until the seventeenth century this narrow lip of land running north from the city of Bordeaux was just marshland!

It's the gravel that makes Médoc wines great. Between the villages of Macau in the south near Bordeaux and St-Seurin-de-Cadourne in the north there are great banks of gravel, providing warm ripening conditions and perfect drainage for the Cabernet Sauvignon grape which dominates the vineyards. This whole area is called the Haut-Médoc – the Upper Médoc – and all the best wines come from here, from one of the half-a-dozen villages with the best gravel banks – Margaux, Listrac, Moulis, St-Julien, Pauillac and St-Estèphe – all with their own AC.

Further north the land becomes flatter, damper, verdant with pasture and dotted with quiet, welcoming villages. But the gravel isn't there any more, its place being taken by damp clay. The wines become fruitier, simpler, but drinkable much younger. This is the Bas-Médoc – the Low Médoc. But the AC is plain Médoc – the growers felt 'Low Médoc' was disparaging – and I can see the point.

AC ENTRIES
Haut-Médoc
Listrac
Margaux
Médoc
Moulis
Pauillac
St-Estèphe
St-Julien

CHÂTEAUX ENTRIES
d'Angludet
Batailley
Beychevelle
Calon-Ségur
Cantemerle
Chasse-Spleen
Cissac
Clarke
Cos d'Estournel
Ducru-Beaucaillou
Fourcas-Hosten
Giscours
Grand-Puy-Lacoste
Gruaud-Larose
Haut-Bages-Libéral
Haut-Batailley
Haut-Marbuzet
d'Issan
Lafite-Rothschild
Lafon-Rochet
Lagrange
la Lagune
Larmande
Larose-Trintaudon
Lascombes
Latour
Léoville-Barton
Léoville-Las-Cases
Léoville-Poyferré
Loudenne
Lynch-Bages
Margaux
Maucaillou
Meyney
Montrose
Mouton-Rothschild
Palmer
de Pez
Pichon-Baron

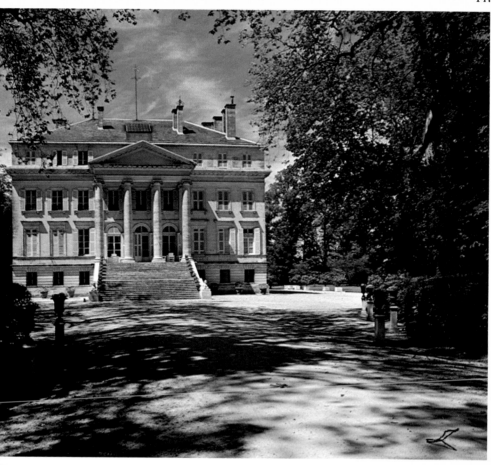

Pichon-Lalande
Pontet-Canet
Potensac
Poujeaux
Prieuré-Lichine
Rausan-Ségla
Sociando-Mallet
Talbot
du Tertre

GRAPE ENTRIES
Cabernet Franc
Cabernet Sauvignon
Merlot

▲ A plane-tree-lined avenue leads impressively to Château Margaux, the top property and only First Growth in the Margaux AC. Lying just north of Bordeaux's industrial suburbs, Margaux is the largest AC in the Médoc and has 21 Classed Growths – more than any other.

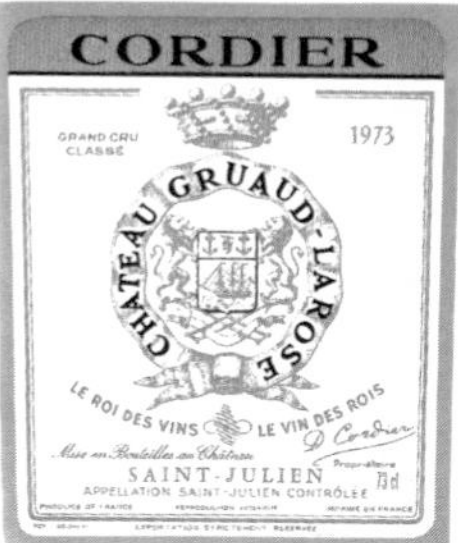

MAUCAILLOU, CH.
Moulis AC, *cru bourgeois*
HAUT-MÉDOC, BORDEAUX

Cabernet Sauvignon, Merlot, Cabernet Franc, Petit Verdot

Maucaillou shows you don't have to have a 'Classed Growth' tag to make top quality wine. Indeed Moulis has several properties which are showing Classed Growth form at the moment. There are two secrets. Firstly, it does have some excellent gravel ridges especially round the village of Grand-Poujeaux where Maucaillou's vineyards are situated. The fruit that comes from there is every bit as good as that of the inland vineyards of St-Julien to the north and Margaux to the south. Secondly, there is a group of dedicated owners in Moulis of which the Dourthe family at Maucaillou is a leading member. The vineyard is 136 acres (55 hectares), with 45 per cent Cabernet Sauvignon, 35 per cent Merlot, 15 per cent Cabernet Franc and five per cent Petit Verdot. And the wine is expertly made using stainless steel equipment followed by up to two years in oak barrels, at least 75 per cent of which are new. The result is a soft, but classically flavoured wine, the fruit all pure blackcurrant fresh off the bush. It matures quickly but ages beautifully for 10–12 years. Best years: 1988, '86, '85, '83, '82, '81, '79, '78.

MAURY AC
LANGUEDOC-ROUSSILLON

Grenache

A *vin doux naturel* red or rosé, made from Grenache grapes grown north of the river Agly and below the Grau de Maury mountain. There are about 5000 acres (2000 hectares) of vineyard producing this strong sweetish, fortified wine – a speciality of the Languedoc-Roussillon – either in a young, vaguely fresh style or the locally-revered but internationally-avoided old *rancio* style.

MAZIS-CHAMBERTIN AC
grand cru
CÔTE DE NUITS, BURGUNDY

Pinot Noir

Mazis-Chambertin is the *grand cru* closest to the village of Gevrey-Chambertin. There are 31 acres (12·6 hectares) and, in the infuriatingly unpredictable world of Burgundy *grands crus*, I find Mazis-Chambertin one of the more reliable. It is not usually as tannic and dark when young as its neighbour, Chambertin Clos-de-Bèze, but does have that damson skin, blackberry pip, crunchy fruit to start with, which, at six to eight years, can develop a heady fragrance – plums, blackcurrants and blackberries all perfumed and ripe – sometimes enriched by the brown sugar sweetness of new oak. Best years: 1988, '87, '85, '83, '82, '80, '78. Best producers: Camus, Hospices de Beaune, Rebourseau, Roty, Armand Rousseau, Tortochot.

MÉDOC AC
BORDEAUX

Cabernet Sauvignon, Cabernet Franc, Merlot and others

This *appellation* covers the northern half of the Médoc peninsula starting beyond St-Seurin-de-Cadourne. The *appellation* should be Bas-Médoc – reflecting the area's downstream position on the Gironde estuary. But *bas* means low – and the growers didn't want the connotation of 'low' quality, especially when their neighbours in the southern part of the peninsula could already use the more attractive title 'Haut-Médoc'. The fact that the 'high' Médoc wines were patently superior to the 'low' ones was regarded by them as irrelevant.

The vineyards cover 7350 acres (2975 hectares) and the AC applies only to red wines, which can be very attractive – dry but juicy, with a little grassy acidity to keep them refreshing and quaffable. This easy-drinking style results from there being very little gravel in the Médoc AC and the Merlot grape dominates in the flat, meadow-like clay vineyards. Most wines are best to drink at three to five years old, but the brilliant Potensac takes ten years' ageing with ease. About 40 per cent of production is controlled by the co-operative movement. Best years: 1988, '85, '83, '82, '81. Best producers: Castéra, Lacombe-Noaillac, les Ormes-Sorbet, Patache d'Aux, Plagnac, Potensac, la Tour-de-By, la Tour-St-Bonnet, Vieux Château Landon.

MENETOU-SALON AC
UPPER LOIRE

🍷 Pinot Noir

🍷 Sauvignon Blanc

Although the village of Menetou-Salon is virtually the neighbour of the grander and far more famous Sancerre, it's a devil of a place to find. You spend an eternity bemusedly poring over your increasingly grubby Michelin map or you ask the locals the way. Since there are more sheep and pigs in these mellow rolling grasslands than people, and since a mixture of mild amusement and impenetrable dialect has never been a recipe for succinct directions, progress is, well, erratic. It's worth making the effort, though, if only to build up a thirst for the AC's extremely attractive Sauvignon whites and Pinot Noir reds and rosés.

Menetou-Salon covers ten villages not far from Sancerre, but light years away in terms of fame and fortune. The wines are something of a *recherché* oddity. There are only 250 acres (100 hectares) of vines so far – although several growers are planting more as they realize that their chalky clay is the same as the best soil in Sancerre and Chablis, and that the ever-increasing prices of Sancerre must give them a chance to score with similar wines at lower prices. And this is exactly what they're doing. The grape varieties are the same as Sancerre. They make very dry, but soft Sauvignon, with a nice hint of gooseberry and blackcurrant leaves in the taste and a pleasant chalky-clean feel. So far they don't equal the best Sancerre, but they are cheaper – and often much more refreshing. The reds quite often have a very attractive, lean but strawberry perfumed style, and can be good and cherry-fresh. Whereas the white Menetou-Salon is a Sancerre country cousin, the reds and rosés, nearly 30 per cent of the production, can be better than many of Sancerre's offerings. Best years (whites): 1988, '87, '86, '85. Best producers: Chatenoy, Chavet, Denis, Mellot, Pellé, Teiller. Best years (reds): 1988, '86, '85. Best producers: des Brangers, Chavet, Pellé.

MERCUREY AC
CÔTE CHALONNAISE, BURGUNDY

🍷 Pinot Noir

🍷 Chardonnay

Easily the biggest and most important of the four main Côte Chalonnaise villages, its 1500 acres (600 hectares) produce more wine than Rully, Givry and Montagny combined. A measure of its importance – or self-importance – is that there is a move afoot to re-christen the Côte Chalonnaise the Région de Mercurey. There is a certain amount of sense in this, because Chalon lies away to the east on the banks of the Saône, and Mercurey is bang in the middle of the vineyards. Whereas much of the Côte Chalonnaise is in the hands of smallholders or independent proprietors, over half of Mercurey's vines are owned by merchant houses, so the wines are the most widely distributed of the region. Red wine production is usually over three million bottles. The flavour is usually a pleasant but pale imitation of the Côte de Beaune just to the north, never very deep in colour, sometimes earthy, but often with a quite attractive cherry and strawberry fruit which can take some ageing. Best years (reds): 1988, '85, '83, '82. Best producers: Chanzy, Faiveley, Juillot, la Mouette, Rodet, Saier, Suremain, Voarick.

The white wine of Mercurey has never had a very good press. It's always accused of being heavy, lifeless, cloddish, lardy – making it sound more like a pile of potato pancakes than a white Burgundy. There isn't a lot of the white, only 130,000 bottles, and the locals rather dismissively whisper that they only plant Chardonnay on ground unsuitable for Pinot Noir – but the wine can be as good as many far more expensive offerings from the more fashionable Côte d'Or. It *is* quite full – but then so is Meursault – and it *does* have a very attractive buttery, nutty, even spicy taste – and so, often, does Meursault! Hmm. I think I'd give it a try, at three to four years old – but not any older. Best years (whites): 1988, '86, '85, '84. Best producers: Chartron & Trébuchet, Faiveley (Clos Rochette), Genot-Boulanger, Juillot, Rodet (Chamirey).

MERLOT

Merlot is one of Bordeaux's two main red grapes, the other being Cabernet Sauvignon. In the Médoc and Graves it was traditionally thought of as the secondary grape, since its wine is softer, richer, more precociously attractive – and, in a wine world which idolized longevity in a red wine, Merlot was normally relegated to the subordinate role of softening up the grand, aggressive Cabernet Sauvignon. Only in St-Émilion and Pomerol, with their cool clay soils, was the easier-ripening Merlot accorded pride of place – but then traditionalists have never thought as highly of the fleshy, comely Pomerol and St-Émilion wines, as of the cold, haughty beauties of the Haut-Médoc.

Times change, though, and throughout the red wine world – now – there is a demand for wines which have the Bordeaux flavours yet which can be drunk young. Merlot wine fits the bill superbly. It is rich, juicy, often blackcurranty, often minty, sometimes almost sweet and buttery, with a taste of fruit-cake raisins. Pomerol wines are now more sought after than Haut-Médoc ones, and with 80,000 acres (32,000 hectares) of vines in the Gironde *département*, Merlot wines outnumber Cabernet Sauvignon, at 42,500 acres (17,200 hectares), by almost two to one. Merlot's ability to ripen on any soil, and to give high yields, have also encouraged its growth elsewhere in the south-west, especially Bergerac, Duras, Buzet, Cahors and Gaillac. But more importantly, it is a recommended grape for the vast swathes of the Midi. The soft, juicy fruit can make a dramatic difference to simple *vin de pays*, and Merlot has been planted throughout the south and even, with great success, in the Ardèche. If you like soft, full-flavoured reds without complications, these southern French Merlots will suit you fine.

MEURSAULT AC
CÔTE DE BEAUNE, BURGUNDY

Pinot Noir

Chardonnay

I'm thinking of a pale golden wine glinting in the cool, bright sunlight. The powerful scent catches the aroma of spring blossoms in the courtyard and mingles tantalizingly with the sweet perfume of fresh-hewn oak casks. I'm tasting Meursault from the latest vintage, still raw and bony, but already promising the smooth-sided succulence which will make the wine cling to my palate – and to my memory in years to come.

I'm thinking of a wine, straw-gold but cut with green, the emptiest bottle in the tasting room as taster after taster has reached for it. The smell is buttery, peachy too, cream coating the fruit, with honey and hazelnuts hiding behind the richness and the distant breakfast smells of coffee and buttered toast. The spittoon is dry. Not even the professionals will spit out this Meursault, now perhaps two years old already so lovely, yet still only hinting at what's to come.

And I'm thinking of sitting with my friends, conversation strangely muted, but the room suffused with beaming pleasures as the deep golden wine weaves its magic. Almost savoury – the rich smoke of toast and roasted almonds and a flash of cinnamon spice, the cream and melted butter of its youth now gone golden, half-way to brown – less luscious but deeper, richer. A conversation, a dream, an ideal, all in itself; Meursault-Charmes, or Meursault-Perrières maybe, the 1978 perhaps or even the '73. White wine perfection.

Ah, if it were all like this – but Burgundy being Burgundy, for every grower striving to excel there's another with his eye on the cash-register, because Meursault, at 1030 acres (417 hectares) the biggest white wine village on the Côte d'Or, is also the most popular. Half-way down the Côte de Beaune, this village is the first, working southwards, of the great white wine villages. Some of its vineyards are a little flat and less well drained, but the general standard of wine *is* high. There are no *grands crus*, but a whole cluster of *premiers crus*. The tiny hamlet of Blagny on the slopes south of Meursault is allowed to sell its lean but classy whites as Meursault-Blagny. Altogether Meursault produces perhaps 2½ million bottles of wine that is lovely to drink young, but better aged for six to ten years. And the less than exceptional vintages are often great successes in Meursault; they haven't had a disaster for 20 years! Best years (whites): 1988, '87, '86, '85, '84, '83, '82. Best producers: Boisson-Vadot, Coche-Debord, Coche-Dury, Jobard, Lafon, Matrot, Michelot-Buisson, Millot-Battault, Pierre Morey, Pitoiset-Urena, Prieur, Roulot.

And what about red Meursault? Well, there is a *little*. Most of it is grown on the Volnay side of the village and if it comes from the *premier cru* Les Santenots vineyard it can be sold as Volnay-Santenots – and it generally is, since the name Volnay means quite a bit in the red wine world. The wine is usually round and earthy – good, but not very 'Volnay'. Red wine is also produced at the southern end of the village, especially around Blagny where it is good, but a little hard, and is sold under the Blagny name. Is any wine sold as Meursault Rouge? Yes, a tiny bit, but since it isn't as good as Blagny or Volnay-Santenots I can understand why most growers prefer to stick to white. Best years (reds): 1988, '85, '83, '82, '79, '78. Best producers: Ampeau, Comte Lafon, Matrot, Potinet-Ampeau.

▼ Wintertime – and a sprinkling of snow lies on the vines in Meursault, one of Burgundy's most famous white wine villages.

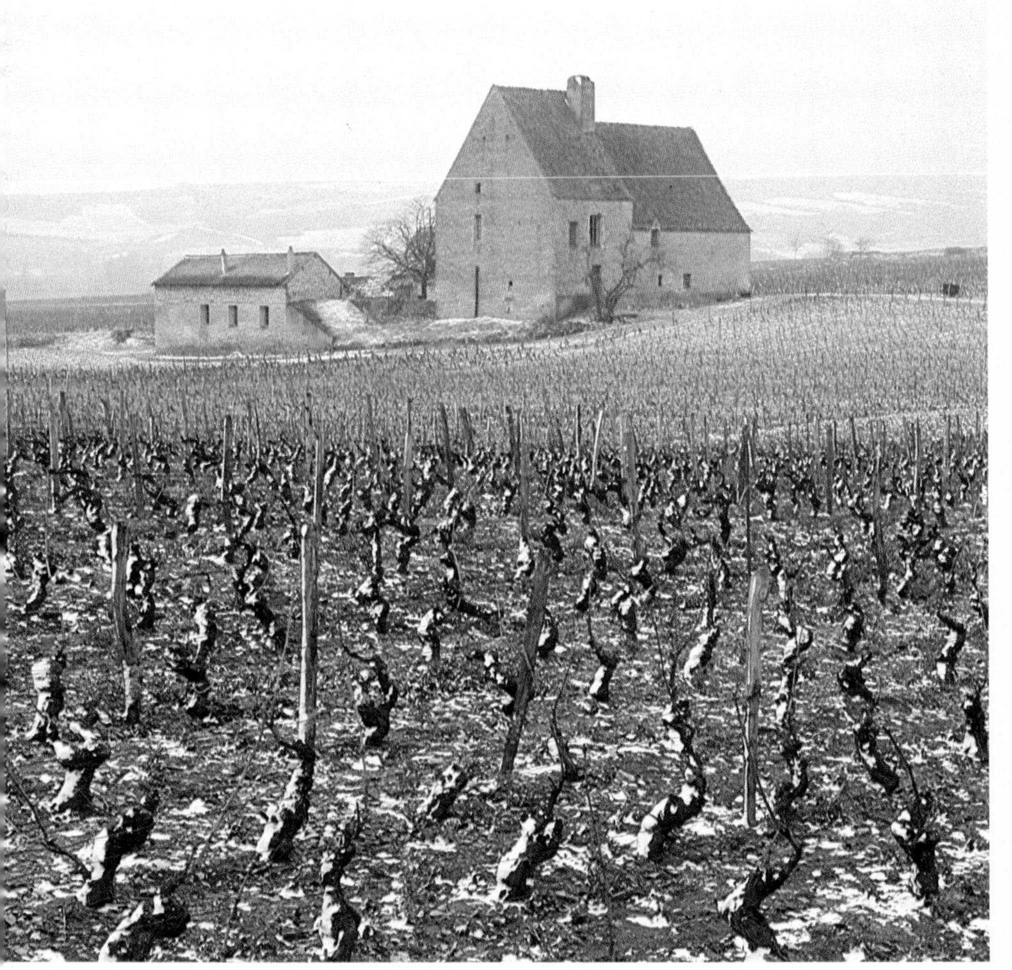

MEYNEY, CH.
St-Estèphe AC, *cru grand bourgeois exceptionnel*
HAUT-MÉDOC, BORDEAUX

Cabernet Sauvignon, Merlot, Cabernet Franc, Petit Verdot

One of those châteaux which has quietly but determinedly been coming up on the inside rails for a number of years. I remember asking the importer a few years ago if I should buy some 1982 *en primeur*, as soon as it was offered, still in barrel. 'Ooh no', he said, 'You don't have to buy wines like Meyney *en primeur*.' Now, you can hardly get it and the price has tripled. Meyney's vineyard is good – 124 acres (50 hectares) with 70 per cent Cabernet Sauvignon, 24 per cent Merlot, four per cent Cabernet Franc and two per cent Petit Verdot, on the same riverside plateau as the Second Growth Montrose. But what has made this wine so reliably fine is the effort made by Cordier, the owners: maximizing the quality and ripeness of the fruit, and ruthlessly selecting only the best vats. The result is big, broad-flavoured wine, generally a little short on nuance but with lovely dark plummy fruit. Best years: 1988, '87, '86, '85, '83, '82, '81, '78, '75. Second wine: Prieur de Meyney.

MINERVOIS AC
LANGUEDOC-ROUSSILLON

Carignan, Grenache, Cinsaut and others

Minervois hasn't quite got the wild 'mountain-man' reputation of Corbières. This is partly because – in recent years – the wines have been relatively light, spicy, dusty and deliciously fruity but not in any way challenging, and partly because with Corbières we all dash off into those unfarmed sub-Pyrenean hills and are soon lost in a timeless twilight world, but with Minervois we generally stay in the Aude valley rootling round the co-operatives and estates within easy reach of civilization.

In fact the high, wind-swept, herb-strewn plateau of the Minervois is exciting and some of the old-style reds reflect this dry-earth, hot-resin fruitiness of the far south. But Minervois' great strength is organization. Big companies like Nicolas and Chantovent have worked hard with local co-operatives to produce good quality, juicy, quaffing wine at reasonable prices. There are 10,000 acres (4050 hectares) of the Minervois AC producing up to 30 million bottles a year, almost all of it red. It is best drunk young, but can age, especially if a little new oak has been used. Most Minervois comes from the co-operatives and is generally good. Other recommended producers: Blomac, Domergue, Festiano, Gourgazaud, Meyzonnier, Paraza, Ste-Eulalie, Vaissière, Villerambert-Julien.

LA MISSION-HAUT-BRION, CH.
Pessac-Léognan AC, *cru classé de Graves*
BORDEAUX

Cabernet Sauvignon, Merlot, Cabernet Franc

One of the properties which, by a show of hands and shouts of 'aye' could be promoted to First Growth. I suppose I'll go along with that but not without qualms, because I always find La Mission wines powerful – almost bullying and hectoring by nature – but never charming, and rarely with that lovely, ruminative flavour-memory which other blockbusters like Latour and Pétrus *do* have. Its strength is in a dark-plums-and-chocolate fruit braided with an earthy dryness which rarely opens out in 10 years and often needs 20 or more to achieve its unsubtle but memorable tangle of tobacco, cedar and herb garden perfumes. The property covers 42 acres (17 hectares), surrounded by Bordeaux's suburbs and sliced through by the Bordeaux-Arcachon main railway line. Best years: 1988, '85, '83, '82, '81, '79, '78, '75, '74.

MOËT & CHANDON
Champagne AC
CHAMPAGNE

Pinot Noir, Chardonnay, Pinot Meunier

If there is one company which rules our perception of Champagne as a drink, it has to be Moët & Chandon, with its enormous production of 1[illegible] million bottles a year, and its domination of so many of the export markets. People seem to be shooting the corks out of gigantic bottles of Moët at every first night, every film award, every Grand Prix victory or glossy showbiz wedding – in fact anywhere there is likely to be a photographer who is likely to get a picture of the event – and a bottle of Moët – into the newspapers. The result is that Moët is the most famou

Champagne in the world yet you hardly ever see an advert – you just see lots of famous people spraying each other with it.

With all this notoriety comes inconsistency – which is a great pity, because when you get a good bottle of Moët non-vintage it is soft, creamy, a little spicy – and absolutely delightful. The vintage is more consistent, and usually has a good strong style to it, though Moët is one of those houses which are apt to release a vintage virtually every year, when some might suggest the quality of the harvest left a bit to be desired. Dom Pérignon is their De Luxe cuvée, famous throughout the night spots of the world. It can be one of the greatest of Champagnes, but it must be given several years age, even after release.

MONBAZILLAC AC
SOUTH-WEST

Sémillon, Sauvignon Blanc, Muscadelle

The leading sweet wine of the Bergerac region, and the only one which is likely to be truly sweet in the style of Sauternes, rather than mildly sweet in a light and unmemorable way. But most Monbazillac nowadays is just that – light, vaguely sweet and entirely forgettable – largely because the noble rot fungus, needed on the overripe grapes to suck out water and concentrate sweetness, doesn't always appear here. Since Monbazillac can't command anything like the price of Sauternes or Barsac, few growers are going to risk losing their crop in the autumn storms simply on the off-chance that noble rot might turn up.

In fact, only a mere handful of properties even consider making traditional rich Monbazillac – most of the eight million bottles produced each year come from the good but unadventurous co-operative. At its best the wine is full and honeyed, with a sweetness of peaches and barley sugar. Lighter versions are likely to be very pale and resemble pleasantly drinkable sweet apples with just a touch of honey. The vineyards, south of Bergerac town, run up a north-facing slope to the impressive Château de Monbazillac (the wine's not as exciting as the architecture). In general drink young, but a real late-harvested example could happily last ten years. Best years: 1988, '86, '85, '83. Best producers: la Borderie, le Fagé, la Jaubertie, Château de Monbazillac, Septy, Treuil-de-Nailhac.

MONBOUSQUET, CH.
St-Émilion AC, *grand cru*
BORDEAUX

Merlot, Cabernet Franc, Cabernet Sauvignon

The only well-known St-Émilion property on the *sables*, the sandy flat lands down by the river Dordogne. The *sables*, generally planted quite recently, do not have the quality potential of the *côtes* (slopes) or the *graves* (gravel plateau). But Monbousquet makes the best of the conditions and produces a delicious, absurdly soft and soothing wine which hardly seems to have any tannin at all, merely a magical burst of honey and butterscotch and blackcurrant which you would expect to fade away with the evening sun, but which in fact can age remarkably well. The 1970 and '75 are still lovely. Best years: 1988, '85, '83, '82, '78.

MONTAGNE-ST-ÉMILION AC
BORDEAUX

Merlot, Cabernet Sauvignon, Cabernet Franc, Malbec

A St-Émilion 'satellite' on the northern borders of both St-Émilion and Pomerol. The wines are rather good and often exhibit quite a bit of the Pomerol plumminess even when quite young. Both Parsac and St-Georges, two small neighbouring communes, have the right to use the Montagne-St-Émilion AC, and in general do so, though some properties in St-Georges, especially the historic Château St-Georges itself, prefer to use the St-Georges-St-Émilion AC. There are 3700 acres (1500 hectares) of vineyard, and the wines are normally ready in four years but age quite well. Best years: 1988, '85, '83, '82, '81, '79. Best producers: Calon, Corbin, Maison-Blanche, Maison-Neuve, Plaisance, Roudier, des Tours, Vieux Château St-André.

MONTAGNY AC
CÔTE CHALONNAISE, BURGUNDY

Chardonnay

Montagny is a white-only AC at the southern end of the Côte Chalonnaise. Since I love white Burgundy, and enthusiastically champion the Côte Chalonnaise as providing decent white Burgundy at a reasonable price, I was always desperately disappointed that Montagny wines had such a dull flavour – bone dry, chalky, lean beyond belief, and showing none of the fullness and ripeness I want from the Chardonnay grape in Burgundy. But then Montagny discovered the 'new barrel'! Just a few months' ageing in a new, or relatively new, oak barrel adds the nuttiness and soft spice which have been conspicuously lacking up until now. And suddenly, I'm getting excited about the wines for the first time.

Montagny has some 750 acres (300 hectares) of vines and an annual production of 400,000 bottles. If you see a wine labelled Montagny *premier cru* don't be fooled into thinking it comes from a superior vineyard site – as you'd assume in the rest of Burgundy. No. Somehow the Montagny growers wangled it that any white wine which reaches 11·5 degrees of alcohol – half a degree more than usual – can call itself *premier cru*. And even worse, the local AC authorities blithely continue to allow it. In general, drink Montagny one to three years after the vintage. Best years: 1988, '86. Best producers: Buxy co-operative, Latour, Martial de Laboulaye, Michel, Roy, Steinmaier, Vachet.

▼ Montagny is the southernmost of the five ACs on the Côte Chalonnaise. Its vineyards, on limestone soil, produce mostly white wine; any red has to be labelled Bourgogne Rouge, not Montagny.

MONTHÉLIE AC
CÔTE DE BEAUNE, BURGUNDY

Pinot Noir

Chardonnay

Monthélie is an attractive village, with 250 acres (100 hectares) of vines, looking down on Meursault from the north. Its steep streets and huddled houses give some clue to the wine's character, which is generally of the strong, herby, rustic, but satisfying type. Monthélie wines have historically been sold as Volnay, the next village to the north-east. That was fine while *appellation* laws allowed it, but when Monthélie had to stand on its own two feet and trade under its own name, it languished in the shadows while barrels of Volnay reached ever higher prices. Which was bad luck on the growers but good news for us: most of Monthélie's 250 acres (100 hectares) of vines have an excellent south-east to south exposure, many of the vines are old, and the wines generally have a lovely chewy, cherry-skin fruit and a slight piny rasp which make good drinking at a good price. Best years (reds): 1988, '87, '85, '83, '82, '79, '78. Best producers: Bouchard Père & Fils, Deschamps, Leflaive, Parent, Potinet-Ampeau, Ropiteau-Mignon, Suremain, Thevenin-Monthélie.

A few rows of Chardonnay vines produce a white Monthélie which has tasted rather dry and lean when I've tried it from the barrel – but I have to admit I haven't tracked down a single *bottle* yet so can't comment on its ageing potential. Best years (whites): 1988, '87, '86, '85.

MONTLOUIS AC
CENTRAL LOIRE

Chenin Blanc

Montlouis is the southern neighbour of Vouvray, within a stone's throw across the river Loire. Montlouis doesn't share the fame of Vouvray and you can sense the growers' resentment at Vouvray's greater renown and higher prices. But the grape is the same – Chenin Blanc; the chalk, limestone, gravel and clay soil is the same; and the styles of wine are the same – dry, medium and sweet whites, and Champagne-method fizz.

Yet the style is a *little* different – the dry wines leaner, the sweet wines developing quite an attractive flavour of nuts and honey, but rarely subduing the high Chenin acidity. Only the sparkling wines (80 per cent of the four million plus bottles produced annually) match Vouvray and, with their cleaner apple fruit sometimes touched by honey, they can improve upon the slightly sterner style of the Vouvray sparklers. The still wines need ageing for five or maybe ten years, but sparkling Montlouis should be drunk young. Best years: 1988, '86, '85, '83, '82, '78, '76, '70. Best producers: Berger, Deletang, Levasseur, Moyer.

LE MONTRACHET AC
CÔTE DE BEAUNE, BURGUNDY

Chardonnay

Given the incredibly meagre amount of Montrachet made – 30,000 bottles in a good year – and the extreme unlikelihood that most wine writers have ever possessed a bottle, or drunk it in its mature state more than once in a blue moon, there have been more adjectives expended on this than on any other wine in the world. Those who love white Burgundy dream of Montrachet and, OK, I do too.

I've tasted it so new that it flowed milky-white from the barrel and stung my mouth with a piercing richness far beyond youthful flavours of fruit – more like an essence coaxed, in minute allowance, deep from the vineyard's earth. I've been faced with it at tastings, so thick in the glass it seemed like syrup, and so coarse and bloated in the mouth – like an elixir of buttered orchard fruit – that I started back with shock only to find some wiser head than mine nodding sagely and saying, 'Don't worry, it needs ten years to sort itself out'. And, just once or twice, I have experienced it at ten and more years old. The sheer concentration of the wine is unchanged. But all the coarseness is gone, and there seems to be a richness which owes nothing to sugar, but everything to the ripest of fruits, the most tantalizing of scents, and the most fragrant of drifting woodsmoke wrapped in triple-thick cream. Dry-sweet, luscious-lean – the most perfect binding of opposites.

Montrachet comes from an 18½-acre (7·5-hectare) vineyard, 1(acres (4 hectares) in Puligny-Montrachet and 8½ (3·5) in Chassagne Montrachet. The land is nothing to look at – poor, stony – but there's thick vein of limestone just below the surface, the drainage i exceptional, and the perfect south to south-east exposure soaks up th sun from dawn to dusk. If you stand among the vines of Montrachet a sunset, a dip in the hills to the west is still allowing the sun's rays t warm the grapes while all the great surrounding vineyards are i shadow. There's one reason at least why their wines have never *quit* reached the peaks of brilliance of Montrachet. Best years: 1988, '87 '86, '85, '84, '83, '82, '78, '71, '70. Best producers: Bouchard Père & Fils Lafon, Laguiche, Pierre Morey, Prieur, Domaine de la Romanée-Conti Thénard.

MONTRAVEL AC, CÔTES DE MONTRAVEL AC, HAUT-MONTRAVEL AC
SOUTH-WEST

Sémillon, Sauvignon Blanc, Muscadelle

White wines from the western fringe of the Bergerac region. Basi Montravel is dryish, while Côtes de Montravel and Haut-Montravel both from hillside vineyards – are sweeter but lack richness. Th Montravel wines, falling uneasily between proper sweet and proper dry are not much in fashion and so production – already low at 300,00 bottles a year – looks likely to decline further. Reds made in the regio are bottled as AC Bergerac.

MONTROSE, CH.
St-Estèphe AC, *2ème cru classé*
HAUT-MÉDOC, BORDEAUX

Cabernet Sauvignon, Merlot, Cabernet Franc

This leading St-Estèphe property of 166 acres (67 hectares) used to b famous, sometimes infamous, for its dark, brooding, Cabernet Sauvig non-dominated style. Twenty years was regarded as a reasonable tim to wait before broaching a bottle, and around 30 years to drink it at it prime. Now I know we used to scoff a bit about how hard it was, how tannic, how slowly it revealed its blackcurrant and pencil-shavings scent but it *was* a classic and we *did* love it. Maybe we made fun of it burliness once too often, because the wine has undergone a sea chang which has markedly reduced its personality. Since 1978 the vintages ar lighter, softer and less substantial, certain to be ready for drinking at te years old, not 20. I really am sorry, because cash-flow accountancy shouldn't affect a famous property like Montrose even if the wine di take 30 years to peak. Montrose used to be thought of as the leadin St-Estèphe. Cos d'Estournel now holds this position, and in great year like 1982, '83 and '85 Montrose is regularly outclassed not only by th top Classed Growths of St-Estèphe but also by leading *crus bourgeoi* like de Pez and Meyney. Best years: 1987, '86, '85, '84, '81, '76.

MOREY-ST-DENIS AC
CÔTE DE NUITS, BURGUNDY

Pinot Noir

Pinot Noir

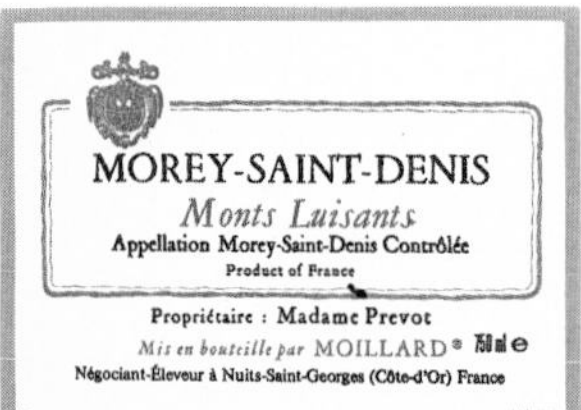

After decades of being treated as Cinderella – squashed betwee Chambolle-Musigny to the south and Gevrey-Chambertin to the north Morey-St-Denis has recently been flexing its muscles, and no commands a price for its wine equal to its more famous neighbour Certainly the vineyards deserve it. There are five *grands cru* (Bonnes-Mares, Clos des Lambrays, Clos de la Roche, Clos de Tart an Clos St-Denis) as well as some very good *premiers crus*, but the entir extent of the village's vineyards is only 329 acres (133 hectares) neighbouring Gevrey-Chambertin, for instance, has 1235 acres (50 hectares) – and so the *négociants* have paid less heed to Morey, simpl because there was less wine to go round. Nowadays most Morey win does come from *négociants*, often blended by the two sma co-operatives which service the village, and much of this is light and dul However there is better Morey, in particular from the *premier cru* an *grand cru* vineyards and usually from single growers. They generall

have a good strawberry or redcurrant fruit, sometimes a little meaty and getting an attractive chocolate and liquorice depth as they age. Best years (reds): 1988, '87, '85, '83, '80, '78. Best producers: Bryczek, Drouhin, Dujac, Lignier, Marchand, Moillard, Ponsot, Tardy.

Believe it or not, there is actually a white Morey-St-Denis. In the Monts-Luisants vineyard to the north of the village, Monsieur Ponsot uses a weird white mutation of Pinot Noir to produce about 3000 bottles of white wine. It can be rather hard and empty to start with, but in hot years it gains a deep, almost overpowering, honeyed nutty weight, which is certainly impressive – but the last time I started on a bottle, none of us could finish it! Best years (whites): 1988, '86, '85, '83, '82.

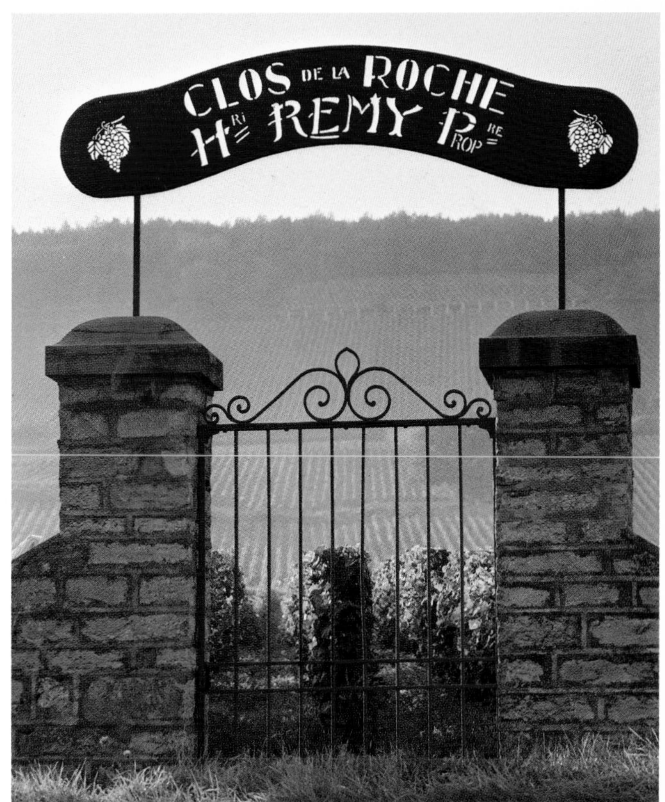

► Clos de la Roche, the largest of the five *grands crus* in Morey-St-Denis. The word *clos*, widely used in Burgundy, describes a vineyard that is (or was) walled. The *roche* seems to have been a huge stone – long since vanished – which played a part in ancient rites.

MORGON AC
BEAUJOLAIS, BURGUNDY

🍷 Gamay

Although Moulin-à-Vent is the Beaujolais *cru* which is supposed to age best and come closest in maturity to a fine Côte d'Or Burgundy, Morgon could easily lay claim to that reputation. Indeed they even have a verb *morgonner* – to 'Morgon'! – which is used to describe how the local wine begins to lose its fresh, plummy fruit after two to three years and evolves into something chocolaty, cocoa-ish and strongly perfumed with cherries or even kirsch. Sounds good? It is. But only the best wines behave like this, usually from a single grower, and from the slopes around Mont du Py. You may see Le Py, Les Chaumes or Le Clachet marked as vineyard names, and snap a bottle up if you do. The majority of Morgon, however, is less special, but it still manages a soft, cherry fruit which is very easy drinking. Best years: 1988, '85, '83, '81, '78. Best producers: Aucoeur, Brun, La Chanaise, Descombes, Jambon, Janodet, Lapierre, Longuepierre, Savoye, Vincent.

MOULIN-À-VENT AC
BEAUJOLAIS, BURGUNDY

Gamay

Moulin-à-Vent would like to be a big, burly, world-famous Burgundy like Chambertin. But sadly it is in the wrong place – a good 150 miles (240km) too far south – and it grows the wrong grape – the Gamay, rather than the much more vaunted Pinot Noir. Undaunted, it keeps on trying, and wine does in fact do a pretty good job of impersonating a fairly full, chocolaty Burgundy – slightly short on perfume, but good and rich, if you leave it for six to ten years to mature. *Moulin-à-Vent* means 'windmill' and that's what the wine is named after – an old building standing in almost 1750 acres (700 hectares) of vines between Romanèche-Thorins and Chénas. Best years: 1988, '87, '85, '83, '81, '79 '78, '76. Best producers: Benoit Trichard, Bloud, Brugne, Champagnon, Charvet, Chauvet, Duboeuf (single domaines), Château des Jacques, Janodet, Siffert, la Tour de Bief. Duboeuf is using new oak barrels experimentally and the first wines out are delicious.

MOULIS AC
HAUT-MÉDOC, BORDEAUX

Cabernet Sauvignon, Cabernet Franc, Merlot and others

The smallest of the six specific ACs within the Haut-Médoc area, at only 964 acres (390 hectares), Moulis had properties included in the 1855 Classification. Much of the wine is excellent, yet never over-priced. The best vineyards are on a gravel plateau centred on the village of Grand-Poujeaux. The wines are beautifully balanced, surprisingly soft behind their early tannin, and delicious to drink at five to six years old, though good examples should age 10–20 years. There's more and more new oak being used to age the wines, to good effect. Best years: 1988, '86, '85, '83, '82, '81, '79, '78. Best properties: Branas, Brillette, Chasse-Spleen, Duplessis-Fabre, Dutruch-Grand-Poujeaux, Gressier-Grand-Poujeaux, Maucaillou, Moulin-à-Vent, Poujeaux.

MOUTON-CADET
Bordeaux AC
HAUT-MÉDOC, BORDEAUX

Cabernet Sauvignon, Cabernet Franc, Merlot

Sémillon, Sauvignon Blanc, Muscadelle

What's a brand name doing in this book? Well, to leave out Mouton-Cadet would be a bit like writing a history of soft drinks and leaving out Coca-Cola! And in any case, is Mouton-Cadet really a brand name? Lots of people think it's a sort of 'younger brother' – *cadet* – of the great Mouton-Rothschild. Well, that's how it started out. In the Great Depression of the 1930s, not only was wine not selling, but the vintages weren't much good; 1930, '31, and '32 were three of the worst ever. Baron Philippe de Rothschild, determined not to release any wine which might harm the reputation of his beloved Château Mouton-Rothschild, blended these three vintages of Mouton-Rothschild together and called it Mouton-Cadet. It was a whopping success, saved his bacon, and is now the most widely-selling red Bordeaux in the world. But the label says Bordeaux AC; that means the wine is blended and comes from the entire Bordeaux region. In the '60s and early '70s it was very classy wine, but nowadays it is perfectly correct but uninspiring, and never cheap. That goes for the white – also AC Bordeaux – too.

MOUTON-ROTHSCHILD, CH.
Pauillac AC, *premier cru classé*
HAUT-MÉDOC, BORDEAUX

Cabernet Sauvignon, Cabernet Franc, Merlot

Baron Philippe de Rothschild died in 1988 and so ended a remarkable era in Bordeaux's history. For 65 years he had managed Mouton-Rothschild, raising it from a rather capricious and run-down Second Growth to one of the most famous wines in the world, achieving promotion to First Growth status in 1973 – the only promotion ever effected within the traditional 1855 Classification! He did this by unremitting commitment to quality, which in great vintages like 196 and '82 paid off so handsomely that Mouton arguably produces Bordeaux's greatest wine. But you can't rely on quality alone if you're determined to force the Bordeaux establishment into admitting you into the top class. So he did it by flair, imagination and brilliant marketing.

The Mouton-Rothschild he created is a 200-acre (80-hectare) estate planted with 85 per cent Cabernet Sauvignon, ten per cent Cabernet Franc and five per cent Merlot on the northern side of Pauillac, but south of Lafite-Rothschild. The high proportion of Cabernet Sauvignon and the perfectly situated gravel banks of the vineyard give a wine which, in most years, is astonishingly exotic and heavy. It manages to transform the cedarwood, cigar-box, pencil-shavings spectrum of dry, restrained fragrances into a steamy, intoxicating swirl of head-turning richness, backed up by a deep, chewy, pure blackcurrant fruit. Mouton is tannic when it's young, often taking 15–20 years to open up fully, but you can always see the richness behind the tough exterior. As well as being superb wine, each year Mouton commissions a different artist to design the label, and most of the modern greats like Chagall, Miró, Picasso and Warhol have had a go. Best years: 1988, '86, '85, '84, '83, '82, '81, '78, '75, '70.

MUSCADET AC
WESTERN LOIRE

Muscadet

Muscadet is now so popular that its name has become a kind of generic term for cheap, dry, French white wine. But in reality, Muscadet can only come from a legally defined area at the mouth of the Loire near Nantes. There isn't an actual town of Muscadet – this is one of the rare occasions in France that a wine takes its name from its grape.

The Melon de Bourgogne grape migrated from Burgundy during the seventeenth century and, en route, changed its name to Muscadet. It became very popular with growers all over the Nantes area and they simply called their wine after the grape – Muscadet. In fact, we don't see much wine just labelled as Muscadet because the bulk of production –

▼ Atlantic weather – damp and mild – characterizes the Muscadet region and helps give the wine its low-acid, light, dry style.

85 per cent – comes from the best area, to the south of the Loire, and so qualifies for the Muscadet de Sèvre-et-Maine AC. Only wine from less suitable vineyards, mostly closer to the sea, carries the plain Muscadet AC. This is usually pretty dull, bland wine, but does have one thing in its favour – a *maximum* alcoholic strength of 12·3 degrees. Since the Muscadet is an early-ripening, low acid grape – though you'd never know it to taste some of the cheaper export versions – this legal maximum is imposed to preserve at least a modicum of freshness in the wine. With that in mind, always drink straight Muscadet very young – even as Muscadet Nouveau, released as early as November.

MUSCADET DE SÈVRE-ET-MAINE AC

WESTERN LOIRE

🍷 Muscadet

The Maine and the Sèvre rivers converge south-east of Nantes before flowing into the Loire and on to the Atlantic ocean, and give their names to the mild, gently hilly region where 85 per cent of Muscadet is made. There's no doubt that the best Muscadet comes from here – but that 85 per cent also includes a lot of wine of no discernible personality except that it is sharply dry and seemingly acid.

Well, Muscadet is dry, but the grape is a low acid variety with a pretty neutral taste. The traditional method of bottling gives the wine quite a full, soft feel which is a revelation to anyone who has always just bought the cheapest available. The wine is bottled directly off its sediment, its lees, and labelled *mise en bouteille sur lie*. When the fermentation is over, the wine is put into a barrel and, instead of being drained off periodically, it just waits, gaining a creamy, yeasty flavour and a slight prickle of carbon dioxide. What *should* then happen is that the wine is drawn off, extremely carefully, into the bottle, without filtering, leaving a layer of sediment in the barrel. But one expert has reckoned that not more than two per cent of supposed *sur lie* Muscadet *is* made like this – and I'm inclined to believe him.

Just occasionally, you find a Muscadet with a creamy softness, livened up with a sharp edge of grapefruit, pepper and lemon – and with just enough prickle to make your tongue tingle. It's a delightful wine, on its own or with the seafood of the region. And although you should really drink Muscadet within the year, these 'true' Muscadets can age for several years, going quite full and nutty with time. Best years: 1988, '87. Best producers: estate bottlings from Michel Bahuaud, Bossard, Chasseloir, Chéreau-Carré, Clos des Roches-Gaudinières, Dimerie, Donatien-Bahuaud, Dorices, Marquis de Goulaine, Métaireau, Sauvion, Touche, Tourmaline.

MUSCADET DES COTEAUX DE LA LOIRE AC

WESTERN LOIRE

🍷 Muscadet

Quite a large area stretching up both banks of the Loire from Nantes towards Angers, but not specially packed with vines, since only five per cent of Muscadet comes from these vineyards. You hardly ever see the wine labelled as such since most exporters find it easier to use the simple Muscadet AC. But if Coteaux de la Loire Muscadet *does* have a special character, it is perhaps a little fuller, and flatter, lacking the fresh zip of the better Sèvre-et-Maine wines.

MUSCAT

It's highly likely that the Muscat is the original wine grape, and that all other varieties descend from this one vine, so it should be treated with great respect by connoisseurs the world over. But sadly it isn't. Muscat suffers from a single fault – its wines are too easy to enjoy: the wine buff can claim no superiority over the ordinary mortal because the delicious grapy, honeyed taste is obvious, delightful and without hidden complexities. To me that makes it very special.

There are three main sorts of Muscat grown in France (though since it makes wonderful eating there are more like 200 members of the Muscat family worldwide). By far the finest is Muscat Blanc à Petits Grains or 'white Muscat with little berries'. In Alsace this used to be the sole Muscat variety, producing pale, fragile but headily perfumed dry white wines like no other in the world. Because of susceptibility to disease so far north, its place in Alsace was largely taken by Muscat Ottonel, but plantings are now on the increase again as the Petits Grains' superior quality is acknowledged. In the northern Rhône it is grown at Die and gives the sublime grapy perfume to the lovely Clairette de Die Tradition sparkling wine, while further south at Beaumes-de-Venise it is responsible for the wonderful rush of grapy, peachy, apples and honey fruit, made more exciting by a whiff of roses, which makes such a perfect after-dinner drink. Although Muscat Blanc à Petits Grains is being usurped as the leading grape in the fortified wines of the Mediterranean coast, it will predominate in good examples.

Muscat Ottonel is a crossbreed created in 1852. It doesn't have quite the perfume of the 'Petits Grains' Muscat, but is more reliable in Alsace where thankfully it doesn't overripen.

Muscat of Alexandria is a big, chubby eating grape which I've seen growing in English glasshouses and happily guzzled numerous times. But the wine doesn't manage to capture that warm clinging scent of the hothouse vine. It does give a high, healthy yield and in the far south it is now three times as heavily planted as Petits Grains in the fortified Muscat centres around Rivesaltes. The heavy, orange marmalade and raisin richness of most of these wines is evidence of this.

The Muscadelle is related to the Muscat family, as its name implies. 5000 acres (2000 hectares) are planted in Bordeaux, and can give a pleasant, honeyed aroma to the rather neutral dry white of the Entre-Deux-Mers as well as adding spice to a Sauternes.

MUSCAT DE BEAUMES-DE-VENISE AC
SOUTHERN RHÔNE

🍷 Muscat à Petits Grains

This is the most delicious manifestation of sweet Muscat in France, and consequently the most expensive. But that's fair enough because the wine is a beauty and in a period in the late 1970s when sweet wines looked to be in terminal decline, the phenomenal success of Muscat de Beaumes-de-Venise gave other sweeties the breathing space they needed to wait for the world's attention to turn their way once more – as it now has.

Beaumes-de-Venise is an attractive little village huddled up against the crags of the Dentelles de Montmirail in the southern Rhône. They've been making Muscat wine there since the Middle Ages. It's what is called a *vin doux naturel* – a fortified wine where the fermentation is arrested by the addition of a slug of high-strength spirit. This preserves the flavour of the unfermented grape juice and accounts for the wine's sweet, grapy taste. In the local bars they throw back shots of their Muscat on the way home from work in the same way as we might stop off at the pub for a beer. They are continually amazed at how their everyday happy-juice has become a revered sweet wine to drink at the end of sophisticated urban dinner parties. Well, I'm not, because the wine is certainly rich, often very rich, full of the flavour of peach and grapes, orange peel, apples and honey, and with a wisp of the scent of roses left hanging in the air. But the secret is that the wine doesn't cloy; it has a fruit acidity and a bright fresh feel which satisfies your thirst as well as stimulates your after-dinner wit. The wine can age, but is best drunk young to get all that lovely grapy perfume at its peak. Best producers: Bernardins, Coyeux, Durban, Guigal, Jaboulet and the Beaumes-de-Venise co-operative.

MUSCAT DE FRONTIGNAN AC
LANGUEDOC-ROUSSILLON

Muscat à Petits Grains

This is the leading Muscat *vin doux naturel* on the Mediterranean coast and comes from Frontignan, a small town south-west of Montpellier in the Hérault. It is supposed to be made 100 per cent from Muscat à Petits Grains, but my palate tells me there *must* be an increasing amount of the coarser Muscat of Alexandria being planted in the vineyards. This would go some way to explaining why much Muscat de Frontignan, though sweet and quite impressive, has a slightly cloying taste, like cooked marmalade, militating against the fresh grapy sweetness. It is a *vin doux naturel* – which means that the grapes are harvested as ripe as possible, partially fermented and then 'muted' by the addition of high-strength spirit. This stops the fermentation and leaves a substantial amount of the grape sweetness still in the wines. Varying between bright gold and a deep orange gold, Muscat de Frontignan is certainly good, but definitely short of the top class. Best producers: la Peyrade, Robiscau.

MUSCAT DE LUNEL AC
LANGUEDOC-ROUSSILLON

Muscat à Petits Grains

Although the little town of Lunel, north-east of Montpellier, boastfully gives itself the title of 'La Cité de Muscat' (the city of Muscat), few people who don't actually live there would agree. Muscat de Lunel is not well-known – both Muscat de Frontignan west of Montpellier, and Muscat de Rivesaltes down towards the Pyrenees, have far higher reputations. That said, however, the fairly small amounts of Muscat de Lunel aren't bad with a very good raisiny flavour and less of the flat marmalady character than the better-known ones exhibit. Best producers: Belle-Côte, Cave Co-operative.

MUSCAT DE MIREVAL AC
LANGUEDOC-ROUSSILLON

Muscat à Petits Grains

Almost never seen outside its own locality, this is one of several fortified Muscat wines (called *vins doux naturels* – natural sweet wines) which pepper the Mediterranean coast between the mouth of the Rhône and Perpignan at the base of the Pyrenees. Mireval is a neighbour of the much better-known Frontignan, but is just a little further inland and the wines, while still sweet and ripe, can have a little more acid freshness and quite an alcoholic kick as well!

MUSCAT DE RIVESALTES AC
LANGUEDOC-ROUSSILLON

Muscat of Alexandria, Muscat à Petits Grains

Rivesaltes, a small town just north of Perpignan, makes good Côtes du Roussillon but its reputation is based on *vins doux naturels* – the traditional fortified wines of the south of France. The best of these is Muscat de Rivesaltes, made primarily from the Muscat of Alexandria grape, a big, rather thick, deep coloured wine, not as aromatic as the best Muscats, and with a sweetness veering between raisins, honey and cooked orange marmalade. Good, but not inspiring. Most other Rivesaltes *vin doux naturel* is based on the red Grenache Noir, but there is a little made from the white Malvoisie, Grenache Blanc and Macabeo which, while not as sweet as the Muscat wines, can be fresher and more appetizing. Best producers: Cazes Frères, Corneilla, Sarda-Malet.

MUSIGNY AC
grand cru
CÔTE DE NUITS, BURGUNDY

Pinot Noir

Chardonnay

This 27-acre (10·7-hectare) *grand cru* vineyard – just to the south of the village on the slopes directly above Clos de Vougeot in the Côte de Nuits – has the ability to produce red wines of such fragrance, such delicacy of texture, that a French monk called Gaston Roupnel described them as 'of silk and lace', the perfume being 'a damp garden, a rose and a violet covered in morning dew'. Lovely isn't it? And, yes, I *do* know what he means. I've found roses and violets, tainted with that earthy dampness of a garden just after dawn, then running through the thrill o

fresh flower scents caught in the breeze of midsummer noons, and later twined through with the autumn smoke of forest bonfires as the wine first breathes, demurely matures and wistfully declines through 20 years or more. Those were Musignys from the 1950s, '60s and early '70s. Musigny is nowadays usually too sweet and too thick for romance remembered. I think the producers' hearts have been hardened by commercial reality.

No such pressures lie behind the creation of white Musigny. Musigny is a red wine *grand cru*, right? Ah yes, but since when have a few silly things like regulations stopped a determined Frenchwoman from having her way? The Comte de Vogüé owns most of the Musigny vines, and makes a famous Musigny red. But what do you do if your wife prefers white? You rip up a few precious Pinot Noir vines and replant with Chardonnay – *et voilà* – you can make white wine – just for your own consumption mind. But you serve it at dinner, your friends plead with you for a bottle or two to buy, and, well, why not? So now there's three-quarters of an acre (0·3 hectare) planted with Chardonnay, producing between 1000 and 2000 bottles a year. The wine *is* good, dry, soft and nutty, and sells for a whopping price – if you can ever find it.

NAIRAC, CH.
Barsac AC, *2ème cru classé*
BORDEAUX

Sémillon, Sauvignon Blanc, Muscadelle

A rising star in Barsac which by dint of enormous effort and considerable investment is now producing a wine reckoned to be on a level with the First Growths – not as intensely perfumed, not as exotically rich, but proudly concentrated, with a fine lanolin richness and buttery honey coating the mouth, and with more spice from new oak barrels than many properties have. Production is rarely more than 24,000 bottles – sometimes a lot less – from this 37-acre (15-hectare) property. The quality-obsessed proprietors ditched all their 1977 and '78 wine as not being good enough and only released 40 per cent of their '79! The influence of ageing in new oak casks, adding spice and even a little tough tannin, make Nairac a good candidate for ageing 10–15 years. Best years: 1988, '86, '83,'82, '81, '80, '76, '74.

NUITS-ST-GEORGES AC
CÔTE DE NUITS, BURGUNDY

Pinot Noir

Pinot Noir

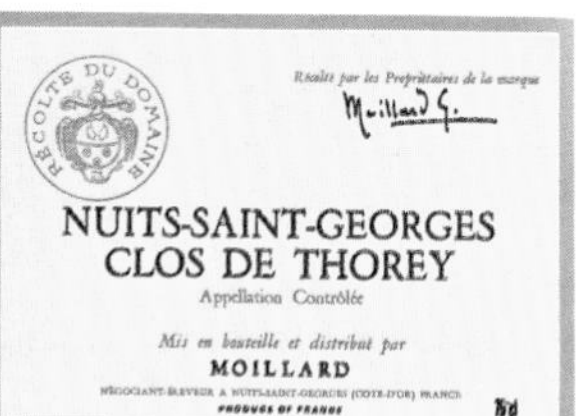

This surely used to be the best-known Côte de Nuits village – at least to the British. In fact, with Châteauneuf-du-Pape and Beaujolais, it was probably the best-known red wine name in the world. That was before 1973, the year European Community (EC) regulations took effect in Britain. Suddenly Nuits-St-Georges, which had been on every hotel and restaurant list in the country, disappeared. The reason was simple. British merchants had rather liked the patriotic ring to 'St-Georges' and the vaguely suggestive feel of 'Nuits', and so, untrammelled by French *appellation* laws, had concocted any old stuff from all stations south to Casablanca and called it Nuits-St-Georges.

When it began to creep back on to wine lists in the late 1970s, Nuits-St-Georges was three times the price and half the colour – but it was the real thing. Nowadays it is one of the few relatively reliable 'village' names in Burgundy. The *appellation*, which includes the village of Prémeaux, is big: 925 acres (375 hectares). Though it has no *grands crus*, it has 38 *premiers crus* – more than any other AC – and many of these are extremely good. The wine can be rather slow to open out, often needing at least five years, but then it gets a lovely dry plumskins chewiness to it which ages to a deep figs-and-pruneskins fruit, chocolaty, smoky and rather decayed. It's delicious, I promise, whatever it sounds like! Best years (reds): 1988, '87, '86, '85, '83, '80, '78, '76. Best producers: Chauvenet, Chevillon, Dubois, Gouges, Grivot, Jadot, Jaffelin, Jayer, Labouré-Roi, Michelot, Moillard, Rion.

There are also minuscule amounts of white Nuits-St-Georges, believe it or not. The few precious bottles made by Domaine Henri Gouges are the most famous whites made in the Côte de Nuits, where the red Pinot Noir is so completely dominant that Monsieur Gouges doesn't even grow Chardonnay and Pinot Blanc but a strange white mutation of Pinot Noir. When he bought the *premier cru* Clos de Poirets vineyard in 1934 he noted with alarm that some of the red Pinot Noir vines were sprouting white grapes. So he took grafts and planted them in the neighbouring Perrière vineyard higher up the slope just below the treeline. Ever since then he has made exceptional white wine, very dry with a savoury, almost Pinot Noir perfume but then growing richer and fatter in your mouth – more like a top wine from the northern Rhône. Strange, but delicious, and hardly like white Burgundy at all. The production is never more than 2500 bottles and often considerably less. There is also a little Chardonnay planted in Clos Arlots, a mile further south, but I've never seen it away from the vineyard itself. Best years (whites): 1988, '87, '86, '85, '84, '83, '82.

PACHERENC DU VIC BILH AC
SOUTH-WEST

Gros Manseng, Petit Manseng, Ruffiac and others

What a name – hardly the most come-hither of titles for a white wine! At the end of World War Two there was scarcely anything left of this ancient vineyard, but luckily it is grown inside the same wine boundaries as Madiran. And as Madiran, also virtually extinct at the end of the war got its act together and expanded, so Pacherenc clawed its way back from the brink. But that name! Well, Pacherenc is local dialect for *piquets en rang* – posts in a line, and Vic Bilh are the local hills. So the name literally translates as 'posts in a line from the Vic Bilh hills' – a reference to the local habit of training vines very high on two-metre posts. Whatever the explanation it still does not do much for my thirst. But actually the wine, sometimes sweetish but usually dry, can have an exciting flavour of pears and apricots – especially if bottled straight off its lees. Only the best estates achieve this and even they make very little, because the total crop is only 90,000 bottles. If you find one, drink it as young as possible. Best producers: Aydie, Crampilh.

PALETTE AC
PROVENCE

Grenache, Mourvèdre, Cinsaut and others

Clairette, Grenache Blanc, Ugni Blanc and others

► Preparing grapes for pressing prior to fermentation at Château Simone.

Pine-needles and resin are what I taste in the wines of Palette – a tiny AC just east of Aix-en-Provence. Not that they actually employ these to make the wine, but the slopes on which the 62 acres (25 hectares) of vines grow are covered in pines and herbs, and for once I do see some possible connection between Provençal wines and the herb-strewn hills round the vineyards. Around 85,000 bottles of red, white and rosé Palette are made each year.

Palette reds and rosés, usually about 60,000 bottles in total, are made from Cinsaut, Mourvèdre and Grenache. The rosé is, well, herby and rather dry. The red: well, herby again. I find it tough and charmless. I'm told it does age, and the local market pays high prices for it, but so far I've had no luck. And pine resin and the rather bitter chewy bits from a herb like thyme are the only kind of memorable flavours I've got from tasting white Palette. But the *appellation* can be proud of one achievement. Given the basic neutral bunch of southern white grapes – Clairette, Grenache Blanc and Ugni Blanc – Château Simone, the only producer of white Palette, has managed to squeeze more flavour out of this trio than any other AC. It must be due to the limestone soil and two years' sojourn in oak barrels. Certainly, there are experts who think Palette is fantastic, but I'm content to admire it from a safe distance and advise people not to smoke when there's an open bottle around. Best producer: Simone.

PALMER, CH.
Margaux AC, *3ème cru classé*
HAUT-MÉDOC, BORDEAUX

Cabernet Sauvignon, Merlot, Cabernet Franc, Petit Verdot

Of all the properties which could justifiably feel underrated by the 1855 Classification, Château Palmer has the best case. Anyone who has the luck to drink this wonderful wine – even in a half-decent vintage – is won over, above all, by its perfume. It is as though every black and red fruit in the land has thrown in a bundle of its ripest flavours: blackcurrant, blackberry, plum, loganberry. But Palmer goes further. There's a rich, almost fat core to the wine; and curling through the fruit and the ripeness are trails of other fragrances – roses, violets, cedar and cigars, all in abundance. The first time I was offered Palmer I was so captivated by its smell I could hardly bear to drink it!

Named after a British major-general who fought in the Napoleonic Wars, it is an 86-acre (35-hectare) site on excellent gravel right next to Château Margaux. The irresistible plump fruit of Palmer is caused by the very high proportion of Merlot (40 per cent), with only 55 per cent Cabernet Sauvignon, three per cent Cabernet Franc and two per cent Petit Verdot. Although Château Margaux has now resumed its position as the greatest property in the Margaux AC, there was a period during the 1960s and most of the '70s when it was Palmer which held aloft the banner of brilliance in the Margaux AC. Best years: 1988, '87, '86, '85, '83, '82, '79, '78, '75, '71, '70. Second wine: Réserve-du-Général.

PAPE-CLÉMENT, CH.
Pessac Léognan AC, *cru classé de Graves*
BORDEAUX

Cabernet Sauvignon, Merlot

At the moment, Pape-Clément only seems to make good wine about once every decade: 1985 is exciting, 1975 outstanding (in a difficult year), 1966 beautifully mature and classic. But once every ten years isn't much of a record for an expensive and famous Graves Classed Growth. The 67-acre (27-hectare) property, named after the French Pope Clément V – whose brother gave it to him in 1300 – was then well-known for its therapeutic spring. Perhaps the owners have recently taken to dosing themselves with the water, because '86 and '85 are highly promising. Let's hope so, since Pape-Clément can mix ripe, sweet fruit with herby and tobaccoey scents in a most delicious way. Best years: 1988, '87, '86, '85, '75, '66.

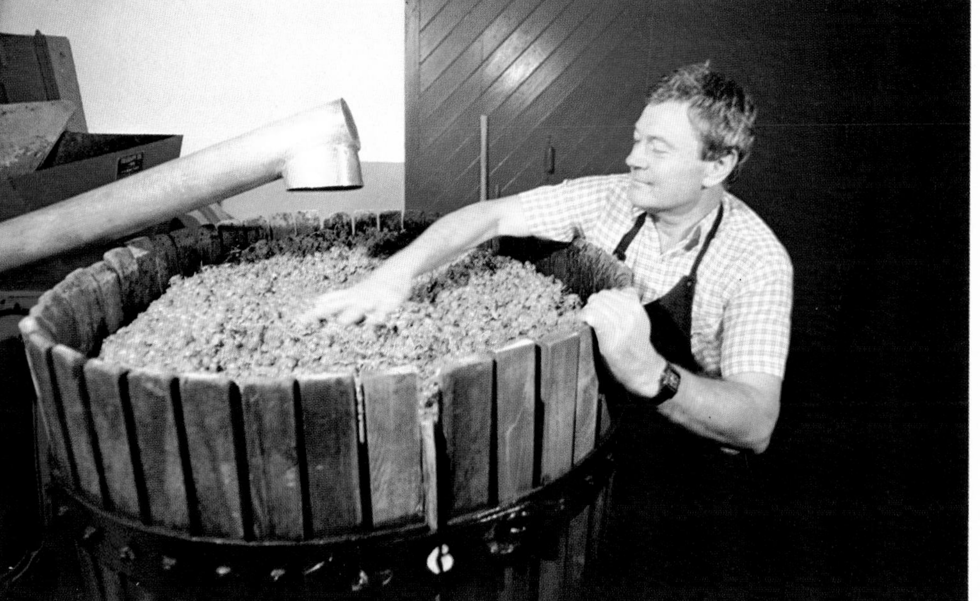

PAUILLAC AC
HAUT-MÉDOC, BORDEAUX

🍷 Cabernet Sauvignon, Merlot, Cabernet Franc and others

If there is a king of red wine grapes it has to be Cabernet Sauvignon. In every corner of the world where there is enough sun to ripen the fruit, it makes dark, dense, rather tough but wonderfully flavoured wines. Yet its heartland is the single village of Pauillac in the Haut-Médoc. Throughout the New World – and in much of southern France, Spain and Italy too – if you ask ambitious winemakers what model they take for Cabernet Sauvignon they will say Latour, Lafite-Rothschild or Mouton-Rothschild – one of the three Pauillac First Growths, each of which, in its different way, is an ultimate expression of Cabernet Sauvignon. There are 2250 acres (900 hectares) of vines in the AC, on deep gravel banks to the north, west and south of the town of Pauillac. This makes Pauillac AC the third biggest commune in the Haut-Médoc. Sleepily huddled at the muddy edge of the Gironde – a faded promenade, an idling boat, a few listless fishermen chatting on the quay, the local restaurant specializing in herrings – you'd never guess that for many this is the Mecca of the red wine world. Apart from the three First Growths, there are 15 other Classed Growths, including the world-famous Pichon-Lalande and Lynch-Bages. The wines go from terse, fretful and austere to blooming with friendly fruit, but the uniting characteristic of blackcurrant fruit and cedar or pencil-shavings perfume is never far distant. Few Pauillacs are ready young and most will last 20 years. Best years: 1988, '86, '85, '83, '82, '81, '79, '78. Best properties: Batailley, Fonbadet, Grand-Puy-Ducasse, Grand-Puy-Lacoste, Haut-Bages-Libéral, Haut-Batailley, Lafite-Rothschild, Latour, Lynch-Bages, Mouton-Rothschild, Pibran, Pichon-Baron, Pichon-Lalande.

PAVIE, CH.
St-Émilion AC, *premier grand cru classé*
BORDEAUX

🍷 Merlot, Cabernet Franc, Cabernet Sauvignon

The biggest of the St-Émilion *premiers grands crus* at 91 acres (37 hectares), enjoys a superb site on steep south-facing slopes just to the south-east of the town. Being biggest was obviously a bit more than Pavie could cope with in the '60s and '70s because none of the wines was outstanding; even the potentially strongest vintages had a soft, simple, buttered-brazil kind of flavour – very attractive but totally one-dimensional. Since 1979 things have bucked up dramatically and Pavie is now one of the most improved properties in St-Émilion. The fruit is still there, but the wines are far more concentrated and, while drinkable young, will happily improve for a decade or more to something very good indeed. Best years: 1988, '87, '85, '83, '82, '81, '79.

PÉCHARMANT AC
SOUTH-WEST

🍷 Merlot, Cabernet Sauvignon, Cabernet Franc, Malbec

Lovely red wines from a small enclave in the Bergerac region east of Bergerac town. The soil is relatively chalky, giving wines that are usually quite light in body but with a delicious, full, piercing flavour of blackcurrants and a most attractive grassy acidity. They are rarely very tannic but are, in general, so well-balanced that good vintages can easily age ten years and end up indistinguishable from a good Haut-Médoc. Recommended. Best years: 1988, '86, '85, '83, '82, '81. Best producers: Clos Peyrelevade, Corbiac, Haut-Pécharmant, Tiregand.

PERNAND-VERGELESSES AC
CÔTE DE BEAUNE, BURGUNDY

🍷 Pinot Noir

🥂 Chardonnay, Aligoté

Another of those off-the-beaten-track Burgundy villages which is consequently not much heard about. Yet Pernand-Vergelesses does have one considerable slice of luck: the great hill of Corton comes round from the east, and at its western end a decent-sized chunk lies inside the Pernand-Vergelesses boundary. Much of the best white Corton-Charlemagne comes from this western end. The red Corton lacks the richness of the wines from the south- and east-facing slopes, and takes longer to mature into a finely-balanced, savoury-rich red. Red sold under

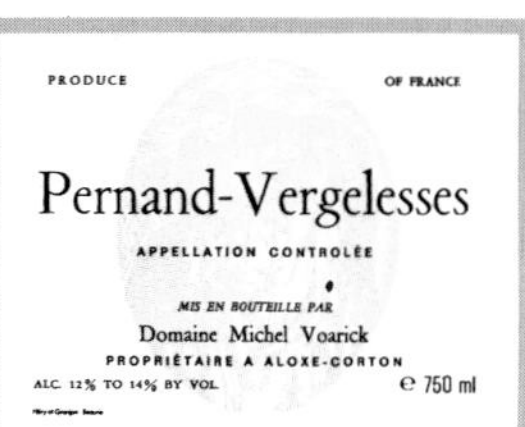

the Pernand-Vergelesses AC is immediately softer, easier, very attractive young with nice raspberry pastille fruit and a slight earthiness, though good to age for six to ten years. The 353 acres (143 hectares) of vineyards produce about 85 per cent red wine and, apart from Le Corton, the best vineyards are Île des Hautes Vergelesses and Les Basses Vergelesses, both *premiers crus*. Best years (reds): 1988, '87, '85, '83, '82, '78. Best producers: Besancenot-Mathouillet, Bonneau du Martray, Chandon de Briailles, Dubreuil-Fontaine, Laleure-Piot, Rapet, Rollin.

Although a sizeable chunk of the white *grand cru* Corton-Charlemagne lies within the parish boundaries, no one ever links poor old Pernand with the heady heights of Corton-Charlemagne because the name Pernand-Vergelesses never appears on the label (*grand cru* vineyards don't have to use their village name). And whereas Aloxe-Corton wines are frequently overpriced, Pernand-Vergelesses can be a bargain – and *that's* a rarity in Burgundy.

Most of the 50,000 bottles of white Pernand come from Chardonnay, and although they're a bit lean and dry to start with, they fatten up beautifully after two to four years in bottle. But there are also some very old plantings of Aligoté (some even used to be in the Corton-Charlemagne vineyards till the authorities found out), and the wine is super – dry, deep, snappy, almost peppery and scoured with lemon peel. *And* they have a vineyard cryptically named 'Under the Wood of Noel and the Pretty Girls', or somesuch! I think there's more to Pernand-Vergelesses than meets the eye! Best years (whites): 1988, '86, '85, '84, '83, '82. Best producers: Bonneau du Martray, Dubreuil-Fontaine, Germain, Guyon, Laleure-Piot, Pavelot, Rapet, Rollin.

PESSAC-LÉOGNAN AC
BORDEAUX

🍷 Cabernet Sauvignon, Cabernet Franc, Merlot and others

🍸 Sémillon, Sauvignon Blanc, Muscadelle

The recent (1987) revision of the AC system in the Graves area to the south of Bordeaux, achieved after years of lobbying, hived off the area immediately to the south of the city – centred on the villages of Pessac and Léognan, but also including the communes of Talence, Cadaujac, Villenave d'Ornon and Martillac as well as four others. This is the area of Graves which includes all the Classed Growths, and has the highest proportion of the classic gravelly soil which gives the Graves its name. Although there is now an exciting quality movement in the southern Graves, there is no doubt that the soil there is far less gravelly, sand and clay become increasingly dominant and both drainage and a decent aspect to the sun become more of a problem. In the north they have been able to call themselves Graves-Léognan, or Graves-Pessac since 1984. But real success came in 1987 with the new Pessac-Léognan AC.

The quality of the Graves reds has long been recognized, even so. Although Cabernet is the main grape, as in the Médoc, more emphasis is placed on the Merlot, and the resulting wines can be softer than Médoc contemporaries. The top half-dozen châteaux are superb, the less well known ones increasingly good. The standard of most whites in the region, however, has been depressingly poor in the past, but with the advent of cool fermentation, controlled yeast selection and the use of new oak barrels for fermentation and ageing of the wines, this is now one of the most exciting areas of France for top class whites. Best years (reds): 1988, '86, '85, '83, '82, '81, '79, '78. Best properties: Domaine de Chevalier, de Fieuzal, Haut-Bailly, Haut-Brion, la Louvière, Malartic-Lagravière, la Mission-Haut-Brion, Rochemorin, Smith-Haut-Lafitte, la Tour-Haut-Brion, la Tour-Martillac. Best years (whites): 1988, '87, '86, '85, '84, '83, '82. Best producers: Domaine de Chevalier, Couhins-Lurton, de Fieuzal, Haut-Brion, Laville-Haut-Brion, La Louvière, Malartic-Lagravière, Pontac-Monplaisir, de Rochemorin, Smith-Haut-Lafitte.

PETIT CHABLIS AC
CHABLIS, BURGUNDY

Chardonnay

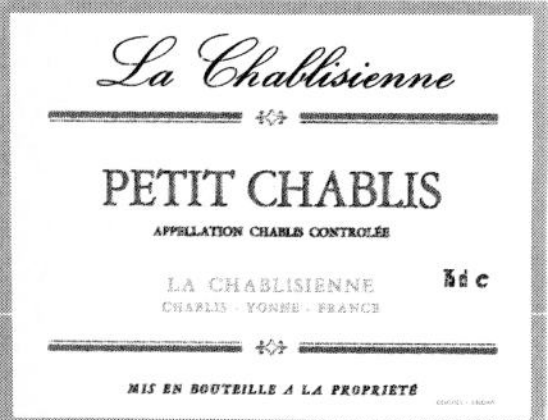

Petit Chablis means little Chablis – and that name fits the bill exactly. Uninspired, rather green, unripe Chardonnay wine from the least good nooks and crannies of the Chablis region. But Petit Chablis does sound demeaning doesn't it? Not good for the ego or the bank balance of the grower. So when there was a surge of interest in white Burgundy and Chablis in the late 1970s and early '80s, a lot of Petit Chablis land, especially that owned by politically-minded growers, was magically deemed worthy of the full Chablis AC – and, quite coincidentally, of an increased price. Had the wine changed in taste? No, but 'Chablis' does look so much nicer on the label, doesn't it?

What's left of Petit Chablis is about 300 acres (120 hectares) – which *must* be pretty feeble if the Chablis growers couldn't get them upgraded. The La Chablisienne co-operative is the best bet for an adequate light Chardonnay – but it's not even a bargain any more, so why bother?

PETIT-VILLAGE, CH.
Pomerol AC
BORDEAUX

Merlot, Cabernet Franc, Cabernet Sauvignon

Not the wine to get in a blind tasting because, although this property produces one of the top Pomerol wines, the style is much sterner and less sumptuous than that of its neighbours. This may partly be because the owner is Bruno Prats, who makes Cos d'Estournel, the outstanding wine of St-Estèphe, and who perhaps brings a little of his *médocain* instinct to bear on his Pomerol property. However, the soil also plays a part. There was a time when half this 27-acre (11-hectare) vineyard was planted with Cabernet Sauvignon, reflecting its gravel content, though now it is 80 per cent Merlot, 10 per cent Cabernet Franc and 10 per cent Cabernet Sauvignon. Some years, like 1982, *are* luscious and rich, but in general it is worth ageing Petit-Village for eight to ten years, even for 10–15 years in vintages like 1975 and '85. Best years: 1988, '85, '83, '82, '81, '79, '78, '75.

PÉTRUS, CH.
Pomerol AC
BORDEAUX

Merlot, Cabernet Franc

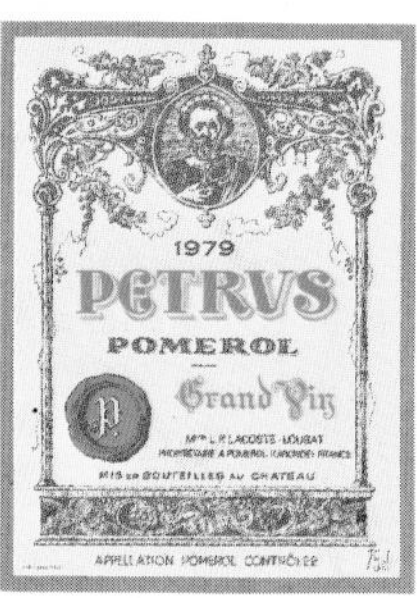

► During the grape-harvest at Château Pétrus, a helicopter dries off rain from the vines. Water on the grapes would dilute the juice and so impair quality.

Château Pétrus is a small, 28-acre (11·5-hectare) estate with charmingly unimpressive buildings in an area that, 30 years ago, used to merit merely a paragraph or two in 'other Bordeaux wines' sections. Yet Pétrus is now the most expensive red wine in the world. Its AC is Pomerol, so recently acclaimed that it still has no 'classification' of quality. If it did, Pétrus would stand alone and magnificent at the very head, and for two reasons.

First, the vineyard: this is situated on an oval of imperceptibly higher land which is virtually solid clay, shot through with nuggets of iron. Only Merlot can flourish in this soil and Pétrus is 95 per cent Merlot. These vines are remarkably old, often up to 70 years of age, which is rare in Pomerol and St-Émilion because the great frost of 1956 destroyed most of the vines and caused wholesale replanting. The owner of Pétrus simply waited patiently for several years while the old vines got their strength back. The result is a concentration of intensely pure fruit.

The second factor in Pétrus' quality is the caring genius of its co-owner, Christian Moueix, and his hugely talented winemaker, Jean-Claude Benouet. They ensure that only totally ripe grapes are picked (they only harvest in the afternoon to avoid dew diluting the juice and in 1987 a helicopter hovered over the vines to dry off vintage rains!); any portion of the wine which doesn't exude Pétrus quality is rejected and the whole crop is then aged in new oak barrels. The result is a wine of powerful, viscous intensity, a celestial syrup of ripe blackcurrants, blackberries, mulberries, plums and cream, overlaid with mint and tobacco scents and the perilous earthy excitement of fresh-dug truffles. Best years: 1988, '87, '86, '85, '83, '82, '81, '80, '79, '75, '71.

DE PEZ, CH.
St-Estèphe AC, *cru bourgeois supérieur*
HAUT-MÉDOC, BORDEAUX

Cabernet Sauvignon, Cabernet Franc, Merlot

I have never tasted a poor bottle of de Pez; nor have I tasted any which made my heart sing, but then ethereal, romantic joys are not St-Estèphe's speciality. Sturdy fruit, slow to evolve, but mouthfilling and satisfying, with a little hint of cedarwood and a good deal of blackcurrant to ride with their earthy taste – that's St-Estèphe's forte. De Pez – for long regarded as St-Estèphe's leading non-classified Growth, but now at least equalled by Meyney and Haut-Marbuzet – adds a leathery, plummy dimension in good vintages. The 57-acre (23-hectare) vineyard, well-placed inland from the Third Growth Calon-Ségur, has a lot of Cabernet Sauvignon (70 per cent), with 15 per cent Cabernet Franc, and 15 per cent Merlot; this goes a long way to explain why good vintages need 15–20 years to mature, and why they have such quality and depth of flavour when they do. Best years: 1988, '86, '85, '83, '82, '79, '78, '75.

PICHON-BARON, CH.
Pauillac AC, *2ème cru classé*
HAUT-MÉDOC, BORDEAUX

Cabernet Sauvignon, Merlot, Malbec

Somehow Pichon-Baron got left behind in the rush. Its Pauillac neighbour, Pichon-Lalande, and its St-Julien neighbours, Léoville-Las-Cases and Léoville-Barton, leapt at the chance offered by the string of fine vintages from 1978. They established a leadership at the top of the Second Growths which now seriously challenges the First Growths for sheer quality and surpasses several of them for consistency. What about Pichon-Baron? Its 74 acres (30 hectares) of vineyards are regarded as superb. Its mixture of 75 per cent Cabernet Sauvignon, 23 per cent Merlot and two per cent Malbec is ideal for making great Pauillac. Yet the wines are medium-weight. I remember thinking how good the 1982 was when I first tasted it – until I tasted the other Pauillac '82s. Since 1987 the wine-making has been taken over by the talented Jean-Michel Cazes of Lynch-Bages. Best years: 1988, '87, '86, '83, '82.

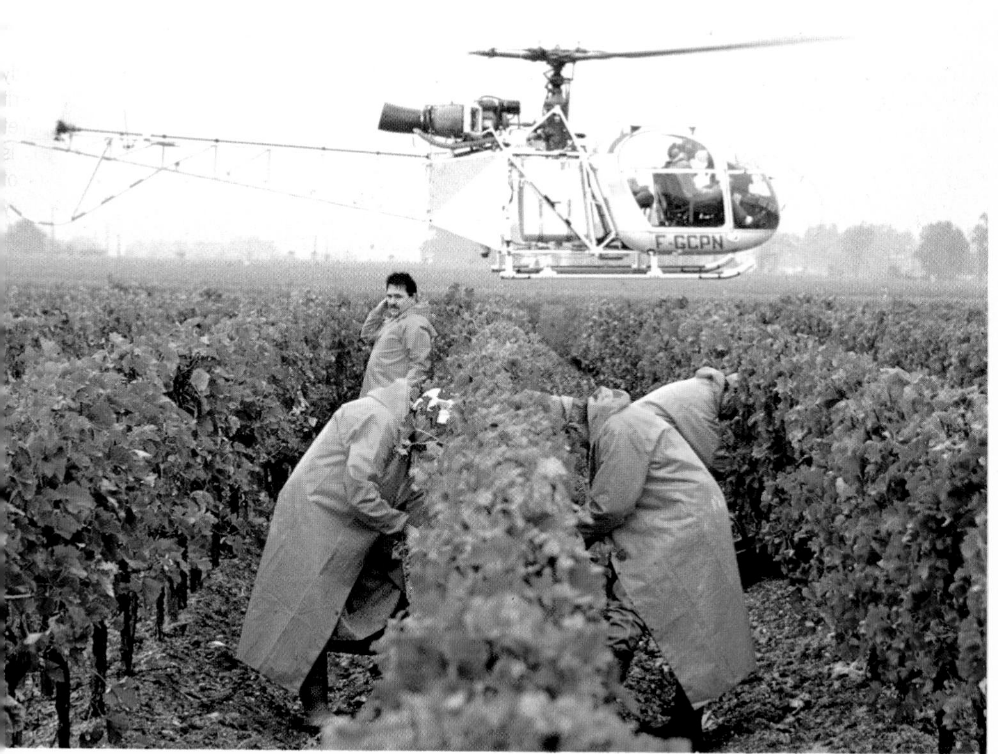

PICHON-LALANDE, CH.
Pauillac AC, *2ème cru classé*
HAUT-MÉDOC, BORDEAUX

Cabernet Sauvignon, Merlot, Cabernet Franc, Petit Verdot

Of all the top-notch wines in the Haut-Médoc, none has so consistently excited me, beguiled me, and totally satisfied me as Pichon-Lalande. The vineyard is on excellent land next to Latour and Léoville-Las-Cases in St-Julien. In fact some of the vines are in St-Julien and this, combined with the highest proportion of Merlot in Pauillac (35 per cent), may account for the sumptuous, fleshy richness of the wine, and its burst of blackcurrant, walnut and vanilla perfume, and I mean perfume – heady, searching – not just smell. But the vineyards are no better than those of the under-achieving brother Pichon-Baron and the real cause of Pichon-Lalande's sensual triumph over the usually austere Pauillac community is the inspired, messianic figure of Madame de Lencquesaing. She took over the property in 1978 and has since led Pichon-Lalande upwards in a wave of passion and involvement. Quite a woman. Quite a wine. Every vintage seems to be good nowadays. And don't be deceived by the lush caress of the rich fruit – there's lots of tannin and acid lurking, and the wines, though wonderful at six to seven years old, will usually last for 20 at least. Best years: 1988, '87, '86, '85, '84, '83, '82, '81, '80, '79, '78, '75. Second wine: Réserve de la Comtesse.

PICPOUL DE PINET VDQS
LANGUEDOC-ROUSSILLON

Picpoul, Clairette, Terret Blanc

Here's our friend the 'lip-stinger' Picpoul again; in the salty, damp vineyards of the Loire estuary where it masquerades as Gros Plant and makes sensationally sour white, it fully deserves the nickname. But Picpoul de Pinet, a beleaguered little Coteaux du Languedoc *cru* between Montpellier and Béziers, is soft and bland, dry, yes, but almost terminally lacking in acidity. What's the problem? Well, it *may* be that the extra sun of the Mediterranean coast ripens the grape well enough for it to *lose* all its acidity – this often happens with Ugni Blanc, which makes a very tart wine further north in Cognac. But it *could* be that this is an entirely different grape! So why would a different grape, producing soft, mild wine, be called 'lip-stinger'? All I can say is that the tracing and identifying of exactly what grape is what is a tortuous and exhausting academic exercise undertaken by about one demented botanist per generation. Anyway, there are about one million bottles produced – and you have to drink it *really* young to get any buzz from it at all.

PINOT BLANC

Pinot Blanc is a chorus member rather than a solo artiste in the grape hierarchy of France. In Italy, however, exciting things are achieved with it, and in the Alto Adige it can outshine even the great Chardonnay. There is a great deal of similarity between the wines of these two varieties, but they are not related – Pinot Blanc is a mutation of the red Pinot Noir, Chardonnay is not. In Burgundy, particularly in the *grand cru* vineyard of Corton where both varieties are planted, Pinot Blanc produces round, fat, apple-creamy wine, positively rich in a warm year, but lacking the exciting balance of flavours which makes Chardonnay so special. However, Pinot Blanc's chief power-base in France is in Alsace where, with the similar-tasting Auxerrois, often called Pinot Blanc for simplicity's sake, it is taking over the 'workhorse' role from Sylvaner and Chasselas. This is good news because not only does the wine have a clear, yeasty, appley taste, sometimes with a slight grapy 'spice' when young, but good examples can also age to a delicious, honeyed fullness after a couple of years. When picked early it is neutral and quite acid – the perfect base material for sparkling wine. Most of Alsace's expanding fizz production, Crémant d'Alsace, now uses Pinot Blanc.

PINOT GRIS

Pinot Gris, or Tokay d'Alsace, isn't a subtle grape, but the fat, broad, honey and raisin flavour of which it is capable is so compelling and indulgent that I'm really not bothered about subtlety. Alsace is where almost all the French plantings are, although its 1500 acres (600 hectares) only represent five per cent of Alsace's total. Almost all the vines are on the steep slopes of the best wine villages, because local winegrowers revere the variety as the best accompaniment for the region's richest dishes. Even a simple co-operative-produced Pinot Gris will have a lick of honey. The acidity is low and the colour deep, but for some reason this doesn't affect the wine's ability to mature. As the quality improves through Vendange Tardive (made from late-harvested grapes) to Sélection de Grains Nobles (intensely sweet grapes affected by noble rot), the honey becomes more and more gooey – but it doesn't become classier or more perfumed. It picks up smoke, it packs in raisins, and overlays this with a thick fat coating like butter oozing through fresh toast. Pinot Gris at its best still has the common touch, rich, fat, intelligible – and irresistible.

The dark-skinned grape occasionally surfaces in Burgundy, where it still clings to its honeyed taste, making a deep, over-golden-coloured wine. In a very welcome survival from the nineteenth century, when the grape was much more widespread in France than it is today, it appears as Malvoisie at Ancenis, in the western Loire; and at Reuilly, west of Sancerre in the upper Loire, it makes some extremely pleasant pale wine which is almost rosé.

PINOT NOIR

◀ Pinot Noir stretching as far as the eye can see – a characteristic Burgundian vinescape. France has more Pinot Noir than any other country.

Burgundy's red grape is very difficult to grow, as anyone who has ever considered giving up Burgundy because the price is so high and the quality so variable will realise. It buds early and ripens early, which makes it suitable for cool climates. But its tight bunches are seriously prone to rot, it reacts to overcropping by producing wine little better than rosé, and yet because its fruit sets very irregularly, it is often pruned for extra quantity. When it *does* set, of course, you're going to overcrop, which means the vine will object and produce pale juice – and so it goes on.

Pinot Noir is a *very* ancient variety, and was probably one of the first successful attempts to isolate and tame a specific wild vine. That was at least 2000 years ago, and yet the wildness is still there. No other vine

mutates so quickly – one authority reckons there are as many as 1000 different Pinot Noir types in Burgundy alone! Yet this savagery is what can make its wine so exciting. Only Syrah has such a variety of flavours to offer. Strawberry, cherry, raspberry and plum predominate in the young wine, but as it ages, the cherry becomes scented, the plums turn to prunes, chocolate and woodsmoke and figs mingle with truffles and over-hung game and the decayed stink of old vegetables. It sounds dreadful but it *is* a shocking flavour, and although many Burgundies never get near it, those that do are more startlingly good than the purer, cleaner flavours of great Bordeaux.

Pinot's sphere of influence is almost entirely in the centre and north of France. It makes light reds or quite tasty rosés in Savoie, Jura, the Loire – especially Sancerre – and Alsace, but its most important contribution outside Burgundy is as a major component of Champagne, occasionally as a rosé, but usually providing the body to fatten out the leaner flavour of Chardonnay. The juice is run off the skins straight after pressing so has almost no colour at all. Altogether there are over 42,000 acres (17,000 hectares) of Pinot Noir in France, one-third of which are in the only place it really has the chance to set the world alight: Burgundy.

POL ROGER
Champagne AC
CHAMPAGNE

Pinot Noir, Chardonnay, Pinot Meunier

The label of Pol Roger non-vintage is bordered in black. Why? As a mark of respect and mourning for Winston Churchill! This may sound far-fetched, but Pol Roger is the most anglophile of companies, and I rather think the current head, Christian de Billy, would take it as a great compliment if you mistook him for an Englishman! Winston Churchill was an avid, indeed voracious consumer of Pol Roger, and it was Pol Roger he was thinking of when he said, in the dark days of World War Two, 'In victory we deserve it, in defeat we need it'.

In 1984, Pol Roger launched a Cuvée Sir Winston Churchill, which, in a period when many special De Luxe Champagnes are proving overpriced disappointments, is a delicious, refined drink worthy of the name. However, most of the production is of the non-vintage White Foil, which is gentle, light and consistently good. They also produce a Vintage, a Vintage Chardonnay, and a Vintage Reserve Special.

POMEROL AC
BORDEAUX

Merlot, Cabernet Franc, Cabernet Sauvignon

When I was at university – not *that* long ago! – there was a restaurant near the river which was a bit on the posh side but was *the* place to take a girl to if you were super-desperate to impress her. There was only one way I could afford to do this – order the cheapest claret on their list with all the self-assured bluster I could manage. I was in luck. It was a bottle simply labelled 'Pomerol' – bottled in Bristol – and I don't think the wine-waiter had any more idea where Pomerol was than I did. But then I didn't care – the wine was so smooth and plummy it should have been twice the price and every sip saw me set my amorous sights a notch higher. Which taught me two things. Firstly, Pomerol has a uniquely smooth, rich taste for a dry red Bordeaux. And secondly, overindulgence in it builds a totally unfounded confidence in one's social skills.

That was Pomerol then. The flavour remains just as seductively rich, but from being a virtually unknown AC 'ooh, somewhere near St-Émilion, I think', it is possibly now the most famous of the Bordeaux regions, in the United States at least; it is certainly the most expensive of the Bordeaux ACs across the board, and the home of the world's most spectacular and exorbitantly expensive red wine – Château Pétrus. Yet Pomerol is the most anonymous of Bordeaux's ACs. You can't tell by looking where it starts – a country lane divides it from the vines of St-Émilion – and you can't tell why it's special.

The unique quality lies in that soil – 1800 acres (730 hectares) of deep, close-packed cloddish clay, interspersed with iron, a little gravel, a little sand, but ultimately it is the clay which makes Pomerol great. The only grape which relishes clay is the Merlot. Most properties have over 80 per cent and the result is superb, inimitable wine – richer than any dry red wine should be, sometimes buttery, sometimes creamy with honeyed spices too; often plummy, but there's blackcurrant there as well, raisins, chocolate, roasted nuts and the disturbing perfume of truffles, with mint to freshen it up. No wonder it's expensive! Best years: 1988, '87, '86, '85, '83, '82, '81, '79, '78. Best properties: Bonalgue, Bon-Pasteur, Certan-de-May, Clinet, Clos René, la Conseillante, l'Évangile, Feytit-Clinet, Lafleur, La Fleur-Pétrus, Petit-Village, Pétrus, le Pin, de Sales, Trotanoy, Vieux-Château-Certan.

POMMARD AC
CÔTE DE BEAUNE, BURGUNDY

Pinot Noir

I'd be more enthusiastic about Pommard if I hadn't had so many bottles at distressingly high prices which were coarse and rough with sullen, scentless flavours. I've had some very good Bourgogne Rouge from the same village's producers which is actually better than their Pommard! Now I'm not asking for suave, silky flavours – Pommard has never been good at that – but I am asking for full, round, beefy flavours, a bit jammy when young but becoming plummy, chocolaty and a little meaty with age. In fact, I want old-fashioned flavours. But *fruit* has to be at the core of the flavour – not just alcohol and tannin and jam. When it's good, Pommard ages well, often for ten years or more. There are no *grands crus* in the 840 acres (340 hectares) of vines which occupy the slopes between Beaune and Volnay, but Les Rugiens Bas, Les Épenots and Les Arvelets (all *premiers crus*) are the best sites. Best years: 1988, '87, '85, '83, '80, '78. Best producers: Gaunoux, Lehaye, Lejeune, Monnier, de Montille, Parent, Château de Pommard, Pothier-Rieusset, Pousse d'Or.

PONTET-CANET, CH.
Pauillac AC, *5ème cru classé*
HAUT-MÉDOC, BORDEAUX

Cabernet Sauvignon, Merlot, Cabernet Franc

Pontet-Canet was, until the mid-1970s, one of the most popular and widely available of the Haut-Médoc Classed Growths. The 185-acre (75-hectare) vineyard next door to Mouton-Rothschild regularly produced the largest amount of wine of any of the Classed Growths, and no wine was château-bottled until 1972; barrels were freely shipped to every sort of bottler to do what they liked with it. The result was cheap, but hardly authentic, claret in considerable quantities. Since 1979 Pontet-Canet has been owned by the Tesserons of the St-Estèphe Fourth Growth Lafon-Rochet, and gradually we are seeing a return to the big, chewy, blackcurrant and sweet-oak style of which Pontet-Canet is capable. Best years: 1988, '86, '85, '83, '82.

POTENSAC, CH.
Médoc AC, *cru grand bourgeois*
BORDEAUX

Cabernet Sauvignon, Merlot, Cabernet Franc

What a pleasure to be able to give an unreserved thumbs-up to a Bordeaux wine. Thumbs-up for quality, thumbs-up for consistency – and thumbs-up for value. There are two keys to Potensac's fabulous success. First, there is a ridge of gravel here. These are rare in the northern Médoc AC but crucial to allow a well-drained vineyard capable of fine wine. Second, the 100-acre (40-hectare) estate is owned and run by Michel Delon, the genius of St-Julien's great Second Growth Léoville-Las-Cases. Alone of all the proprietors in the lowly Médoc AC, he draws out a richness, a concentration and a complexity of blackcurrant, vanilla and spice flavour which during the 1980s has regularly surpassed many Classed Growths for quality. Potensac can be drunk at four to five years old, but fine vintages will improve for at least ten, the 1982 for up to twice that. Best years: 1988, '86, '85, '83, '82, '81, '80, '79, '78, '76.

POUILLY-FUISSÉ AC
MÂCONNAIS, BURGUNDY

Chardonnay

The wine I love to hate. There must be more examples of flagrantly over-priced, second-rate Pouilly-Fuissé on the market than any other wine. American demand is the problem. The name caught on there in a most dramatic way, and what was admittedly the leading wine of the Mâconnais – but not a patch on a decent Meursault or Puligny-Montrachet – demanded, and obtained, a price higher than either. Well, a weaker dollar has put paid to that; prices dropped 50 per cent in 1986 and even more drastically since. Now the wine, although still expensive, is beginning to find a vaguely sensible price level.

Pouilly-Fuissé is a dry white wine from the vineyards of five villages – Pouilly, Fuissé (yes, you did see a comma, they're two different villages!), Vergisson, Chaintré and Solutré. The vineyards are beautiful – clustered under the startling rock outcrop of Solutré. Many are ideally situated to produce fine wine, but the overbearing importance of the Chaintré co-op, which processes over 95 per cent of the AC's crop, and the cynical disregard for quality by the merchants who buy three-quarters of the wine for their own-label requirements, has meant that most growers can get a good living by simply milking their vineyards of every last grape. This would explain why less than 1500 acres (600 hectares) of vines manage to produce 5·6 million bottles a year.

Luckily, two or three per cent of the AC is in the hands of committed growers who care passionately about the quality that can make Pouilly-Fuissé a great wine. They restrict their yields, use only ripe grapes, employ wooden barrels (almost unheard of at the Chaintré co-op) to ferment and mature their wines, and the result is great wine – buttery, nutty, the fruit full of peach and melon and banana, and all this enriched with the spice of cloves and cinnamon and a generous splash of honey. These wines can be wonderful at two years old but often age beautifully for up to ten years. Best years: 1988, '87, '86, '85, '83. Best producers: Corsin, Feret, Château Fuissé (Vincent), Guffens-Heynen, Leger-Plumet, Luquet, Noblet.

► The vineyards of Pouilly-Fuissé, in the Mâconnais, are dominated by the spectacular cliff of Solutré.

POUILLY-FUMÉ AC
UPPER LOIRE

Sauvignon Blanc

That 'fumé' in the title means 'smoky', and there's no doubt that a good Pouilly-Fumé has a strong pungent smell. The old-time wine writers used to say it had a whiff of gunflint about it. But the smokiness which *I* find is that fabulous, fresh yet acrid stench of roasting coffee.

The only grape allowed is the Sauvignon Blanc, which is famous for its gooseberry, grassy-green, even asparagus flavours, and what gives the extra smokiness in Pouilly is that many of its vineyards – covering 1500 acres (600 hectares) on slopes near the town of Pouilly-sur-Loire – are on a particularly flinty soil called silex. The wines produced on this type of soil are tremendously full, meaty even, and filled with the heady perfume of lychees and elderflower.

However, by no means all Pouilly-Fumé wines are as exciting as this, and dramatic price rises in recent years – even for the most basic wines from the less good vineyards – have meant that this is an AC of great potential quality, but one whose ordinary wines are very over-priced. The best wines come from the hamlets of Les Berthiers and Les Loges: look for these names, and the word 'silex' on the label. Pouilly-Fumé may also be labelled Pouilly-Blanc-Fumé or Blanc Fumé de Pouilly. Best years: 1988, '87, '86, '85. Best producers: Bailly, Didier Dagueneau (his 'silex' is superb), de Ladoucette (his Baron de L is a crazy price but very good), Redde, Saget, Tracy.

POUILLY-LOCHÉ AC, POUILLY-VINZELLES AC
MÂCONNAIS, BURGUNDY

Chardonnay

Loché and Vinzelles are two perfectly decent Mâconnais villages with vines on the flatter land just to the east of Fuissé. Funnily enough, the growers of Vinzelles tried to organize their own AC in 1922 – long before Pouilly-Fuissé – but as Pouilly-Fuissé's Midas touch turned every bottling run into a money-minting extravaganza, it seemed obvious that adding Pouilly to their own names might prove profitable. That's the angle. So does it work? Yes, Pouilly-Vinzelles and Pouilly-Loché are more expensive than equivalent wines like Mâcon-Viré. And no, the quality of the wine – largely processed by the Loché co-op, but sold as Pouilly-Vinzelles regardless of which village it came from – is not a patch on a good Pouilly-Fuissé, and indeed no better than the normal Mâcon-Clessé or whatever. Once again we're in the impasse of a highly efficient co-op doing a highly efficient processing job, but with everyone getting too greedy and not asking themselves – do I *really* deserve that price, shouldn't I try to make better wine first?

POUILLY-SUR-LOIRE AC
UPPER LOIRE

Chasselas

Pouilly-sur-Loire is the town which gives its name to the famous Pouilly-Fumé, one of the world's leading whites from the Sauvignon Blanc grape. However, 15 per cent of its vineyards are planted not with Sauvignon but with Chasselas – the area's traditional grape for hundreds of years – and these wines can only take the Pouilly-sur-Loire AC.

Chasselas is not much of a grape – it gives light, frail, tasteless whites whose only worth lies in their youthfulness, though it makes quite a pleasant eating grape. The reason it still survives, despite being both less good and less popular than the Sauvignon, is that some Pouilly land is not suitable for Sauvignon. But with rocketing prices for the Sauvignon-based Pouilly-Fumé tempting growers, irresistibly, to plant Sauvignon wherever remotely possible, it will soon only be the *totally* unsuitable land which grows Chasselas. Production of Pouilly-sur-Loire is about 300,000 bottles annually and falling. The declining production is no great loss to the wine world, because even now the only examples with any character are from producers who pass the Chasselas wine over Sauvignon lees to pick up a bit of flavour! Drink as young as possible.

POUJEAUX, CH.
Moulis AC, *cru grand bourgeois exceptionnel*
HAUT-MÉDOC, BORDEAUX

Cabernet Sauvignon, Merlot, Cabernet Franc, Petit Verdot

Poujeaux is one of the properties whose ever-improving wine-making standards are propelling the Moulis AC more and more into the limelight. It's a big property – at 125 acres (50 hectares) second only in size to Chasse-Spleen among Moulis' châteaux – and is beautifully located on the gravel banks around the village of Grand-Poujeaux. Although its reputation is for dry, long-lived wines, recent vintages have been richer, more supple, with a delicious chunky fruit, new-oak sweetness and a slight scent of tobacco. This more accurately reflects the very high percentage of Merlot in the vineyard – 35 per cent, with the same amount of Cabernet Sauvignon, 15 per cent Cabernet Franc, and an unusually large amount of the late-ripening Petit Verdot, 15 per cent. Indeed the Petit Verdot may be a major reason why, though Poujeaux is attractive at only six to seven years old, good vintages can easily last 20–30 years. Best years: 1988, '86, '85, '83, '82, '81, '78.

PREMIÈRES CÔTES DE BLAYE AC
BORDEAUX

Merlot, Cabernet Sauvignon, Cabernet Franc, Malbec

Sémillon, Sauvignon Blanc, Muscadelle

Not one of my favourite Bordeaux regions, but there are definite signs of improvement. Up till now the problems have been a lack of that acid bite and tannic grip which make red Bordeaux special. The wines have been smudgy, sludgy things, jammy and sweet to taste and earthy of texture. Premières Côtes de Blaye is the supposedly superior AC for reds and whites from the Blayais, a wine area of 6700 acres (2700 hectares) on the opposite side of the Gironde to Lamarque in the Haut-Médoc. (Technically, AC Blaye or Blayais is also allowed in this area. In practice, virtually all the red wines are sold as Premières Côtes.) The AC for whites permits only three grape varieties, as against seven for Côtes de Blaye. The wines can be dry, medium or even sweet, but in practice almost all of the best dry ones use the Côtes de Blaye AC. Don't go out of your way to try these, but if you find one, drink it as young as possible.

Although vines were planted here long before they were in the Médoc, any wine fame the Premières Côtes de Blaye once had is long gone, and Blaye itself, a rather attractive little town, is best known for its citadel and the car ferry to Lamarque. Still, things *are* improving and the following châteaux are beginning to make attractive, rather fresher reds from Cabernet which are ready at two to three years, but can age for two or three more if you want: Bas Vallon, Bourdieu, Charron, l'Escadre, Grand-Barrail, Haut-Sociondo, Jonqueyres, Peybonhomme.

PREMIÈRES CÔTES DE BORDEAUX AC
BORDEAUX

Merlot, Cabernet Sauvignon, Cabernet Franc

Sémillon, Sauvignon Blanc, Muscadelle

Premières Côtes de Bordeaux has some of the most captivating scenery in Bordeaux. This lovely hill-tousled AC stretches for 38 miles (60km) down the right bank of the Garonne river. Time and again as you breast a hill you find yourself at the top of steep slopes running down to the Garonne, with an unparalleled view across to the famous properties of Graves and Sauternes – on the opposite bank.

The Premières Côtes de Bordeaux has always been thought of as sweet white territory, especially since it has three communes – Cadillac, Loupiac, and Ste-Croix-du-Mont – which do specialize in 'Sauternes look-alike' sweeties. But as the fashion for sweet wines faded during the '70s, more and more growers turned to red wine with a good deal of success. In the last ten years white plantations have dropped by over 20 per cent to about 1730 acres (700 hectares). Most of this white, however, only qualifies for Bordeaux Sec AC, since the Premières Côtes AC requires a minimum of four grams of sugar per litre of wine. This isn't a lot, but it *is* too much for growers who are trying to make fashionable dry-as-a-bone whites. The result is that reds forge ahead. There are now 3845 acres (1556 hectares) of red vineyards.

In the north, near Bordeaux, a certain amount of *clairet* is made – light red, halfway to rosé for quick drinking. However, as the vineyards mature, a very attractive juicy fruit quality is becoming evident, and – with investment in better equipment, including some oak barrels for ageing – the future looks bright for the Côtes. Reds and rosés are usually delicious at two to three years old but should last for five to six; the whites, especially the dry ones, won't last that long. Best years (reds): 1988, '86, '85, '83, '82. Best properties: Brethous, Cayla, Fayau, Grand-Mouëys, du Juge, Peyrat, Reynon, la Roche, Tanesse. Best years (whites): 1988, '87, '86. Best producers: Birot, Grand Mouëys, du Juge (in the Premières Côtes, though they may release their wines under the simple Bordeaux AC), Lamothe, Reynon, Tanesse.

PRIEURÉ-LICHINE, CH.
Margaux AC, *4ème cru classé*
HAUT-MÉDOC, BORDEAUX

Cabernet Sauvignon, Merlot, Cabernet Franc, Petit Verdot

If you're short of something to do on Christmas Day, no problem. Nothing on this Easter? I've the answer. I've also the answer for New Year's Day, Ash Wednesday, Labour Day, May Day, Hallowe'en, or any other day you care to mention. You go to visit Château Prieuré-Lichine in Bordeaux because this property is open 365 days a year! I must say I find it pretty astonishing. But then Prieuré-Lichine has never been an ordinary château. Alexis Lichine, who was probably the greatest promoter and apostle of French wines this century, owned and ruled the property until his death in 1989. This extraordinary man virtually single-handedly created the American market for high quality, estate-bottled wines from France. This zeal to press the flesh and pop the top of a bottle in persuasive mood is what kept his property – 143 acres (58 hectares) spread all over Cantenac and Margaux – open all year round. The wine is increasingly good in the '80s, adding a little weight to the gentle, perfumed style typical of the property. It is usually ready quite young, but keeps well for 10–15 years. Best years: 1988, '86, '85, '83, '82, '78, '71.

PUISSEGUIN-ST-ÉMILION AC
BORDEAUX

Merlot, Cabernet Franc, Cabernet Sauvignon, Malbec

One of the smaller St-Émilion satellites lying to the north-east of the town of St-Émilion, in charming, gently hilly countryside, with vineyards covering 1600 acres (650 hectares). The wines are usually fairly solid, without being inspiring; they have an attractive chunky fruit but are a bit short on perfume and excitement. Even so, they're usually good, full-bodied drinking at three to five years. There is an important co-operative. Best years: 1988, '87, '85, '83, '82. Best properties: Beaulieu, Bel-Air, Durand-Laplagne, des Laurets, Vieux-Château-Guibeau.

PULIGNY-MONTRACHET AC
CÔTE DE BEAUNE, BURGUNDY

Chardonnay

If you feel a thirst coming on in Puligny-Montrachet, making a beeline for the Café du Centre won't do you much good. Although the sign is still there, the café has been closed for years. In fact all the cafés and bars in Puligny are shut. It's a strange feeling! Puligny-Montrachet – the home of what most people reckon is the greatest dry white wine in the world – and yet you can't get a drink there for love or money! Maybe it's because prices for Puligny's superb whites have risen to such astronomical heights overseas that growers jealously guard every single bottle to earn their dollars, pounds and Swiss francs. But the real reason is probably to be found in the fact that this dull little village has been declining in population for years as the mighty merchants of neighbouring Beaune buy up the land to guarantee their supplies of wine, and families whose forebears have worked the vineyards for generations must shuffle off townwards in search of work.

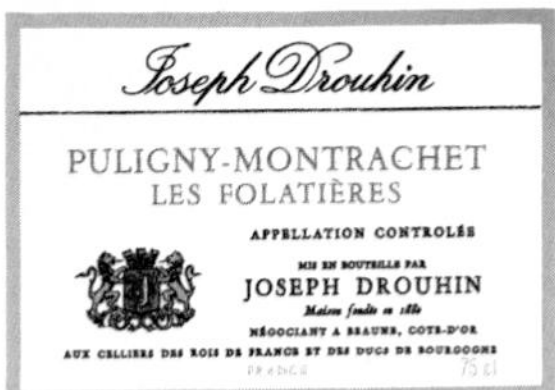

But the mediocrity of the village cannot dim the brilliance of its best vineyards. Altogether there are 580 acres (235 hectares) of vines – about 97 per cent white Chardonnay, producing 1·2 million bottles a year. The pinnacle is the *grand cru* Le Montrachet, an ordinary-looking 18½-acre (7·5-hectare) vineyard which manages to produce such a wine that Alexandre Dumas said it should only be drunk 'on one's knees with head uncovered' while its smell has been likened to 'a religious cantata resounding through the vaults of a Gothic cathedral'! Stirring stuff, eh!

There are three other *grands crus*, almost as good but less spiritual – Abide With Me at a Wembley Cup Final perhaps – and ten *premiers crus* which are still among the most exciting wines in Burgundy. These take up all the best slopes above the village, and although the flatter land is allowed the Puligny-Montrachet AC, the result is less thrilling.

Good vintages really need five years to show what all the fuss is about, while the *premiers crus* and *grands crus* wines may need ten years and can last for 20 or more. Best years: 1988, '87, '86, '85, '84, '83, '82, '79, '78. Best producers: Bachelet-Ramonet, Boisson-Vadot, Boyer-Devèze, Carillon, Chartron & Trebuchet, Drouhin, Jadot, Labouré-Roi, Laguiche, Leflaive, Château de Puligny-Montrachet, Ramonet-Prudhon, Rodet, Roux, Sauzet, Thénard.

PYRÉNÉES-ORIENTALES
LANGUEDOC-ROUSSILLON

Pyrénées-Orientales is the torrid, gale-scoured, southernmost French *département*, climbing up to the Spanish border in a succession of thin-aired high passes which start in alarming but visually exhilarating style on the sheer cliffs above the Mediterranean, and end shrouded in clouds near Andorra. Total wine production is usually about 55 million bottles, over half of which are *vin de pays*. The ACs are firstly, the *vins doux naturels* – sweet, fortified wines, usually from the Grenache or Muscat grape, of which Rivesaltes and Banyuls are the best known; the dark red Collioure, based on the Grenache, from near the Spanish border; and Côtes du Roussillon and Côtes du Roussillon-Villages, whose reds and rosés are some of the south's best cheap wines. The extreme climate is much better suited to red than white, but there is some quite attractive Côtes du Roussillon white from the Macabeo grape occasionally improved by a little Malvoisie. The Vin de Pays des Pyrénées-Orientales designation covers the *département*, though there are five zonal *vins de pays* of which 'Catalan' is the most important. There are also about 1½ million bottles of white Vin de Pays des Pyrénées-Orientales which aren't terribly exciting and *must* be drunk very young. The one white wine glory of the *département* is nearer a deep gold in colour – the Muscat de Rivesaltes, full, rich, gooey, winning no prizes for perfume, but thick and grapy nonetheless.

Unlike other southern *vins de pays*, there is little experimental vine planting, but a few estates, like La Barrera and Mas Chichet, are making exciting use of Merlot and Cabernet Sauvignon.

► The snow-thick peaks of the Pyrenees form a spectacular backdrop to the ancient region of Roussillon (now the Pyrénées-Orientales *département*). Roussillon vineyards, the most southerly in France, produce a distinctive variety of wines, ranging from the ripe raisin-rich *vins doux naturels* to light, fruity-fresh *vins de pays* – increasingly made by carbonic maceration.

QUARTS DE CHAUME AC *grand cru*
CENTRAL LOIRE

🍷 Chenin Blanc

Sample a young Quarts de Chaume, and you'd never know that you were experiencing one of the world's greatest sweet wines in its infancy. Whereas most dessert wines at least taste rich right from the start, Quarts de Chaume can be rather nuttily dull, vaguely sweet in a crisp apple kind of way and acidic – above all, acidic. This is thanks to the Chenin grape – the most fiercely, raspingly acidic of all France's great grapes, frequently used to make dry whites so strangled with their own sourness they never recover. But on the 100 acres (40 hectares) of gentle slopes protected by a low horseshoe of hills around the village of Chaume, the Chenin finds one of its most special microclimates.

This is the *grand cru* Quarts de Chaume, a little enclave inside the larger Coteaux du Layon AC. The vineyards slope south to the little Layon river, and if the sun shines, the grapes – protected from northerly chill – ripen more than any others in the Loire. And as the mists of autumn begin to twine and curl off the river, the magic noble rot fungus concentrates the richness to as great a degree as in Sauternes. And yet the acidity remains proud and unmoved. They have to go through the vineyard several times so as to pick only the grapes affected by 'noble rot', and this contributes to Quarts de Chaume having the lowest maximum yield of any AC in France – 22 hectolitres per hectare; in many years they don't even achieve that. The winter often closes in as the pickers toil through the vineyard for a last time, and in the next few months the wine ferments quietly till the spring, when it is bottled.

The result is all fruit and no oak influence. And it lasts for as long as any sweet wine in the world – thanks to Chenin's acidity. It *may* seem dull for its first few years, but after ten the pale gold becomes tinged with orange, the apple sweetness blends with apricot and peach . . . and in the full sunset glow of 20 years' maturity, honey fills out the perfume of the peach – with a bitter twist of nut kernel roughness and the dark, fascinating intensity of quince jelly. The wine may then stay in this happy state for another 20 years. Production of this classic is less than 100,000 bottles, and the price is now rising fast. Best years: 1988, '85, '83, '82, '81, '78, '76, '70, '69, '66, '64, '59, '47. Best producers: Baumard, Bellerive, Echarderie, Suronde.

QUINCY AC
UPPER LOIRE

🍷 Sauvignon Blanc

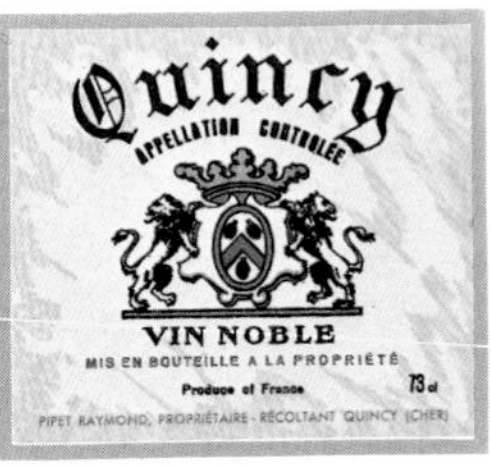

Sometimes Quincy seems to pack more unmistakable Sauvignon flavour into its bottles than any other French wine. I know we're supposed to find gooseberry and asparagus and nettles in Sancerre and Pouilly-Fumé – but those wines have become so popular and the vineyards so burdened with overproduction, that we rarely do. Yet Quincy always reeks of gooseberry and asparagus and nettles – and yes, you guessed, Quincy is *not* popular: in fact you hardly ever see it at all. But if you really want a nostril-full of unashamed Sauvignon, it's worth seeking out.

There isn't much of it, though. The vineyards – clustered along the left bank of the river Cher, just west of Bourges – produce only 450,000 bottles of this intensely flavoured dry white. You can age it for a year or two, but it won't improve, merely become slightly less outrageous. And if I buy Quincy I'm usually in the mood to be outraged! Best years: 1988, '87, '86. Best producers: Jaumier, Mardon, Pichard, Pipet.

RAHOUL, CH.
Graves AC
BORDEAUX

🍷 Merlot, Cabernet Sauvignon

🍷 Sémillon

This is a property which is showing that the unfashionable southern end of the Graves can make exciting wine. Château Rahoul, a tiny vineyard at Portets – in the low-lying Graves vineyards next to the Garonne river, and well away from the best sites of Pessac-Léognan – has achieved remarkable renown, given that its 6 acres (2·5 hectares) of vines produce only about 12,000 bottles a year. The explanation lies in its erstwhile winemaker, the talented and innovative Peter Vinding-Diers, a Dane who came to Bordeaux in 1978 and stayed to run the estate for the next ten years. By scrupulous wine-making and considerable use of new oak barrels, Vinding-Diers produced a rich, plummy, vanilla and coconut-scented red which is almost more New World than it is Bordeaux. Lovely at three years old, the Merlot-dominated wine will age for ten, and each vintage seems better than the last.

Vinding-Diers has, if anything, been even *more* revolutionary in his work with white wine. By using stainless steel, cool fermentation, carefully selected yeast strains, and maturation in new oak barrels, he has produced wines of such intense pineapple, coconut, apricot and vanilla flavours that the Classed Growth winemakers now look to him as an example of how *they* should be making their wine. And this has been accomplished with 100 per cent Sémillon, disdaining the more trendy Sauvignon and showing that, given the right treatment, the Sémillon can actually make the deeper, more complex-flavoured wine. White Rahoul is lovely young but ages beautifully for five years plus. It's worth the wait Best years (reds): 1988, '86, '85, '83, '82, '81, '79. Best years (whites) 1988, '87, '86, '85, '84.

RASTEAU
Côtes du Rhône-Rasteau AC
SOUTHERN RHÔNE

🍷🍷 Grenache, Syrah, Cinsaut, Mourvèdre

🍷 Clairette, Roussanne, Bourboulenc

An important Côtes du Rhône-Village east of Cairanne and north-east c Châteauneuf-du-Pape. Its reds – mostly from the stony slopes at th foot of the Dentelles de Montmirail rocks – are usually fairl old-fashioned, taking several years to soften, and rarely having the fres burst of spice and raspberry which makes some of the other 'Villages' s attractive when young.

Even more old-fashioned is the speciality of Rasteau – a *vin dou naturel* made from very ripe Grenache grapes which are fermented fc three to four days only. Then pure alcohol is added to kill the yeasts an stop fermentation and this remains, giving a rich, raisins-and-grape-skir flavour to the wine. It is usually red – or rather a deep tawny after som ageing – but there is also a 'white', which is made by draining the juic off the skins at the start of fermentation. If it is left in barrel for sever years it is then called *rancio* and tastes a bit like raspberry jam, raisir and tired toffee all mixed up.

RAUSAN-SÉGLA, CH.
Margaux AC, *2ème cru classé*
HAUT-MÉDOC, BORDEAUX

Cabernet Sauvignon, Merlot, Cabernet Franc, Petit Verdot

Before 1983 my comments on Rausan-Ségla would have been sharp and to the point. Something like, 'This is supposed to be the top Second Growth, within spitting distance of Margaux, Mouton-Rothschild and the other greats. So why is it that in most years it is making wine a Fifth Growth would be ashamed of? Lack of care, lack of commitment, lack of respect for the consumer, that's what.' (I would still apply the same kind of remarks to the next Second Growth in line, the neighbouring Rauzan-Gassies, which explains why it doesn't have its own entry.)

A new broom, in the shape of Monsieur Jacques Théo arrived; he promptly rejected half the crop as totally inadequate, phoned up Bordeaux's most famous wine-doctor Professor Peynaud for advice and then set about producing one of the finest '83s in the whole Margaux AC. He made a fair stab at the difficult '84, and then produced a superb '85 and a marvellous '86. The wines are marked by a rich blackcurrant fruit, almost tarry, thick tannins and weight, excellent woody spice and real concentration. There are 111 acres (45 hectares) of vines, 55 per cent Cabernet Sauvignon, 32 per cent Merlot, 11 per cent Cabernet Franc, two per cent Petit Verdot. Don't buy any of the wines of the 1970s, but since 1983 Rausan-Ségla is a worthy Second Growth. Best years: 1988, '86, '85, '83.

REGNIÉ AC
BEAUJOLAIS, BURGUNDY

Gamay

'Lucky' is what I call Regnié and its neighbour Durette whose combined vineyards are now confirmed as the tenth Beaujolais *cru*. *Cru* is a virtually untranslatable French word, but it means approximately 'a parcel of land and its crop of grapes'. This may be a whole village as in Chénas, or it may be a group of villages as in Brouilly, but what distinguishes each 'patch' of land or *cru* in Beaujolais is that the wines have consistently been of a higher standard than the general run. For this reason the wines can sport their own specific AC.

The other nine *crus* without doubt deserve their position, but I'm not yet convinced by Regnié. The vineyards are just west of Morgon and Brouilly, and the light, attractive wine is much closer to Brouilly in style. I *have* had some pleasant bottles, but in poor years like '84 the wines have definitely not rated *cru* status, and even in the great year '85 there were some strangely unattractive attempts. Best years: 1988, '85. Best producers: Cinquin, Crêt des Bruyères, Duboeuf, Durand, Gérarde, Magrin.

REUILLY AC
UPPER LOIRE

 Pinot Noir, Pinot Gris

Sauvignon Blanc

A friend of mine once told me there was a grower in Reuilly called Oliver Cromwell. And there was! It took me ages to track down a bottle and when I finally got the cork out I'm afraid it was pretty unmemorable. Even so, at least it had made me find out where Reuilly is. It is really in the middle of nowhere – west of Bourges in the featureless but vaguely soothing agricultural land which is typical of the middle of France. White, red and rosé are produced from the 150 acres (60 hectares) of vines on the banks of the river Arnon. There is a little rather pallid red from the Pinot Noir, but the speciality is rosé from either Pinot Noir or Pinot Gris. The best are from Pinot Gris, very pale pink, quite soft but with a lovely, fresh, slightly grapy fruit.

Sauvignon Blanc goes into the white, and since Sancerre is about 37 miles (60km) to the east, you'd expect a similarity. In fact the very high limestone element in the soil makes good Reuilly extremely dry, but with an attractive nettles, gooseberry nip to the fruit. The best Reuilly is never as good as the best Sancerre, but most Reuilly is better than poor Sancerre, so if you see a bottle do try it – it's cheaper too. Best producers: Beurdin, Cordier, Lafond, Martin.

RHÔNE

It's one of those trick questions: 'What is the most northerly wine grown in the Rhône Valley?' Tricky indeed! It isn't even in France – it's in the Valais high up in the Swiss Alps! We always forget that the Rhône starts out as a Swiss river, ambling through Lake Geneva before hurtling southwards into France.

Well, as far as the AC Côtes du Rhône is concerned, we're right. This *appellation* starts below Vienne, which is just south of Lyon, but nowhere near Switzerland, and finishes just south of Avignon. Below this the river sprawls out and fragments into marshlands which soon become the wild Camargue swamps. 'Côtes du Rhône' does, after all, mean 'Rhône slopes', or at least 'Rhône banks', and south of Avignon, there isn't much of either. But between Avignon in the south and Vienne in the north there's enough excitement to show the Rhône as one of France's greatest wine regions.

This central section of the valley splits naturally into two parts. The north doesn't produce much wine, but the little that does appear is of a remarkable individuality. On the vertigo-inducing slopes of Côte-Rôtie at Ampuis, the Syrah grape produces sensuously fragrant long-lasting reds, while at Tain-l'Hermitage the great hill of Hermitage produces what they used to call France's 'manliest' wine. St-Joseph and Crozes-Hermitage also make excellent reds, while Cornas, a few miles south, makes a marvellous monster red too. The white Viognier grape yields perfumed, delicate wine at Condrieu and the tiny AC Château Grillet.

There is a gap as the valley widens and flattens, and the slopes give way to vast expanses of land, rising a little into the hills both east and west but, in general, flat, with vines sweltering under the sun. Most of these vineyards are either Côtes du Rhône or Côtes du Rhône-Villages, reds, whites and rosés, but there are also various specific ACs. Red Gigondas is to the east, crunched up against the jagged Dentelles de Montmirail peaks. Southwest are rosés Lirac and Tavel. This is also the home of luscious, golden Muscat de Beaumes-de-Venise. But the most well-known name of all is south of Orange – at Châteauneuf-du-Pape.

► The uniquely stony soil of Châteauneuf-du-Pape retains the sun's heat, helping the grapes to ripen. Behind stands the ruined papal palace which gives the vineyard its name. It was here that the first rules were drawn up regulating French wine production.

Châteauneuf-du-Pape
75 cl
Domaine du
Vieux Télégraphe
APPELLATION CHATEAUNEUF-DU-PAPE CONTROLÉE
MIS EN BOUTEILLE AU DOMAINE
GAEC H. BRUNIER ET FILS, PROPRIETAIRES-RECOLTANTS
ROUTE DE CHATEAUNEUF-DU-PAPE 84370 BEDARRIDES FRANCE

PRODUIT DE FRANCE
CONDRIEU
APPELLATION CONDRIEU CONTROLÉE
Mis en bouteille à la Propriété
750ml
Georges VERNAY, VITICULTEUR A CONDRIEU (Rhône)

LES VIGNERONS
LAUDUN
CÔTES DU RHÔNE-VILLAGES
APPELLATION
CÔTES DU RHÔNE - VILLAGES
CONTRÔLÉE
MIS EN BOUTEILLE A LA PROPRIÉTÉ
A F 30290/047 PAR U.C.V.F. BAGNOLS-s/CÈZE, FRANCE
PRODUIT DE FRANCE

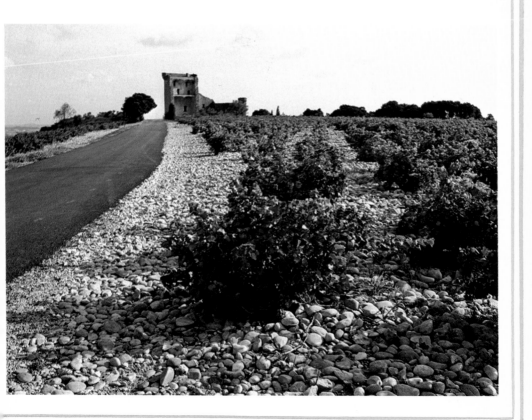

RICHEBOURG AC
grand cru
CÔTE DE NUITS, BURGUNDY

🍷 Pinot Noir

What a name! It has resonances of tremendous opulence, of sumptuous velvet and silk-smooth flesh, of scents dark and musky, of dishes based on fatted calves and cream served to corpulent prelates and princes. This 20-acre (8-hectare) *grand cru* at the northern end of Vosne-Romanée does produce a rich, fleshy wine, its bouquet all flowers and sweet, ripe fruit and its flavour an intensity of spice and perfumed plums which fattens into chocolate and figs and cream as it ages. Because the name is so evocative, there are occasionally bottles – usually with a Beaune or Nuits-St-Georges merchant's name on them – which really don't do justice to the vineyard; but most domaine-bottlings are exceptional. Best years: 1988, '87, '85, '84, '83, '82, '80, '78. Best producers: Domaine de la Romanée-Conti, Gros, Jayer, Noëllat.

RIESLING

Riesling is a German grape and one does wonder whether France's long-standing historical mistrust of Germany has to answer for the Riesling's almost total absence from the French wine scene. It is an important grape in Alsace, which has twice been under German rule since 1870, and whose traditions in grape-growing are intermingled with those of Germany. Elsewhere in France there is a tiny experimental patch at the Listel mega-winery near Montpellier in the Midi and a technically outlawed plot at Doisy-Daëne in Barsac that makes an unmistakable floral contribution to the excellent dry white.

Otherwise, nothing. The Riesling is proscribed, banned, beneath contempt and what a pity – it's a great grape variety, able to offer a tremendous boost in floral perfumes and grapy fruit flavours to many of the duller French whites. The Californians often add Riesling to the less good Chardonnay to give it some personality. I've tasted a lot of Mâcon Blanc-Villages recently that would benefit from such 'outrageous' bending of the laws. So we're left with Alsace, where there are over 5000 acres (2000 hectares), 16 per cent of Alsace's total, and most of the best vineyards are at least partially planted with Riesling.

The wine is almost always dry, with a strong lemon and lime acidity, and a green apple crispness when young, which fills out to a strange but exciting richness with a few years' age. The fruit takes on the flavour of nuts flecked with drops of honey – not enough to make it seem rich, but just the right amount to smooth out its steely cutting edge. Occasionally, late-harvest Vendange Tardive or 'noble rot' Sélection de Grains Nobles wines are made from Riesling and these are bigger, broader, more intense, with a beautiful and characteristic Riesling pungency.

RIEUSSEC, CH.
Sauternes AC, *premier cru classé*
BORDEAUX

🍷 Sémillon, Sauvignon Blanc, Muscadelle

Apart from the peerless and scarcely affordable Château d'Yquem, Rieussec is often the richest, most succulently self-indulgent wine of Sauternes. If Rieussec has a fault it is that this gorgeous flowing tide of exotic sweet fruit is not always held in check by the stern hand of good acidity. Yet there is such a riot of pineapple and peach and honey to wallow in, that it is difficult not to say – oh, what the hell, maybe it won't last quite as long as d'Yquem or Guiraud, but it's so irresistible that I really couldn't care. In fact the 153 acres (62 hectares), on high ground just inside the parish boundary of Fargues, lie alongside d'Yquem and, since the property was bought in 1984 by the Rothschilds of Lafite-Rothschild (Pauillac), I wonder if they are going to try to challenge d'Yquem. I hope not, because the wine is already wonderfully rich and satisfying – and I can just occasionally afford a bottle. I've never been able to afford a bottle of d'Yquem! There is a very rare special selection called Crème de Tête which is quite remarkable, and a dry wine called 'R' which isn't. Best years: 1988, '86, '85, '83, '81, '79, '76, '75.

RIVESALTES AC
LANGUEDOC-ROUSSILLON

Grenache

Muscat of Alexandria, Muscat à Petits Grains

The fame of Rivesaltes, a small town just north of Perpignan, lies in two wines. The local firm of Cazes Frères makes an outstanding red *nouveau*, using the carbonic maceration method of vinification. And it is the home of some of the south's best *vins doux naturels*. The most famous of these are deep and gold, from the Muscat grape, but red and rosé wines are made from Grenache. If stored for several years in barrel they add a barley sugar, burnt toffee taste to the Grenache's original plummy grapiness which is strangely attractive. The Rivesaltes AC covers 86 of Roussillon's 118 communes, and about five million bottles of Rivesaltes VDN are produced. Best producers: Cazes Frères, Sarda-Malet, Vignerons Catalans.

LA RIVIÈRE, CH.
Fronsac AC
BORDEAUX

Merlot, Cabernet Sauvignon, Cabernet Franc, Malbec

You have to hand it to Monsieur Borie, who owns this 109-acre (44-hectare) Fronsac estate – he knows how to market his wine. He is always setting up tastings against wines like Classed Growth St-Émilions and Haut-Médocs – and walking off with the plaudits. Totally independent arbiters have also included La Rivière in blind tastings and it has consistently bested more expensive, more renowned wines. Actually the wines *are* good, and they do age remarkably well. Use of at least one-third new oak barrels each year and a good number of very old vines must play a part in this. Best years: 1988, '85, '83, '82, '78.

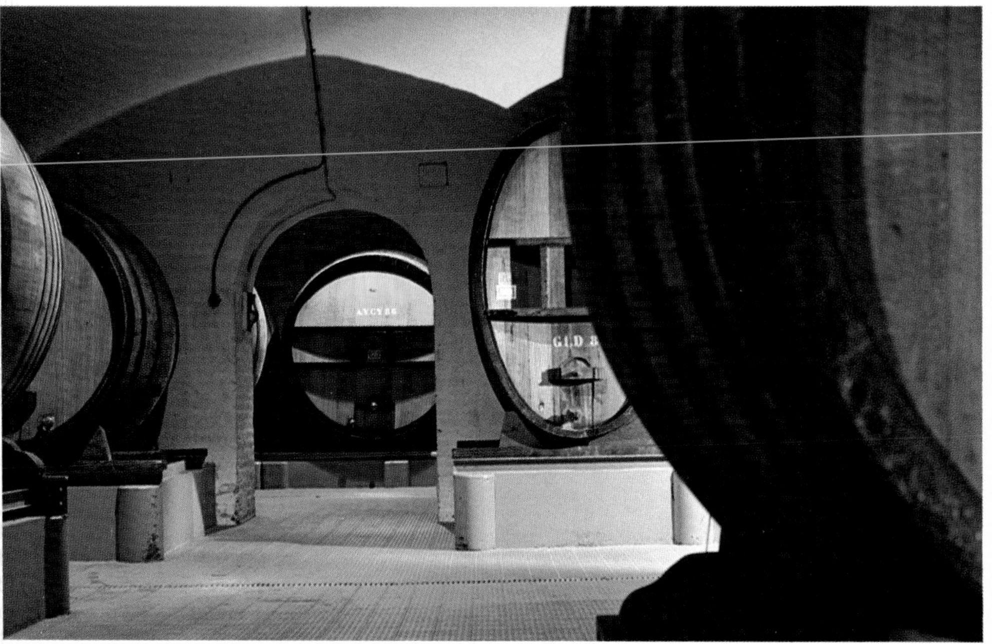

LOUIS ROEDERER
Champagne AC
CHAMPAGNE

Pinot Noir, Chardonnay, Pinot Meunier

▲ Cellars for reserve wine at the Champagne house of Louis Roederer.

This company has the reputation of having the best winemaker in Champagne. Obviously the word's got around, because the chief problem with Roederer is to try to find a bottle which is mature enough for you to experience its full splendour. The number of times I've had Roederer and said – yes, the quality is fabulous, but I wish it had just a little more age – doesn't bear thinking about. But despite that, the quality is extraordinarily good, and the green edges which afflict so much over-young Champagne are soothed and softened here by the spicy ripeness of the fruit.

They also make a big, exciting Vintage, and the famous Roederer Cristal, which comes in a clear bottle originally designed for the Russian tsar, and is usually delicious. Another strong point is that Louis Roederer make the best medium and sweet Champagnes on the market. They need ageing to show their class, but can be rich and honeyed and not at all cloying – unlike most sweet Champagnes, which are feeble stuff.

LA ROMANÉE AC, ROMANÉE-CONTI AC, ROMANÉE-ST-VIVANT AC *grands crus*

CÔTE DE NUITS, BURGUNDY

🍷 Pinot Noir

Three of the five *grands crus* in the Burgundy village of Vosne-Romanée. La Romanée is the smallest AC in France, covering a touch over 2 acres (0·84 hectares). This tiny little scrap of magic dirt doesn't produce wines of the class of the other Vosne-Romanée *grands crus*. While the wines made by its neighbour Domaine de la Romanée-Conti are all rich flavours and exciting perfumes, La Romanée, wholly owned by Liger-Belair, is strangely lean and glum. Best years: 1988, '85, '80, '78.

Romanée-Conti is the cloud-capped pinnacle of Burgundy for many extremely wealthy Burgundy lovers. They tell me it has an almost satiny texture, that its bouquet shimmers with the fragrance of sweet-briar and its orgy of wonderful scents and exotic opulence has been known to strike wine-writers dumb and imbue sommeliers with solicitous friendliness. I'm not really the chap to comment on all that, because I've only had Romanée-Conti once. It was the 1985 and I thought it was delicious, but Romanée-Conti is only 4½ acres (1·8 hectares) and only produces 7000 well-heeled bottles in a good year. Since there are sure to be at least 7000 well-heeled Burgundy fanatics desperate for a slurp at any price, it was actually jolly nice of the owners to open a bottle of '85 for me at all. It's wholly owned by the Domaine de la Romanée-Conti.

Romanée-St-Vivant was the first of the great *grands crus* of Vosne-Romanée to excite me and yet is the one which has proved most troublesome to love in recent vintages. I first came across it in the early '70s. I kept being offered it really young, hardly off the vine, and I thought it was fantastic, rich, unctuously soft with that heavy-lidded decadence of fresh *foie gras* and Sauternes. This, mark you, in a dry red wine! Well, I was hooked, and after a long barren period when I had to do things like work for a living and pay the rent, I was reintroduced to Romanée-St-Vivant with the vintages of the '80s. Maybe it's me, but the wine doesn't seem so rich any more. Perhaps it is simply that this 24-acre (9·54-hectare) vineyard, crunched up to the houses of Vosne-Romanée below Richebourg, is no longer having to pander to the instant gratification market and at 10–15 years these wines *will* show the keenly balanced brilliance of which the vineyard is capable. I hope so. Best years: 1988, '87, '85, '84, '83, '80, '78, '76. Best producers: Arnoux, Latour, Noëllat, Domaine de la Romanée-Conti.

ROSÉ D'ANJOU AC, CABERNET D'ANJOU AC & ROSÉ DE LOIRE AC

CENTRAL LOIRE

🍷🍷 Groslot, Cabernet Franc, Cabernet Sauvignon and others

Rosé d'Anjou is usually somewhere between off-dry and reasonably sweet. It is produced predominantly from the Groslot grape – a pretty ordinary performer that doesn't give much colour or much flavour. When the wine is fresh, not too sweet, and not ruined by a gross over-application of the antiseptic sulphur dioxide (which is the case with most cheap Anjou rosé), it has a lovely, slightly nuts-and-apple flavour with a slight blue cast to its bright pink colour. Drier rosés, usually made from Cabernet Franc grapes and higher in alcohol than Rosé d'Anjou are called Cabernet d'Anjou. This can be delicious if it is fresh, with a rather smoky, grassy flavour. There is also a Rosé de Loire which is drier than Rosé d'Anjou. This can come from Anjou, Saumur or Touraine and must contain 30 per cent Cabernet. It can be a lovely, grassy drink but, again, get it as young as possible and chill it well.

ROSÉ DES RICEYS AC
CHAMPAGNE

Pinot Noir

A real oddball rosé. It comes from Les Riceys in the very south of the Champagne AC region. It is made from Pinot Noir as a still wine – but only in the ripest years. The wine is a strange sort of dark golden pink, and tastes full, rather nutty, or, if the locals are to be believed, 'of gooseberries'. There's hardly any of it – only about 7500 bottles. And it's fiendishly expensive. So why do they make it? They probably get fed up with drinking Champagne. Best producers: Bonnet, Horiot.

ROSETTE AC
SOUTH-WEST

Sémillon, Sauvignon Blanc, Muscadelle

Hurry, hurry, hurry! Rosette is fading fast. Well, don't give yourself a hernia in the rush, because Rosette isn't *that* splendid, but this tiny AC for semi-sweet wines from the hills just north and west of Bergerac is now down to 20,000 bottles. And each year local pundits predict that *this* is the year the AC will die out completely. Somehow it still hangs on, and the wine can be lightly sweet in a rather whimsical way – as befits an AC which is rapidly becoming a mere afterthought. Best years: 1988, '86, '85. Best producer: Puypezat.

RUCHOTTES-CHAMBERTIN AC
grand cru
CÔTE DE NUITS, BURGUNDY

Pinot Noir

The smallest of Gevrey-Chambertin's *grands crus* at less than 8 acres (3 hectares), squeezed up into the hillside directly north of Clos-de-Bèze. The result is that Ruchottes is often intensely coloured and full of deep, slow-evolving fruit, but also with a good tannin and acidity. After ten years it does show that mix of perfumed plum and dark, figgy prune richness which is at the heart of Gevrey-Chambertin *grands crus*. Best years: 1988, '87, '85, '83, '82, '80, '78. Best producers: Mugneret, Roumier, Rousseau.

RULLY AC
CÔTE CHALONNAISE, BURGUNDY

Pinot Noir

Chardonnay

An example of a little-known village hauling itself up by the bootstraps. Rully is the northernmost of the Côte Chalonnaise ACs (though Bouzeron, with its special AC for Aligoté, is further north still), and in reputation is more of a white wine village than a red. In fact the amounts of red and white produced are roughly equal, and Rully – at the northern end of the Côte Chalonnaise – is one of the few areas in Burgundy where there is room for expansion, with some very promising steep slopes facing east to south-east, recently planted and coming into full production.

The vines of Rully, covering 620 acres (250 hectares), once provided thin light base wine for the village's thriving fizz industry, which meant the village had no real reputation for its still wines. This all changed in the '70s as the prices of both red and white Burgundy from the Côte d'Or, just a few miles to the north, began to go crazy – not only was there a lot of new planting in Rully, but the bubbly-makers began to bring in their wines from elsewhere, leaving Rully's own vineyards to capitalize on a sudden demand for good quality, reasonably-priced Burgundy. Red Rully is light, with a pleasant, if fleeting, strawberry and cherry perfume. Certainly I'd like a bit more body in the wines, but at two to four years they can be very refreshing. You may see *premier cru* on some labels but such epithets have little importance here, and several of the best vineyards are not *premiers crus*, so I shouldn't worry about it. Best years (reds): 1988, '87, '85, '83. Best producers: Chanzy, Cogny, Delorme, Duvernay, Noël-Bouton.

Rully has always made fairly light whites, due to its limestone-dominated soil, but in recent vintages the wines have become fuller, rather nutty, their appley acidity jazzed up by an attractive hint of honey. As some growers also begin to use oak barrels, we should start to see an increasing amount of exciting wine, at a price nearer to a Mâcon

Blanc-Villages than a Meursault. Some wines sport the name of a vineyard – probably one of the 19 *premiers crus*, but, as is usual in the Côte Chalonnaise, the term *premier cru* doesn't mean a lot. Best years (whites): 1988, '86, '85, '83, '82. Best producers: Belleville, Bêtes, Brelière, Chanzy, Cogny, Delorme, Dury, Duvernay, Faiveley, Jaffelin, Noël-Bouton.

ST-AMAND, CH.
Sauternes AC, *cru bourgeois*
BORDEAUX

Sémillon, Sauvignon Blanc

One of the few non-Classed Growth properties which regularly manages to produce big, rich, classic Sauternes – *and* which doesn't charge the earth. The 54-acre (22-hectare) estate is in the commune of Preignac – right next to the little river Ciron, whose autumn mists have so much to do with the formation of noble rot on the grapes. The wine is also sold as Château la Chartreuse. Best years: 1988, '86, '83, '81, '80.

ST-AMOUR AC
BEAUJOLAIS, BURGUNDY

Gamay

What a lovely name. The Love Saint. Obviously this northernmost of the Beaujolais *crus* has missed its vocation: it ought to be a honeymoon retreat. The calf-eyed couples would certainly find it quiet: there isn't even a village inn! So perhaps the inhabitants are better off making a particularly juicy, soft-fruited Beaujolais, perfumed, peachy, ready to drink within the year, but lasting well for two or three. The village is just inside the Saône-et-Loire *département* (all the others are in the Rhône *département*) and so is theoretically in the Mâconnais. Indeed any white wine from its 568 acres (230 hectares) can legally be called St-Véran, but the red is so delicious, and the vineyard area so restricted, that [illegible] wouldn't like to see white plantings increase. There is no co-operative at St-Amour, and several *négociant* offerings are better than average. Best producers: Billards, Domaine du Paradis, Duboeuf, Patissier (Guy and Jean), Poitevin, Revillon, Saillant, Château de St-Amour.

ST-AUBIN AC
CÔTE DE BEAUNE, BURGUNDY

🍷 Pinot Noir

🍷 Chardonnay

This is my sort of Burgundy village! It's not actually on the Côte d'Or's Golden Slope but in its own cleft, just up the hill from Puligny-Montrachet and next to the village of Gamay, which means that prices are comparatively low, and despite recent replanting, there are lots of old vineyards producing quite big, chewy-fruited reds. There *is* a fair bit of old Gamay – which can't be used for St-Aubin AC, but which makes the Gamay/Pinot Noir blend Bourgogne Passe-Tout-Grain particularly tasty here. In fact most of the 300 acres (120 hectares) of vineyards are on good east to south-east facing slopes, and two-thirds of them are classified *premiers crus* – and they deserve it. Les Frionnes and Les Murgers des Dents de Chien (love that name) are two of the best. Best years (reds): 1988, '87, '85, '83, '82. Best producers: Bachelet, Clerget, Colin, Lamy, Prudhon, Roux, Thomas.

It's a great pity that perhaps only one-third of the vineyard area is planted in white grapes because the lean, racy fruit combined with a delicious toasty, biscuity perfume from a little oak ageing makes these wines as good as many Chassagne-Montrachets or Meursaults. They're delicious young, but are better after five years' ageing. I sometimes wonder whether St-Aubin isn't in fact the patron saint of the white Burgundy lover with limited means, because the wines of St-Aubin are always delicious, and are never overpriced. Best years (whites): 1988, '86, '85, '83, '82. Best producers: Bachelet, Clerget, Colin, Duvernay, Jadot, Jaffelin, Lamy, Lamy-Pillot, Albert Morey, Roux, Thomas.

ST-CHINIAN AC
LANGUEDOC-ROUSSILLON

🍷 Carignan, Grenache, Cinsaut and others

With Faugères, this was the first of the red wines of the Hérault *département* to break away from the pack and start making a name for itself. In the hill villages back from the coast, the rocky slopes can produce strong, spicy reds with a fair amount of fruit and *far* more personality than the run of the Hérault mill – particularly when carbonic maceration has been employed at least partially. About 14 million bottles of St-Chinian are produced from around 25,000 acres (10,000 hectares) of vines in the hills above Béziers, but the potential is for twice that. Carignan is the main grape, but increasingly Grenache, Syrah and Mourvèdre are being planted. The wines can be drunk very young but age happily for two to three years. Though they have a good, strong taste, they are usually a little lighter-bodied than neighbouring Faugères, and as yet not quite so consistent. Best years: 1988, '86. Best producers: Calmette, Clos Bagatelle, Coujan, Jougla, co-operatives at Rieu-Berlou and Roquebrun.

STE-CROIX-DU-MONT AC
BORDEAUX

🍷 Sémillon, Sauvignon Blanc, Muscadelle

◀ Morning mists left from Ste-Croix-du-Mont. In autumn similar mists encourage the growth of noble rot – vital to the creation of the AC's sweet wine.

The best of the three sweet wine ACs (Loupiac and Cadillac are the others) which gaze jealously across at Sauternes and Barsac from the other – wrong – side of the Garonne. The views are magnificent as the vines tumble down what look to be perfectly sited, south-west-facing slopes. But to make great sweet wine, sunshine isn't enough: you must have the clammy, humid autumn days which encourage the noble rot to shrivel your grapes and concentrate their sugar. The little river Ciron running though Sauternes creates these conditions, but the wide Garonne is far less likely to waft morning mists towards Ste-Croix-du-Mont. Even so, the 1050 acres (425 hectares) of vines do occasionally produce splendidly rich wines, but more often the wine is mildly sweet – very good as an aperitif or with hors d'oeuvres, but not really luscious enough for the end of a meal. And those 1050 acres aren't all even trying to produce sweet wine – many growers have switched to dry whites to gain a more reliable income. Best years: 1988, '86, '85, '83. Best producers: Loubens, Barbe-Maurin, Lousteau-Vieil, de Tastes.

ST-ÉMILION AND POMEROL

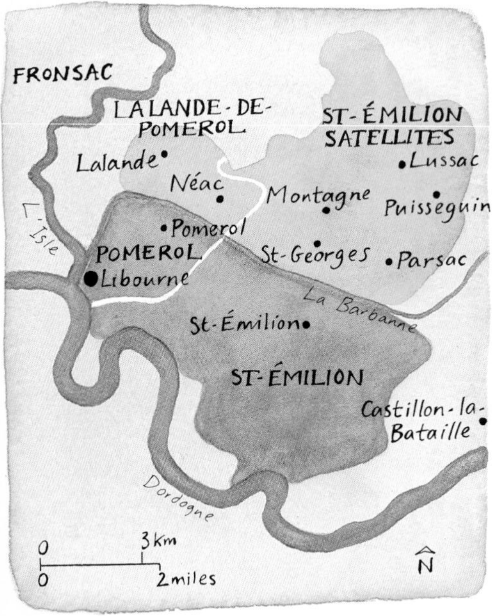

St-Émilion and Pomerol make the greatest red wines on the right bank of the Dordogne in Bordeaux. Indeed the hill town of St-Émilion, huddled into clefts of rock above the vineyards, is the most historic wine region in Bordeaux. Over 1700 years ago the Romans were planting the steep south-facing slopes just outside the town, and leading properties, like Château la Gaffelière and Château Ausone (whose vineyards once belonged to the Roman poet Ausonius) can trace their records as far back as the second century.

The finest vineyards with most of the famous names are on the steep sites round the town, the *côtes* vineyards ('the slopes'). But there is a second large area of St-Émilion to the west towards the town of Libourne called the *graves* which contains two of St-Émilion's greatest properties – Château Cheval-Blanc and Figeac. The *graves* refers to a gravel ridge occupied by both of these properties on a plateau which is otherwise noted for heavy clay soil. Merlot dominates the vineyards.

The clay comes into its own in Pomerol, which begins right next to Cheval-Blanc and continues westward to the outskirts of Libourne. There are no fancy buildings, no signs of affluence and renown here, yet the world's most expensive wine – Château Pétrus – is made in a tiny building in the heart of Pomerol and the rich, sumptuous flavours of the Merlot-based wine are echoed by numerous other properties crammed into the tiny space, none as great as Pétrus, but many giving more than just a suggestion of the power and succulence which make Pétrus so exciting.

Both Pomerol and St-Émilion have 'satellite' ACs – employing a hyphenated version of the famous name. Lalande-de-Pomerol produces good soft wines directly to the north of Pomerol. North of St-Émilion a group of ACs all produce sturdy but fruity reds – Lussac-St-Émilion, Montagne-St-Émilion (also the preferred AC for most wines in neighbouring Parsac-St-Émilion and St-Georges-St-Émilion) and Puisseguin-St-Émilion.

◀ Château Fonplégade, a *grand cru classé* situated on *côtes* vineyards south-west of the town of St-Émilion.

AC ENTRIES
- Lalande de Pomerol
- Lussac-St-Émilion
- Montagne-St-Émilion
- Pomerol
- Puisseguin-St-Émilion
- St-Émilion
- St-Georges-St-Émilion

CHÂTEAUX ENTRIES
- l'Angélus
- l'Arrosée
- Ausone
- Balestard-la-Tonnelle
- Belair
- Canon
- Clos René
- la Dominique
- l'Évangile
- Figeac
- Lafleur
- Latour-à-Pomerol
- Magdelaine
- Monbousquet
- Pavie
- Petit-Village
- Pétrus
- de Sales
- Siaurac
- Trotanoy
- Vieux-Château-Certan

GRAPE ENTRIES
- Cabernet Franc
- Cabernet Sauvignon
- Merlot

ST-ÉMILION AC, ST-ÉMILION *grand cru* AC
BORDEAUX

🍷 Merlot, Cabernet Franc, Cabernet Sauvignon, Malbec

If William the Conqueror had decided to take some Bordeaux wines to England with him when he laid low poor old Harold at Hastings in 1066 there's a good chance his triumphant tipple would have been St-Émilion because the Brits have been drinking it for over 800 years. And I can see why it became so popular so quickly, because the one thing that marks the flavour of St-Émilion is a gorgeous softness, a buttery toffeeish sweetness, and a fruit whose flavour owes more to the dark chewy richness of raisins in a fruit cake, than to the leaner more demanding tastes of the wines of the Graves and Médoc.

The *appellation* is centred on the Roman town of St-Émilion on the right bank of the Dordogne, east of Bordeaux. The vines cover 130 acres (53 hectares) in eight different communes, although the best lie within the boundaries of the St-Émilion commune itself. It is a region of smallholdings, with over 1000 different properties, the smallest being Château le Couvent actually in the town of St-Émilion. Consequently, the co-operative is of great importance, and vinifies over 20 per cent of the entire St-Émilion crop to a consistently high standard.

There has been a classification system for St-Émilion wines since 1954, which allows for promotion and demotion every ten years. St-Émilion *premier cru classé* applies to the top 11 properties, and St-Émilion *grand cru classé* covers 64 wines, although both figures are re-appraised each decade. Below this level comes 200 or so St-Émilion *grands crus*, and the rest are straight St-Émilion.

The classification used to be enshrined in the AC, but since 1985 there are only two ACs – St-Émilion *grand cru* for the top 90 or so wines and St-Émilion for the rest. Now I can add up – just – and this looks to me as though a wine not in the top 90 can call itself *grand cru* although its AC is merely St-Émilion. Yes, that's *exactly* what it looks like!

Best years: 1988, '87, 86, '85, '83, '82, '81, '79, 78. Best producers: l'Angélus, l'Arrosée, Ausone, Balestard-la-Tonnelle, Belair, Berliquet, Canon, Cheval-Blanc, la Dominique, Figeac, Fonplégade, Franc-Mayne, Larmande, Magdelaine, Monbousquet, Pavie, la Gaffelière, Pavie Decesse, la Tour du Pin Figeac, Tertre Rôteboeuf, Troplong Mondot.

ST-ESTÈPHE AC
HAUT-MÉDOC, BORDEAUX

🍷 Cabernet Sauvignon, Cabernet Franc, Merlot and others

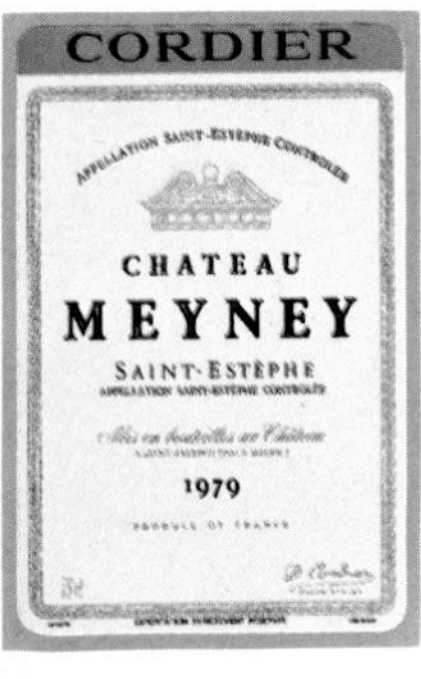

The wines of St-Estèphe are frequently accorded only grudging praise. I can understand this if the wines are being judged on their perfume and elegance: St-Estèphe's style is no match for St-Julien and Margaux here. I can also understand it if it is sheer concentration of fruit and personality that matter: St-Estèphe's broad-shouldered, tweedy character is far less memorable and less dignified than that of Pauillac. Yet, in its old-fashioned tweed and plus-fours way, St-Estèphe is the most reliable and the least overpriced of the Haut-Médoc's specific ACs.

It is a large AC at 2700 acres (1100 hectares), but the most recently established of the great Haut-Médoc areas, partly because the gravel soil which gives all the finest wines in Pauillac, St-Julien and Margaux is much less prevalent here – clay clogs your shoes as you wander these vineyards. It also has a cooler climate than the other main villages and the vines may ripen a week later than those in Margaux. This means that most of the properties have a fairly high proportion of the earlier-ripening Merlot, though Cabernet Sauvignon is still the leading grape. St-Estèphe has only five Classed Growths, due partly to the clay soils, and partly to the late development of the area. Many vineyards were not fully established by 1855. Several non-classified properties consistently make fine wine of Classed Growth quality.

St-Estèphe wines are not the most likeable wines straight off. They have high tannin levels, and a definite earthy scratch in their texture. Give them time, however, and those sought-after flavours of blackcurrant and cedarwood do peek out – but rarely with the brazen beauty of a Pauillac or a St-Julien. There is some evidence of a softer style of wine-making being tried out, but although this is fine for the lesser properties, for the leading châteaux the end result is a bit half-hearted and St-Estèphe's best efforts are still in the brawny mould, demanding 10–20 years ageing for full development. Best years: 1988, '86, '85, '83, '82, '79, '78, '76, '75. Best properties: Andron-Blanquet, Calon-Ségur, Cos d'Estournel, Haut-Marbuzet, Lafon-Rochet, Meyney, Montrose, les Ormes-de-Pez, de Pez.

ST-GEORGES-ST-ÉMILION AC
BORDEAUX

Merlot, Cabernet Franc, Cabernet Sauvignon, Malbec

Probably the best of the satellite St-Émilion ACs. The wines can be the epitome of Merlot softness – all buttered brazil nuts and fruitcake and soft plums, but well able to age for six to ten years if called on to do so. Best years: 1988, '85, '83, '82. Best properties: Bélair-Montaiguillon, Calon (sometimes sold as Montagne St-Émilion), Cap d'Or, Château St-Georges (one of the most impressive buildings in the whole region as well as lovely wine), Maquin St-Georges, Tour-du-Pas-St-Georges.

ST-JOSEPH AC
NORTHERN RHÔNE

Syrah, Roussanne, Marsanne

Marsanne, Roussanne

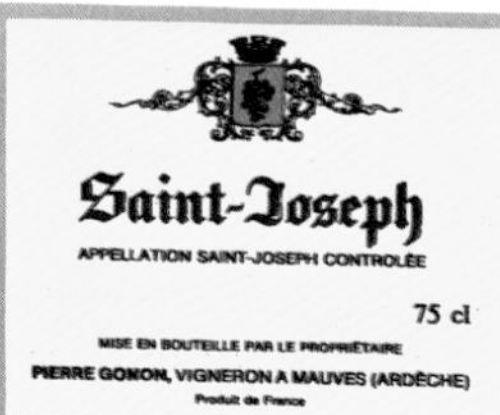

If ever the Syrah wished to show the smiling side of its nature in the northern Rhône it would have to be at St-Joseph. I have never had an unfriendly St-Joseph, and most of them have been an absolute riot of rich, mouthfilling fruit and an irresistible blackcurrant richness. I was at a Paris Wine Fair with Jean Lenoir who has invented a system of identifying wine smells called Le Nez du Vin (the nose of wine). 'Show me the purest example of blackcurrant', I cried, expecting to be shunted towards some wonderful Cabernet Sauvignon-based Classed Growth Bordeaux. He led me to Monsieur Coursodon's stand and ordered a glass of his 1980 St-Joseph. Pure, heavenly blackcurrants, *crème de cassis*, blackcurrant jam, blackcurrant sorbet. Mmmm!

St-Joseph used to be limited to the granite slopes of half-a-dozen right-bank villages centred on Mauves just south of Hermitage. All the best St-Joseph still comes from there. But, infuriatingly, the AC was extended in 1969 to take in another 20 communes on flat land north of Tournon and Hermitage. Their wine isn't anything like as good, although it's still a jolly nice drink. Ah well. St-Joseph is brilliant at only one to two years old; it can age for up to ten from the area round Mauves, but you'll gradually lose that wonderful fruit, so I'd drink it before five years old. Average production is about 1,300,000 bottles, 94 per cent red, six per cent white. Best years (reds): 1988, '85, '83, '82, '80. Best producers: Chave, Coursodon, Gonon, Gripa, Grippat, Jaboulet (le Grand Pompée), Marsanne, St-Désirat-Champagne co-operative (for the lighter style).

At their best, St-Joseph whites have an astonishing flavour half-way between the peach and apricot headiness of a Condrieu and the buttery richness of a good Meursault. At worst, they are flat, hollow wines with no fruit or acidity. And somewhere in between is a pleasant, flowery, apple-scented wine for chilling and drinking without too much ceremony at a year old or so. The worst is simply the result of bad wine-making. The 'in-between' is the result of bang up-to-date wine-making.

The best are the old-style wines, made from low-yielding vines round Tournon and Mauves, matured in old oak and capable of lasting 20 years. They are rich, heavy, scented with sandalwood, woodsmoke and peaches, and tasting of toast and brazil nuts draped in butter caramel – with a strong acidity gnawing at a central kernel of fruit that is as dry yet rich as preserved apricots. Sadly, there aren't many examples of these. Best years (whites): 1988, '87, '86, '85, '83. Best producers: Courbis, Florentin, Grippat, Trollot.

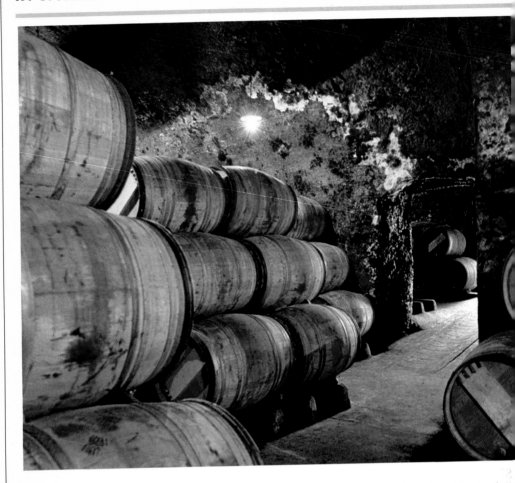

ST-JULIEN AC
HAUT-MÉDOC, BORDEAUX

🍷 Cabernet Sauvignon, Cabernet Franc, Merlot

▲ The cellars at Château Langoa-Barton. Léoville-Barton wine is made at Langoa, owned by the same family.

If someone said to me 'show me the perfect red Bordeaux', this is wher I would look first. Not because they are the most fragrant. Margau often has a more beguiling perfume. Not because they are the mos sumptuous – Pomerol and St-Émilion regularly produce richer reds. An not because they are the grandest – the great Pauillacs have a massiv concentration of flavour St-Julien rarely approaches. No, it is becaus St-Julien wines have the perfect balance between substance an delicacy, between opulence and austerity, between the necessar harshness of youth and the lean-limbed genius of maturity. Although th great Pauillacs are the models for winemakers across the world, if were the perfect Bordeaux they sought to emulate, St-Julien should b their target.

There's not very much of it; at 1850 acres (750 hectares) it is th smallest of the four main Haut-Médoc communes, but almost all of it vineyard land of the highest class, 75 per cent of the land being taken u by 11 Classed Growths. The Second Growths, Léoville-Las-Case Ducru-Beaucaillou and Gruaud-Larose are the leaders, and not f behind are Léoville-Barton and Beychevelle. The third group, als making excellent wine, is Talbot, Branaire-Ducru, St-Pierre, Lango Barton and the recently revived Lagrange. Only Léoville-Poyfer continues to be erratic. Despite that, the overall quality in St-Julien higher than in any other Bordeaux AC. Best years: 1988, '86, '85, '8 '82, '81, '79, '78, '75.

ST-NICOLAS-DE-BOURGUEIL AC
CENTRAL LOIRE

Cabernet Franc, Cabernet Sauvignon

An enclave of 1250 acres (500 hectares) in the Bourgueil area of Touraine producing two million bottles of red and rosé wine. Cabernet Franc is usually the sole grape used although sometimes a bit of Cabernet Sauvignon creeps in. Almost all the wine is red and it has the sharp, piercing, raspberry and blackcurrant flavours of neighbouring Bourgueil and Chinon. The wines are generally pretty dry, prone to be a little tannic and have an earthy background which is pleasant enough, though I'd prefer less earth and more fruit. They are drinkable quite young – two to three years – and will last seven to ten years from warm vintages. Best years: 1988, '86, '85, '83. Best producers: J-P Mabileau, Joël Taluau.

ST-PÉRAY AC, ST-PÉRAY MOUSSEUX AC
NORTHERN RHÔNE

Marsanne, Roussanne

The community of St-Péray is a dormitory town for the city of Valence, directly across the Rhône. So it's a bit of a surprise to discover that a century ago St-Péray was the producer of France's most famous sparkling wine – after Champagne, of course. Sparkling wine is supposed to be lively, vivacious, witty stuff – but not only is St-Péray depressingly suburban, it is also in the hot Rhône valley, and it seems extremely unlikely that the 150 acres (60 hectares) of vineyards which remain can produce the light, acid wine favoured by fizz-makers.

Well, they can't. The Marsanne and Roussanne grapes make big round wines which undergo the Champagne method and turn out as – big round wines with fizz in them! The whole production is only 260,000 bottles, and most of that goes no further than the local bars and restaurants. There is a little still white, usually dry and stolid, but occasionally more exciting. Admittedly big and broad, the wine can have a lovely golden feel of nuts and honey, and fruit just touched with the spice of apricots and quince, with a flicker of orange peel at the end. This is Marsanne at its best, and it is too good to make into fizz – but such flavours, I'm afraid, are still very much the exception. Best years: 1988, '87, '86, '85. Best producers: Chaboud, Clape, Juge, Thiers, Voge.

ST-PIERRE, CH.
St-Julien AC
HAUT-MÉDOC, BORDEAUX

Cabernet Sauvignon, Merlot, Cabernet Franc

After a century of anonymity, Château St-Pierre (previously St-Pierre-Sevaistre) has stepped forward to claim its place in the sun. It used to be undervalued, and in years like 1970, '75, '79 and '81 you got superb quality at half the price of the better-known St-Juliens. It isn't a big property, only 50 acres (20 hectares), but the vines, close to Branaire and Beychevelle, are well-sited and old. The wine often lacks the startling beauty of the best St-Julien but makes up for this with a full, gentle, almost honeyed weight of flavour, plums and blackberries and soft vanilla backed up by unassertive but effective tannins. It is often ready quite young, and since 1982 and new ownership has had a lusher feel. Top vintages can easily improve for 20 years. Best years: 1988, '86, '85, '83, '81, '79, '75.

ST-POURÇAIN-SUR-SIOULE VDQS
UPPER LOIRE

Gamay, Pinot Noir

Tressallier, Chardonnay, Sauvignon Blanc

If you've ever had the misfortune to sample Vichy-St-Yorre, you'll begin to understand the gastronomic distress inflicted upon health-fad tourists taking the waters at Vichy. And you'll agree that the local wine need not be measured against the highest international standards, since after a couple of days spent glugging Vichy water – overpoweringly salty and minerally – even the feeblest brew would be welcomed with open arms.

Well, feebleness isn't the problem at St-Pourçain-sur-Sioule, with about 1000 acres (400 hectares) of vines 15 miles north of Vichy. This tiny VDQS sits inside the great loop of the Loire river as it turns south towards its source. The reds and rosés, based on Pinot Noir and Gamay, can have quite a pleasant fruit to them when young, although it may take more than a single glass to get used to the rather earthy taste.

The white wines, although very light, are not short of flavour: it's just that the flavour is generally sharp, rather acidic and infected with a deeply strange smokiness, rather like wet hay trying to catch fire. I can only presume this is due to the local Tressallier grape. Best producers: Pétillat, Ray.

ST-ROMAIN AC
CÔTE DE BEAUNE, BURGUNDY

Pinot Noir

Chardonnay

St-Romain is better known for barrels than wine, since François Frères, barrel-makers to the Domaine de la Romanée-Conti and a whole string of other top estates, are situated here. Actually there isn't much room for vines, since St-Romain is at the rocky head of a little side valley running up through Auxey-Duresses from Meursault, and the difficult growing conditions mean there are more trees than vines around. Only 350 acres (140 hectares) out of a possible 5000 (2000) are cultivated, but the poor geological situation results in its being the only Côte de Beaune AC to have no *premiers crus*. In fact, but for kind officialdom and a certain historical reputation for quality, St-Romain would have had to content itself with the lowly Hautes-Côtes de Beaune AC. About 55 per cent of production is red, and though they often have a slightly unnerving earthiness which can verge on the resinous, they also have a firm, bitter-sweet cherrystone fruit – and can age very well for five to seven years. Best years (reds): 1988, '87, '85, '83, '82. Best producers: Bazenet, Buisson, Thévenin, Thévenin-Monthélie.

White St-Romain tastes more like a Chablis than a Meursault, although Meursault is only a few miles away. The wine is flinty dry, hinting at ripeness but held back by a rather herby, stony personality which can be quite refreshing but is unlikely to charm your socks off. If you do see one of the 200,000 bottles of white around, it's worth a try – and will probably age well for a good five years or more. Best years (whites): 1988, '86, '85, '83, '82. Best producers: Bazenet, Buisson, Gras, Taupenot, Thévenin-Monthélie.

ST-VÉRAN AC
MÂCONNAIS, BURGUNDY

Chardonnay

Until 1971 the Mâconnais had one star white AC – Pouilly-Fuissé – and then merely a welter of Mâcon-Villages; in the south, there was also a certain amount of Beaujolais Blanc shared with the Beaujolais communes of Leynes, St-Vérand (yes, there *is* a 'd') and St-Amour. It was clear, however, that these three villages – and five others tightly grouped round the Pouilly-Fuissé AC – were far better than the general run, more closely resembling the classier examples of Pouilly-Fuissé than the normally anonymous glut of Mâcon-Villages. So in 1971 they were given their own AC – St-Véran – and it immediately came to be thought of as a Pouilly-Fuissé understudy.

Often, however, it is much more than that, because while the best Pouilly-Fuissés are superb, the majority veer between adequate and disgraceful – whereas the overall quality of St-Véran is good and the price is fair. The United States has not caught on to St-Véran as a Pouilly-Fuissé look-alike so it's generally less than half the price. Oak is very rarely used in St-Véran, revealing the gentle Mâconnais Chardonnay at its clearest and best – gentle and very fresh, but with a richness combining bananas, apples, pineapples, peaches and even musky grapes, softened with a yeasty creaminess. All that appears during the first year of the wine's life, and though the wines will age they don't gain a great deal from extra maturity. Best years: 1988, '87, '86, '85. Best producers: Chagny, Corsin, Depardon, Duboeuf, Gregoire, Loron, Lycée Agricole de Davayé, Tissier, Vincent, and the co-operative at Prissé.

DE SALES, CH.
Pomerol AC
BORDEAUX

Merlot, Cabernet Franc, Cabernet Sauvignon

At 117 acres (47·5 hectares), this is Pomerol's biggest property, with a lovely château building – commonplace in the Haut-Médoc, but almost unheard of in artisanal Pomerol where every square inch of land is occupied by precious vines. This spaciousness is assisted by the fact that de Sales is right at the north-western tip of the AC, away from the brilliant centre with its superstar châteaux clustered round Château Pétrus, and the soil is sandier with a fair sprinkling of gravel too. The wines never have the tingling excitement of the best Pomerols, but they don't have a blood-pressure-raising price tag either. They are full, round, plummy, rather luscious and smooth for a red wine, quick to mature, but certainly able to age ten years in the bottle. Best years: 1988, '85, '83, '82, '81, '79, '78.

SANCERRE AC
UPPER LOIRE

Pinot Noir

Sauvignon Blanc

Sancerre is such a well-known name nowadays, that I find it difficult to accept that the first wine book I got hold of, less than 20 years ago – a famous and much respected discourse of 300 pages on the wines of France – accorded Sancerre precisely *five* lines. It didn't say what grapes were used, what colour the wines were, what they tasted like, whether they should be drunk young or old . . . Merely five lines to say Sancerre existed. Funny how fashion veers one way then the other!

The omni-thirsty Henry IV is on record as saying that Sancerre was the best wine he'd ever drunk and that if all his subjects were to drink it there'd be no more religious wars. Louis XVI said much the same thing a short while before the French Revolution proved otherwise. And then, about 20 years ago, some Paris journalists (always on the lookout for a new fad wine) noticed the high mound of Sancerre rising powerfully above the upper reaches of the Loire, tasted the wines from its steep chalk and flint vineyards, and tore back to Paris with the news – Sancerre was the tangiest, zippiest, super-freshest, ultra-modernest white wine in France and they were 'crazy' about it.

Sancerre mania broke out – firstly with the white, which can indeed be a wonderful refreshing drink, tasting of nettles, asparagus and gooseberries, and a whiff of brewing coffee, and then with the far less exciting reds and rosés. This is all excellent news for the growers, but Sancerre is now *the* expense account white and consequently is *always* expensive. Since it can provide the perfect expression of the bright green tang of the Sauvignon grape, perhaps we shouldn't complain too much, except that all over France and in Italy, Spain, America, Australia and New Zealand, growers have shown that they too can produce the snappy, high-acid, thirst-quenching whites which Sancerre epitomizes. But even so, a Sancerre from a village like Bué, Chavignol, Verdigny or Ménétréol, made by a good grower in a vintage which wasn't too hot, and drunk before it is two years old, can be one of the most deliciously refreshing white wines of France. Best years (whites): 1988, 87, '86, '85. Best producers: Bailly-Reverdy, Bourgeois, Francis Cotat, Paul Cotat, Daulny, Alain Dezat, Pierre Dezat, Dupuy-Chavignol, Lalone, Merlin, Migeon, Millérioux, Natter, Picard, Roger, Vacheron, Vatan.

Sancerre is really much better at growing white wine than red or rosé (a point emphasized by the fact that red and rosé Sancerre only gained their AC in 1959, 23 years after the white). Still, it certainly must be profitable because many of the new plantings in the region are for Pinot Noir, the only permitted red grape. But with very few exceptions, Pinot Noir doesn't ripen enough here to give interesting red wine, partly because it is usually planted on the less successful north-facing slopes. The rosé is usually very dry, sometimes with a hint of fruit, but I can't see a lot of point to it. Best producers: Bailly-Reverdy, André Dezat, Fouassier, Roger, Vacheron.

SANTENAY AC
CÔTE DE BEAUNE, BURGUNDY

Pinot Noir

Chardonnay

Produce of France
Grand Vin de Bourgogne
SANTENAY
GRAND CLOS ROUSSEAU
APPELLATION CONTRÔLÉE
Mis en bouteille à la Propriété par
Bernard MOREY
Viticulteur à Chassagne-Montrachet (Côte-d'Or)
75 cl

You can almost taste the Côte de Beaune winding down in the red wines of Santenay. The challenging, powerful fruit of the wines of Aloxe-Corton or Pommard is missing, the soft, perfumed beauty of Volnay and Beaune doesn't seem to surface with any regularity, yet the village *is* an important one, and there *are* good wines. In fact, Santenay is really a little town, well-known since Roman times for its therapeutic springs. There are 939 acres (380 hectares) of vines, mostly to the north-east and south-west, and 99 per cent of them are Pinot Noir. The vineyards to the north-east, well sloped towards the morning sun, give the best wine – rarely heavy and sometimes a little stony and dry, but reasonably fruity and reasonably priced. Though Santenay reds often 'feel' good, and promise a good ripe flavour, the final result is usually just a little disappointing. Occasionally a full, rather savoury style appears from a vineyard like Les Gravières and it is worth ageing Santenay for at least four to six years in the hope that the wine will open out. Sometimes it does: sometimes it doesn't. Best years: 1988, '87, '85, '83, '82, '78. Best producers (reds): Belland, Clair, Fleurot-Larose, Girardin, Lequin-Roussot, Mestre, Bernard Morey, Pousse d'Or, Prieur-Brunet, Roux.

About 40,000 bottles of white Santenay are produced each year. Most of these are drunk locally, since Santenay has a casino – and a spa – to boost demand. The wine isn't bad but that rather earthy – even muddy – lack of definition which affects a lot of the red Santenay is also likely to be present in the white. The best results, as with the red, come from the Les Gravières *premier cru* on the border with Chassagne-Montrachet, one of Burgundy's top white wine villages. Best years: 1988, '86, '85, '83. Best producers (whites): Lequin-Roussot, Maufoux, Prieur-Brunet.

SAUMUR AC
CENTRAL LOIRE

Cabernet Franc, Cabernet Sauvignon, Pineau d'Aunis

Chenin Blanc, Chardonnay, Sauvignon Blanc

You only have to taste the basic still white wine of Saumur to realize why most of it is rapidly transformed into fizz – it is thin, harsh, acid stuff, often showing off the Chenin grape at its graceless worst. The shining exception to this comes from the St-Cyr-en-Bourg co-operative, whose still Saumur Blanc is tart and crisp, but packed with fruit, and worth looking out for.

The region is also quite important as a producer of light, rather sharp reds. Thirty-eight villages around Saumur have the right to the AC. Cabernet Franc is the main grape, sometimes blended with Cabernet Sauvignon or Pineau d'Aunis and the result is usually a fairly thin wine, slightly earthy, but with a fairly good, direct, raw blackcurrant fruit. The wine softens with age but doesn't particularly improve. There is a little off-dry rosé made, generally sold under the title Cabernet de Saumur, at its most approachable in warmer years when the grapes ripen properly. Best years: 1988, '85, '83, '82. Best producers: Fourrier, Pérols, St-Cyr-en-Bourg co-operative.

SAUMUR-CHAMPIGNY AC
CENTRAL LOIRE

Cabernet Franc, Cabernet Sauvignon, Pineau d'Aunis

Saumur's best red wine area deservedly sports its own AC. The vineyards are to the east of Saumur on a chalk and limestone plateau 200 feet (60 metres) above the left bank of the Loire. Cabernet is the dominant grape, and in hot years the wine can be superb, never heavy but with a piercing scent of blackcurrants and raspberries easily overpowering the earthy finish. Absolutely delicious young, it can happily age six to ten years, losing some of its sharpness and seeming to get sweeter with maturity. Best years: 1988, '85, '83, '82, '78. Best producers: Chaintres, Duveau, Filliatreau (especially his Vieilles Vignes cuvée – unbelievably delicious), Legrand, St-Cyr-en-Bourg co-operative, Sanzay.

SAUMUR MOUSSEUX AC
CENTRAL LOIRE

Chenin Blanc, Chardonnay, Cabernet Franc

For many years the sparkling wines of Saumur – made by the Champagne method since 1811, and for more than a century actually sold as Champagne – were regarded as the natural cheap alternative to Champagne. However, the Chenin base wine doesn't have the ability of Champagne's Chardonnay or Pinot Noir to start harsh and dry yet fill out, after a few years, to something gentle and honeyed. Nor does it pick up the creamy, toasty flavours of the yeast cells which lie in the bottle during the second fermentation, and which are a mark of true Champagne. So you could use it as a substitute for *cheap* Champagne (classy Champagne taste-alikes are Crémant de Bourgogne or Crémant d'Alsace). Efforts are now being made to produce a rather more charming wine, and the addition of Chardonnay and Cabernet Franc (red but pressed as white) does make for softer, more interesting results. Small quantities of rosé are also made. Saumur can be vintage, but is usually non-vintage and the title *Saumur d'origine* is generally used on the label. Best producers: Ackerman-Laurance, Bouvet-Ladubay, Gratien & Meyer, Langlois-Château, St-Cyr-en-Bourg co-operative.

SAUTERNES AC
BORDEAUX

Sémillon, Sauvignon Blanc, Muscadelle

What marks out this small enclave of vineyards is the particular susceptibility of its grape to go rotten before they are picked in the autumn. That sounds a bit daft, but I'll explain. If you ripen a grape fully during a good summer, it will have enough sugar to convert to a lot of alcohol during fermentation, but the wine will be dry. Even if you stop the fermentation artificially before it has finished and leave some of the sweetness in, it won't be very intense or exciting. What you need to do if you're going to get a really sweet wine is to have so much sugar in the grapes that the yeasts ferment out as much as they can, yet you are still left with masses of unfermented sugar to provide rich concentration.

That's where the 'rot' comes in. There is a particular sort of rot (called 'noble') which attacks grapes and instead of ruining the flavour, eats into the skin, then sucks out the water in the grape, leaving behind most of the sugar, which then gets more and more concentrated, and may end up twice as strong as in a normally ripe grape. These squidgy, messy grapes actually make great sweet wine. They may contain up to 25 degrees or more of potential alcohol in their sugar, and since the yeasts cannot work at a higher alcoholic strength than 14 to 15 degrees – all the rest remains as sweetness. The result is a wine of high alcoholic strength and deep, mouth-coating richness full of flavours like pineapples, peaches, syrup and spice.

For this rot to develop you need special climatic conditions, alternating humidity and heat. The little river Ciron runs along the northern boundary of Sauternes, and in a good autumn, fog rises off the river in the morning, only to be burnt away by the sun later in the day and there you have it – humidity and heat. Sauternes, and its neighbouring AC Barsac, are two of the very few areas in France where this happens naturally (the river Layon in the Loire valley can also achieve it). In some vintages the 'rot' doesn't really develop, and then it is not possible to make intensely sweet wine, although it may still be sold as Sauternes, and can be a pleasant, adequately sweet drink. It is always expensive, though, because the permitted yield is extremely low at 25 hectolitres per hectare – about half that of a Haut-Médoc red wine. Good vintages should be aged for five to ten years and often twice as long. Best years: 1988, '86, '83, '81, '80, '76, '75, '71, '70. Best producers: Bastor-Lamontagne, de Fargues, Gilette, Guiraud, les Justices, Lafaurie-Peyraguey, Lamothe-Guignard, de Malle, Rabaud-Promis (since 1983), Rayne-Vigneau (since 1983), Rieussec, St-Amand/Chartreuse, Suduiraut, d'Yquem.

Sauternes and Other Sweet Bordeaux Wines

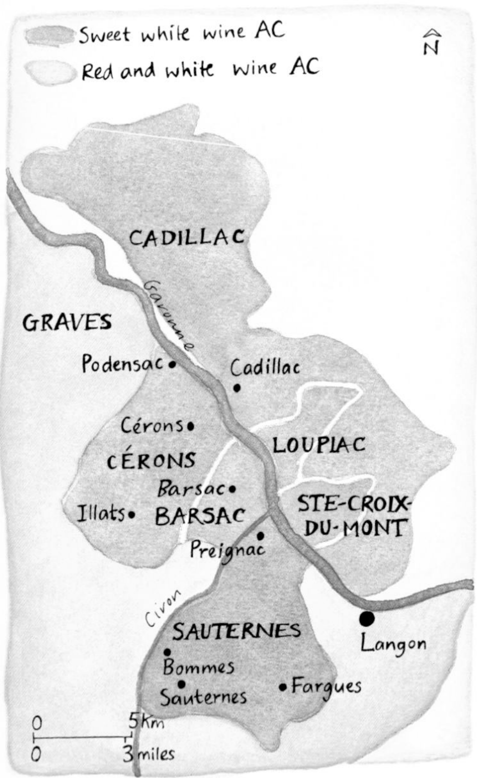

Somehow the names Sauternes and Barsac have come to mean sweet gooey wines without much character, to be sold off to anyone who doesn't like dry wines. This implies that they are easy to make, cheap to produce, and incapable of achieving any memorable personality. Nothing could be further from the truth.

The production of fine sweet white wine is an exhausting, risk-laden and extremely expensive affair, requiring nerves of steel, a huge bank balance, and just the right mix of grape varieties, vineyard sites and local climatic conditions. Bordeaux has half-a-dozen localities where, to a greater or lesser extent, the vineyards and the climate get the balance right.

Greatest of these are Barsac and Sauternes. Just north of the town of Langon, the little river Ciron sidles up from the south to join the river Garonne. On the Ciron's east bank lie the vineyards of Sauternes and on its west bank those of Barsac. Adjoining Barsac to the north is Cérons, whose speciality is a light sweet white but increasingly Cérons vineyards are now producing reds and dry whites (which are not allowed the Cérons AC). On the opposite bank of the Garonne are Cadillac, Loupiac and Ste-Croix-du-Mont whose speciality is also sweet white, but whose vineyards rarely produce anything of the concentration of a good Sauternes.

Sauternes and Barsac produce the most exciting sweet wines because their vineyards are regularly attacked by 'noble rot', a form of fungus which settles on the skins of the grapes and feeds off the water inside. This dramatically reduces the amount of juice, but what is left is extra concentrated in sugar and flavour. Noble rot occurs only in the autumn, and needs a mixture of humidity and warmth to take root. In warm autumns, fogs rise every morning, only to be burnt off later in the day by the sun's heat – the perfect combination. Cérons and the ACs on the Garonne's right bank get these conditions to a much lesser degree.

Noble rot usually strikes late in the autumn, if at all, so storms are an ever-present threat since a couple of days' heavy rain can dilute the juice and bloat the grapes. In some years the whole crop can be ruined. Also, noble rot does not strike consistently. On one bunch, some grapes may be totally rotted, some may be partially affected and some untouched. So the top properties have to go through the vines time after time snipping off only the most affected bunches, or sometimes only the most rotted single grapes on a bunch! Very expensive, very time-consuming. When you realize that a single vine may produce as little as one glass of wine, as against the bottle or more that a producer of dry wine could expect, it becomes painfully obvious that we've been underestimating – and underpricing – these great wines for far too long.

AC ENTRIES

Barsac

Cadillac

Loupiac

Ste-Croix-du-Mont

Sauternes

CHÂTEAUX ENTRIES

Bastor-Lamontagne

Broustet

Climens

Coutet

Doisy-Daëne

Doisy-Védrines

De Fargues

Gilette

Guiraud

Lafaurie-Peyraguey

de Malle

Nairac

Rieussec

St-Amand

Suduiraut

d'Yquem

GRAPE ENTRIES

Sauvignon Blanc

Sémillon

▲ Poppies bring a blaze of colour to this vineyard at Preignac – the largest of the five villages included in the Sauternes AC.

SAUVIGNON BLANC

Sauvignon Blanc's strength and weakness are the same – its uncanny suitability to the mood of the '80s. Its wine is sharp, snapping with green, tangy flavours – fresh mown grass, nettles crushed underfoot, blackcurrant leaves – bright, brash, refreshing and ever so easy to understand. Sometimes the wine is riper and deeper – with flavours of gooseberry, of asparagus, a whiff of roasting coffee carried on the wind – but still the effect remains the same. Which is great for how the world feels now. But 20 years ago Sauvignon Blanc was chiefly known as a dull component of boring Bordeaux Blanc. And 20 years from now we may have become bored with it, because the one thing Sauvignon hasn't yet revealed is complexity and extra nuances of flavour. With age, Sauvignon just keeps on tasting the same – older, more tired, less fruity, but basically the same.

Right now, though, it is *the* easy-drinking white grape, along with Chardonnay. Sancerre and Pouilly-Fumé are its two most famous products, but all along the Loire it softens the tricky Chenin Blanc, and in Touraine it is frequently seen unblended. Its traditional importance in Bordeaux has been to add zip to Sémillon, but increasingly Bordeaux Blanc is being produced from 100 per cent Sauvignon. The examples from Bergerac and Côtes de Duras are often more successful, and there is no doubt that the most exciting white Graves and Sauternes are those in which Sauvignon blends with Sémillon. Elsewhere, Sauvignon crops up in the centre of France in VDQS wines like Sauvignon de St-Bris and Sauvignon du Haut-Poitou, and is frequently included in new plantations in the far south to add zing to the heavy, dull whites of the Mediterranean basin.

SAUVIGNON DE ST-BRIS VDQS
CHABLIS, BURGUNDY

🍷 Sauvignon Blanc

Success seems to be going to the head of Sauvignon de St-Bris, a little outcrop of Loire flavours in a Chardonnay stronghold. A few years ago this tangy, deliciously sharp, gooseberry-tasting white from St-Bris-le-Vineux, just south-west of Chablis, seemed a perfect example of Sauvignon, at a price way below Sancerre and Pouilly-Fumé. The last couple of vintages, however, have brought disappointment after disappointment; full, heavy wines, not entirely clean, and woefully short of zip. And at prices not so far short of Sancerre. Such erratic quality won't help the wine's claim to AC status, so far denied it because Sauvignon is not a permitted grape in the AC Bourgogne area. Best years: 1988, '86, '85. Best producers: Brocard, Sorin, Tapit.

SAVENNIÈRES AC
CENTRAL LOIRE

🍷 Chenin Blanc

Savennières is often hailed as the crowning dry wine glory of the Chenin grape – and there are two vineyards designated *grand cru* which further enhance this theory. But as frequently happens with the Chenin, the wine is so rough and unfriendly when young, and the maturation period is so painfully slow – often occupying 15 years, sometimes more – that it is difficult to embrace Savennières' undoubted quality in an entirely whole-hearted way. Attempts by one or two growers to produce a more immediately soft and fruity wine aren't entirely convincing either, since a good chunk of baby has been thrown out with the bath water.

The AC's 150 acres (60 hectares) are on perilously steep slopes on the north bank of the Loire, opposite the little river Layon, and production veers between 70,000 and 170,000 bottles – the wide variation is caused by a particularly capricious microclimate. Because Savennières used traditionally to be a sweet wine, the AC laws only allow a very low yield of 30 hectolitres per hectare, and demand a very high minimum alcohol of 12 degrees. This results in much wine having to be declassified to Anjou AC in cooler years.

Young Savennières is totally, gum-judderingly dry – the sensation is of feeling rather than tasting, as the steely, ice-bright wine sweeps over your palate. But they do get there in the end. Even if it takes a decade or two, honey begins to soften the steel, and the creaminess of nuts soothes the gaunt herb-harsh dryness. But even at the peak of maturity, there'll still be an acid freshness – part late-winter flowers and their leaves, part the zesty snap of lemon peel.

The two *grand cru* vineyards have their own ACs. They are Savennières-Coulée-de-Serrant, a 15-acre (6-hectare) plot which definitely makes the subtlest and most refined wine; and another similarly sized block of vines, Savennières-la-Roche-aux-Moines, whose wines are a little lighter, but also extremely good. Best years: 1988, '85, '83, '82, '78, '76, '71, '70, '69, '66. Best producers: Baumard, Bizolière, Brincard, Chamboureau, Clos de la Coulée-de-Serrant, Closel, Épiré.

▼ Coulée-de-Serrant, one of the two Savennières *grands crus*. The tiny AC, on the north bank of the Loire, make the most elegant dry whites in Anjou.

SAVIGNY-LÈS-BEAUNE AC
CÔTE DE BEAUNE, BURGUNDY

Pinot Noir

Chardonnay, Pinot Blanc

Although Savigny-lès-Beaune is off the main 'Côte', in the side valley through which the Autoroute du Soleil now leaps southwards, its parish boundaries are far flung, spreading right down to Beaune, and across to Aloxe-Corton. The 1000 acres (400 hectares) of vines in the AC represent the third largest red wine production on the Côte de Beaune, after Beaune and Pommard. The vines follow the cleft in the hills, facing both north-east and south to south-east. This less than perfect aspect does show in the wines, which are usually fairly light with a slightly minerally streak, but there is also a very pleasant strawberry fruit. Savigny whites aren't terribly impressive when young, but manage to show a bit of dry, nutty class after three or four years. Barely 40–50,000 bottles of white are made each year. Best years (reds): 1988, '87, '85, '83, '82, '80, '78. Best producers: Bize, Camus-Bruchon, Écard-Guyot, Fougeray, Girardin, Guillemot, Pavelot-Glantenay, Tollot-Beaut.

SAVOIE

▼ Mountains surround the scattered vineyards of Savoie. In this mainly white wine area, the AC/*vin de pays* regulations permit the addition of 20% white grapes to some red wines.

Savoie's high, alpine vineyards, tumbling down from the snow-capped peaks, are obvious candidates for making fresh, snappy whites, and this is what they do best. Except for the extremely pallid wines of Crépy, Savoie whites have got loads of taste, mainly thanks to the Altesse grape (also known as Roussette) – a fiery, spicy variety which was brought from Cyprus in the Middle Ages. Together with the dullish Jacquère, and the lean but tasty Chardonnay and Aligoté, this is grown on various sites down the embryo Rhône valley between Geneva and Lac du Bourget, and on the south-east and south-west-facing curve of mountain slopes below Chambéry. The result is an intensely fruity white – but it isn't soft, easy fruit, it's grapefruit, it's pepper, it's pear and apricot skins, with high, sharp acid and the twirl of tobacco smoke. They also make a fair number of very attractive light reds and rosés, and one deep, strong red which could happily hold its head up in the Rhône valley. Most of the best reds, from Gamay, Pinot Noir and Mondeuse, come from a group of villages near Chambéry, where the mountains curve round into the Isère valley. The Gamay isn't special and often ends up as rosé whereas the Pinot Noir can make lovely, fragile reds, scented with flowers and strawberry fruit. But the true star is Mondeuse, which makes an improbably deep, chewy red full of plum and mulberries and a slightly tarry darkness. The better wines are AC Vin de Savoie, which covers the wines of the whole Savoie and Haut-Savoie *départements*, as well as a few little patches of Ain and Isère. Drink the whites young, keep the best reds – five to ten years for the really good stuff.

ÉMILLON

Sémillon is a bit like a tennis player who can never win at singles, but comes to life brilliantly at doubles and wins title after title. With a couple of exceptions in Bordeaux – the dry Château Rahoul in Graves and the sweet Doisy-Daëne in Barsac (both of which are 100 per cent Sémillon), all France's best Sémillon-based wines are blended with Sauvignon Blanc. They complement each other perfectly. The Sauvignon benefits immeasurably from the weightier Sémillon, while the latter's lumpishness is transformed into a smooth, waxy, lanolin consistency. And its low acid, flabby fruit is woken by the green grass Sauvignon and broadens out into a lovely flavour of nuts and honey. All the great Graves *crus classés* are based on this formula.

Sémillon has another crucial character trait – it has a thin skin and can rot easily. Normally this would be regarded as a serious disadvantage, but in the Sauternes and Barsac regions, the grape is attacked by a particular type of fungus called 'noble rot' which sucks out the water but intensifies the sugar and acid. The result is the greatest range of sweet wines in the world, most of them made from at least 80 per cent Sémillon (the rest being Sauvignon and Muscadelle).

Sémillon's somewhat neutral character comes through in flavours which are not at all grapy, but are rich with pineapple, peach, syrup, butterscotch and barley sugar. Almost all France's Sémillon is grown in the south-west, and Bordeaux has so much of it that it ranks as France's second most planted white variety with over 49,000 acres (20,000 hectares) of vineyard devoted to it. The Bordeaux satellites of Bergerac, Buzet and Duras and, to a lesser extent, other south-west wines make up most of the rest. However, it is also being planted experimentally in the far south to add some flavour to France's most widely planted grape – the tasteless Ugni Blanc.

EYSSEL MOUSSEUX AC

AVOIE

Molette, Altesse (Roussette)

Seyssel is the best known of the Savoie villages, mainly became it is the headquarters of the region's sparkling wine industry – and we used to see quite a bit of sparkling Seyssel over here. Now, this really was feather-light, water-white fizz and made a fabulous summer Sunday gulper. But the vineyards of Seyssel are extremely limited – under 250 acres (100 hectares) of chalky limestone slopes on the banks of the Rhône. However, the ambitions of the local fizzers were distinctly beady-eyed and as sales grew and grew, the use of local grapes dropped and dropped. Finally we were left with heavy, sickly fizz of no style whatsoever – a disgrace to the Seyssel tradition.

Luckily, good sense has now prevailed and real Seyssel Mousseux AC – the lovely sharp peppery bite of the Molette and Altesse grapes smoothed out with a creamy yeast – is back on the market and tasting even better than in its previous heyday over a decade ago. The wines are often released with a vintage date and are worth seeking out. There is a little still white Seyssel AC, from the Altesse grape – very light and slightly floral – but it isn't as interesting as the racy, dry, Altesse whites from Chambéry and the Isère valley further south in Savoie. Best producers: Mollex, Varichon & Clerc.

IAURAC, CH.
alande-de-Pomerol AC

ORDEAUX

Merlot, Cabernet Franc, abernet Sauvignon

A leading Lalande-de-Pomerol property of 57 acres (23 hectares). The wines are full, rounded but reasonably tannic – excellent to drink young for their rather soupy richness, but much better to age for five to ten years because it probably ages better than any other Lalande de Pomerol. I've got half bottles of the 1966 and '67 which still have a delicious delicate blackcurrant scent, going a little musty like old lace in a shuttered room, but still lovely. Best years: 1988, '85, '83, '82, '78, '75.

SMITH-HAUT-LAFITTE, CH.
Pessac-Léognan AC, *cru classé de Graves*
BORDEAUX

🍷 Cabernet Sauvignon, Merlot, Cabernet Franc

🍸 Sauvignon Blanc

The property is one of the region's biggest at 111 acres (45 hectares) producing about 250,000 bottles of red (and some white) from a vineyard of 73 per cent Cabernet Sauvignon, 11 per cent Cabernet Franc and 16 per cent Merlot. The soil is good and gravelly on a swell of ground to the north of Martillac, but the red wine just doesn't 'sing', and is always a bit short on personality and a little lean. It lasts well enough but it never seems to get very exciting and if anything is marked by a persistent streak of green gooseberryish acidity. It is owned by Eschenauer, a Bordeaux shipping company and the same group which has revolutionized Rausan-Ségla in the last few years. Certainly the 1985, '86 and '88 vintages show distinct signs of improvement, so hopefully Eschenauer's redoubtable Monsieur Théo has begun to waggle his magic wand over Smith-Haut-Lafitte too. Best years (reds): 1988, '86, '85, '83, '82, '78.

But if the red has been dawdling, the whites have certainly geared up to a sprint. Before 1985, the white wine-making here was pedestrian and uninspired; since 1985 it has taken off and – using barrel fermentation and maturation in new oak – has shot Smith to the forefront of modern Bordeaux whites. Today the château stands as a shining example of what investment and commitment can do to a wine. A few years ago if you asked me to describe a boring Graves style white I'd have said it was sulphury, flabby, fruitless, unrefreshing – just like Smith-Haut-Lafitte. Today, if you ask me to describe the brilliant, exciting flavours which are flowing out of the Pessac-Léognan region, I'd say they're packed with apricot and crunchy grapefruit, sharpened up by a nettly bite and a smoky aroma of roasting coffee, and rounded out with a delicious savoury creaminess rather like *fromage blanc* – just like Smith-Haut-Lafitte! I was with a wine merchant at Smith-Haut-Lafitte last year and he was saying he didn't think the export market was ready for this type of wine yet. I beg to disagree. This is pure class and as bang up-to-date as it is possible to be. It's also a smack in the eye for the Burgundians because these wines are better than all but the best Côte d'Or whites – and half the price. So far only 15 acres (6 hectares) – out of Smith-Haut-Lafitte's total of 126 acres (51 hectares) in the commune of Martillac – are planted with white grapes – 100 per cent Sauvignon – although a further 15 acres are planned. Interestingly, the white is not 'classified' since there were no white grapes at all when the Graves Classification was decided in 1959, but the white is now easily outstripping the red for quality. Best years (whites): 1988, '87, '86, '85.

SOCIANDO-MALLET, CH.
Haut-Médoc AC, *cru grand bourgeois*
HAUT-MÉDOC, BORDEAUX

🍷 Cabernet Sauvignon, Merlot, Cabernet Franc

A rising star if ever I saw one. When I first visited the château at St-Seurin-de-Cadourne, holding lonely vigil over the last really decent gravel outcrop of the Haut-Médoc, I was not prepared for the beady-eyed, furious passion of the owner, Monsieur Gautreau, for his wine. And I wasn't prepared for the magnificent quality of this wine whose name I'd hardly even heard before. Dark, brooding, tannic, dry but with every sign of great, classic claret flavours to come if you could hang on for 10–15 years. So hats off to Monsieur Gautreau for his dedication and for believing in his wine which now easily attains the quality of a Classed Growth, and is rapidly approaching Classed Growth prices too.

The vineyard is 75 acres (30 hectares), 60 per cent Cabernet Sauvignon, 30 per cent Merlot and 10 per cent Cabernet Franc. Annual production is up to 220,000 bottles. Fifty per cent of the oak barrels used to mature the wine are new; this is an unusually high percentage and really *very* rare for a non-Classed Growth. Best years: 1988, '86, '85, '83, '82, '78, '76, '75.

SUDUIRAUT, CH.
Sauternes AC, *premier cru classé*
BORDEAUX

🍷 Sémillon, Sauvignon Blanc

Although d'Yquem is universally acclaimed as the greatest wine in Sauternes, its neighbour to the north, Château Suduiraut, is probably the smart money's bet for the role of runner-up. Suduiraut has a fresher, more perfumed quality than the other chief contender, d'Yquem's neighbour to the east, Château Rieussec – and if Rieussec is sometimes more blatantly sumptuous, Suduiraut counters this with a viscous ripeness which coats your mouth as if the whole were wrapped in melted butter and cream. Add to this a delicious fruit like pineapples and peaches soaked in syrup, and you can get some idea of the expansive, luscious flavours of which Suduiraut is capable.

Strangely, although Suduiraut made excellent wine in the two difficult vintages of '79 and '82, in the two super vintages of '83 and '86 the wine, although good, was less thrilling than I expected. The large 175-acre (70-hectare) estate usually produces about 120,000 bottles a year, and though the wines are delicious at only a few years old, the richness and excitement increase enormously after a decade or so. It really is worth the wait. Best years: 1988, '86, '83, '82, '79, '76.

▼ Harvest time at Château Suduiraut. On the horizon is its illustrious neighbour, Château d'Yquem.

SYLVANER

Sylvaner is very much a grape variety on the wane. Alsace is now the only part of France with any plantations, and it is being brushed aside by the more immediately attractive Pinot Blanc. The problem with Sylvaner is that it just doesn't actually taste of anything very much, and its wine is often marked out solely by being rather appley in a green, skinsy kind of way.

Since Pinot Blanc can give highly attractive rather creamy flavours to a wine almost as soon as it is bottled, and since Sylvaner's main advantage has always been its ability to produce big yields on uninspired vineyard land, something which the Pinot Blanc can *also* do, you can see why it is that fewer and fewer producers are offering any wines based on Sylvaner for sale, while at the same time more and more producers in Sylvaner's Alsatian heartland – guess what I'm going to say? – are offering a varietal Pinot Blanc.

SYRAH

► The hillside vineyards of Hermitage, overlooking the Rhône, are so steep that a restraining hand is needed on this trailer-load of harvested Syrah grapes.

I adore this grape and have done ever since I first tasted a Hermitage 1972 bottled by French merchants Nicolas years ago. Hermitage is usually made entirely from Syrah and it was the startling mixture of flavours which got me hooked. So savage to start with – the tannin tugging at your gums, the tarry, peppery brashness overlaid with a thick hot jammy fruit – that you feel sure the wine will never be remotely civilized. Yet the change does come. The tar and pepper subside into a smoky, leathery perfume, while the tannins drop away to reveal a wonderful sweet fruit – blackberries, blackcurrants, raspberries and plums – the black chewiness of dark treacle and liquorice, the slightly bitter edge of pine, the soothing texture of cream. All this may take five years, it may take ten or even 20, but it is one of wine's great conjuring tricks and puts Syrah into the front line of the world's red grapes.

Its home base is the northern Rhône, in particular the ACs of Hermitage, Côte-Rôtie, Cornas, St-Joseph and Crozes-Hermitage, in which it is the only red grape permitted. Its other traditional role has been as an improver vine in the southern Rhône and especially Châteauneuf-du-Pape, where it is used to add backbone and toughness to the fleshier Grenache. And it has now found a new role – as an improver to all the lifeless vineyards of the far south. The dark, tannic character and good plummy fruit can make a massive difference to a dull Midi blend, and many of the southern ACs as well as the burgeoning *vins de pays* use Syrah to great effect. Syrah now accounts for almost two per cent of French red grape plantings, with nearly 50,000 acres (20,000 hectares).

LA TÂCHE AC
grand cru
CÔTE DE NUITS, BURGUNDY

🍷 Pinot Noir

With Romanée-Conti, La Tâche is at the very peak of Vosne-Romanée *grands crus*, and similarly owned by Domaine de la Romanée-Conti. But there's a lot more La Tâche – 15 acres (6·1 hectares) as against 4½ acres (1·8 hectares) – and production is generally around 24,000 bottles. The vineyard's position is superb, just yards south of Romanée-Conti, fractionally more south-east, at the perfect altitude between 800 and 1000 feet (250 and 300 metres). For me, it is the greatest of these marvellous Vosne-Romanée *grands crus*. It has the rare ability to provide layer on layer of flavours, different scents and sweetnesses endlessly satisfying yet challenging, an exotic richness of fruit as heady as ripe plums soaked in brandy, and a spice of smoke, cinnamon, mace, the blackest of dark chocolate . . . La Tâche is a great sensation for the palate, the brain, but especially for the heart because it is the most sensuous and emotional of all Burgundy's great wines. Keep it for ten years or you'll only experience a fraction of the pleasure in store. Best years: 1988, '87, '85, '84, '83, '82, '80, '79, '78.

TAITTINGER
Champagne AC
CHAMPAGNE

🍷🥂 Pinot Noir, Chardonnay, Pinot Meunier

For many years I was infuriated by the fact that the top of the line Taittinger Comtes de Champagne Blanc de Blancs was one of the most memorable wines produced in Champagne, while their non-vintage Brut – the one I could afford to buy – was dull, lifeless and extremely short on fun, which is what I'm usually after in a simple non-vintage fizz. Well there's been a very welcome change of direction. The ordinary non-vintage is now soft, honeyed, beautifully balanced between fresh acidity and spice, and showing the relatively high percentage of Chardonnay the company uses.

The marketing men have found a way to create yet another ultra-de-luxe – this one called Vintage Collection – each vintage in a specially-commissioned modern art bottle. The wines are certainly good, but so far I've found the packaging slightly off-putting.

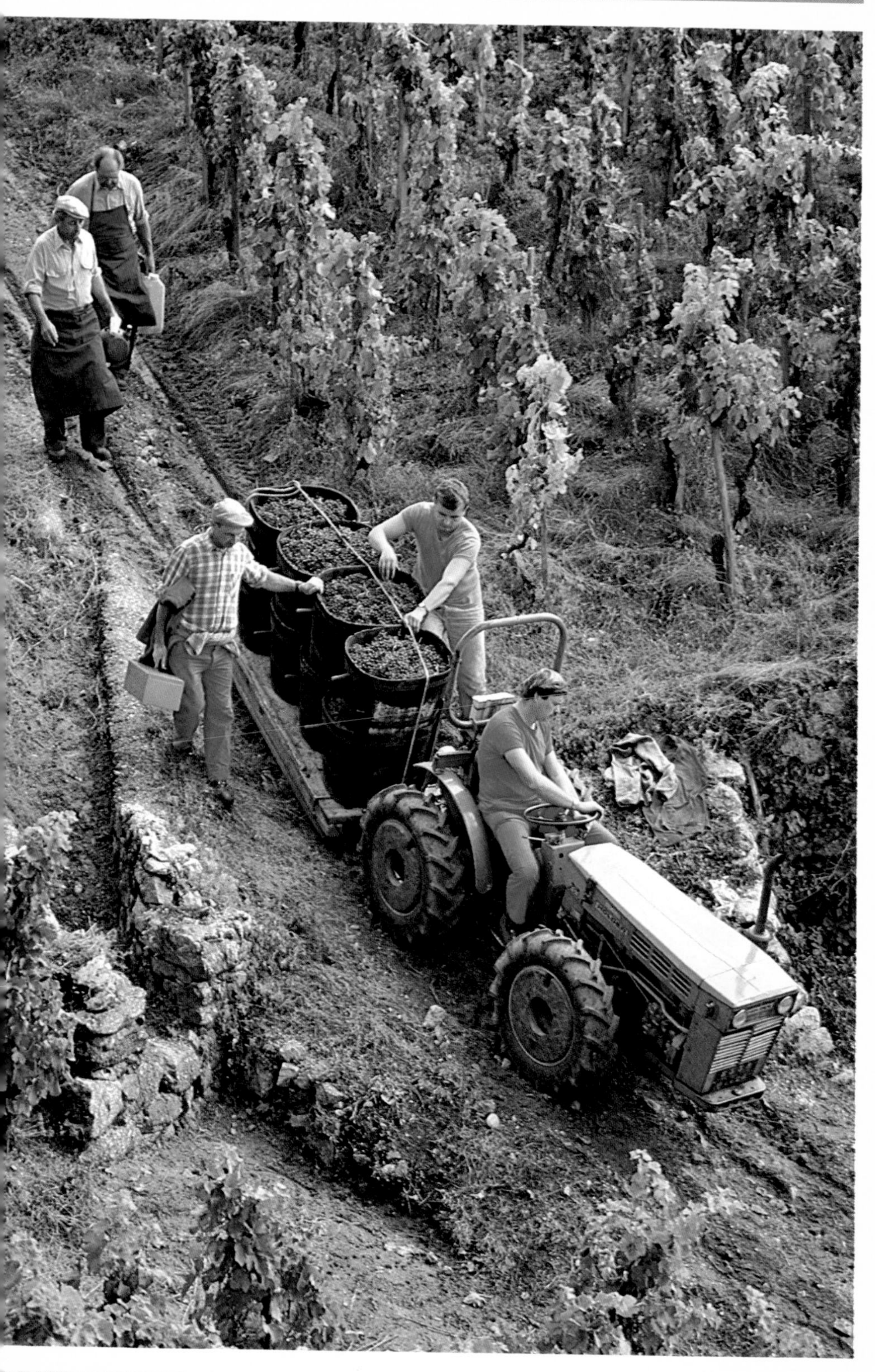

TALBOT, CH.
St-Julien AC, *4ème cru classé*
BORDEAUX

🍷 Cabernet Sauvignon, Merlot, Cabernet Franc, Petit Verdot

Talbot is a superb Fourth Growth which really should be upgraded to a Second. It's a *very* big estate – 250 acres (100 hectares), planted 71 per cent Cabernet Sauvignon, 20 per cent Merlot, five per cent Cabernet Franc and four per cent Petit Verdot. It occupies a single chunk of land bang in the middle of the AC.

The wine is big, soft-centred but sturdy, capable of ageing extremely well for 10–20 years, going from rather rich, almost sweet beginnings to a maturity of plums, blackcurrants and cigar-box scent – yet never to quite the same extent as sister-château Gruaud-Larose. But then Gruaud-Larose *is* a Second Growth. Best years: 1988, '86, '85, '84, '83, '82, '81, '79, '78. Second wine: Connétable Talbot.

TAVEL AC
SOUTHERN RHÔNE

🍷 Grenache, Cinsaut, Clairette and others

An oddity for southern France in that the Tavel AC applies only to one colour of wine – pink. Tavel boasts a hefty degree of alcohol as well as a big, strong, dry taste. But if rosé is supposed to be bright, cheerful and refreshing I'm afraid Tavel misses the mark because it just takes itself too seriously; it's too adult – which reminds me: it's also generally too old by the time it gets to the shops. One year old is fine, but I frequently come across examples at nearer three years old which have lost their pretty pink bloom and gone orange at the edges!

The vineyards, west of Orange and north-west of Avignon, are quite extensive at 1900 acres (750 hectares). Grenache is the dominant grape and gives ripe juicy flavours to the young wine, as usual kept from getting really fleshy and exciting by its side-kick Cinsaut. Altogether nine grapes are allowed, including Syrah and Mourvèdre, but these two are the important ones. The best producers allow the grapes to soak with the juice for a few hours before fermentation to add colour as well as perfume and flavour. Best years: 1988, '86, '85. Best producers: Aqueria, Génestière, Trinquevedel, Vieux Moulin.

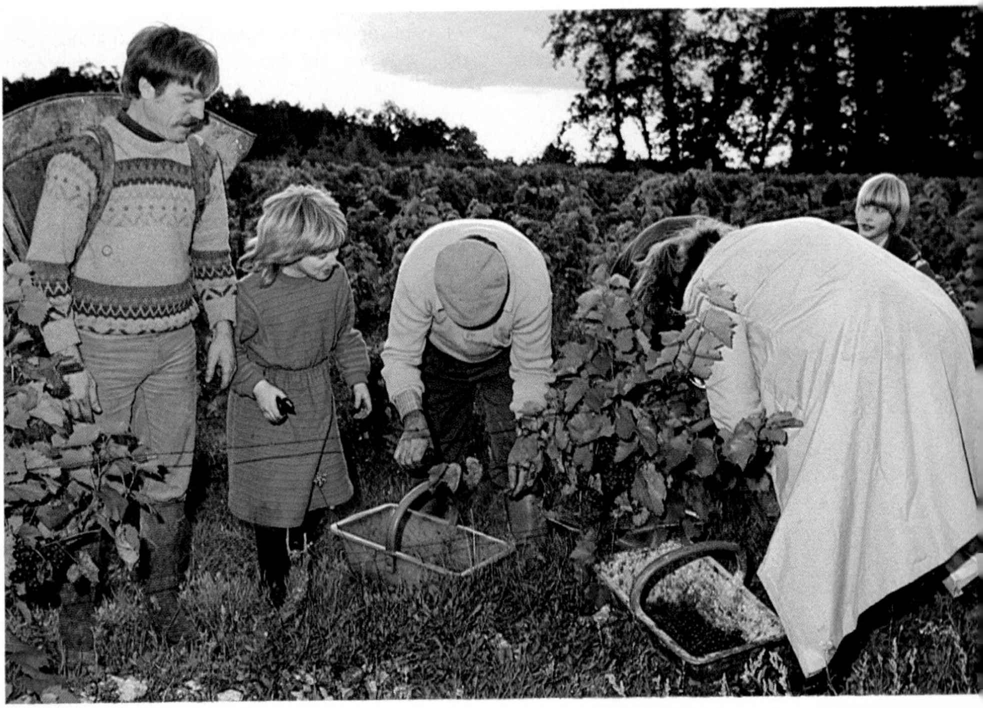

DU TERTRE, CH.
Margaux AC, *5ème cru classé*
HAUT-MÉDOC, BORDEAUX

Cabernet Sauvignon, Cabernet Franc, Merlot

At last du Tertre is gaining recognition – which it really does deserve, because stuck out in the wilds of Arsac, on the edge of the Margaux AC, you're not exactly going to benefit from any passing trade. But this 120-acre (48-hectare) vineyard is atop a knoll (*tertre* means 'knoll') on the highest ground in the AC, with extremely gravelly soil.

The mixture of 80 per cent Cabernet Sauvignon, 10 per cent Cabernet Franc and 10 per cent Merlot could be expected to produce hard, difficult, slow-maturing wine, but in fact du Tertre shows wonderful fruit, with strawberries, blackcurrants and mulberries apparent right from the start. There is tannin too, certainly, but also a glycerine ripeness coating your mouth and a marvellous cedar, strawberry and blackcurrant scent building up after a few years. It's usually delicious at five to six years old, but will happily age 10–15 years, maybe more. Best years: 1988, '86, '85, '83, '82, '80, '79, '78.

TOURAINE AC
CENTRAL LOIRE

Gamay, Cabernet Franc, Cabernet Sauvignon and others

Sauvignon Blanc, Chenin Blanc

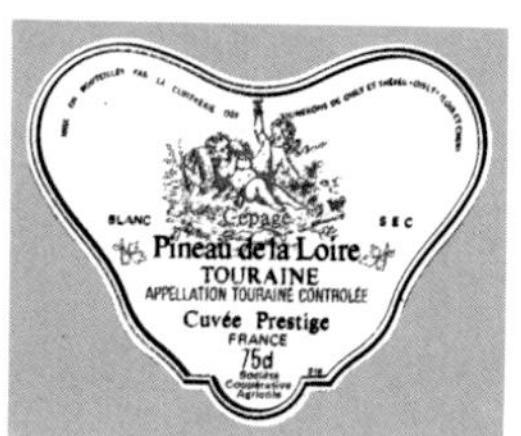

Touraine is the most interesting of the Loire's wine provinces. All the best wines have their own specific *appellations* – the reds are Chinon, Bourgueil and St-Nicolas-de-Bourgueil. The chief white ACs are Vouvray, Montlouis and Jasnières.

However, there is still a large amount of wine made, red, white and rosé, which merely qualifies for the Touraine AC, a fairly general AC covering 60 miles (97km) of the Loire valley to the east and west of Tours, the region's capital, and taking in sections of the Loir-et-Cher, Indre-et-Loire and Indre *départements*. Altogether there are 28,500 acres (11,500 hectares) of AC vineyards, divided half and half between white and red or rosé.

The red grapes used reflect Touraine's position on the Loire, between the wine cultures of Bordeaux and Burgundy. The Loire grapes Grolleau and Pineau d'Aunis are used for rosé only, whereas the Bordeaux grapes Cabernet Sauvignon, Cabernet Franc and Malbec (here known as Cot), the Pinot Noir from Burgundy and the Gamay from Beaujolais are used for rosés and reds. Most of the reds are from Gamay and in hot years can be juicy, rough-fruited wines, but they usually have a rather rooty overtone which can spoil the pleasure. Cabernet, too, is often a bit green, but can give quite pure-tasting wine.

Fairly good white wines come from the Chenin (often called Pineau de la Loire here), but the best are from Sauvignon. Dry, tangy, with a light apple and gooseberry fruit and a flicker of nettly acidity, Sauvignon de Touraine can be a good Sancerre substitute at half the price.

There are three villages which can add their names to Touraine AC on the label. Touraine-Amboise is a surprisingly good red from the Cot, made in an area of high chalk cliffs on the south bank of the river. Touraine Azay-le-Rideau is pink or white – the rosé, based on the Grolleau, is merely adequate and can be raspingly dry or slightly sweet; the whites, dry and off-dry, are fair in quality.

Touraine-Mesland has 1530 acres (620 hectares) of good vineyard on the north bank to the west of Blois that produces red wines from the Gamay which, especially when made with at least partial carbonic maceration, can be Touraine's best. Rosé is fair. Best years (reds): 1988, '87, '86, '85. Best producers (reds and rosés): Brossillon (Mesland), Charmoise, Corbillières, Denay (Amboise), Girault-Artois (Mesland), Octavie, Oisly-et-Thésée co-operative.

Touraine white wines should be drunk in the year following the vintage, though Chenin ones can last longer. Best years: 1988, '87, '86, '85. Best producers: Barbou, Baron Briare, Aimé Boucher, Bougrier, Charmoise, Octavie, Oisly & Thésée co-operative; Pavy (Azay-le-Rideau); Brossillon, Girault-Artois (Mesland); Denay, Dutertre (Amboise).

◀ Picking red grapes in the Loire. Although Touraine is mainly white-wine country, it also produces light, fresh reds.

LA TOUR-MARTILLAC, CH.
Pessac-Léognan AC, *cru classé de Graves*
BORDEAUX

🍷 Cabernet Sauvignon, Merlot, Cabernet Franc

🍷 Sémillon, Sauvignon Blanc

A Pessac-Léognan Classed Growth which has positively cultivated its old-fashioned image – both in its sturdy, unforthcoming wine styles and in the simple rustic charm of the peaceful little château, hidden away from the hurly-burly at the southern edge of Martillac.

The property rather seems to have been left behind by the wave of improvement sweeping through the region. This is a pity, because the owner Monsieur Kressmann has vines dating from the 1920s. He also determinedly follows organic practice in the vineyard and such an attitude should bring about deep, dark, well-structured wines for the long haul, but somehow they just lack chutzpah – their flavours are rather full and blank and their chunky feel is never matched by good dollops of fruit. But there does seem to be an improvement in the '80s. Best years (reds): 1988, '86, '85, '83, '82.

Only 10 acres (4 hectares) of the 57 acres (23 hectares) are planted with white grapes, but again, some of these are extremely old. I've always found the wine a bit stodgy, but since 1986 new style vinification and the employment of new oak barrels have combined to create a delicious, long-flavoured, apricotty dry white wine. Given that the vines yield small amounts of well-flavoured, concentrated juice, La Tour Martillac will be a property to watch from now on. Best years (whites): 1988, '87, '86.

TOURTEAU-CHOLLET, CH.
Graves AC
BORDEAUX

🍷 Cabernet Sauvignon, Merlot

Another example of how the less fashionable parts of the Graves, south of Pessac-Léognan, are taking up the quality banner and running with it. This 75-acre (30-hectare) property is in Arbanats, on the river Garonne to the south of Portets. Since the beginning of the 1980s (including the difficult years '80 and '84) the wines have been full, dry, slightly earthy but with good compact fruit – ready at three to four years old, but much better after six or seven. Best years: 1988, '86, '85, '83, '82, '81.

TROTANOY, CH.
Pomerol AC
BORDEAUX

🍷 Merlot, Cabernet Franc

Trotanoy puts itself up as Pétrus' main challenger for the title King of Pomerol but, except in vintages like 1978 (when Pétrus was inexplicably disappointing) and 1962 (when Trotanoy was an enormous, broad flavoured wine, smacking of chocolate and hazelnuts, brown sugar and blackberry jam), it is going to have to content itself with a crown prince role.

It's tremendous stuff, though, and another example (along with Pétrus, Lafleur, Latour-à-Pomerol and a gaggle of others) of the brilliant touch of Jean-Pierre Moueix and his son Christian. They own this 19-acre (7·5-hectare) property to the west of Pétrus on slightly more gravelly soil, and though the plantings of 85 per cent Merlot and 15 per cent Cabernet Franc do give a rich, massively impressive, Pétrus-like wine, they are also likely to have a tempering of leather and tobacco scent and just lack the magic mingling of sweetness, spice and perfume which make Pétrus so memorable. One of the great Pomerols, not *the* greatest. Best years: 1988, '85, '83, '82, '81, '79, '78, '76, '75.

TURSAN VDQS
SOUTH-WEST

🍷🍷 Tannat, Cabernet Franc, Cabernet Sauvignon

🍷 Baroque

Adequate reds, rosés and whites from south of the Adour river on the edge of Landes. The district backs on to Côtes de St-Mont and Madiran and the red Tannat grape – which makes Madiran so dour and charmless when it is young – is also evident in Tursan, backed up by Cabernet Franc and Cabernet Sauvignon. So it isn't surprising that the reds resemble a rather shadowy Madiran. The rosés, too, have the 'lack of fruit' problem of Madiran and although I'd drink them (and the whites) if I were passing through, I wouldn't seek them out.

VACQUEYRAS
Côtes du Rhône-Villages AC
SOUTHERN RHÔNE

Grenache, Syrah, Cinsaut, Mourvèdre

▼ The dramatic profile of the Dentelles de Montmirail rising above the terraced vineyards of Vacqueyras.

The most important and consistently successful of the Côtes du Rhône-Villages communes, now edging its way towards its own fully fledged individual AC. The village itself is rather a large one, liable to be raucous in summer and silent as a tomb in winter, and is on the flat land just south of Gigondas. However the vineyards sweep up towards the jagged Dentelles de Montmirail and produce red wines of a lovely dark colour, a round warm spicy bouquet and a fruit which happily mixes plums and raspberries with the wind-dried dust of the south. Lovely at two to three years; good producers' wines from good vintages will age well for ten years or more. Best years: 1988, '86, '85, '83, '81, '80, '78. Best producers: Couroulu, Fourmone, Jaboulet, Lambertins, Montmirail, Pascal, Roques, Vacqueyras co-operative.

VEUVE CLICQUOT
Champagne AC
CHAMPAGNE

Pinot Noir, Chardonnay, Pinot Meunier

Widows have featured prominently in the affairs of the Champagne houses, but when someone talks of 'The Widow' in Champagne, they are sure to be talking of the Widow Clicquot – Veuve Clicquot. Not only was she Champagne's dominant figure at the beginning of the nineteenth century, but she invented the process of *remuage* – the last factor in the equation needed to get clear Champagne rather than cloudy.

The problem is, to make Champagne fizz, a second fermentation is induced inside the bottle – but this produces loads of sludgy dead yeast cells, which stick to the glass and have to be removed. So Veuve Clicquot invented an A-shaped frame, with holes on both sides. The bottles are put in neck first and over the weeks turned and tapped against the wood, gradually going from 45 degrees to vertical, upside-down. The sludge has been coaxed on to the cork, and it's a comparatively easy job to whip out the cork and its sludge as you turn the bottle upright. It sounds so simple, but until this *remuage* process was invented, between 1814 and 1818, Champagne had to be shipped out with all the gunge still in it.

Luckily, the Veuve Clicquot wine lives up to the widow's standards. The non-vintage is full, toasty, slight honeyed and quite weighty for a sparkling wine. There is also a Vintage which resembles the non-vintage but is even fuller, and a De Luxe, called Grande Dame after the original widow, which is impressive stuff.

VIEUX-CHÂTEAU-CERTAN, CH.
Pomerol AC
BORDEAUX

Merlot, Cabernet Franc, Cabernet Sauvignon, Malbec

If Trotanoy now disputes the title of runner-up to Pétrus in the Pomerol hierarchy, traditionally that position has always been occupied by Vieux-Château-Certan. But whereas Trotanoy often seems to ape Pétrus, Vieux-Château-Certan goes out of its way to be different. It is owned by the Thienpont (not Moueix) family, for one thing. And, although it is only a few hundred yards down the road, its soil is obviously different, mixing sand and gravel with its clay.

But most importantly it has only 50 per cent Merlot as against Pétrus' 95 per cent. The rest of the 34-acre (13·6-hectare) vineyard is 25 per cent Cabernet Franc, 20 per cent Cabernet Sauvignon and five per cent Malbec, and it is this unusually strong presence of Cabernet for Pomerol which makes Vieux-Château-Certan drier, leaner, less gushing, less sumptuous, less Rubens flesh and sheer indulgence. What you do get is a slow-developing, tannic wine, which gradually builds up over 15–20 years into an exciting 'Médoc' blend of blackcurrant and cedarwood perfume just set off by the brown sugar and roasted nuts of Pomerol. A bottle of '52 Vieux-Château-Certan was the first blind wine-tasting prize I ever won in my life. (I don't know why they gave it to me though – I confidently said the wine was a Latour!) Best years: 1988, '87, '86, '85, '83, '82, '81, '75.

VIN DE CORSE AC
CORSICA

Nielluccio, Sciacarello and others

Vermentino

Corsica has been slower than mainland southern France to catch on to the new wave of wine technology – and with it the tremendous possibilities of making good wine even where the sun is baking the ground dry long before noon. The problems lie in the dogged traditionalism of most of the owners of the best-sited vineyards, and the carpet-bagging mentality of many of the vine-growers from French North Africa who re-settled during the 1960s on the flat eastern plains. With commendable agricultural skill, but little oenological interest, they turned eastern Corsica into a grape basket of grand proportions. As a wine venture it was a disaster – the heavy, unsubtle reds were merely shipped north to add a little beef to the feeble Midi brews, and since 1976 one third of the vineyards have been uprooted.

However, on this heavenly island which effortlessly lives up to its title Île de Beauté (the name of its *vin de pays* too), there are many fine hillside vineyards, producing good fruit – primarily the local red

▼ The Patrimonio area in the north of Corsica produces some of the island's better wines and can add its name to the Vin de Corse AC.

Nielluccio and Sciacarello varieties. White Vermentino has possibilities too. What is lacking is good wine-making. Most reds are volatile and oxidized, most rosés and whites flabby and dull, and the famed *maquis* herb perfume more likely to be a polite description of the pong left by a dirty wooden barrel. Yet the advances in wine-making techniques are tailor-made for the blistering climate of Corsica and its fairly flavourless grape varieties.

The greatest enemy during fermentation is overheating of the juice, as all the aroma and fruit flavour are then, quite literally, boiled off. Overheating also creates the conditions for acetic acid – vinegar – to form. The greatest enemy during storage is, again, too much heat, since it can promote bacterial growth, especially in unclean conditions. Yet it's perfectly possible to combat these problems by the use of refrigeration, selected yeasts, controlled temperature fermentation and storage – and the employment of stainless steel instead of wood.

Things are improving on Corsica, but very slowly. At a recent tasting of Ajaccio wines, the fruit was obviously good on most of the estates, but the wines all turned out unbalanced and past it – except for the expensive but highly proficient Comte Peraldi. Most of the white Corsica ACs employ Ugni Blanc and Vermentino (though the best wines are 100 per cent Vermentino). Interesting results are extremely rare, but Vin de Corse Coteaux du Cap Corse AC, in the far north-east, and Vin de Corse Calvi AC, in the north-west, can produce fair stuff. Otherwise the Vin de Corse Porto Vecchio AC is the most reliable – if that's the word! And if you're in this lovely island, do try the sweet Muscats – especially from Cap Corse and Patrimonio – they're deep, rich grapy wines, but they don't have an AC. Daft. Of the 30 million bottles of Corsican wine produced, about 2½ million are white. Best producers (whites): Leccia, Clos Nicrosi, Peraldi, Torraccia, UVAL co-operatives.

Corsican wines are supposed to age well, but except from a producer like Peraldi, I'd drink them as young as possible. The better areas – Ajaccio, Calvi, Cap Corse, Figari, Patrimonio, Porto Vecchio, Sartène – are allowed to add their name to Vin de Corse. Outside the AC areas, co-operative groups and in particular Sica UVAL are planting mainstream French grapes like Cabernet and Syrah, Chenin and Chardonnay – and having considerable success. I'm not one to support the dilution of traditional grape types, but maybe the Nielluccio and Sciacarello just aren't terribly brilliant. Best producers (reds): Cantone, Couvent d'Alzipratu, Dominique Gentile, Peraldi, Sica UVAL, Torraccia.

VIN DE L'ORLÉANAIS VDQS

UPPER LOIRE

Pinot Noir, Pinot Meunier, Cabernet Sauvignon

Chardonnay, Pinot Blanc

Orléans is the vinegar capital of France. Situated on the northernmost point of the Loire's long arc across France, and perilously close to the point where grapes just won't ripen at all, it looks to be a very sound location for such an enterprise! Yet, as recently as the last century, red Orléans wine was regarded as one of France's outstanding drinks and it was a favourite of the French court for several centuries. Well, the weather must have been a lot better then because most of the 700,000 bottles produced from 370 acres (150 hectares) on both sides of the Loire are a *very* pale rosé of distinctly fragile constitution. They call it Gris Meunier d'Orléans, and it's the only time Pinot Meunier appears under its own name, unblended, in France. (There's Pinot Noir and Cabernet Franc too, but I think I'd go elsewhere for them.) There are also about 60,000 bottles of white made from Pinot Blanc and Chardonnay (here called Auvernat) and, astonishingly, the Clos de St-Fiacre somehow manages to produce one of the most delightful, deliciously drinkable Chardonnays in the whole of France. Drink whites and rosés as young as possible. Best producer: Clos de St-Fiacre.

VIN DE PAYS DES BOUCHES-DU-RHÔNE
PROVENCE

Grenache, Cinsaut, Carignan

Ugni Blanc, Clairette and others

This *département*, which stretches across the wide Rhône delta, produces about 15 million bottles a year of Vin de Pays des Bouches-du-Rhône – mostly red, with some rosé and a little white. The best wines come from the area round Aix, although the mysterious, wild marshes of the Camargue contribute about a quarter of the total. The wines are rarely very exciting, although the reds, when made by an up-to-date co-operative, can have a pleasant, dusty, strawberry fruit which makes for undemanding drinking.

VIN DE PAYS DES SABLES DU GOLFE DU LION
LANGUEDOC-ROUSSILLON

Cabernet Sauvignon, Cinsaut, Grenache and others

Ugni Blanc, Clairette, Marsanne and others

This splendid title translates as 'the Sands of the Gulf of the Lion'. Well, the Gulf of the Lion is the whole of the gentle loop of shore-line that swings round from Marseille to Béziers, and the *vin de pays* comes from the coastal vineyards through most of that area, covering three *départements* – Bouches-du-Rhône, Gard and Hérault – and producing in total about 16 million bottles: 35 per cent red, 40 per cent rosé or *gris* (very pale rosé) and 25 per cent white.

By far the most important producer is the Domaines Viticoles des Salins du Midi – which uses the brand name Listel. Basically a salt company producing enormous amounts of salt from the Rhône delta marshes, the Salins du Midi are also, astonishingly, the biggest vineyard owners in France with a staggering 4750 acres (1900 hectares) out on the sandbars of the Camargue. Among numerous claims to fame – like, how you grow anything on sand in the middle of a salty swamp – they are France's largest producer of Cabernet Sauvignon!

Listel wines probably are the best in the area, though they are by no means memorable – but they're not expensive either. The very pale *gris* can be good but *must* be drunk ultra-young and I prefer the slightly darker rosés. Grenache, Cinsaut and Carignan are the main grapes in the region, but there are good plantings of Syrah, Merlot – and obviously, Cabernet Sauvignon.

Despite the Mediterranean climate, the company produces the best white *vin de pays* in southern France, employing the usual Ugni Blanc and Clairette, but also getting tremendous results out of Marsanne, Muscat, Sauvignon Blanc and Chardonnay. The wines are best drunk very young, but I stumbled over – literally! – a four-year-old Sauvignon the other day and it was actually better than a six-month-old version I'd recently tasted. There's also a pleasantly grapy Pétillant de Raisin, lightly fizzy and refreshingly low in alcohol – it weighs in at under three per cent alcohol!

VIN DE PAYS D'OC
LANGUEDOC-ROUSSILLON

Carignan, Cinsaut, Grenache

Ugni Blanc, Macabeo, Bourboulenc

In the olden days, one part of France expressed 'yes' by saying *oui*; another part, spread round the Mediterranean basin said *oc*. 'Some more wine, Asterix?' 'Oc please'. Well, sort of. But on that simple difference of how to say 'yes', France came to be divided. Languedoc – the modern name for much of the south of France – means 'Language of Oc'! So the regional Vin de Pays d'Oc covers the Rhône and Provence as well as Languedoc-Roussillon. However, most wines in the region either have AC or VDQS status, or prefer to use more clearly defined departmental *vins de pays*, such as Vin de Pays de l'Aude for wines made throughout the Aude *département*, or zonal *vins de pays* such as Vin de Pays de la Vallée du Paradis for a specific mini-region in the south of the Aude *département*. About ten million bottles declare themselves as Vin de Pays d'Oc; the reds and rosés, mostly from Carignan, Cinsaut and Grenache, come into the cheap and cheerful category. Drink them young. The million or so bottles of white Vin de Pays d'Oc are unlikely to be very exciting.

VIN DE PAYS DU COMTÉ TOLOSAN
SOUTH-WEST

🍷🍷 Cabernet Sauvignon, Cabernet Franc, Merlot, Malbec

🍷 Sauvignon Blanc, Sémillon, Colombard and others

This *vin de pays régional* covers the enormous area of the entire south-west, but it is a comment on how the traditional ACs and VDQSs are successfully catering for the needs of both traditional and innovative winemakers that the production only totals 2½ million bottles from what is arguably the most important wine area in France. For example, Bordeaux is covered by the regulations, but all quality wines in Bordeaux are *appellation contrôlée*. Even so, there are large numbers of unplanted but suitable vineyard sites in this large and interesting south-westerly area, with plenty of opportunity for good clean reds from traditional Bordeaux varieties and whites from grapes like Sauvignon, Sémillon and Colombard. As yet we rarely see these labels but I'm sure we'll see more of them in the next few years.

VIN DE PAYS DU GARD
LANGUEDOC-ROUSSILLON

🍷🍷 Carignan, Cinsaut, Grenache and others

🍷 Clairette, Ugni Blanc, Bourboulenc and others

The smallest of the 'big three' departmental *vins de pays* in France's Midi, producing about 30 million bottles, mainly reds and rosés. Because the Gard *département* takes in the southern end of the Rhône valley as it fans out into the Mediterranean, the wines are often supposed to have something of a Rhône quality. That would be flattering them. There is a lot of Carignan planted and not enough of the top grapes Syrah, Mourvèdre, Cabernet Sauvignon and Merlot – although plantings are increasing. Consequently, most Gard red is light, slightly spicy, but often with a gamy earthiness flattening the fruit. The rosés are often better and, drunk young and fresh, can be very attractive. The quality of the whites is good where modern technology intervenes.

VIN DE PAYS DU JARDIN DE LA FRANCE
LOIRE

🍷🍷 Cabernet Franc, Cabernet Sauvignon, Cot and others

🍷 Chenin Blanc, Sauvignon Blanc, Chardonnay and others

What a lovely name for a wine – Garden of France. Well, it's an apt title as this is the regional country wine title for the Loire valley, which has for centuries been regarded as France's market garden. Altogether it covers 13 *départements*; although each one is entitled to its own departmental *vin de pays* title, many of them prefer to market their wines under the 'Jardin de la France' umbrella. Production in the largest of the French regional *vins de pays* often exceeds 30 million bottles – mostly white and usually very cheap.

The Chenin and the Sauvignon are the most common grapes, but various growers are exploiting the laxness of the regulations to produce Chardonnay wines (not permitted by Loire ACs), often with excellent results – crisp, a little sharp sometimes, but with the crucial Chardonnay creaminess just enough in evidence. (The Jardin de la France title is particularly useful in the Anjou and Muscadet ACs where the Chardonnay has proved it can ripen well.) These are wines to drink young and the Sauvignons and Chardonnays, in particular, can be very attractive. The few reds and rosés – usually from the Gamay, but occasionally from Pinot Noir or Cabernet – are generally light and sharp; fine drunk young and chilled on the banks of some Loire tributary like the Layon or the Cher, but not to be sought out for more 'substantial' experiences.

VIN DE SAVOIE AC
SAVOIE

🍷🍷 Mondeuse, Gamay, Pinot Noir

🍷 Altesse, Jacquère, Chardonnay and others

Apart from Crépy and Seyssel, which have their own ACs, most Savoie wines are simply labelled Vin de Savoie AC, or Vin de Savoie plus the name of a village. The best of these are Abymes, Apremont, Arbin, Chignin, Cruet and Montmélian.

The vines here have to contend with holiday housing, ski-lifts, and fairly intense agriculture – so they tend to sprout up all over the region, whenever there's a south-facing slope not yet nabbed for a ski jump. There are 3700 acres (1500 hectares) altogether, producing about 8·3

million bottles, most of it white. You can age the wines for a year or two, especially those with some Chardonnay in them – but they lose their thrilling snap of tangy fruit, so I can't see any point.

There is some good sparkling wine made, but most of that comes under its own AC at Seyssel, although Ayze, south-east of Geneva, also has a reputation for it – and its own AC. The best reds are made from the Mondeuse; plummy, chewy wines capable of ageing. Best years: 1988, '87, '86. Best producers: Cavaillé, Monin, Monterminod, Neyroud, Ollivier, Perret, Perrier, André Quénard, Raymond Quénard, Rocailles, Tiollier, le Vigneron Savoyard.

VIOGNIER

▲ The Viognier-planted terraces of Château Grillet rise steeply above the river Rhône.

You might question my sanity in including the Viognier grape as one of France's leading varieties when there are fewer than 75 acres (30 hectares) planted in the whole of the country and fewer than 10 acres (4 hectares) in the rest of the world put together. Ah, but never mind the quantity, taste the wine – if you can find any! The vine is an incredibly poor yielder of grapes, producing less than any other dry white wine variety, and markedly prone to disease. Consequently the two tiny Rhône vineyards – Château Grillet and Condrieu – which make 100 per cent Viognier wines are among the rarest in the world.

Every year or two I manage to get hold of a bottle of Condrieu, I open it, and the room is swamped with a perfume as meadow-fresh as it is autumn-rich. One writer calls that perfume May-blossom – and I sort of know what he means, because it is like that first exhausted gulp of air as you clamber to the top of a steep hill in spring-time, and the breeze-blown fragrance of the mountain flowers is heady and intoxicating. Taste the wine and you'll swear it's sweet – but it isn't! That rich fruit is like apricot skins and ripe pears all squashed together and smothered with a fatness almost like fresh yoghurt. Strange? Yes. Special? Very.

Viognier also occurs in the Côte-Rôtie, just north of Condrieu, where it can be blended in with Syrah adding its exotic, evocative fragrance to produce one of France's greatest red wines. *Can* be, but few growers have more than five per cent of it today. The Viognier is also planted in minute quantities in the Southern Rhône, and in the Hérault at Mas de Daumas Gassac, but is not as yet producing wine with any noticeable Viognier characteristics.

VOLNAY AC & VOLNAY-SANTENOTS AC
CÔTE DE BEAUNE, BURGUNDY

Pinot Noir

Until the eighteenth century, Volnay produced Burgundy's Nouveau, much the same way as Beaujolais does now. The wine was extremely pale and was snapped up for high prices as soon as it had settled down after fermentation. French kings drank quite a bit of it, which is always good for trade.

The soil has a fair bit of chalk and limestone, particularly in the higher vineyards – normally the cue for planting white vines, but there isn't a white vine in Volnay's 531 acres (215 hectares). There are, in fact, two main styles of Volnay. One *is* light, or perfumed in a delicious cherry and strawberry way, sometimes even lifted by a floral scent. However, there are also some wines of tremendous, juicy, plummy power, particularly from the lower vineyards like Champans and Santenots (which is actually in Meursault but is called Volnay-Santenots). Drinkable at three to four years old, but unless the wine is very light this is usually a pity, because lovely flavours can develop between seven and ten years. Best years: 1988, '87, '85, '83, '82, '80, '78. Best producers: Blain-Gagnard, Clerget, Comte Lafon, Delagrange, Glantenay, Lafarge, Marquis d'Angerville, de Montille, Potinet-Ampeau, Pousse d'Or, Vaudoisey-Mutinde.

VOSNE-ROMANÉE AC
CÔTE DE NUITS, BURGUNDY

Pinot Noir

They call it the greatest village in Burgundy – simply because it has an incomparable clutch of five *grands crus* at its heart. I'd only go so far as saying the greatest village in the Côte de Nuits – partly because the Côte de Beaune has Puligny-Montrachet, home of the greatest dry white wines in the world, and partly because the Côte de Nuit's other contender – Gevrey-Chambertin, with its large string of *grands crus* – is relentlessly failing to realize its potential at the moment.

There are 600 acres (240 hectares) of vineyards of which just under 66 acres (27 hectares) are Vosne-Romanée's *grands crus* themselves, but this figure rises to 163 acres (66 hectares) if the *grands crus* of Échézeaux and Grands-Échézeaux (technically belonging to the village Flagey-Échézeaux) are included in the total, as is usual. However a village's reputation is not just made on its *grands crus*. There are 119 acres (48 hectares) of *premiers crus* which match other villages' *grands crus* in quality. Best of these are Malconsorts and Suchots. And the fact that all of Vosne-Romanée's other AC land is on the slopes to the west of the N74 road, rather than slipping across to the inferior plains beyond, also helps to keep the wine quality high.

The mix of exciting, red-fruit ripeness with a delicious tangle of spices and smoke, sometimes even showing a distinctly savoury edge and a whiff of mint and eucalyptus, and finally ageing to the deep, decaying pleasures of prunes, brown sugar and chocolate, moist autumn dampness and well-hung game – all these make Vosne-Romanée red wine one of the world's really exciting experiences. In good years the wines should have at least six years' age. Ten to fifteen would be better. Lighter years still need five to eight. Best years: 1988, '87, '86, '85, '84, '83, '82, '80, '78, '76. Best producers: Domaine de la Romanée-Conti, Engel, Grivot, Gros, Hudelot-Noëllat, Jayer, Lamarche, Martin-Noblet, Moillard, Mugneret-Gibourg, Rion.

Vins de Pays

The phrase *vins de pays* implies that these are the traditional wines of the country districts of France which have been created and enjoyed for centuries by the locals. The reality is a little different. The vast majority of *vins de pays* are impressively modern and forward-looking.

The name *vin de pays* was conceived as a dependable category of French wine only in 1968. Until then, in many parts of the country – especially the far south – there was a serious problem of overproduction of very mediocre wine and no incentives available to the grower to improve quality since all the wines were consigned to the anonymity of the blending vats of various shippers and merchants. Matters have definitely improved since then.

The aim was to encourage quality, and to provide a specific guarantee of geographical origin for the wines. In this the *vin de pays* system follows the example set by the two top quality tiers in French wines (see page 14). In effect, *vin de pays* became the third tier of quality control, following similar guidelines based on geographical origin, yield of grapes per hectare, minimum alcohol levels and choice of grape varieties.

There are three geographically defined categories, each one becoming more specific. *Vins de pays régionaux* covers a whole region encompassing several *départements*. There are only three of these and any wine grown in the region concerned may qualify. *Vin de pays départementaux* cover the wines of an entire *département*. There are 35 of these. *Vin de pays de zone* is the most specific category, and relates only to the wines of a specific community or locality. Altogether these account for about 14 per cent of French wine production.

Yield is higher than for ACs since the *vins de pays* are only just beginning to create a reputation and cannot as yet command high prices, and alcoholic strength is generally lower.

The grape varieties are specified to eliminate the worst sorts, but the crucial element here is that excellent varieties excluded from a region's ACs but capable of producing high-quality wine are included. Consequently, for example, we are seeing excellent white Chardonnay from the Loire and Languedoc-Roussillon – grape varieties previously virtually unknown there. Increasingly the *vin de pays* is labelled with the grape variety – and these are now the source of some of France's best-value flavours.

REGIONAL WINES
Vin de Pays d'Oc
Vin de Pays du Comté Tolosan
Vin de Pays du Jardin de la France
DEPARTMENTAL WINES
Aude
Bouches-du-Rhône
Gard
l'Hérault
Pyrénées-Orientales
ZONAL WINES
Charentais
Coteaux de l'Ardèche
Coteaux de Peyriac
Côtes de Gascogne
l'Île de Beauté
Sables du Golfe du Lion
l'Yonne

► Timeless terraces of vines and olives in the Hérault, which has more vineyards than any other *département* in France. Although it has several AC and VDQS wines, the Hérault is primarily *vin de pays* country. Its own departmental *vin de pays* is traditionally based on the rough, sullen Carignan grape but is being improved by planting other varieties – including the Bordeaux classics Cabernet Sauvignon and Merlot – and by the use of carbonic maceration.

VOUGEOT AC
CÔTE DE NUITS, BURGUNDY

🍷 Pinot Noir

🍸 Chardonnay

When I first saw a bottle of Vougeot I thought the label was faulty because I was so accustomed to seeing Clos de Vougeot, that plain Vougeot just didn't look right. But there are 30 acres (12 hectares) of Vougeot vines outside the walls of the famous Clos, producing about 70,000 bottles of wine, divided six to one in red's favour. It's not bad stuff – full and slightly solid to start but gaining a really good chocolaty richness with a few years age – and it's a *lot* cheaper than Clos de Vougeot – but then, what isn't? *Premiers crus* Clos de la Perrière and Les Petits Vougeots are best. Best years: 1988, '87, '86, '85. Best producer: Bertagna.

VOUVRAY AC
CENTRAL LOIRE

🍸 Chenin Blanc

The excruciatingly high acidity of the Chenin grape is both the main problem with young Vouvray, and also the support system which allows the best examples to last 50 years. The grapes in this decidedly one-grape town grow in 3700 acres (1500 hectares) of picturesque vineyards east of Tours, on a limestone and chalk clay soil – which yields intensely flavoured juice, but, in cool years when the grapes don't ripen, creates even more acidity. Unripe grapes traditionally go to make Vouvray Mousseux AC, produced by the Champagne method and usually of a high standard. However, the still wines are more exciting. They can be dry – in which case they'll be bitingly sharp to start with, but beautifully rounded out into a dry buttermilk and nuts flavour after ten years or so. And they can be sweet (*moelleux*) – the noble rot occasionally infects the grape late in October and the results are wines of peach and honey soft sweetness but ever-present acidity.

Vouvray's greatest role is as a medium-dry wine. Cheap Vouvray has spoilt our appreciation of this style, but when it is properly made from a single domaine, it will start out with the usual rasping acidity, but slowly, perhaps over 20 years, build up an exciting smoky peach, pears and quince fullness – again kept fresh by an acidity as insistent but tongue-tingling as the skin of a green apple. Such wines are some of the cheapest classics on the block. Best years: 1988, '85, '83, '82, '78, '76, '75, '70, '69. Best producers: Bidaudières, Brédif, Foreau, Freslier, Huet, Jarry, Poniatowski.

L'YONNE, VIN DE PAYS DE
CHABLIS, BURGUNDY

🍸 Chardonnay, Aligoté, Sacy, Sauvignon Blanc

Certainly the Chablis vineyards, Burgundy's most northerly, grouped along the banks of the Serein river about 80 miles (130 kilometres) north-west of Dijon and the Côte d'Or and within the Yonne *département*, can produce world-class wine from the Chardonnay grape but there are several other little areas of historic importance here, even if their vineyards have now diminished to such an extent that they are looked on as mere oddities.

Vin de Pays de l'Yonne usually applies to wines from young vines in the Chablis region or wines from Chardonnay, Aligoté, Sacy or Sauvignon which don't qualify for any better category. These are normally very light and rather tart, but can be refreshing in a sharp kind of way on a hot summer's day.

D'YQUEM, CH.
Sauternes AC, *grand premier cru*
BORDEAUX

🍸 Sémillon, Sauvignon Blanc

Last but by no means least. In fact, many people would rate Château d'Yquem as the greatest wine in Bordeaux and maybe even the greatest wine in France. Certainly if we're talking about total commitment to quality and a no-compromise approach to wine-making, you simply cannot fault d'Yquem – the supreme example of the majestic sweet wines of Sauternes. In 1855, when Bordeaux was busy classifying wine d'Yquem was accorded a sort of 'first of firsts' position as against the

▲ Château d'Yquem, the most prestigious producer in Sauternes, also makes a dry white wine, called 'Y', which can only qualify for the Bordeaux Blanc AC.

other famous First Growths like Margaux, Latour, and, of course, several other top Sauternes. D'Yquem's title was *grand premier cru* – Great First Growth – the only wine accorded this title. This shows that d'Yquem was regarded as supreme all those years ago – and its position hasn't changed since.

The vineyard is large – 250 acres (100 hectares), planted with Sémillon (80 per cent) and Sauvignon (20 per cent) – but production is tiny, rarely reaching 65,000 bottles. When you note that Château La Tour Blanche – another Sauternes First Growth – manages to produce 65,000 bottles from only 75 acres (30 hectares), you begin to understand the sacrifice for quality which takes place. Only fully 'noble-rotted' grapes are picked – often berry by berry! This means that the pickers may have to go through the vineyard as many as eleven times, and that the vintage doesn't finish till the freezing winter days of December.

Noble rot concentrates the juice but radically reduces the volume. Although the Sauternes AC allows a yield of 25 hectolitres per hectare – which is already very low – at d'Yquem the yield is more like eight hectolitres per hectare. This works out at a glass of wine per vine (a great red wine estate might easily produce a bottle of wine per vine). This precious liquid gold is then fermented in new oak barrels – and left to mature in them for three-and-a-half years, before bottling and eventual release.

If the wine isn't at the very least outstanding, and preferably incomparable, it isn't released as d'Yquem. In 1964, '72 and '74 the entire crop was declassified; in '79, 60 per cent and in '78, 85 per cent were refused the Château label. The result is a frantically expensive wine which is nonetheless in constant demand, because for sheer richness, for exotic flavours of vanilla, pineapple, melons, peaches and coconut, enveloped in a caramel richness so viscous and lush your mouth feels coated with succulence for an eternity after swallowing the wine . . . for all that, and for an ability to age a decade, a generation, a century even . . . no wine in the world can touch d'Yquem. Best years: 1988, '86, '83, '81, '80, '76, '75, '71, '67, '62.

BOTTLES, CORKS AND LABELS
RED AND ROSÉ WINES

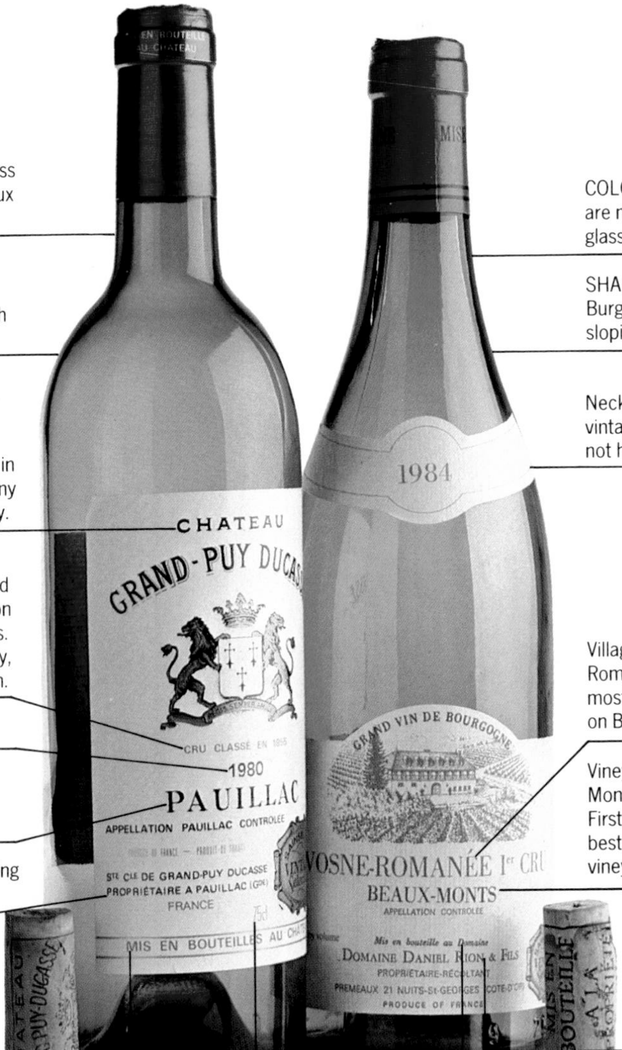
COLOUR Dark green glass is traditional for Bordeaux red wines.
SHAPE The classic Bordeaux bottle has high shoulders.
The estate – although *château* means 'castle', in Bordeaux it applies to any wine-producing property.
Classed Growth, as listed in the 1855 Classification of top Médoc properties. The label doesn't specify, but this is a Fifth Growth.
Vintage.
Pauillac is a leading commune in the Haut-Médoc with its own AC.
Name of company owning the property.
Cork stamped with the estate name.
Contents in bottle.
Estate-bottled – obligatory for *cru classé* wines in the Médoc.
COLOUR Burgundy bottles are made of olive-green glass.
SHAPE The classic Burgundy bottle has low, sloping 'shoulders'.
Neck label showing the vintage; many wines do not have a neck label.
Village name: Vosne-Romanée is one of the most famous communes on Burgundy's Côte d'Or.
Vineyard name: Beaux Monts is a *premier cru*, First Growth – the second best quality level for vineyards in Burgundy.
Cork stamped with 'estate- bottled'.
Name of the producer owning the vineyard.
Bottled on the estate.
CHATEAU
GRAND-PUY DUCASSE
CRU CLASSÉ EN 1855
1980
PAUILLAC
APPELLATION PAUILLAC CONTROLÉE
STE CIE DE GRAND-PUY DUCASSE
PROPRIÉTAIRE A PAUILLAC (GDE)
FRANCE
MIS EN BOUTEILLES AU CHATEAU
1984
GRAND VIN DE BOURGOGNE
VOSNE-ROMANÉE 1er CRU
BEAUX-MONTS
APPELLATION CONTROLÉE
DOMAINE DANIEL RION & FILS
PROPRIÉTAIRE-RÉCOLTANT
PREMEAUX 21 NUITS-ST-GEORGES CÔTE-D'OR
PRODUCE OF FRANCE

'ou can learn something about a wine simply ›y looking at the bottle – certain regions have raditional shapes and colours. And you can earn a great deal more by understanding the abel, which carries a range of essential information, some of it required by law, and some ›rovided at the discretion of the winemaker, ›roducer or *négociant*.

BOTTLES, CORKS AND LABELS WHITE WINES

COLOUR In Bordeaux, clear glass is used for sweet wines such as Sauternes, and also for some dry whites. Green glass always denotes a dry wine.

SHAPE The traditional Bordeaux bottle has high, square shoulders.

The wine-producing estate.

First Growth, as listed in the 1855 Classification of Sauternes properties.

Vintage.

The appellation contrôlée.

COLOUR Unusually dark for a Burgundy bottle. A lighter, olive-green is mor

SHAPE The classic Burgundy bottle has low, sloping shoulders.

Neck label with vintage and producer's name.

The village name – Pulign Montrachet is world famous for its *grand cru* wines as well as its own village label.

Bottle contents.

Name of producer.

SHAPE Alsace bottles are distinctively tall and slender.

COLOUR Alsace wines are bottled in green glass.

Neck label showing the vintage.

The *appellation contrôlée.*

Name of producer.

The grape variety – Gewürztraminer. Most Alsace wines are single grape 'varietals'.

Bottle contents. Although 700ml (70cl) is traditional to Alsace, the EC is standardizing bottle size to 750ml (75cl).

SHAPE Champagne bottles are similar to Burgundy bottles but they have a heavy lip for securing the wire muzzle.

Foil capsule showing the producer's name. A capsule keeps the cork clean, helps stop it drying out and protects it from weevils.

Neck label indicating dryness; 'extra dry' is the second-driest category of Champagne after 'brut'.

COLOUR Champagne bottle glass is dark green to protect the contents from light; it is also thicker than usual to withstand pressure.

Champagne is the only AC not required to have the words *appellation contrôlée* on the label.

Épernay, on the river Marne, is one of the main towns in the Champagne region.

The producer – one of the top Champagne houses.

The 'mushroom' cork is traditional to Champagne. A metal cap covers the top of the cork to prevent the wire muzzle cutting into it.

Storing and Serving Red Wines

STORING Most wine, unless it's really getting on in years, is pretty resilient stuff. Although it won't *like* being stored next to the central heating boiler it'll probably survive for a few weeks at least. But if the wine is at *all* special, it's worth taking a few precautions.

That is, if you need to store the stuff at all! Despite the feeling that the older the bottle the better, this just isn't the case with most modern wine: nowadays nearly all wine is ready to drink the moment it appears on the shop shelf. Reds *may* benefit from a little ageing, especially those based on the Cabernet Sauvignon and Syrah grapes, but – except for the top wines of Bordeaux and the northern Rhône – these are also generally ready to drink by the time they are put on sale.

However, if you still want to store a few bottles – find somewhere with an even temperature which is fairly quiet and not too dry. The traditional basement cellar is ideal for this, but few houses have one nowadays, so a broom cupboard, a disused fireplace, or the space under the stairs may have to do. Lay the wines on their sides to stop the corks drying out, and preferably shield them from direct light. The cooler the place is, within reason, the slower the wines will develop: somewhere between 50°F and 55°F (10°C and 13°C) is ideal. But avoiding sudden changes in temperature is the most important thing.

SERVING Most red wine is best served at room temperature – but that's 60°F (15°C) or so – cooler than many centrally-heated houses. It's better to serve reds slightly too cool than too warm because you can always warm wine up by cupping the glass in your hand. *Don't* do anything dramatic to change a wine's temperature like leaving it in front of the fire. It'll probably blow its cork and taste like grape soup. Light, new reds such as Beaujolais can take up to an hour in the fridge, but that's not essential. Rosés should be well-chilled to very chilled indeed! *Any* wine can be decanted just for the fun of it, and some wines do get softer and rounder after a couple of hours' decanting. But no wine *demands* it. Even an old wine which has thrown a sediment can be poured out successfully from the bottle – do it slowly, avoiding any sudden movements which might make the wine slop about. But if you do decide to decant, it's best to stand the bottle upright for a couple of days to let the sediment settle. Just before you want to drink it – within an hour or two – open it, and with a candle or torch under the neck of the bottle, pour gently in one single motion until you see an arrowhead of sediment arrive at the lip. If you do it carefully you'll only waste about half a glass – and that can go into the gravy. There's one final thing – use nice big glasses which you fill to between one-third and one-half. And after you've finished with them, hand-wash them in very hot water, taking particular care to rinse away any traces of washing-up liquid.

TASTING Well, we're going to drink it rather than swish it round our mouths and spit it out like the professional tasters do. But take a moment to look at the colour – some reds have a lovely hue – and do register the smell, which is often memorable. Then take a decent mouthful, and hold the wine in your mouth for a few moments, breathing through your nose. As the wine warms up in your mouth and the aromas rise into your nasal cavity, you'll get at least ten times the pleasure than if you'd just glugged it back!

FOOD AND WINE The last thing I intend to do is start laying down laws about what you must or must not drink with this or that food. No, that's up to you to decide, and if you like Burgundy with your fish course – why not! The thing to remember is – it's *your* palate doing the tasting, so if the flavours seem to go well together – then they do. For you at least!

Even so, let's look at a few guidelines which may help us decide what we're *likely* to enjoy most. Take rosés first. So long as they're fresh and young and well chilled, these are the perfect all-purpose wines. Their slight hint of red-wine fruit makes them happy with meat

dishes, yet the absence of red-wine toughness makes them good partners for salads or fish. A really nice rosé is the perfect picnic choice when a single wine has to accompany the entire contents of the hamper.

Red wines are *not* quite as adaptable – largely because of their tannin. Tannin is the tough, rather cold-tea bitter edge that most reds have, especially from areas like Bordeaux and the northern Rhône, and especially from the Cabernet Sauvignon grape. Tannin makes most fish taste metallic, and becomes drier and more rasping with sweet things. So red wine with dessert doesn't usually work and tannic reds are unlikely to suit meat dishes in sweet sauces like *duck à l'orange*.

On the other hand, tannin does cut through fat so the fattier cuts of lamb and beef are often good with quite tough reds (though pork goes better with a white). And if you want to drink red with spicy food, a rough young red can become positively mellow.

Bordeaux-type reds, with their tannins and acidity, often act as appetite-whetters. Burgundy and Beaujolais have far less tannin and react differently with food. If you've got some well-hung game, or well-hung red meat, the slightly gamy and plum-perfumed flavours of Burgundy will often complement it perfectly. And if you want the one really all-purpose and affordable French red which will go with anything from omelette to oxtail, turkey to taramasalata – it's Beaujolais. The reason is its gush of fresh fruit – the most unquenchable of flavours in a wine.

Storing and Serving White Wines

STORING Wine of any colour can stand up to a fair amount of ill-treatment, but there's no doubt we have a better chance of really enjoying it if we treat it with at least a modicum of consideration. After all, a decent wine is a living thing, it is evolving, undergoing physical change in the bottle, both as a reaction to movement, temperature, light, even noise, and as a natural part of the ageing process. Indeed, if there is a general rule it is that the older a bottle of wine the more you must cherish it and involve it in the minimum amount of stress. A really young bottle can bounce about in the car for days, almost bake to death on the back seat in the sun, then almost freeze to death in the fridge – and still taste reasonable – not as good as it could – but reasonable.

White wines in general do not benefit from ageing as much as reds, and many light fruity whites from Alsace, the Loire, Entre-Deux-Mers, and the Mâconnais may well lose their freshness if kept for more than a few months. However, the fuller type of Alsace wines, Chablis and Côte d'Or Burgundy, the leading Loire wines from the Chenin grape, and top Graves, Barsac and Sauternes, can all age superbly, and often improve dramatically with a few years' storage.

You don't need to store your whites separately from your reds, but they tend to be more fragile, and more light-sensitive. For this reason most good white wines are put into green glass – Burgundy and Champagne are good examples. The only exception is sweet Sauternes, which for some reason has always been bottled in clear glass.

SERVING White wine doesn't need to be decanted – though it can look lovely in cut glass – but the temperature will affect the flavour. One rule of thumb is the cheaper the wine, the colder it should be! For wines that you're actually proud of serving, don't chill them too much, and do it gradually. Half an hour in the deep freeze is not so good as two hours in the refrigerator. Sparkling wines *can* be chilled right down, because it preserves the bubble in the wine. Sauvignon wines from the Loire and Bordeaux can take two to three hours in the fridge because of their green acid edge; Muscadet can take the same kind of treatment. Alsace wine and sweet wines start losing their perfume if you give them more than two hours chilling, and good Burgundies and white Rhônes really shouldn't have more than about an hour or so because they begin to lose their attractive round nuttiness. If you *do* want to chill a wine down in a hurry – fill a jug or bucket with ice *and* water – you'll be amazed at how quickly the wine's temperature drops!

TASTING We describe them all as white but you don't need to look hard to see that white wine varies from the palest, almost water-white colour of Muscadet to the rich toffee-yellow of a mature Sauternes. In between are dozens of variations – but in general my advice is avoid too dark a colour in an inexpensive wine – it probably means that sherry-like effects have taken over. White wine – even mature white wine – should always smell clean and fresh. A scent of vanilla probably means that the wine has been aged in new oak.

FOOD The wonderful thing about white wine is that it's a do-anything, go-anywhere, anytime kind of drink. You can enjoy it with or without food, before, during and after a meal, and, to be honest, it'll go pretty happily with almost any dish you can think of. OK, I suppose a dry, light Muscadet isn't exactly going to titillate the tastebuds parked up against a Black Forest gâteau and a light Bordeaux Blanc is going to get pretty walloped in a fist-fight with a vindaloo, but, in the main, white wine is wonderfully adaptable.

Remember, these are just guidelines. If you like to drink Beaujolais with your sea bass, or Muscadet with your mutton – fine! I may very well join you.

First, Champagne is the perfect aperitif. It gees you up, makes you feel special and perks up the appetite no end. If you want to drink it right through your meal – and you can afford it – do just that. If not, a good Blanquette de Limoux or perhaps a sparkling Saumur would do the trick.

Light food is generally better with light wine, because the delicate flavours of, say, seafood can easily be overpowered by a big Meursault. And the salty tang of oysters and mussels *will* clash with a strong-flavoured wine. So a good Muscadet or Entre-Deux-Mers is often the best wine to serve with a starter. If you've got a meaty first course – pâté, charcuterie – I'd go for Alsace whites every time. And I find that salads go best with Sauvignon wines, and for the slighty fatty flavours of eggs and cooked cheese, dry sparkling wines would again be my first choice.

Grilled fish is delicious with Chablis, Sancerre or, again, a good Muscadet. Fish with a rich sauce needs a weightier wine, and Côte d'Or white Burgundies, top-quality Graves or white Châteauneuf-du-Pape are best. Chicken and pork *both* go well with white wines – especially Alsace Pinot Gris and Gewürztraminer, and full-bodied wines from the Chardonnay grape. Beef, lamb and game are best with red wines, but big Chardonnays and Alsace wines are pretty good, too.

As for desserts – Sauternes, Muscat de Beaumes-de-Venise or the lovely Clairette de Die Tradition fizz are spot on. In fact anything Muscat-based is good. And, contrary to the usual belief that red wine is best with cheese, white is usually better, and sweet whites are best of all with the palate-blasting efforts of a Roquefort or a Stilton.

Vintages – Red Wines

BORDEAUX	88	87	86	85	84	83	82	81	80	79
Margaux	7⇧	5⇧	8⇧	8⇧	5⇧	9⇧	8●	6●	4★	7★
St-Julien	7⇧	6⇧	8⇧	8⇧	5⇧	8⇧	10⇧	7●	4★	7★
Pauillac	6⇧	6⇧	8⇧	8⇧	5⇧	8⇧	10⇧	7●	4★	7★
St-Estèphe	6⇧	5⇧	8⇧	8⇧	4⇧	8⇧	9⇧	6●	4★	7★
Listrac/Moulis	7⇧	5⇧	7⇧	8⇧	4●	8⇧	9●	6●	4★	6★
Graves/Pessac-Léognan	7⇧	5⇧	7⇧	8⇧	5●	8⇧	9●	8●	5★	7★
St-Émilion	8⇧	6⇧	7⇧	10⇧	3●	8●	10●	6●	4★	7★
Pomerol	8⇧	6⇧	8⇧	10⇧	3●	8●	10●	6●	4★	8★
BURGUNDY	**88**	**87**	**86**	**85**	**84**	**83**	**82**	**81**	**80**	**79**
Côte de Nuits	8⇧	9⇧	7⇧	10●	6★	7●	6★	3★	6★	5⇩
Hautes-Côtes de Nuits	6⇧	8⇧	6●	8★	4⇩	7★	6★	3⇩	4⇩	5⇩
Côte de Beaune	8⇧	8⇧	7⇧	9●	5★	7●	6★	3⇩	6⇩	6⇩
Hautes-Côtes de Beaune	6⇧	7⇧	6●	8★	3⇩	6★	6⇩	3⇩	3⇩	6⇩
Beaujolais Cru	9●	9★	6★	10★	4⇩	8★	5⇩	7⇩	4⇩	7⇩
Côte Chalonnaise	8⇧	7●	5●	8★	5★	6★	6⇩	3⇩	5⇩	5⇩
LOIRE	**88**	**87**	**86**	**85**	**84**	**83**	**82**	**81**	**80**	**79**
Anjou Rouge	8●	6●	5★	9★	3⇩	8★	7★	6⇩	2⇩	4⇩
Bourgueil	9⇧	6⇧	6●	9●	3●	8●	7★	6⇩	3⇩	5⇩
Chinon	9⇧	6⇧	7●	10●	4●	9★	8★	6⇩	3⇩	5⇩
Sancerre	8⇧	5●	6★	9★	4⇩	8⇩	7⇩	6⇩	3⇩	5⇩
RHÔNE	**88**	**87**	**86**	**85**	**84**	**83**	**82**	**81**	**80**	**79**
Hermitage	9⇧	7⇧	7⇧	9⇧	5●	10⇧	7●	4★	7★	6★
Côte-Rôtie	8⇧	7⇧	6⇧	10⇧	4●	9⇧	7●	4★	6★	6★
Châteauneuf-du-Pape	8⇧	4⇧	7●	8●	6★	7★	5★	6★	6★	6⇩
Crozes-Hermitage	8⇧	6●	6●	8★	4★	8★	6★	4⇩	4⇩	5⇩
Cornas	8⇧	6⇧	6⇧	9●	4●	9●	7●	5★	5★	6★
St-Joseph	8⇧	6●	6●	9★	4★	9★	7★	4⇩	8⇩	6⇩

Vintages – White Wines

ALSACE	88	87	86	85	84	83	82	81	80	79
Alsace Grand Cru	8△	6★	5★	10★	4★	10●	5★	7▽	4▽	6▽
Vendange Tardive	7△	5△	5△	9●	3★	10●	–	–	–	–
BORDEAUX	88	87	86	85	84	83	82	81	80	79
Bordeaux Blanc	9★	7★	8▽	7▽	5▽	8▽	6▽	7▽	4▽	7▽
Graves/Pessac-Léognan	9△	7●	8●	7★	6★	8★	7★	7▽	4▽	8▽
Sauternes	7△	4△	10△	6△	4★	9△	5★	6★	6★	5★
BURGUNDY	88	87	86	85	84	83	82	81	80	79
Bourgogne Blanc	8●	6★	9★	7★	4▽	7▽	7▽	5▽	4▽	6▽
Chablis	7●	8★	9★	8★	6★	8★	6▽	8★	4▽	5▽
Côte de Beaune	8●	7△	10●	8●	6★	7★	7★	5▽	4▽	7▽
Côte Chalonnaise	7●	6△	9●	8●	5★	7★	7★	5▽	4▽	7▽
Mâconnais	8●	7★	9★	8★	5▽	8▽	6▽	7▽	4▽	6▽
CHAMPAGNE	8△	4△	7△	9●	2●	8●	9●	6★	4★	8★
LOIRE	88	87	86	85	84	83	82	81	80	79
Muscadet	8★	9★	8★	7▽	7▽	6▽	6▽	7▽	5▽	6▽
Sancerre	8●	7★	9★	6★	7★	8▽	5▽	8▽	4▽	5▽
Vouvray	8△	6△	7△	9△	4△	9△	7●	6●	4●	6★
Bonnezeaux	7△	5△	6△	10△	4△	9△	7●	5●	4★	6●
RHÔNE	88	87	86	85	84	83	82	81	80	79
Hermitage	9△	8△	7△	8△	6●	9△	8●	6●	6★	7●
Condrieu	8●	6●	7★	9★	7★	9★	7▽	7▽	6▽	7▽
Châteauneuf-du-Pape	8●	6★	8★	7▽	5▽	7▽	6▽	8▽	7▽	6▽

HOW TO READ THE CHART △ = not ready ● = just ready ★ = at peak ▽ = past its best

The numerals represent an overall rating for each year, based on a score out of ten, bearing in mind of course, that such measures can only ever be broad generalizations. There will be many variations with individual wines and producers, and in fact the top producers can succeed in making good wine in bad years – by being very careful with their grape selection.

GLOSSARY

ACIDITY Naturally present in grapes, it gives red wine an appetizing 'grip' and whites a refreshing tang. In excess, it can make a wine seem very sharp – but if there's too little, the wine will be flabby.

AGEING Essential for fine wines and for softening many everyday reds. Storing the wine in wooden barrels then keeping it in bottle, perhaps for months or years, has a mellowing effect on a wine's various elements.

ALCOHOLIC CONTENT Alcoholic strength of wine, usually expressed as a percentage of the total volume.

ALCOHOLIC FERMENTATION Process whereby yeasts convert grape sugars into alcohol, transforming grape juice into wine.

APPELLATION D'ORIGINE CONTRÔLÉE Official designation in France guaranteeing a wine by geographical origin, grape variety and production method; abbreviated as AC or AOC.

ASSEMBLAGE Final cask-to-cask blending of fine wines in Bordeaux and Champagne.

BARRIQUE Oak barrel holding 225 litres, used for ageing wine and sometimes for fermenting it too.

BLANC DE BLANCS White wine, especially Champagne, made only from white grapes. The rarer *blanc de noirs* is white wine made only from black grapes.

BRUT Dry, though not as dry as Extra Brut. Usually seen on Champagne labels.

CARBONIC MACERATION Wine-making method traditional to Beaujolais. The grapes, whole and uncrushed, are fermented in a closed vat to give a well-coloured, fruity wine for early drinking.

CAVE French for 'cellar'.

CHAI The building in which wine is stored before bottling. A Bordeaux term.

CHAMBRER To bring (red) wines to room temperature, ready for drinking.

CHAMPAGNE METHOD Traditional way of making sparkling wine by inducing a second fermentation in the bottle.

CHAPTALIZATION Legal addition of sugar during fermentation to increase alcoholic strength.

CHÂTEAU A wine-producing estate (literally 'castle'). Applied to all sizes of property, particularly in Bordeaux.

CLARET English name for red Bordeaux.

CLIMAT Specifically defined area of vineyard, often very small. A Burgundian term.

CLOS Term for a vineyard that is (or was) wall-enclosed; traditional to Burgundy.

COMMUNE Village. Many French *appellations contrôlées* are based round the produce of a single commune.

CO-OPERATIVE Winery run collectively by a group of growers.

CÔTES, COTEAUX Slopes. Hillside vineyards generally produce better wine than low-lying ones.

CRÉMANT Champagne-method sparkling wine from Alsace, Burgundy and the Loire. In Champagne, applies to wines purposely produced with fewer bubbles.

CRU French for 'growth'. Used to describe a single vineyard, normally with an additional quality reference as in *grand cru*.

CRU BOURGEOIS In Bordeaux, a quality rating immediately below *cru classé*.

CRU CLASSÉ Literally 'classed growth', indicating that a vineyard is included in the top-quality rating system of its region.

CUVE CLOSE Method of making sparkling wine in which the second fermentation takes place in closed tanks – not in bottle.

CUVÉE Usually indicates a blend, which may mean different grape varieties or simply the putting together of the best barrels of wine for a producer's label.

DEMI-SEC Despite what you might think, *demi-sec* means medium tending to sweet, rather than medium-dry.

DOMAINE Estate, especially in Burgundy.

DOUX Sweet.

ÉLEVAGE Term covering all wine-making stages between fermentation and bottling.

EN PRIMEUR Wine offered for sale immediately after the vintage, still in cask. Often – but not always – the best way to buy top-class reds.

ESTATE-BOTTLED Wine bottled on the premises where it has been made. This may be indicated on the label as *mis en bouteilles* followed by *au domaine, au château* or *par* with the name of the producer.

FINING Clarifying wine by adding coagulants, traditionally egg-whites, to the surface. As these fall through the wine they collect impurities.

FORTIFIED WINE Wine strengthened by the addition of extra alcohol.

FÛTS DE CHÊNE Oak casks. Sometimes seen on the label as '*élevé en fûts de chêne*' – matured in oak.

GRAND CRU 'Great growth'; the top quality classification in Burgundy, used less precisely in Alsace, Bordeaux and Champagne.

GRAND VIN Used in Bordeaux to indicate a producer's top wine. Usually bears a château name.

HECTARE Metric measure of area equal to 10,000 square metres (2·471 acres).

LEES Coarse sediment – dead yeasts, etc – thrown by wine in a cask and left behind after racking.

MOUSSEUX Sparkling.

NÉGOCIANT Merchant or shipper who buys in wine from growers, then matures, maybe blends and bottles it for sale.

NOBLE ROT The *Botrytis cinerea* fungus which, in warm autumn weather, can attack white grapes, shrivel them and thus concentrate the sugars to produce quality sweet wines such as Sauternes.

OAK Traditional wood for wine casks. During ageing or fermenting it gives flavours, such as vanillin and tannin, to the wines. The newer the wood, the greater its impact.

OENOLOGIST Wine scientist or technician.

OXIDATION Over-exposure of wine to air causing bacterial decay and loss of fruit. Often characterized by a rather sherry-like aroma.

PÉTILLANT Semi-sparkling wine.

PHYLLOXERA Vine aphid (*Phylloxera vastatrix*) which devastated viticulture worldwide in the late 1800s. Since then, the vulnerable European *Vitis vinifera* has been grafted onto phylloxera-resistant American rootstocks.

PREMIER CRU 'First growth'; the top quality classification in Bordeaux, but second to *grand cru* in Burgundy. Also used, not always with the same precision, elsewhere in France.

PRIMEUR 'New wine'; wine of the most recent vintage, especially Beaujolais.

RACKING Gradual clarification of wine by transferring it from one barrel to another, leaving sediments behind.

RÉCOLTANT Grower. He may either make his own wine or sell the grapes to a merchant.

SEC Dry.

SECOND WINE Wine from a designated vineyard which is sold separately from the main production, under a different name, for a variety of technical reasons. Usually lighter and quicker-maturing than the main wine.

TANNIN Bitter element in red wine, derived from grape skins, stems and oak barrels; softens with ageing and is essential for the wine's development and staying power.

VENDANGE TARDIVE High-quality wine from Alsace, sometimes sweetish, made from late-picked grapes with extra concentrated flavour. Only made in the best vintages.

VIEILLES VIGNES Or *vieille vigne*. A wine made from mature vines.

VIN DÉLIMITÉ DE QUALITÉ SUPÉRIEURE Second category of French quality control for wines, below AC; abbreviated as VDQS.

VIN DE PAYS French 'country wine'. Although it is the third and bottom category for quality, it includes some first-class wines which don't follow local AC regulations. Wines made from high-quality grapes which are not traditional to the area would come into this category.

VIN DOUX NATUREL Sweet wine fortified with grape spirit; abbreviated as VDN. Mostly from the Midi.

INDEX

A page reference in *italics* indicates main entry.

ACKNOWLEDGEMENTS

Photographs supplied by Michel Guillard/Scope *1*, Jean-Paul Ferrero/Explorer *2*, Mike Busselle *5*, Patrick Eagar *7*, Jon Wyand *11 left*, Patrick Eagar *11 right*, Mike Busselle *13*, Patrick Eagar *15*, Michel Guillard/Scope *17* and *18*, Jacques Guillard/Scope *21*, Francis Jalain/Explorer *22, 29* and *32*, Mike Busselle *34*, Anthony Blake *36*, Michel Guillard/Scope *40* and *42*, Landscape Only *48*, Patrick Eagar *50*, Francis Jalain/Explorer *56*, Mick Rock/Cephas *58*, Hug/Explorer *63*, Luc Girard/Explorer *69*, Michel Guillard/Scope *72*, Jacques Guillard/Scope *79* and *80*, Mick Rock/Cephas *83*, Patrick Eagar *86*, Mike Busselle *91* and *92*, Mick Rock/Cephas *95*, Mike Busselle *97* and *101*, Landscape Only *103*, Michel Guillard/Scope *108*, Jean-Daniel Sudres/Scope *110*, Patrick Eagar *114*, Michel Guillard/Scope *120*, Mick Rock/Cephas *126*, Jean-Daniel Sudres/Scope *128*, Frédéric Hadengue/Scope *131*, Jacques Guillard/Scope *137*, Landscape Only *138*, Mike Busselle *142*, Francis Jalain/Explorer *147*, Mike Busselle *151*, Mick Rock/Cephas *154* and *157*, Anthony Blake *159*, Jacques Guillard/Scope *165*, Patrick Eagar *169*, Henri Veiller/Explorer *170*, Patrick Eagar *174*, Jean-Daniel Sudres/Scope *179*, Mike Busselle *183*, Anthony Blake *185*, Michel Guillard/Scope *188*, Anthony Blake *190*, Patrick Eagar *194*, Mike Busselle *201*, Anthony Blake *203*, Manix/Explorer *204*, Patrick Eagar *207*, Jacques Guillard/Scope *209*, Richard Platt *210*, Jacques Guillard/Scope *213*, Michel Guillard/Scope *214*, Francis Jalain/Explorer *218*, Jean-Paul Ferrero/Explorer *221*, Mike Busselle *223*, Christian Errath/Explorer *240*

Managing Editor Sandy Carr
Editor Fiona Wild
Art Editor Ruth Prentice
Deputy Editors Catherine Dell, Fiona Holman
Deputy Art Editors Alison Donovan, Alison Shackleton
Editorial Assistants Mary Pickles, Mary Hitch, Ray Granger
Consultant Rosemary George MW
Indexer Naomi Good
Maps Diane Fisher
Illustrations Peter Byatt, Robina Green, Stan North